Reform Without Liberalization

D0348441

Reform
Without Liberalization
China's National People's Congress and
the Politics of Institutional Change

KEVIN J. O'BRIEN

Ohio State University

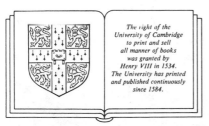

The right of the
University of Cambridge
to print and sell
all manner of books
was granted by
Henry VIII in 1534.
The University has printed
and published continuously
since 1584.

CAMBRIDGE UNIVERSITY PRESS

New York
Cambridge   Port Chester   Melbourne   Sydney

Published by the Press Syndicate of the University of Cambridge
The Pitt Building, Trumpington Street, Cambridge CB2 1RP
40 West 20th Street, New York, NY 10011, USA
10 Stamford Road, Oakleigh, Melbourne 3166, Australia

© Cambridge University Press 1990

First published 1990

Printed in the United States of America

Library of Congress Cataloging-in-Publication Data

O'Brien, Kevin J.
    Reform without liberalization : China's National People's Congress
and the politics of institutional change / Kevin J. O'Brien.
        p.   cm.
    Includes bibliographical references and index.
    ISBN 0-521-38086-3
    1. China. Ch'üan kuo jen min tai piao ta hui.   2. China—Politics
and government—1949-   I. Title.
JQ1513.027   1990
328.51'072—dc20   90-1911
                                                         CIP

ISBN 0-521-38086-3 hardcovers

To my parents,

Dolores A. O'Brien and Joseph A. O'Brien

Contents

Part III The NPC under Deng

Acknowledgments

This book began as a dissertation on Chinese legislative politics, completed at Yale University in 1987. At the outset, valuable comments from Joseph LaPalombara, Robert Dahl, and Jim Scott helped define the project and sharpen the focus. As the research progressed, Dan Kelliher, John Bryan Starr, and Hong Yung Lee read drafts of the manuscript and offered perceptive criticisms concerning organization and points of interpretation, as well as suggestions on how later chapters should proceed. To all these mentors and friends, I offer my sincere gratitude.

After I decided to focus the manuscript on institutional change, Pat Patterson, Larry Baum, Bill Liddle, Richard Baum, Zheng Shiping, and several anonymous referees patiently read draft chapters, provided detailed recommendations, and saved me from many errors. Their collective comments reshaped my understanding of legislative functions and immeasurably improved my treatment of structural and systemic reforms.

Although many friends and colleagues assisted throughout, my greatest intellectual debt is to Vivienne Shue, for introducing me to Chinese politics and for guiding this project from beginning to end. Her insights, interest, and encouragement made my work possible and enjoyable, and provided me with a model of what it means to be a teacher, scholar, and adviser.

My field research in China was supported by the Ohio State University Office of Research and Graduate Studies, the Office of International Affairs, the College of Social and Behavioral Sciences, the Department of Political Science, and the East Asian Studies Center. A fruitful overseas stay would have been inconceivable without the cooperation of the Chinese People's Institute of Foreign Affairs, the All-China Journalists' Association, and the National People's Congress. In particular, He Zhigeng, of the Chinese People's Institute of Foreign Affairs, was a ready and able friend, sounding board, and negotiator, who won permissions and set up interviews that I never thought possible. Special thanks should also be given to leading mem-

bers of the NPCSC General Office and Legislative Affairs Commission and
a researcher in the Chinese Academy of Social Sciences Political Science
Institute, who graciously consented to long interviews and gave me valuable
information on the staff and internal operation of the NPC. Professor Wang
Shuwen, a member of the NPC Law Committee, also kindly spoke with me
for several hours in the Great Hall of the People in March 1989. Li Fan,
Chinese embassy officials, and members of the International Liaison Department of the All-China Journalists' Association were instrumental in securing permission to attend press conferences at the 1989 NPC and in gaining
entry to small-group meetings. Two China-based correspondents, Chang
Shao Wei of *Ta Kung Pao* and John Pomfret of the Associated Press, gen-
erously offered their time and their interpretations of the 1988 and 1989
plenary sessions.

For research assistance, I would like to note the contributions of Carmen
Lee of the Ohio State University Library and Maureen Malone Jones of
Sterling Library, both of whom tirelessly and speedily located and obtained
difficult-to-find materials without which this work could not have been done.
Graduate assistants at Ohio State, including Eunbong Choi, Eunsook Chung,
Liz Reyer, and John Zurovchak, provided essential help gathering materials,
proofreading the manuscript, and preparing the index.

I am thankful to the Comparative Legislative Research Center for permission to base Chapter 7 on an article published in *Legislative Studies
Quarterly*. Chapter 8 builds on a paper that appeared in *Studies in Comparative Communism*.

To Betsy, for her patience, her faith, and her ear for bad metaphors, I
am most grateful of all.

We cannot imagine a democracy, even proletarian democracy, without representative institutions, but we can and must imagine democracy without parliamentarism.

Lenin, 1918

The problems we face in implementing reforms are far greater than those we encounter in opening our country. In political reforms we can affirm one point: We have to adhere to the system of the National People's Congress and not the American system of the separation of three powers.

Deng Xiaoping, June 9, 1989

PART I
Introduction

1

Chinese legislatures and political change

Chinese legislatures have had a short and turbulent history. First established in the final decade of the Qing Dynasty (1644–1911), popular assemblies have rarely acquired considerable power, persisted for long, or drawn the attention of foreign scholars. The national legislature set up under the Communists is no exception. Since its founding in 1954, the National People's Congress (NPC) has "traversed a winding and tortuous road of development,"[1] with more than its share of detours and wrong turns. A period of legislative activity and reform in the mid-1950s ended suddenly when a series of policy shifts reversed a trend toward institutionalization and reliance on law. For two decades, political campaigns, from the Anti-Rightist Movement (1957–8) to the Great Leap Forward (1958–60) to the Cultural Revolution (1966–76), interrupted legislative development and ultimately drove the NPC into inactivity. For the last ten years of Mao Zedong's life, a legislature whose ancestry was in the "revisionist" Soviet Union and the "capitalist" West had no place in the Chinese political system; it was ignored and scorned, called a "rubber stamp" or a "phony organ of idle talk."[2]

Then, in the autumn of 1976, Mao died. His passing ushered in a new era in Chinese politics – one that brought a reassessment of past policies and a series of political reforms, including revival and strengthening of the NPC. Beginning in 1978, party leaders convened people's congresses each year and encouraged lively debate. Legislative committees were reestablished and NPC involvement in law making, oversight, representation, and regime-support activities reached and surpassed the level of the mid-1950s. Even after the promulgation of a new constitution in 1982 and the military suppression of 1989, discussions continued on the proper role of a legislature in a socialist, one-party state and reform proposals continued to appear.

Few western scholars, however, have investigated legislative renewal or its implications, save as one small part of the political reform program.[3] What can be learned from direct focus on the NPC, its demise and its rebirth remains to be explored.

An indicator of change

Legislative development (or decay) is a component of political change.[4] In nations with weak legislatures just as in those with strong legislatures, growth or decline of an assembly's institutional importance alters the pattern of rule. In socialist systems in particular, the health of a legislature reveals much about the state of mass-elite relations and the division of tasks among government organs. When a socialist legislature is impotent or ignored, law making, supervision, representation, and regime-support activities are dispensed with or carried out elsewhere. When a legislature is rising and active, it assumes a range of responsibilities and may serve as a testing ground to develop and refine techniques of rule. In China, the NPC's ups and downs have coincided with changes in the policy-making environment and have heralded (or reflected) changes in the way leaders interact with the citizenry and with each other. Throughout its history, the NPC has been a window on evolving party–society and party–state relations that has shed light on the broad character of the Chinese polity – how open or closed it is, how exclusive or inclusive it may be becoming.[5]

In one institution in miniature, the forces of change and continuity have met. At different times, reform or reaction has prevailed. But the underlying question, posed at the end of the Qing dynasty and still troubling to this day, has remained the same: What must be done to build China into a strong and prosperous nation? Through our legislative window, three separate but intersecting alternatives can be discerned.

First, the path of liberalization. Advocates of liberalization in modern China have achieved prominence on several different occasions – in the 1910s, during the Hundred Flowers Movement in the mid-1950s, in the early years of the post-Mao thaw, and for a short period prior to Zhao Ziyang's 1989 removal. In the legislature, their ascendance has been marked by lively criticism and calls for structural reform. Liberal reformers, at various times, have sought to limit central power and to transform the legislature into an institution with an established role in policy making. They have envisioned outside control over leaders and regular influence over policy: they have aimed to build a legislature that has the ability to veto misguided policies and the power to remove incompetent or corrupt leaders. They have sought to strengthen the nation by diffusing power. When permitted to do so, liberalizers have urged leaders to be more responsive and have championed

electoral reform and elite accountability; they have supported close legislator–constituent ties and active representation of individual, partial, and
national interests. Despite repeated setbacks, several generations of liberal-
minded reformers have periodically reintroduced the idea of popularizing
autocratic rule and allowing limited political competition. Though never
strong in numbers, advocates of liberalization have galvanized the nation
with bold proposals and have explored the outer bounds of permissible
debate.

A second option discussed for many years has been that of rationalization.
Less far reaching than liberalization, rationalization involves routinizing and
legalizing political power and circumscribing the authority of individual leaders. Proponents of this strategy have emphasized fixed legal codes, formal
rules, and a "rational division of labor" among government organs. They
have recommended clarifying jurisdictions to prevent overconcentration of
power and to increase government efficiency. Less interested in diffusing
power than liberalizers, rationalizers have focused on increasing the capabilities of the state and institutionalizing political power. They have sought
a predictable and orderly political system in which the duties and rights of
government officials and ordinary citizens are clearly spelled out in regulations and laws. In the legislature, they have been particularly concerned
with managing intraelite relations and have stressed the importance of law
making and government supervision. The rationalizing impulse has been
evident at various times in the modern era, and was a strong current for
much of the 1980s.[6]

A third course, relevant only to China under communist rule, can be
considered under the rubric of "inclusion." Inclusion, as Kenneth Jowitt
uses the term, refers to measures adopted by the leaders of a one-party,
Leninist state that institutionally acknowledge social diversity and grant
limited access and influence to nonparty forces, but do not require functioning electoral machinery or imply any right to organized opposition. Inclusion might be thought of as a promise to be consulted – a right to a
presence in policy making, if not always a regular, guaranteed role. It involves enlarging the united front[7] and institutionalizing legitimacy – using
the legislature (as well as other organizations) to integrate the political community and to organize it around one-party rule. It entails heading off an-
tisystem ideas by cooptation rather than coercion and expanding the internal
boundaries of the regime to preempt political challenges and protect party
rule.[8] Over the years, the NPC has been a prime venue to witness changing
approaches to inclusion. At times, the leadership has used the NPC to
exclude the putative "enemies of socialism" and to pursue class-based pro-

grams. At other times, the legislature has been used to win over these same enemies, when their cooperation was deemed necessary to realize leadership goals.

Periodically, all of these options – liberalization, rationalization, and inclusion – have come onto the agenda in ways that touched the legislature. Appropriate reforms have been suggested, accepted, rejected, revoked, and reconsidered. Two steps forward have been followed by one step back – or three steps back. By tracing legislative change, we gain insight into the trajectory of Chinese political development and consider recurring choices that confront leaders of an illiberal polity as they seek to modernize. From one position in the political system, we assess where the nation has been and where it may be heading.

A preview of the argument

The position of the NPC on the eve of Zhao's fall suggested conditional steps toward rationalization and inclusion, combined with continuing rejection of liberalization. Despite notable efforts to reduce capriciousness and to broaden the base of the regime, the reforms of the 1980s did little to increase political competition or to institutionalize responsiveness. In the NPC, legislators often discussed improving one-party rule; few suggested ending it. A legislator's ability to press minority views or to agitate for individual, group, or sectional interests continued to hinge on leadership sufferance rather than right or unquestioned custom. Long-standing structural obstacles to legislative liberalization (including unfree elections; large chamber size; brief, infrequent plenary sessions; and weak committees) remained partly in place, and legislative functions (e.g., propaganda, education, socialization, mobilization), entrusted under Mao, continue to be embedded in the NPC's structure and in the minds of Congress leaders and other elites. Legislative influence, as in the past, was granted only when it was broadly supportive and the NPC existed to provide informal consultation rather than formal restraint. Reforms had not recast the NPC into a popular, representative assembly; those who anticipated such a transformation had lost sight of the realities of party rule and the entrenched historical, structural, and ideological obstacles that impede Chinese legislative change.

Though Deng and his associates firmly rejected liberalization several times during the 1980s, they expressed concern with rationalization through efforts to regularize policy making and to guarantee policy implementation. This shift was visible in the NPC in organizational changes that (1) strengthened the NPC Standing Committee and expanded its scope of action, (2) increased specialization, procedural regularity, and full-time staff, and (3) improved internal organization. The NPC of the 1980s devoted proportionately less time to symbolic, educational, informational, and mobilizational functions and more time to law making and supervision. Although the legislature rarely rejected executive proposals or initiated bills, the NPC and its committees occasionally drafted legislation, often revised and edited it, and always oversaw the drafting process. The Standing Committee, Law Committee, and Legislative Affairs Commission, in particular, assumed an active role in clarifying and elaborating general directives and in modifying laws to ensure their feasibility and implementation.

After decisions were made and promulgated, legislators frequently criticized state bureaucrats and conducted inspection tours of policy implementation. The NPC began to act as a clearinghouse, often a proxy for the party, that gathered information on local and central departments that were not implementing policy and that defined and supervised handling of unconstitutional and illegal behavior. Information was channeled to decision makers to help them refine their directives and to improve local compliance. The objective of rationalizing law making and supervision was to reduce arbitrariness, hastiness, and nonconformity, and to check overoptimism and sloganeering; the hope was that the legislature could play a part in restoring balance and stability to a system whose motive forces had long been imbalance and instability.

At the same time, Deng-era NPC representative and regime-support activities indicated selective adoption of inclusionary approaches. Movement toward inclusion was evident in the use of the NPC to broaden the united front and to institutionalize legitimacy. Members of formerly disparaged social groups were encouraged to speak out and spirited debates were allowed in exchange for consent to one-party rule and willingness to propagate party policy. The composition of the NPC and its committees was changed to include additional scholars, technical experts, rich peasants, and "tails of capitalism." By allowing social and economic elites to meet with high cadres and to express dissatisfaction, the party was seeking to show that it could incorporate a variety of societal interests – that the united front included all loyal citizens and that advantages accrued to those who accepted party rule. By allowing legislators to undertake representative activities, including obtaining benefits for individual constituents and requesting redistribution of resources to regions or social groups, reform leaders, particularly Zhao Ziyang and Hu Yaobang, displayed a more sophisticated understanding of strategies that generate legitimacy among the skeptical, the alienated, and the apathetic and of means to organize the political community around the principle of one-party rule. In exchange for a right to disagree and to articulate group interests, first generation post-Mao leaders expected deputies to penetrate society, to build legitimacy, and to contribute to system maintenance. Reformers offered members of key social groups inclusion to soften demands and to preserve an illiberal state. Limited inclusion thus appeared as a substitute for liberalization, not as a sign of it.[9]

Since 1954, the legislature, an emblem of liberal democratic rule, has been struggling to find a place in an illiberal and undemocratic state. To understand the significance and consequences of this undertaking, we must explore how historical events, past decisions, ideological propensities, organizational arrangements, and functional imperatives shaped the NPC and determined its role. We must understand the repertoire of choices available to several generations of national leaders and the ways in which history, structure, and function have interacted to make some forms of institutional and systemic change more likely than others.[10]

A note on method

Nelson Polsby outlines two approaches commonly used to study legislatures and legislative activities. Functionalists look across the political system for agencies and occasions on which law making is performed. Structuralists focus on the legislature itself and enumerate the many functions legislatures actually account for.[11] Functionalists discuss legislatures incidentally, albeit in a rich and complex mesh of institutional interrelationships. Structuralists investigate legislatures systematically, but with scant reference to other organizations engaged in similar work. Both approaches are functionalist in an important sense – they look for functions performed by institutions. Neither, however, is particularly well suited to identify institutional and systemic change; one provides a cross section at a given moment, the other lacks a sense of system.

Students of socialist legislatures often adopt a structural approach, emphasizing the internal organization of a legislature and the functions it performs – including rule making, representation, and a host of regime-support activities. Though a natural and necessary first step, an exclusively structural orientation reveals what a legislature does but not how important it is to the political system. We can agree that the legislature plays a role in mobilizing non-elites and in integrating and legitimizing the polity without understanding what particular contribution it makes to achieving ends simultaneously pursued in many places and ways. In William Welsh's view, single-minded focus on the legislature itself encourages portrayal of other institutions in terms of their relationship to the legislature rather than their role in the allocation of values:

The overall impression is what one might receive from being sequentially presented with small bits of a large photograph, arranged in no particular order and presented in no particular sequence. The picture is all there, but some segments of it have been enlarged dramatically, whereas others have been reduced. There is no frame or schema that can be used to put the pieces of the picture back in their proper places.[12]

Putting legislatures back into a functional and processual context, however, is not without problems, frequently of a reductionist nature. The dangers of a strict functionalist approach are well known. Over twenty years ago Michel Crozier wrote:

Functionalists always run the risk of indulging in a self-deceiving, conservative, and complacent commentary on the status quo. When analyzing the tendency to remain stable and to perpetuate itself manifested by a complex set of interrelationships they often forget how a system has developed and why it will ultimately have to change. ... Functionalists usually forget to discuss why, when, how, and under what circumstances strains that had heretofore reinforced the hold of the central pattern become too burdensome for it and force it to transform itself or even disappear.[13]

In studying the NPC, functionalism would draw us to a series of "yes–no" questions on rule making, mostly answered "no." We would primarily learn what the NPC was not. Directed away from questions on history, ideology, and structure, we could not assess the institutional impact of the legislature; moreover, we could "analyze how change has been integrated within the system, but not how the system itself could change."[14]

Exploring many functions carried out by one institution or one function carried out by many institutions is not sufficient. Both structural and functional approaches give incomplete answers to the question of how the legislature performs *assorted* functions in a political system in which *many bodies* share responsibility for the same tasks.

An integrated historical-structural study of legislative activity and legislatures investigates all functions associated with legislatures and all structures associated with legislative activities. Analysis across institutions complements analysis of the history, ideologies, structure, and power relationships within each institution. Only through such an approach can we explain how the NPC fits into the political system and why and how it performs certain functions at certain times. Only by combining features of structural and functional approaches, and adding an oft-lacking longitudinal dimension to both, can we uncover the contradictions inherent in Chinese legislative theory and practice and the possibilities for change stirring within.

The analysis to come only follows this research plan in broad outline, because examining all the NPC's rivals in their full complexity, over time, is beyond my scope. Nonetheless, sections on ideological constructs and systemic relationships (Chapters 4, 5, 7, and 8) supplement a basically structural approach, help explain the causes of NPC decay and destruction (Chapters 3 to 5), and prepare the stage for study of the legislature's revival and transformation (Chapters 6 to 8). The aim is to round out the picture sketched by NPC history (Chapters 2, 3, and 6) and internal organization (Chapters 4 and 7) with two snapshots of the legislature's position in the political system – one in Mao's China (Chapter 5), and one in Deng's China (Chapter 8). This method does not do full justice to change, nor treat it as the continuous function that it is. It does, however, isolate trends and illuminate the "strains that uphold the central pattern" – strains that made the NPC what it was from 1954–76 and predicated the direction, speed, and magnitude of changes since.

An historical-structural analysis involves study of a legislature's past, including periods of decline and impotence. Due attention to weakness reveals historical, structural, and ideological constraints and shows the many gradations within the category illiberal legislature. It also provides a baseline against which strengthening can be assessed – small, but significant, efforts to upgrade the legislature are not lost in a sea of unrealistic comparisons. A weak legislature's past brings to light opportunities missed, reforms discussed but not implemented, and reforms implemented but not maintained; this is important because yesterday's nonissues and "almost issues" often reappear as today's agenda for reform.[15]

Study of history also uncovers the events that shaped the way elites think about legislatures – events that opened certain avenues of development, and closed off, or at least made much less likely, other avenues. Historical analysis clarifies the genetic stock of an institution and shows how making one choice at time t can impede or facilitate making a second choice at time $t + 1$.[16] Historical analysis shows how the past channels and constrains change: how it presents options, creates habits, and teaches lessons. Though history does not supply definitive causal links, it continually impinges on the present and reminds us of the culture into which the NPC was thrust. It helps us perceive the context in which institutions operate and the inefficiencies that slow or prevent the attainment of a lasting equilibrium.[17] Researching the NPC's past (and that of earlier assemblies) illuminates the contradictory expectations present at the legislature's founding and the external jolts that affected its development. Study of the NPC over time also shows that change is often transitory and must be reaffirmed if it is to persist.

Structural analysis complements historical analysis. Structural analysis entails discussion of the Leninist Chinese political system and the Stalinist legislature established in 1954. It brings to the fore a web of institutional relationships and communist precepts that circumscribe legislative development – some of which are changing, some of which are not. Structural analysis draws attention to organizational impediments within the NPC, which over the years prevented it from becoming an effective political actor. It highlights the institutional manifestations of past choices and the prevailing systemic and ideological background against which change occurs. Structural analysis, broadly construed, delimits boundaries and a framework for action, and it suggests obstacles that must be overcome if the NPC is to carry out the tasks it is now assigned.

In the final analysis, a changing legislature attests to a changing polity. The NPC is embedded in an historical and structural context and it is part of the change of that context[18]; it is a product of functional demands of the past and a survivor into a present whose functional imperatives are quite different.[19] Altered legislative involvement in law making, supervision, representation, and regime support signals a systemwide redivision of political tasks. Knowing a legislature's role in a maturing, socialist system, we better understand the system and the forces for change brewing within.

2
Origins of the NPC

In China, the first half of the twentieth century was a time of ideological and institutional reorientation. Though often remembered for decay and disarray, this period was also one of ferment and soul searching. Amid a debilitating crisis, elites and candidate elites began to question political truths and to promote unconventional strategies to enhance national power, popularize autocratic rule, and achieve control over local society. Intellectuals, officials, and revolutionaries all acknowledged that past attempts to cope with foreign incursions and domestic fragmentation had failed, and they sought new means to reinvigorate the Chinese state and to reassert China's position in the world.

If crisis posed the challenge, aspiring state builders shaped the nation's response. By 1949 the critical pass had been negotiated. Wholesale transformation of the mode of governing established institutional forms, powers, and precedents that reduced the incongruence between the state structure and the domestic and international environment.[1] China's Communist leaders rewrote the compact between state and society, successfully reversing the flow of power into local and foreign hands and reconstituting the political center.

But the process of reintegration and rebuilding was neither smooth nor incremental: it was fitful, full of false starts and contradictory impulses. Beginning early in the century, rival state builders turned to liberal democracy, authoritarian socialism, and traditional Chinese political formulas for guidance; structures and functions cumulated and imperfect solutions to imperfectly understood problems created new problems, propensities, and approaches to try (and to avoid). Elite preferences and institutional capabilities were continually evolving and although most borrowed ideologies and institutions were found lacking, and many solutions were patently dysfunctional, each policy initiative and structural experiment left institutional and ideological vestiges to be worked with (or against) in the next round of state building.[2]

This chapter discusses early Chinese assemblies and the historical conditions that gave rise to the NPC. It shows the NPC to be the institutional culmination of experiments with legislatures that drew from western liberal, Soviet socialist, and Chinese authoritarian experience. It links the crisis that enveloped China and the disintegration of the preexisting regime to changing expectations of what a legislature should be. It probes the lingering effects of inherited attitudes and institutional arrangements on a government born in revolution.

Constitutionalism and national assemblies, 1898–1925

In the late 1890s, after decades of foreign penetration and humiliation, a group of Chinese intellectuals decided that the time had come to look outward for a solution to China's problems. Kang Youwei, and other reformers, carefully studied newly translated texts and "concluded that Western secrets of wealth and power consisted not only of technological knowledge but included political theories and sociopolitical institutions that China would also have to emulate."[3] In 1898 Kang memorialized the Emperor that the strength of nations hinges on "the establishment of constitutions and the opening of national assemblies," and rhetorically asked, "Can these nations be anything but strong when their rulers and the millions of their people are united in a single body?"[4] Kang noted that China had near equivalents to Western executive and judicial bodies, but it lacked an organ that exercised deliberative power; he suggested creating an embryonic cabinet, including a liaison bureau (*luhui ju*), which would prepare the way for a true, national assembly.[5] Only through institutional modernization, Kang argued, could China regain its autonomy and its rightful place among nations.

Although the Hundred Days' Reform of 1898 ended abruptly with the imprisonment, exile, or execution of many reformers, the idea that a constitution ensured and augmented national power spread. In the first decade of the new century, when reformist pressures and revolutionary activities intensified, the Court itself embraced constitutionalism. Literati and officials alike were impressed by Japan's victory over Russia in 1905; even diehard autocrats took note of a Japanese monarchy that "owed its vitality not just to a loyal and efficient bureaucracy and military, but to the parliament which helped . . . pay for these instruments."[6] In July 1905 several Court officials were sent abroad to investigate constitutional systems, and on return they recommended establishing a constitutional monarchy. An imperial edict issued in September 1906 seemed to place the Emperor among the reformers. In words that could have been Kang Youwei's, the edict decreed:

That other countries are wealthy and strong is primarily due to the adoption of a constitution, by which all the people are united in one body and in constant communication, sane and sound opinions are extensively sought after and adopted, powers are well divided and well defined, and financial matters and legislation are discussed and decided upon by the people.[7]

The edict envisioned a constitutional polity in which supreme authority was vested in the crown but all questions of government were considered by a popular assembly.

In 1907 the Court promised a transitional assembly within three years and a full parliament by 1916. Publicly, the Court agreed with the emerging consensus that a parliament would strengthen and unify the nation and enable China to free itself from foreign influence. Privately, Court officials expected a parliament to raise money and rally constitutionalist officials and literati to defend the imperial system. Imperial support for a parliament would, it was hoped, defuse revolutionary pressures and deflect other threatening demands, such as that for a cabinet. The 1908 "Principles of a Constitution" contained no reference to a cabinet, but considerable detail on the proposed parliament. The Court apparently preferred the "remote and less well-known perils of a parliament over the immediate and seemingly familiar perils of a cabinet."[8] Hiding behind a raft of organizational details necessary to form a national parliament (e.g., a census), the Court intended to prolong the preparatory period and to accompany concessions to constitutionalism with redoubled efforts to concentrate power and to strengthen the center's hold over political change.[9]

Despite Court insincerity, by 1910 the demand for constitutionalism had become "the rage throughout the country."[10] Individuals across the political spectrum supported establishing a western-style representative system within a constitutional monarchy. The provincial elite saw a representative system as a way to protect provincial interests; new industrialists, businessmen, and professionals saw an assembly as a means to gain influence where they had little before.[11] Even some revolutionaries took note. From 1907–10 the Petition-for-a-Parliament movement mobilized hundreds of thousands of Chinese and induced the Court to reduce the preparatory time for a full parliament from nine to six years.[12]

In 1908 the first provincial assemblies convened; in 1910 the National Legislative Council met. Although Fincher argues that the assemblies had "enormous nuisance value" and cemented a counterelite determined to have some say in centralization plans,[13] the assemblies had few of the powers associated with western-style legislatures. According to the "Principles of the Constitution," the National Legislative Council was primarily an advisory organ to the Emperor whose laws did not come into effect without approval and promulgation by the Emperor. The Council could impeach officials for unlawful conduct, but had no regular powers over appointment and removal. Members did not enjoy freedom of speech in the assembly and the Emperor could convene, adjourn, postpone, or dissolve the Council at will.[14] Through the parliament, the Court sought to quiet constitutionalist and revolutionary agitation without altering autocratic rule.

The overthrow of the monarchy in 1911 initiated China's Republican era and removed the main obstacle to parliamentary development. But even with the Emperor gone, the road to parliamentary development was not clear. Uncertainty and advice from abroad led to an experiment with representative government and autonomous political parties based on western models,[15] but within a very short time, fears that intense party competition would cause political stalemate and insufferable delays induced many moderates, reactionaries, and progressives to conclude that liberal politics was premature or unsuited to Chinese conditions. In 1912 a coalition of political parties came out against "unprincipled" party competition and promised to struggle for the common good. All the major political actors felt compelled to promise that party government would end internal strife.[16] Ironically, "the country imported a Western ideology founded on individualism and conflict because of its presumed ability to overcome individualism and conflict."[17] A parliament was still desired, but one that would foster cooperation and harmony and one that would concentrate power rather than divide it. In postimperial China a parliament would draw the nation together and legitimate the government; it would both enhance state power and make it more popular.

The National Assembly convened on schedule in April 1913. But the Assembly (and four others convened under seven different constitutions or basic laws) fell far short of expectations. Legislators lived a life of conspicuous consumption and party machines dominated elections. Andrew Nathan explains that persistent factionalism led politicians who believed in constitutionalism to destroy it. Instead of uniting the state and citizens in a new consensus, the National Assembly amplified dissension and disorder. Small factions within successive assemblies refused to cooperate and the Assembly was unable to pass laws, supervise the budget, or bargain effectively with the cabinet. Most rules pertaining to government organization and policy were promulgated by the President in the form of administrative measures.

President Yuan Shih-k'ai, for example, secured a foreign loan without prior National Assembly approval, flagrantly violating the Assembly's legally constituted powers. He also bribed, physically coerced, and arrested deputies under emergency powers. For long periods, government was carried on with no parliament in session, simply because it was not necessary for the conduct of public affairs.[18]

Yuan's attacks and party politics sullied the Assembly's reputation. Parliament could not fulfill its mandate of simultaneously representing rival social and political forces and building unity. Assemblymen could not put aside private interests and petty disagreements to reinstill a sense of national purpose. Erstwhile monarchists soon gathered behind Yuan and echoed his claim that republican government would bring disorder, threats to foreign interests, and foreign intervention. Among the revolutionaries, Sun Yat-sen concluded that a period of tutelage had to precede parliamentarianism – that for a time opposition could not be opposition, but only a helpmate of the ruling clique. The vested interests, liberties, and privileges institutionalized by parliaments stood in the way of the drastic changes needed to make China strong and wealthy. Most elites agreed that enlightened despotism of some sort was needed to unite China and to build a strong center. By the mid-1910s, even remaining western-style liberals favored strengthening the state and making the chief executive the initiator of legislation.[19]

Few mourned the dissolution of parliament in 1914 or welcomed its return in 1917. In the new parliament factional maneuvering reappeared, and efforts to build a consensus were no more successful than in the old assembly. Factional struggles in 1922–3 and the open purchase of the presidency by Cao Kun ushered in "the decisive stage of China's disillusionment with constitutional republicanism."[20] The last parliament of the Peking Regime closed in 1925, long after momentum for representative democracy at the national level had dissipated.[21]

John Fincher argues that early experiments in Chinese democracy, when viewed in relation to the Russian Dumas or the rise of western assemblies, were relatively successful and disprove the assertion that Chinese political culture was unreceptive to democracy.[22] Andrew Nathan, looking primarily at the period 1918–23, indicts both elite political culture and the urgency of China's problems. Nathan points to "informal political rules" and "short-term tactical requirements of a chosen political game" that produced factional alignments and "disintegrative behavior" at a time when unity was paramount. By 1923, Nathan concludes, it was clear that nonhierarchical organizations (e.g., parliamentary parties) could not save China: diffused power resulted in chaos. A strong, unambiguous focus of loyalty was needed.[23]

National disintegration belied attachment to legal processes or to an immobile legislature that accurately reflected political and social disunity.

In 1950, Qian Duansheng, a Harvard-trained political scientist (Ph.D. 1924), wrote of "understandable contempt" for political parties and concluded:

The experience of constitution-making during the period of the Peking Regime [1911–23] had therefore meant nothing to the people of China. It had not provided political stability nor improved their material well-being. It had only enabled the politically unscrupulous to take advantage of constitutions to promote their selfish and personal interests, almost invariably to the detriment of the national interest.[24]

If the failure of constitutionalism meant little to the Chinese people, it meant much to those who would lead China in coming generations. As early as 1914, Li Dazhao and Chen Duxiu, two of the men who would later found the Chinese Communist Party (CCP), resolved that "political parties... work for the interests of an exclusive minority or class" and they criticized parliaments and parties as "bloodsuckers."[25] Some years later, Mao Zedong would conclude that " 'dreams' about learning from the West were shattered ... not only by imperialist aggression, but by the ineffectiveness of Western solutions in the Chinese context."[26] Fear of backsliding into disorder would animate Mao and his colleagues to seek a more effective government built on extraconstitutional bases. On an ideological plane, "the loss of liberal meaning, of dividing the world into constitutional and nonconstitutional states, opened up the possibility of reexperiencing the world in terms of oppressed and imperialist peoples."[27] Out of a failed political democracy, symbolized by inefficient, obstructionist, splintered national assemblies, the CCP's vision of a united party leading a united China grew.

Legislatures under the Guomindang

More than twenty years would pass between the end of the Peking Regime and Communist accession to power – years in which Chiang Kai-shek and the Nationalist Party (Guomindang) ruled China. Under Chiang, China had its first taste of legislative assemblies in a one-party system. This experience reinforced centralizing trends and further channeled reform toward authoritarian alternatives that offered the hope of transcending liberalism (and the weak state) by adopting institutional forms more compatible with Chinese traditions.[28]

In the early 1920s, the founder of the Guomindang, Sun Yat-sen, turned to the Soviet Union for advice on party organization and tactics. "Soviet antiparliamentarian doctrines" coupled with "revulsion (over) the failures of the Chinese Parliament" heightened Sun's disdain for democracy, both at home and abroad.[29] Domestically, he put his faith in a strong executive who would lead China through a period of political tutelage. The five-Yuan[30] system he proposed outwardly resembled a separation of powers, but owed more to traditional Chinese notions of a unitary state. According to Qian Duansheng:

> Sun Yat-sen deplored checks and balances, and thought that the five organs in possession of the powers should work in unison. But he failed to define how the president holding an office which he envisaged as one of importance could resist the temptation to interfere with some or even dominate all of them.[31]

As for the Legislative Yuan, Sun intended it to be a simple organ of legislation, devoid of other powers. Members would lack the right to censure or impeach, and powers of initiative and referendum were to be parceled out to a separate National Assembly.

Sun Yat-sen died suddenly in 1925. Three years later, after successfully unifying the country, Chiang Kai-shek formed a government based on Sun's teachings. But without Sun's leadership and with politics dominated by factional alliances and personal and military power, the five Yuan could not function as effective state organs. State institutions had minimal autonomy under a Nationalist government based on the principle of party dictatorship.[32] The Guomindang thoroughly penetrated and controlled each Yuan, and Chiang postponed the transition to constitutional democracy indefinitely, pending administrative consolidation and years of political tutelage. In the face of pressure from Japan and regional militarists, Chiang argued it was necessary to curtail individual freedoms and to construct an efficient and farsighted government free from constitutional restraints. For Chiang, unity and the ability to act took precedence over broad representation.

As set up in 1928, the Legislative Yuan had 49 appointed members and was primarily a drafting bureau. Although it passed a number of laws that provided a legislative foundation for the Nationalist state, it met only several hours each week and "was not known for its hard work." Its members were "mediocre and apolitical" and "the more ambitious left rather than be stalemated." Committee members knew they had no authority to challenge Chiang and saw little reason to review proposals carefully. Legislators occasionally censured the Executive Yuan, but only when it was in retreat; they could not maintain pressure against resistance.[33] Successive constitutional drafts prepared and reviewed from 1931 to 1936 were increasingly

authoritarian, and each granted greater policy-making and appointment powers to Chiang.

The National Assembly was not established until 1938. Elections were
tightly controlled by the Guomindang machine in the provinces. During
sessions, members occasionally attacked and embarrassed officials but seldom persuaded the government to change its conduct. Interpellations put
pressure on officials to heed public opinion, though the sharpest questions
were reserved for the weakest ministers and dismissal was not a realistic
hope. Members rarely exercised budgetary powers or the right to approve
important policies. The Assembly organized investigations, but findings and
proposals carried no official weight. In short order, the four councils held
from 1938 to 1948 "grew progressively (more) impotent and disappointing."[34]

It is unlikely that the existence or activities of the Guomindang legislative
organs drew much attention from CCP leaders in the 1930s and 1940s; even
Communists who took part in the National Assembly often abstained or
boycotted sessions. After 1949, of course, the CCP repealed all Guomindang
laws and abolished both the Legislative Yuan and the National Assembly.
Chiang's government, as the last in a century-long succession of governments
unable to bridle local elites or repel foreign aggression, symbolized what
was wrong with China and provided the standard from which the Communists diverged. This does not mean, however, that the CCP negated the
Guomindang completely, or were their mirror image. The new regime developed partly as a reaction to the mistakes of its predecessor and partly as
a continuation of historical and cultural factors that transcend choice. Institutional arrangements in socialist China were the product of a long process
of state building. If the Communists repudiated what Chiang did, they did
not entirely separate themselves from how he did it.

Important structures and routines developed during China's first experience with a one-party state included indifferent constitutional enforcement,
ambiguous party-state relations, and use of a legislature as a "home for the
unemployed."[35] Later, the CCP would build a more effective one-party
system, based on a different ideology and different policy priorities. But
from Chiang they learned that in times of crisis, a legislature under a single
party, like one with many parties, could not be the institution where competing interests met and shaped state policy. Under conditions of foreign
intervention, revolt, and civil war, the locus of power had to shift toward
an active and united executive.

Despite these inauspicious beginnings, the future of Chinese legislatures
was not set. Doors were opening as others closed. In their base areas, the

Communists were experimenting with new state forms and grappling with questions that bedevil every political party – questions about building power, implementing policy, and mobilizing support.

Assemblies in the Jiangxi Soviet, 1931–4

By the 1930s, disillusionment with democracy was widespread and faith in institutional solutions to China's problems was waning. For many Chinese, it was no longer a question of how to find a path to constitutional democracy, but what to seek instead. Marxists, among others, openly impugned constitutionalism and legislative primacy and raised the centralization of power as an end in itself. For the CCP, popular assemblies and law-making bodies would exist (if at all) in an authoritarian environment where few of the assumptions and practices of parliamentary democracy were observed.

Although Marxists dominated Chinese intellectual activity in the 1930s, the form that Marxism would take in China remained to be determined. Contending groups within the CCP envisaged different paths to Communist victory. The "Returned Students," back from training in Moscow, looked to the Soviet Union's urban-based strategy; Mao, ensconced in the newly formed Jiangxi Soviet, was developing organizational theories and practices that implied reliance on the peasantry and eventual encirclement of the cities.[36] According to Ilpyong Kim, the two groups, out of necessity, cooperated in the years 1931–4. As the geographical center of the revolution shifted, the Returned Students needed Mao's support and influence in the base areas, and Mao needed the imprimatur bestowed on the Students in Moscow and the backing of leaders who outranked him in the party hierarchy.[37]

On matters of state structure, the Returned Students dominated. Although Mao was the first Chairman of the Chinese Soviet Republic, his hand was not evident in either the constitution of 1931 and 1934. Conceivably, in 1931 he may not have had sufficient power or he may have judged it premature to press for a legal statement of his ideas on the mass line and peasant revolution. He also may have felt that he had finally arrived in a place where Soviet experiences applied.[38] Whatever the case, the constitution and representative organs adopted for the Chinese Soviet Republic closely followed those of the Soviet Union. From the 1924 Soviet constitution, the Chinese Communists borrowed a system of administration headed by a Congress of Soviets, with regional and local soviets below it, indirect election of higher congresses, exclusion of the bourgeoisie from elections, and representation ratios weighted against peasants.[39]

The Chinese Communists also followed the Soviet lead and opted for a large national assembly that met infrequently. Although the Congress was empowered "to discuss and decide on laws and future development plans," it was not a decision-making organ. Instead, it "summarized experiences, united and centralized all organization and work" and provided a tangible alternative to Guomindang government structures. Sessions were largely informational, and deputies, after returning home, helped implement policy and gauge local reaction.[40] Especially after enlargement in 1934,[41] the Congress failed to exercise "supreme power" and served primarily as a "sounding board for mass participation." Formally subordinate administrative bodies made policy.[42]

The historical significance of the two Congresses centers on their role in Mao's rise to leadership of the CCP. Mao won control of the new government at the 1931 Congress, partly through manipulation of election committees, and was able to frustrate the plan of the Returned Students to change his rural policies. From 1931–4 Mao's standing in the party and Red Army eroded, but he retained control of the government until the Returned Students convened the 1934 Congress and wrested this counterweight to the party away from him. Maoists were removed from the government and Mao maintained his position only by acquiescing to the leadership of the Returned Students. The first two National Congresses, thus "far from being stepping stones on Mao's road to power, were in reality evidence of his temporary decline."[43] By 1934 Mao probably felt ambivalent about representative assemblies; a body that had served him well in 1931 had been used against him in 1934.

The Jiangxi Soviet Congress was no more a native institution than its republican predecessors. By western, liberal standards it also had no better claim to status as a functioning legislature or representative assembly – perhaps less. But to Chinese Communists, it was a marked improvement over past assemblies. Unlike early Chinese parliaments, the Congresses of the Chinese Soviet Republic facilitated rule; they did not fan disunity or slow policy making. Congresses drew the party leadership together, unified the people behind party rule, and encouraged nonparty members to participate in politics. The party center was strong, and assemblies, though not remarkably influential, contributed to that strength. At a time of intense competition between the Guomindang and Communists, congresses established a primitive state structure that mobilized peasants and drew them into the processes of local government.[44] Building on their understanding of Chinese legislative history and Russian Soviet experience, CCP leaders had begun to map out a role for popular assemblies in an illiberal polity.

Assemblies and New Democracy

After Mao won undisputed control of the CCP in 1935, he began to adapt Marxism to Chinese conditions. One Yanan era (1937–45) innovation that affected representative assemblies sprang from a tactical decision to emphasize cooperation over class conflict. Surrounded by enemies, Mao sought allies and promised those who joined a stake in the revolution. In two essays, "On New Democracy" (1940) and "On Coalition Government" (1945), Mao developed the idea of a "transitional form of state to be adopted in the revolutions of the colonial and semicolonial countries," in which the state would resemble neither liberal democracies nor the Soviet Union, but would instead rest on a "joint dictatorship of several anti-imperialist classes."[45] In this period of "New Democracy," non-Communists would help the guerrillas win and consolidate power, and the Communist Party would respect and accommodate nonparty social groups.

Mao held that a system of popularly elected people's congresses, from township to nation, laid a foundation for New Democracy and that universal suffrage ensured proper representation for each revolutionary class according to its status in the state.[46] People's congresses would draw all patriotic Chinese into a united front, determine major policies, and elect governments, and so allow the people to take part in state affairs. Though some opponents would be excluded, Mao saw "no reason to refuse to cooperate with all political parties, social groups, and individuals, provided their attitude toward the Communist Party is cooperative."[47] In the name of broadening the revolution's popular base, compromise would be possible.

In 1937 and 1941, the CCP acted on Mao's words. Party officials drafted an election law imbued with the spirit of participation and devoid of references to class struggle or other Marxist categories. The party gave full political rights to former class enemies and convened elections in Communist-controlled districts. Particularly in 1941, efforts were made to include progressive non-Communists and moderates among the candidates. But results of this experiment in election were inconclusive. An impending Japanese offensive in 1937 drew official attention away from the elections before completion of the four-stage process. The councils created in 1941 met infrequently, focused on policy implementation rather than formulation, and were often supplanted by small-group meetings of high-level cadres. In Yanan, "elected government was never the ultimate authority; it was but one facet of New Democratic politics in which power was shared by the party, the bureaucracy, the army, and mass organizations."[48] Although theory outpaced practice in Yanan and the intended role of popular assemblies was not fully brought out, elections and elected bodies mobilized potential allies, spread information, and built support for Communist rule.

Fulfilling promises of formal inclusion, however, and real, institutional influence for non-Communists awaited more stable political conditions and a final sorting out of what Yanan had meant. For it the Yanan legacy offered the promise of a broad united front, it also showed that representative assemblies were only one means to achieve it. Appropriate cadre behavior and the mass line popularized Communist rule without recourse to institutionalized assemblies or legal codes. Many of Mao's writings suggested that if cadres adopted a correct work style, then political education, representation and mass influence would be adequately served. In this view, representative assemblies only supplemented face-to-face, informal contact and were of distinctly secondary importance.

Even so, Mao recognized that the end of the civil war and nationwide rule required new approaches, and he continued to develop his ideas on the role of representative institutions. By 1945, he imagined a future in which the CCP would establish popularly elected congresses as one component of "a new democratic type of state and government with a union of several democratic classes."[49]

On the eve of victory, Mao explained the extent of collaboration planned with non-Communist forces. In "On the People's Democratic Dictatorship" (1949), he expanded the ranks of "the people" to include the petty bourgeoisie and national bourgeoisie. But at the same time, he downplayed populist elements of the Yanan way and defended "leaning to one side" and reliance on the Soviet Union as "our best teacher." He called for strengthening the state apparatus – particularly the army, police, and courts – to enforce dictatorship over remaining enemies and reactionaries. He referred to the state as "an instrument for the oppression of antagonistic classes," as "violence and not benevolence."[50] With victory in sight, Mao's foremost concern had shifted from building a united front to protecting the revolution, and predictably, the coercive potential of state organs overwhelmed their representative significance.

After assuming power, the Communists were slow to clarify what role representative institutions would play. Although Chinese leaders looked to the Soviet Union for organizational guidance and modeled many state institutions after those of the Soviet Union, they did not set up an equivalent to the Supreme Soviet. The leadership agreed to establish a National People's Congress, and discussions took place in August 1948, but in September 1949, the Chinese People's Political Consultative Conference (CPPCC) convened to legitimate the founding of the new state and to organize a government.[51] The CPPCC adopted "The Common Program" (a proto-constitution) and was charged with carrying out the authority of the NPC until a constitution and electoral law were written and the people's congress system established. The CPPCC included representatives of fourteen "patriotic parties" as well as "independent democratic personages"; it was, however, only a provisional state organ. Once elections were held and the NPC established, it would be transformed into a united-front organization that gave informal, nonbinding advice. Until then, with military mop-up, agrarian reform, and penetration of CCP cadres incomplete, representation and legislative duties would be turned over to party leaders and "patriotic personages" who would not challenge or embarrass the new regime.

During the nation's first five years, the CPPCC's decisions had the force of law. Cooperation of non-Communist luminaries in the CPPCC reflected the broad nationalist appeal of the revolution and the popular support the new regime enjoyed, and it also reassured former capitalists and the technical intelligentsia that moderate policies would follow.[52] The CPPCC was a temporary national assembly that symbolized the multiclass alliance upon which the state rested; it was a precursor to the NPC that blended the form of a legislature with the functions of a united-front organization.

When the NPC was finally established in 1954, it lagged behind the times. An outgrowth of New Democracy, its founding roughly coincided with the end of that era and the beginning of socialist construction. A symbol of political mediation, it came into being as the CCP consolidated one-party rule and launched campaigns against counterrevolutionaries. If memories of Yanan lingered, conditions had changed. The revolution was won and domestic, Communist power was vast and secure. The stumbling first steps toward socialist transformation in 1953 had confirmed the need for more devoted Communists and better leadership to carry out policies far more contentious than resistance to the Japanese and land reform. In the early 1950s, the revolution was still unfinished, and leadership priorities revolved around building and concentrating power. Like China's early parliaments, the NPC came onto the scene at a time when political realities militated against liberalism, and like its predecessors, the NPC was designed to foster unity and centralization.

The CCP, unlike the Imperial Court, however, formed a parliament from a position of strength. It was no longer obliged to court allies of dubious loyalty, who supported overthrowing the Guomindang but might oppose future CCP policies. The NPC was meant to serve the united front, but not at the expense of party power.

For these reasons, and even more compelling international considerations, the Chinese turned to the Soviet Union for guidance in establishing a system of popular assemblies. The NPC's structure reflected Soviet legal tutelage and Soviet formulations on legalizing Communist rule and institutionalizing representation. Like the Supreme Soviet, the NPC would be a modern embodiment of the Paris Commune that combined legislation and administration and demonstrated the fiction of separation of powers and the inefficiency of checks and balances. It would serve as the centerpiece of a unitary state that brought into play the creativity and initiative of the masses and enabled them to govern directly. Antibureaucratic and staffed by by unpaid amateurs (who returned to their work after finishing state duties), the NPC would actively organize diverse interests, iron out conflicts, and prove the wisdom and popularity of party rule. Unlike bourgeois assemblies, which were derided as capitalist-dominated "centers of idle talk" (*qingtan guan*), the NPC would represent the people's will, and an assembly devoted to integration, legitimation, mobilization, and socialization would also engage in law making, supervision, and representation without interfering with the dominant role of the party.[53]

In terms of Chinese parliamentary experience, the model of the Jiangxi Soviet Congresses had prevailed over the possibilities *and* ambiguities implied in the Yanan experience.[54] The parliaments of the early twentieth century remained examples of organizational structures to avoid.

That the NPC would not be a liberal democratic legislature was unquestioned. The Communists did not need to compromise, and so set up a legislature in which they would never be forced to. Yet the same power that constrained the NPC also gave the party unprecedented security and confidence. Counterrevolutionaries still existed, but not in great numbers. Some local elites and ordinary people were not yet converted to socialism, but this simply awaited further political education. In the halcyon days of the mid-1950s, party leaders believed they could be both popular and strong – that the government could be effective yet "established on the trust of the masses rather than their fearfulness."[55] Initial conformity to Soviet and authoritarian Chinese models did not fix the NPC's development path or erase all memories of Yanan and early republican assemblies. A tension remained between the Soviet-inspired NPC structure and ideas of some Chinese concerning the role of representative institutions. This became apparent within several years, when Mao enlarged the united front and encouraged outside criticism, and legal scholars and cadres resurrected proposals that resonated with China's past.

PART II
The NPC under Mao

3
Development, doubts, and decline

The 1954 constitution and the NPC organic law established the NPC and granted it an array of powers that paralleled those of the Supreme Soviet and East European assemblies.[1] The constitution deemed the NPC "the only legislative authority in the country," "the highest organ of state authority," and the sole body empowered to amend the constitution. As the only legally sovereign organ and a conduit for mass political participation, the NPC legalized Communist rule and represented popular sovereignty within the Chinese constitutional myth. It stood beside the vanguard party and symbolized accountability and a united political community. A working model of democratic centralism, the NPC embodied socialist democracy and boosted party legitimacy. Its primary task was mobilizing citizens and offering them a chance to participate in governing an exclusive, class-based Leninist state in the form of a dictatorship of the proletariat.

As the nation's law maker, the NPC shared the right to initiate legislation with the state chairman, vice chairman, and the highest state executive organ – the State Council. The State Council was given the power to issue decrees and orders that did not contravene the constitution or laws passed by the NPC, but the NPC had the power to revise or annul decisions of any state organ that it judged to be in conflict with the constitution.

The NPC was also empowered to form and oversee the upper reaches of the state apparatus. The constitution accorded the legislature the authority to elect and remove central government officials, including the state chairman, vice chairman, premiers, members of the State Council, and leading members of the Supreme People's Court and Supreme Procurator. At yearly plenary sessions, deputies were to deliberate over and pass the state budget, final accounts, and economic plans. Deputies were given the right to question members of the State Council, ministries, and commissions, and to ask them for information. Those questioned were obliged to reply. NPC leaders, at their discretion, were empowered to appoint commissions of inquiry to

29

investigate problems of their choosing and the full body was authorized to decide on questions of war and peace. Last on a long list, the legislature was granted "such other functions and powers as the National People's Congress considers necessary."

To better exercise its powers, the NPC was given a Standing Committee. The NPCSC would conduct elections of NPC deputies, convene sessions, interpret laws, adopt decrees, meet twice each month and exercise all non-lawmaking powers of the NPC between plenary sessions. Since NPC sessions were to be infrequent and brief, the NPCSC would be the heart of the legislature. With its broad powers and the right to appoint committees and conduct inquiries, the NPCSC would be well-placed to influence policy and to supervise other organs of state.[2]

On paper, the NPC and its Standing Committee had resources and power. No funding decisions were to be made without NPC participation, and all state agencies were subordinate to the legislature. Authority over law making was complete and jurisdiction unbounded. Representation, in its Communist formulation, was to be guaranteed by deputies who remained employed in full-time jobs and had contact with their constituents in daily life.

Yet evolution of the NPC into a legislature that exercised power and represented the people was far from certain. To grow beyond a united-front organ limited to mobilization, propaganda, and socialization work depended on three related developments. First, the party had to reexamine its approach to law and activate NPC law making. In the past, Chinese Communists had governed through party policy without notable recourse to codification or legal norms. This had to change: law (in the sense of formal, detailed, written sets of rules) had to secure a place and a purpose in the political system. China's leaders had to develop an appreciation for precision and specification and to see worth in using legal means to guide and restrict officials, to control the public, to publicize and enforce policies, and to monitor policy implementation. Legal processes had to find a niche next to political movements, class struggle, and revolutionary justice.[3] Lawyers and judges had to be trained and decisions had to be made on how (if at all) law differed from party policy in scope, stability, and binding force.[4]

Marxian theory and Soviet practice, of course, provided counsel on the role of law during socialist construction. But it was ambiguous, or at least counsel open to several interpretations. On the one hand, law was derivative and fated to wither away once class distinctions were abolished through proletarian revolution. On the other hand, while awaiting this occurrence, law was politics; law was an integral part of the superstructure that protected the interests of the dominant class. After the proletarian revolution, law would exist for a time as a tool of class struggle – an elastic, flexible instrument of social engineering used to transform society in accordance with the revolutionary ideology. Law was thus one of many weapons available for suppressing class enemies and effecting the transition to communism.[5]

But this perception of law as inescapable and useful was not universally shared within the party. For many Chinese Communists, history proved that laws were unnecessary during a revolutionary struggle; theory stated that laws were unnecessary in the future communist state. Skeptics remained unconvinced that in the interim, during the period of socialist construction, law and law-making bodies were indispensable instruments of proletarian rule.[6]

Second, the CCP had to encourage the development of a separate state apparatus for the NPC to oversee. Although the constitution placed the NPC at the apex of the state structure, the preamble reaffirmed the leadership of the party and party statutes pointedly did not exclude members who served in the NPC from party discipline. The NPC did not have jurisdiction over party committees, and if party and state organs were indistinguishable, legislative oversight would evaporate and be replaced by party discipline. The NPC provided an alternate channel of control over parts of the bureaucracy; for the NPC to serve the party, without unduly constraining it, it had to have a clearly defined nonparty target at least partially staffed by nonparty functionaries.

Third, and most important, leadership support for the NPC had to remain high, to give the legislature time to gain prestige and to accrue powers and functions. Before the NPC could develop a coherent, institutional identity, it had to survive its first few years. The NPC had to make peace with external forces that could easily topple it or usurp its mission. The NPC was a latecomer and an interloper. Its participation in policy making and rule making complicated party roles; its status as legislator and administrator encroached on bureaucratic territory; its representative, integrative, and legitimizing roles duplicated party and CPPCC functions. For decades, Chinese leaders had experimented with legislatures, never finding one that was entirely satisfactory. At its founding, few knew what the NPC would or could do. Inspired by the Soviet Union, it might have followed the lead of other socialist legislatures. Or, it might have built on latent, home-grown expectations and absorbed tasks initially assigned to other institutions.

This chapter explains how political twists and turns, what the Chinese call "subjective reasons," buffeted the NPC from 1954–76, first expanding and then narrowing its mandate. Chapter 4 discusses the consequences of the NPC's Soviet-derived structure on the legislature's search for organizational definition. Chapter 5 blends history, structure and legislative theory to bring out the contradictions that defined the NPC under Mao.

"Healthy development"

The First Session of the First NPC opened in September 1954 amid great fanfare. The nationwide radio network carried the legislature's proceedings to China's distant provinces and the daily press covered the session in detail. The First NPC had 1,226 deputies, elected in the summer of 1954 by provincial-level people's congress deputies, and seated after certification by the NPC Credentials Committee. Early in the session, delegates approved an NPCSC of 81 members, formally established two permanent committees – the Nationalities Committee and the Bills Committee – and convened a Budget Committee that would meet for the duration of the session. Staff support was provided by the NPCSC General Office (*bangongting*), whose director and five vice directors managed a staff of several hundred professionals divided among eight offices (Legal, Research, Translation and Editing, Secretary's, Advisory, Nationalities, People's Reception, and General Affairs) devoted to research, issuing and distributing documents, and coordinating routine, day-to-day work.[7]

After introductory speeches, deputies turned to substantive work. They elected or confirmed the nomination of 227 state officials[8] and deliberated over and passed the constitution and five organic laws: those of the NPC, Supreme People's Court, Supreme People's Procurator, State Council, Local People's Congresses,[9] and Local People's Governments. (These laws defined the central and local state structure and established channels of accountability and rules for interaction.) Throughout the session deputies listened to reports on the government's work, and though ordinary deputies had the right to speak on any topic, and several hundred did, only 39 proposals were submitted to the Motions Examination Committee.[10] At this first session, deputies did not address oral or written questions to ministers, voted by a show of hands (except on the constitution), and passed all measures unanimously. Moreover, they endorsed all laws and decrees enacted from 1949 to 1954 that did not contravene the new constitution.

Although Mao Zedong hailed the session as a "milestone in the historical development of the People's Republic of China,"[11] ceremony dominated over substance. The constitution did not found the state or codify power relations developed in the regime's first five years. Instead, it established new organs of state power that replaced or modified existing political machinery. The NPC's first session at best redefined formal power relationships and indicated in what direction the state system might evolve. Only time would indicate if more than names and titles had changed.

Chinese scholars, writing after the Cultural Revolution, identify 1954–6 as years of healthy development of the people's congress system and steady progress in law making.[12] Though they are excessive in their praise and overanxious to sharpen the contrast with later years, there is no doubt that the mid-1950s were the heyday of Chinese legal and legislative development. Zeng Lin highlights the mobilizational role of congresses: "through the mid-1950s the people's congress system was unceasingly perfected and consolidated, and it played a large role in uniting the people, forming a united force, and perfecting socialist revolution and development under party leadership."[13] Chen Shouyi, an early (1955–8) editor of China's foremost political-legal journal (*Zhengfa Yanjiu*), focuses on law making:

On the basis of the 1954 constitution, after the five important organic laws were drafted, other laws were drafted on Advanced Producer Cooperatives and the transformation of capitalist industry and commerce, and although temporary and far from perfect, they were formulated step by step in response to the needs of state building, proceeding from China's current conditions, summing up experiences, and advancing from the simple to the complex. . . . During the seven or eight years following the founding of the state, the development of the country's legal system was basically healthy, its orientation was correct, and its achievements were conspicuous.[14]

As regards the NPC, activities of the NPCSC and individual deputies between sessions stood out. In its first four and one-half years, the NPCSC met 109 times and listened to work reports on 37 occasions.[15] Many of its decisions fleshed out constitutional provisions and explained how to implement the organic laws. For example, at its Seventeenth Session in 1955, the NPCSC passed a resolution on legal interpretation, deciding that powers would be shared among the NPCSC, the Judicial Committee of the Supreme Court, the Chinese Academy of Science, and the editorial board of *People's Daily*.[16] Though this provision was vague and included two nonstate organs in state work, it indicated leadership commitment to defining relations between the party and state executive, judicial, and representative bodies, and interest in untangling, or at least clarifying, overlapping powers.

In the mid-1950s, the NPCSC also adopted measures to involve deputies more deeply in legislative work and to turn the NPC into a working, if not full-time, organ of state power. In particular, deputies were encouraged to be more active between sessions. In February 1955, the NPCSC formed special offices to furnish free secretarial help to deputies. Later in 1955, the NPCSC instructed deputies to carry out twice-yearly investigation tours in their electoral unit, place of origin, or other places of their choosing. Only those who were too old, ill, or engaged in work that could not be interrupted were exempted. According to a deputy secretary general of the First NPC, inspections were designed "to play a supervisory and promotional role, to make the most of achievements and correct mistakes, to overcome bureaucratism and subjectivism, and to prevent leadership organs from becoming separate from the masses." On the first tour in May 1955, deputies visited 23 provincial-level regions for an average of 15 to 20 days. In November 1955, CPPCC members were included, and units in all 29 regions received inspections ranging from one month to six weeks.[17]

The NPCSC made the longer second tour possible when it agreed to pay deputies' travel expenses. At the time of the first tour, deputies only received 50 yuan/month working expenses and no regular salary,[18] and likely were hesitant to incur expenses that would not be reimbursed.

Inspections followed a set format: first, the deputy received an introduction to the unit; he or she then convened a discussion (*zuotanhui*), conducted individual interviews and on-the-spot investigations. Next, the inspector summed up results, exchanged opinions with the unit's leaders, and made proposals; lastly, the deputy relayed recommendations to the NPCSC, local people's congress, local government, procurator or courts, and wrote a report for the NPCSC.

Statistics from the second tour suggest that deputy reports touched on important issues. Of 676 reports, 18% concerned culture and education, 13% medicine and health, 12% state commercial and industrial enterprises, 11% socialist transformation of capitalist commercial enterprises, 8% agricultural cooperativization, 7% socialist transformation of handicraft enterprises, 6% united grain purchase, with the remaining quarter on subjects such as transportation, nationalities, overseas Chinese, local cadre work style, neighborhood and judicial work, and the suppression of counterrevolutionaries.[19]

Commentators in the mid-1950s emphasized the contribution inspection tours made to combating local bureaucratism. Inspections, it was said, provided an opportunity for citizens to channel complaints about local leadership through NPC deputies, who then did their best to "wake up" (*qingxing*) the leadership.[20] Chinese sources tell us that tours educated deputies, gave them a basis to speak at plenary sessions, and helped them "promptly reflect the needs of objective reality in legislative work."[21] Of course, it should not be forgotten that inspections took place against a background of party dominance, which limited what deputies could "reflect" and supplied an official view of "objective reality" – yet they were not meaningless exercises. Within bounds, deputies, in the name of the people and a more efficacious political system, had the right and ability to bring problems to the attention of decision makers. According to an informed Hong Kong analyst:

In the mid-1950's NPC deputies received respect, could go anywhere for inspections and interviews and local party committees didn't dare casually neglect their opinions. . . . There was an atmosphere that regarded deputies as the masses' spokesmen and not that of the party committee.[22]

Inspectors identified local problems, upbraided miscreants, and promised change. Through NPC deputies, the leadership strove to show their displeasure with immoral and incompetent local administrators and their responsiveness to the needs of the people.

At the same time, the between-session duties of deputies grew, NPC lawmaking capabilities expanded. In order "to promote state work" and "promptly deal with urgent matters,"[23] the NPC in July 1955 authorized the NPCSC to draw up special regulations and laws of a "partial nature" (*bufen xingzhi*). Some three years later, the NPCSC was further empowered to revise clauses and make new provisions between NPC sessions on the basis of the developing situation and work needs. These provisions signaled a break with the practice of the Soviet Union, which strictly limited the powers of the Supreme Soviet's Presidium, and increased the likelihood legislative work would proceed during the 50 weeks each year the NPC was not in session.[24] Most importantly, these amendments demonstrated leadership resolve to develop a working legislative system, in which policy passed through state bodies before it became law.

The 1955 and 1956 NPC sessions provided further evidence of official support for a more active national assembly. At its second session, the NPC passed its first substantive law – the military service law. It also dissolved two provinces and reviewed and passed the Yellow River Management Act and the just-finished final draft of the First Five Year Plan. Over 280 civil servants attended deputy group meetings to explain the draft and to provide additional materials.[25] Although approval came two years after the plan had officially begun and few changes were made, plenary debate reportedly took place on deputy proposals that opposed socialist industrialization or demanded a slower pace.[26]

At the 1955 NPC session, Zhou Enlai reported to the Congress on the 39 motions submitted by deputies in 1954.[27] He said that motions on topics such as harnessing the Yangtze and railway construction had all been "carefully studied"; some had been handed over to relevant departments for "gradual application"; while others could not "immediately be put into effect due to various limitations." Ministers and other officials addressed the session on work in their fields and 147 spoke on assorted topics.[28] The media covered the session closely and released an unprecedented amount of information on government operations. Press reports emphasized accomplishments, but did not ignore problems. Zhou and Chen, with their comments at the NPC, put the party's credibility on the line and displayed considerable confidence, explaining what could be done and why certain motions and suggestions could not be carried out.

The 1956 NPC saw the first serious legislative criticism of government work. One hundred fifty-six deputies gave speeches at the session, of which only 28 were work reports by government officials. Deputies put forward numerous proposals and criticisms on the central–local division of power, finance, work benefits, and bureaucratism. On the closing day of the session, Vice Premier Chen Yun and Premier Zhou Enlai responded. Chen admitted mistakes in commercial work, especially on the proper handling of private factories' profits, and suggested remedies. He also recognized that his proposed solutions would raise more questions and answered some of these. Chen then replied to questions on revenue needed from joint-state enterprises and acknowledged that the government had not submitted sufficient data to make the facts clear to deputies. He provided more information to show that the state plan on this item could be fulfilled. Following Chen, Zhou Enlai accepted criticisms and opinions raised by deputies, and agreed that the division of power between central and local authorities needed better definition. He recognized the problem of "the higher the cadre the more likely to be separated from the masses," and agreed that local authorities should be given more explicit powers. Zhou also addressed standard-of-living and social welfare issues and promised raises for urban workers and renewed efforts to solve a growing housing shortage.[29]

Concerns expressed by deputies at the 1956 NPC reflected those of important segments of Chinese society, including former capitalists, nonparty local officials, intellectuals, and urban workers: four groups crucial to socialist development but potentially hostile to communist rule. Deputies did not simply praise the new society, or pretend that the party was above reproach. And the government's response suggested that the party would not make all decisions internally, but would allow nonparty social groups some say in China's socialist development.

Through the legislature, the Chinese Communists had begun to assert their independence from Moscow and to recall the lessons of Yanan. Though still working within a structure modeled after the early Supreme Soviet and its pre–1936 predecessors, Mao denied the necessity of a period of Soviet-style dictatorship of the proletariat, and maintained that class enemies and fence-sitters could be educated to accept socialism.[30] The NPC was one means to win over the suspicious. In the view of a contemporary Chinese commentator, "intense struggle and debate" were present and necessary at the NPC, "because victories on the ideological and political front were not yet completely won."[31] Former enemies and bourgeois intellectuals could be given their say, for ultimately they would come around. On a policy such as socialization of business enterprises, deputies of capitalist background took part in discussions and made suggestions, and thus incurred the obligation to explain to colleagues who opposed nationalization why the policy was patriotic and necessary. In the name of nationwide, multiclass unity, limited dissonance in the NPC was tolerated and limited inclusion was offered.

Only the naive would have suggested that the Chinese political system was evolving into a pluralist parliamentary system. Yet it would have been equally mistaken to dismiss the NPC as a rubber stamp. Surely it had not played a decisive role in policy formulation. Nor could one say the NPC always spoke for the people or strictly held the state apparatus accountable. But the legislature had elite support and was carving out a role for itself in the policy process as a forum for policy review, where deputies enunciated problems on people's minds and party and state officials admitted mistakes and publicly committed themselves to improvement. Without actually sharing its power, the CCP, through the NPC, was showing that a one-party state did not imply arbitrary and capricious rule and that inclusive policies could be pursued simultaneously with power consolidation. Party leaders had chosen to justify themselves to their critics and were confident that explanations (and even concessions) would not undermine their rule, but would instead broaden the united front.[32] Given Chinese and Soviet legislative traditions, the virulent antiliberalism implicit in Marxism–Leninism, and the inevitable insecurity of newly established leaders, a stronger NPC would have been surprising. As an otherwise critical Hong Kong author put it: "in general, the first three NPC sessions had the spirit of a country run by joint consultation, and were heartening steps in making a more democratic system."[33]

"Reform in the air"

Two months after the 1956 NPC, at the Eighth Party Congress, China's leaders reaffirmed their promise "to perfect the legal system." According to the Party Congress' concluding resolution, a new era was beginning – one in which law would play a large role. The resolution explained:

Since the socialist revolution has been essentially completed, and the main task shifted from the liberation of the productive forces to their protection and development, we must further strengthen the people's democratic legal system and consolidate order in socialist construction. The state must work out comprehensive law codes, systematically and step by step, according to need.[34]

At the Congress, NPC Chairman Liu Shaoqi spoke of the urgent need for legal development, and Dong Biwu, a Politburo member, head of the Supreme Court, and one of the founders of the party, recommended revising pre-1954 laws on counterrevolutionaries and taxes and enacting basic criminal, labor, and land-use laws.[35] All appearances suggested that the party was committed to rationalizing its authority and codifying its policies.

What this meant for the legislature became clear in November 1956, when at an NPCSC meeting, Liu Shaoqi proposed to alter and strengthen the NPC committee structure.[36] He suggested creating eight standing committees under the NPC, with branches at the local level, to act as a supreme, national supervisory system. In the following months, Peng Zhen, the secretary general of the NPC, drew up plans to implement Liu's proposal and reported back to the NPCSC. Peng recommended setting up permanent legislative committees responsible for political-legal affairs, finance, heavy industry, light industry, agriculture, education, and foreign affairs – committees that would parallel the structure of the State Council and ministries and enable deputies to pose cogent and penetrating questions to officials.[37] Liu and Peng, and probably others, wanted more out of a legislative system than unreconstructed Stalinist institutions could provide. They wanted the NPC to oversee a growing state bureaucracy and to ensure that party policies were faithfully carried out. Like previous legislative reformers and systemic rationalizers, they sought to strengthen the legislature to strengthen the state.

In early 1957, however, Mao's call to "let one hundred flowers blossom and one hundred schools of thought contend" suddenly shifted reform to a far more radical track. NPC deputies and many others responded to Mao's request for outside help with party rectification and spoke out forthrightly on political reform, including that of the NPC itself. A loose alliance of state officials, NPC deputies, democratic party members, and scholars argued "that China's organizational problems could not be solved by either rationalization or rectification, but required that mass organizations be given a degree of control over party and state."[38] In March 1957, one of the more

prominent critics, Minister of Communications and NPC deputy Zhang Bojun, suggested that the CPPCC be turned into a democratic link in a strengthened parliamentary system: the upper chamber of a national assembly in
which the NPC was the lower house.[39] Later in the spring, Zhang suggested
creating a "political design institute" (*zhengzhi sheji yuan*), comprised mainly
of members of the CPPCC National Committee and the NPCSC, which the
party would call in to discuss important problems and policies.[40] Though
radical in appearance, Zhang's proposals only went a step further than those
of Liu and Peng. Zhang probably had no illusions about true independence
of the CPPCC or NPC; he, on behalf of all nonparty state officials, was
merely eager to grasp whatever influence the party offered.[41] In historical
terms, Zhang was attempting to collect on the promise of inclusion tendered
in Yanan; it's unlikely he thought possible or desirable liberal, party politics.

Others, however, did not show Zhang's restraint. Many democratic party
members, who were in the NPC but not the government, reviewed the
NPC's record and urged sweeping changes. Encouraged by Mao and Deng
Xiaoping's words that "democratic personages can provide a kind of supervision over our party which cannot easily be provided by party members
alone,"[42] they saw an opportunity to gain influence in a strengthened NPCSC
beyond that available in the downgraded CPPCC. They took Mao at his
word and for six weeks heaped criticism on the party, becoming bolder as
newspapers continued to publish their comments and top officials remained
silent.

Four of the more liberal Hundred Flowers-era critiques of the NPC came
from NPC deputies who were also members of the Guomindang Revolutionary Committee.[43] Early in May 1957, Shao Lizi said that democratic
party members could not effectively voice opinions at NPCSC and CPPCC
meetings because they were not informed beforehand of the matters to be
discussed, and had no time to study them during the session. He proposed
that members be informed in advance of the agenda. Wang Kunlun, a deputy
mayor of Beijing, agreed that NPCSC members did not fully understand
state work, and could only give general opinions on the state budget and
economic plans. He concluded that NPCSC discussion and approval of major
policies were nothing more than a "gesture."

As May progressed, party treatment of the NPC was criticized in increasingly explicit language. Wang Kunlun and Huang Shaohong questioned party
respect for the NPC, and pointed out that NPCSC quorums were difficult
to achieve, largely because of CCP members' absenteeism. They noted that
at NPCSC meetings, often only democratic personages spoke, while party
members sat silent. Wang asked, "Does this indicate that the party has

already discussed and made its decision on the matters concerned?" Huang wondered if party members of the NPCSC regarded NPC passage as a necessary but inconsequential formality.

As their confidence increased, democratic party members/NPC deputies offered suggestions on how to strengthen the NPC, going far beyond what Liu, Peng, and Zhang envisioned. Tan Tiwu called for radical structural changes; she proposed that departments within the CCP be made into committees under the NPCSC. Reform, in her view, entailed limiting party flexibility and enlarging NPC competence at party expense.

In late May, university scholars and party members joined the critics. Wu Jialin, a lecturer at People's University, said to the Society of Politics and Law: "the highest directive organs of the central government have no clear concept of legality," and cited as examples the unconstitutional delegation of partial legislative powers to the NPCSC and its illegal creation of the Xinjiang Uighur Autonomous Area. Wu recommended reversal of the 1955 authorization decision, lest "untold troubles" arise when "those below follow the bad example of those above." Although an arguable interpretation of the constitution, Wu's remarks found support among other legal scholars and marked the first public accusation that the NPCSC had acted illegally.[44]

Other scholars and legal cadres criticized party control of NPC nomination lists and portrayed voters as "blind followers" with deputies the product of "disguised appointment." Appeals were heard for free elections and free campaigning. Some critics suggested that inadequate time made NPC debate impossible or perfunctory. All agreed that the NPC, as constituted, was "undemocratic."[45]

Finally, and most alarming, on June 10, 1957, a professor and head of the Shenyang University Communist Youth League assailed party manipulation of the NPC. As reported in *Shenyang Daily* the next day, Zhang Bosheng said:

The NPC is nothing but a mud idol, while all power is in the hands of the party center. The NPC merely carries out the formality of raising hands and passing resolutions. In all these years, one has seldom seen an NPCSC member put forward an important motion, though occasionally one has seen some of them publish unimportant notes on inspection tours in the press. Is this not laughable? They saw only what the party said and saw nothing when the party did not say anything. Why did the NPC deputies see no contradictions among the people during their inspection tours? . . . The party must be removed from its position of superiority to the NPC and the government, the government must be placed below the NPC, and the NPC must be made an organ of genuine power.[46]

The critics had spoken. Using explicitly liberal constructs, they had openly ridiculed the political system and had shown a lack of understanding of why the NPC was set up and what it was expected to do. No leader had ever suggested that the party should be anything other than superior to the NPC. How could China achieve socialism if the vanguard party was subordinate to a representative assembly? The leadership saw no option but to suppress such "anti-Party" ideas. It could not ignore spiralling criticism that challenged fundamental tenets of communist rule.

Evidence exists that senior party leaders opposed the interpretation Mao gave to the Hundred Flowers policy in early 1957.[47] Perhaps Mao's more conservative colleagues realized that the remolding of class enemies and intellectuals was not complete – that reform proposals would go beyond removing the pathologies of a Soviet-based system and raise liberal alternatives that, in their view, had long ago been proved bankrupt. Perhaps they also sensed it was premature to shift from consolidation to inclusion, from rule based on domination and command mobilization to rule based on organizational manipulation of articulate audiences, from denying the whole people representation and legitimation to awarding it.[48]

In any case, by June 1957, orthodox Leninists had their opening. Over-exuberant critics, underground presses, and demonstrations threatened social and political stability and left Mao vulnerable to charges of "undermining the supreme authority of the party, compromising ideological principles of Marxism–Leninism, encouraging ultrademocracy, anarchism, and social disorder, and allowing enemies of socialism to vent their spleen." Mao had not been able to "secure the social constraint and political support necessary for a balanced fusion of a Leninist polity and a system of effective democratic liberties."[49]

In the party's view, many NPC deputies, like their predecessors in the 1910s, were not working to unify the people and strengthen the state. Quite the contrary; they had become a divisive force. Mao's hope for unanimous support for one-party rule overestimated the Communists' popularity; given a say, all would not choose communist rule unchanged in any substantial way. The CCP faced either loosening its grip on power or restricting channels of dissent. Without further pause, leadership priorities shifted from party rectification to social control.

Crackdown and the 1957 NPC

In 1957 a few persons with ulterior motives took advantage of our party's rectification campaign to attack the party's leadership and the dictatorship of the proletariat. They stridently called for a system in which everyone takes turn serving, like players in a Mahjong game. They wanted to throw the Communist Party out of office and put into practice the bourgeois bicameral system in an attempt to nullify the great fruits of our revolution.[50]

On May 25, 1957 Mao told Communist Youth League delegates that all words and actions that deviated from socialism were mistaken; that same day, the NPCSC postponed the opening of the NPC from June 3 to June 20. Roderick MacFarquhar observes: "very possibly the Chinese leaders felt that in the prevailing atmosphere the Congress might turn into an embarrassingly official platform for denunciation of their policies." He also suggests that they may have feared student demonstrations.[51] On June 19, the NPCSC put off the NPC once again, and instead held a week of preparatory meetings.

The first preparatory meeting had lasted one day in 1956 and had been convened to discuss pending legislation and other items on the agenda. The preparatory meetings in 1957 served a different function. Deputies studied the just-published, newly restrictive version of Mao's February speech, "On the Correct Handling of Contradictions Among the People," and party leaders explained insertions and deletions, seeking "to stiffen deputies' resolve to participate wholeheartedly in the forthcoming denunciation of erring friends and colleagues."[52] The preparatory meetings offered party leaders an opportunity to explain a controversial matter to deputies and to rehearse them on their part in the coming crackdown. Many deputies went into the preparatory meetings rightists or sympathizers. When they emerged, they knew the tide had changed, but not who would be swept away by it.

Ten days before the preparatory meetings began, *People's Daily* had published the first of a series of sixteen editorials denouncing "rightists." At first, however, names were not given, and it was unclear whether the sweep would touch outspoken NPC deputies and affect the impending congress. On one hand, the lead *People's Daily* editorial on the day the NPC opened contained a veiled threat:

Some people are not prepared to extol the creative achievements of the people, and this is their freedom. But nobody has the right to obliterate objective facts. What attitude will the people's deputies take toward the fruits of the struggle of the masses of the people? We believe that at least the overwhelming majority of the deputies will give a correct answer to these various questions.[53]

On the other hand, the editorial continued in a fashion sure to draw out more rightists:

In the various previous sessions many deputies made frank and beneficial criticisms of the work of the state. At this session, there is all the more need for development of serious criticism. . . . Some people think that since we have to affirm our achievements and criticize the rightists, then it seems not desirable at the same time to carry out criticism and self-criticism. This is clearly a misunderstanding.[54]

For the first ten days of the session, Mao's Hundred Flowers continued to bloom. Premier Zhou Enlai's government work report defended the regime's record, but was temperate in language, generally avoiding use of epithets such as "bourgeois rightist."[55] *People's Daily* printed a deputy's report on his inspection tour, which contained sharp criticisms of local officials and election procedures.[56] According to a scribe for the Guangdong delegation, small-group discussions were quite lively during these first days; deputies questioned an official about firing his gun at a peasant and grilled an official with a long revolutionary history on her bureaucratism. The top party officials present listened closely to all criticisms, and deputies made many suggestions.[57]

In the beginning of July, however, the atmosphere changed. Tension increased and deputies who made comments in the morning retracted them in the afternoon. Gradually, several deputies, who would later be labeled rightists, became the talk of the session and mention of helping party rectification ceased.[58] Deputies increasingly attacked other deputies who had criticized the party during the early stages of the rectification campaign. The accused rightists resisted for a time, but eventually gave in. Either verbally or in written form, deputies one after another made self-criticisms, admitted mistakes, recounted old crimes, and asked for pardon and punishment for their "antiparty, antisocialist, and antipopular views." The climax came on July 13 and July 15, with the surrender of the best known rightists, including NPC critics Zhang Bojun and Tan Tiwu.[59]

A *People's Daily* editorial on the NPC's closing praised the session as "well held" and an "impetus to all phases of work." It declared: "The deputies as a whole expressed deep indignation against the rightists and demonstrated warm support for the Communist Party line." It claimed that the deputies' "righteous and forthright criticism compelled the rightists among the deputies to bow their heads and admit their guilt. . . . The majority of intellectuals, industrialists and merchants among the deputies supported socialism in this struggle. Moreover, the struggle enabled them to get a clearer view of things."[60] Undoubtedly, among the things deputies saw clearer were the dangers of criticizing the party and the futility of seeking more power for nonparty bodies. The liberal interregnum was coming to an end. Shortly after the NPC closed, the leadership would launch a massive Anti-Rightist Campaign that wrenched the nation back onto a more orthodox Leninist path.

The 1957 session was a turning point both for China and the NPC. Few observers doubt that the party decided to separate out the rightists before the Congress and then orchestrated their criticism.[61] The spectacle of deputies denouncing each other and ultimately admitting guilt resembled Stalinist show trials more than the proceedings of a national legislature. Deputies who followed Mao's instructions to criticize the party were humiliated, and proposals to strengthen the NPC were discredited along with their proponents. 1957 was a watershed year after which NPC decline began.[62] Slogans such as "amateurs cannot lead experts," "political design institute," and "rotating persons" all demanded legislative strengthening and obliquely opposed one-party dictatorship. When the party bludgeoned the critics into submission and then initiated the Anti-Rightist Movement, this soured the political atmosphere.[63] The party asked NPC deputies to speak, and then labeled those who did antiparty or antisocialist. Comment on party–state relations, local bureaucratism, and party members who sought special privileges brought disgrace. After 1957, "almost all NPC deputies were very reluctant to voice opinions, and as for large or small officials, who dared expose them?"[64] Dissent had become dangerous; prudence directed deputies to speak in one voice.

In 1957, the NPC displayed high sensitivity to external pressures and the party showed a willingness to build unity through coercion if cooptation and persuasion failed. Several months of liberalization produced a backlash whose effects lingered for decades. After 1957, serious exploration of how to implement a socialist constitution in the Chinese context halted. NPC supervisory work languished and spokesmen for social groups abandoned their charge. In a telling remark at the 1958 NPC, Gao Chongmin summarized the "penetrating socialist education" received by intellectuals during the antirightist struggle thusly: "the Communist Party and socialism cannot be opposed, and the transformation of one's political stand, bowing one's head before the working people, and following the Communist Party in taking the road of socialism provide the sole outlet."[65] Central party and government officials had used the NPC to launch a movement that weakened the NPC and closed avenues of legislative development.

After 1957, the NPC would not be a forum for nonparty government officials, intellectuals, democratic party members, or former capitalists to express their views or to urge the party to reform or compromise. Doubtful converts would not question party dominance again under the bright lights of national publicity. The leadership would sacrifice the benefits of further legislative development before it would allow the NPC to undermine party rule. Unwilling to accept the risks of upgrading a legislature, the CCP would follow Stalin's example: pay lip service to responsiveness and building a broadly based united front, but stock the NPC with true believers and party loyalists.

Undermining the NPC

Organizational unraveling of the NPC began shortly after the 1957 session. Provincial congresses quickly revoked the credentials of sixteen deputies, and the NPC Credentials Committee recommended that thirty-eight additional rightists be removed. The thirty-eight accused rightists were deprived of the right to attend the 1958 session pending final action, and eventually all their mandates were canceled. Of the five deputies who publicly urged strengthening the NPC, Tan Tiwu was one of the first sixteen to lose her position and Zhang Bojun and Huang Shaohong were among the latter thirty-eight.[66] Wang Kunlun and Shao Lizi continued in their posts. Although electoral units recalled deputies according to legally prescribed procedures, involvement of the party center was transparent. Few could believe claims that the recalled deputies were "renounced" (*paoqi*) by their electoral units, or that their recall was "proof of the system's democraticness."[67] Stung by criticism, the party had reasserted control over NPC personnel and had issued a warning to remaining deputies, making the limits of NPC autonomy apparent to all.

Critics in universities and research institutes also suffered. Proposals to strengthen the NPC disappeared from the daily and legal press and were replaced by long, detailed articles that defended prevailing nomination and election procedures and refuted charges that the NPC was a "mud idol" or "mere formality," or that the NPCSC had violated the law.[68] Wu Jialin, and many other legal scholars, like their allies within the NPC, were disgraced. An authoritative *People's Daily* article deemed Wu's analysis of NPCSC illegality evidence of "extreme hostility . . . toward the NPC and socialist legality, indicating a desire to overthrow the political and legal system, to usurp party leadership authority, and to carry out bourgeois restoration."[69] Even Qian Duansheng, President of the Beijing College of Politics and Law and a long-time international spokesman on Chinese law, was implicated as a member of an antiparty clique and dismissed from his posts.

The events of 1957 also shook the NPCSC. In November 1957, in order to reduce waste of time and manpower, the NPCSC decided to permit provinces and provincial-level cities to hold only one congress each year.[70] In 1958, the NPCSC revoked each deputy's 50 yuan/month working expenses and required vouchers for every official purchase.[71] That same year, the frequency of NPCSC meetings decreased from thirty-seven to thirteen. In general, the legal and legislative systems entered a period of stagnation and interference in which "construction of state power gradually received little attention and . . . democracy in national political life was not systematized and legalized, but instead was damaged."[72] One western author speaks of a "leadership return to an approach that implied the complete negation of law."[73] Why did law making falter and NPC supervision virtually disappear? Even timid deputies could ratify laws and codify party policy; and the NPC could oversee the state for the party, if not for the people. As we have seen, a Soviet-style legislature was not entirely without potential.

To explain NPC inactivity, we must recall that profound changes were occurring in China in 1958, with effects that rippled through to legislative circles. By 1958, Mao's doubts about the Soviet model of development had crystallized and he believed institutionalization interfered with construction. To speed development, Mao strengthened party committees and set out to involve them directly in policy implementation and administration. Over time, this shift would undercut the NPC as the party supplanted state organs and the leadership abandoned legal rule.

According to Liao Gailong, a researcher in the Central Committee Policy Research Office, leaders in the late 1950s came to think that socialism meant concentration of power in the hands of the Party Central Committee.[74] Party organs gradually took over state tasks and regarded state organs as subordinate. Setting a course maintained through the Cultural Revolution, cadres held several party and government posts, mixed party and state functions, and allowed the party to replace the government. A first party secretary often headed a state administrative organ, or a party committee set up its own organ to handle routine state affairs.[75] Despite constitutional provisions, the oversight functions of the NPC and local congresses gravitated toward party organs. Mention of the division of work between the party and state became a "forbidden zone" and those who questioned the party–state fusion were attacked in 1959 in another struggle against "rightist opportunists."[76]

At the national level, party organs supplanted the State Council. The party monopolized leadership and gradually withdrew its confidence in nonparty state officials. Party leadership was deemed the soul of the people's congress system and party involvement in all levels of people's congresses was applauded.[77] Of course, NPC supervisory powers atrophied; party committees dominated state representative and executive organs, had their own channels of control, and had no obligation to accept outside oversight. Any use of external checks receded in favor of party penetration of all public organs. Direct party control, via personnel overlap and discipline inspection committees, guaranteed efficiency and reliable implementation; independent supervision by people's deputies was unnecessary and possibly obstructive. Under a strong party, balky state officials and meddling NPC deputies would not be allowed to impede socialist construction.

Nor would laws interfere with development or limit leadership flexibility. In late 1956, Mao had chided the Soviets for failing to develop democratic procedures and for neglecting socialist legality.[78] In 1958, however, Mao himself showed little respect for law's restraining force. On a decision that dramatically changed the local administrative structure of the state, Mao said: "Have the people's communes violated the constitution? The issue of integrating politics and the commune, for example, was not passed by the People's Congress, nor is it in the constitution. Many parts of the constitution are obsolete."[79] The attitude of the political elite toward law was shifting. Opponents of the Eighth Party Congress decision to build a perfect legislative system met less opposition after the Anti-Rightist Campaign and the revival of guerrilla-style leadership that accompanied the Great Leap Forward. The call to overcome complacency with past achievements and to recognize that traditional Chinese and early communist attitudes toward law were no longer appropriate fell on deaf ears. By one count, the daily press during the first six months of 1959 carried fewer than twenty articles on any aspect of law.[80] The dormant, but not forgotten, anti-institutional, anti-legal thread in Chinese socialism was gaining in strength.

Though silent at the time, Chinese legal theorists now write extensively on this period. In political and legal circles, they explain, the influence of leftism grew and led to criticism of the principles of democracy and legality enunciated in the constitution. Law was opposed to party policy and handling the people's affairs in accordance with law was regarded as a "law first" bourgeois point of view.[81] Elements within China's leadership advocated legal nihilism (*falü xuwuzhuyi*), which held that form had no significance and Marxism was China's basic law. The legal nihilists extolled mass movements and intense class struggle and believed that democracy and legality "tied the hands and feet" of the leadership. They opposed codification and legalization and put their faith in party policy.[82] They obstructed legislative work and vilified fixed legal codes as "transferred from capitalist countries," "revisionist," and "Guomindang."[83]

The causes of legal nihilism were complex and varied – linked to factors as diverse as Chinese culture, party history, and changing Sino–Soviet relations. Some leaders, we are told, were influenced by the traditional Confucian belittlement of law, and accepted legality only to placate the Soviets. Others fondly remembered CCP successes before 1954, achieved through party policies and without a legislative system, and felt a complete set of laws inhibited party creativity in changing conditions.[84] The break from the Soviet economic model and return to guerrilla-style leadership in 1958 encouraged a resurgence of these early communist and traditional Confucian attitudes and called into question all structures established under Soviet tutelage. Desire for a speedy and indigenous path to socialism led the Chinese to renounce Soviet-style legality and to return to a pattern of rule based on their guerrilla experiences. Although the Great Leap Forward was hailed as a revolutionary innovation, in the legal field, it represented a step back to pre-1949 beliefs and approaches.

By 1959, law was simply a manifestation of party policy that changed when policy changed. Party pronouncements played the role given in most systems to statutory law and legal organs merely implemented and executed party policy. Permanent, unchanging rules were not permitted to slow revolutionary progress (i.e., the Great Leap Forward) and commitment to a conception of law as elastic and everchanging meant that law in the sense of norm no longer existed.[85]

The end of law, of course, disrupted state legal and legislative work. After transfers and new job specifications were written, "the activity and prestige of almost all the legal organs fell sharply."[86] At the beginning of the Anti-Rightist Movement, the State Council Legislative Affairs Bureau (which drafted most regulations and many laws) closed, and planned provincial-level ministry legal offices were not established or gradually ceased to operate.[87] The Ministry of Justice was abolished in April 1959 and the Political-Legal Affairs Group of the Central Committee became a department in which staff members were encouraged to devote spare time to productive labor.[88] Researchers at the Institute of Law of the Chinese Academy of Science were sent to the countryside to investigate the masses and the relationship between theory and practice, and were encouraged to combine collection of materials with physical labor.[89] Hundred Flowers-era critics of incomplete legal codes and slow progress in legal work disappeared, and remaining legal theorists distanced themselves from work or themes associated with their disgraced colleagues.

In the universities, political-legal institutes continued to operate, but focused on politics and ideology rather than law. Many teachers and students were sent to the countryside and law courses and students dwindled in number. The publication of legal materials declined both in quantity and quality.

The stock of the legal specialists had fallen. The party leadership removed many of the legal scholars trained in Republican China or the West, including some who had been instrumental in writing the constitution. Instead of a "rigid system" of law that did not accord with "permanent revolution," leaders advocated "mass-centered law," in which the people were encouraged to take part in abolishing and revising "irrational laws, regulations, and institutions that have lost touch with the times."[90] New members of the reorganized Law Department at People's University argued that a "so-called complete system of laws" was "harmful to construction" and "opposed to the spirit of permanent revolution."[91]

The NPC had lost its fountainhead. Legal nihilism had weakened the NPC and party replacement of the state had caused a complete standstill in the nation's legislative work. Legal drafting stopped, and with it NPC participation in codification and ratification; the Standing Committee's staff was reduced to just over 100 people.[92] From 1954–7, it had appeared that the party would use the NPC to create an aura of legitimacy around its rule, in Merle Fainsod's words, "to clothe the party thesis in the garb of constitutional legality."[93] By 1959, the party no longer sought to legalize its rule and did not value stability and rationality in and of themselves. Codification fixed policies that might be changed tomorrow. NPC ratification became associated with reactionary, bourgeois-style rule. In the new way of thinking, the party staked its support on correct policies and dispensed with formal approval by representatives of the people. From 1957–65, no laws were passed and all NPC resolutions were "secondary technical bills as a rule mechanically confirming reports or edicts originating in some other organ."[94]

Political winds had again shaken the NPC. If the 1957 Anti-Rightist Movement and tighter party control of state organs undercut NPC representation and supervision, legal nihilism ended law making. Yet NPC sessions and activities continued until 1966. Stripped of most duties and cowed out of their early activism, deputies devoted more and more time to mobilization, propaganda, and socialization.

Failed mobilization

The three NPC sessions from 1958 to 1960 form a group. Their proceedings and atmosphere differed from the NPC's first four sessions and reflected the unfolding and subsequent collapse of the Great Leap Forward. Ironically, as Mao made his greatest break from Marxist–Leninist economic theory, the NPC became a rather ordinary socialist legislature. Political pressure for unity and repudiation of the Hundred Flowers stifled discussion and debate and transformed the NPC into a simple tool of mobilization, propaganda, and socialization.

People's Daily spoke of the 1958 Congress as "a prelude to a new leap forward of the national economy" at which "a number of deputies gave an impressive account of plans, conditions and experiences in the leap forward on each front of socialist construction."[95] Ideological content infused deputies' speeches, as efforts turned to building support for new and untested policies. More than in previous years, deputies spoke not of or for existing social groups, but of vanguard individuals who would lead China to a new society:

At this National People's Congress, industrial and labor models, in their speeches, reported on the revolutionary vigor and heroic exploits of workers and peasants throughout the country in the big production leap forward, as well as their great revolutionary fervor for the socialist cause described in newspapers during the recent period.[96]

In 1958, the NPC discussed contentious issues, such as language reform and minorities' policy, and leaders appeared committed to relatively modest economic goals; in 1959 and 1960, a different pattern emerged:

The old model aimed at producing a glorious picture of progress and at the end of the report added deficiencies yet to be overcome. The new model omits the second part and the picture resembles Byzantine medieval paintings with their radiant gold backgrounds.[97]

Reports in 1959 admitted few failures, mistakes, or serious problems in economic work. Zhou Enlai's statements on planning, coordination, and manpower management hinted at difficulties and the retreat already under way, but he also praised the general line and called for another Great Leap in 1959 to achieve the fantastic targets set in December 1958. Zhou's ambivalence was not found in most other speeches, including that by the Minister of Finance, who refuted criticisms of economic hardship and urban shortages, and presented statistics that showed life for peasants was improving. The Finance Minister also claimed that transportation and distribution bottlenecks had already been resolved.[98]

Published deputy speeches, by and large, praised the Leap with remarkably few reservations. They spoke of "brilliant achievements" in 1958 and asserted it was "absolutely possible" to launch a still greater leap forward in 1959. They expressed confidence that targets for steel, coal, grain and cotton would be fulfilled or overfulfilled.[99] At a feverish time, deputies were white hot. Several years before, many deputies had lagged behind the leadership and had argued for slower socialist transformation; now, many urged immediate communization.[100]

In the fall of 1959, Mao rebuffed Marshall Peng Dehuai's challenge and inaugurated a second, radical phase of the Great Leap. At the 1960 NPC, deputies' optimism remained high and many advocated extending the Leap. *People's Daily* reported: "it is clear from the speeches made by many deputies that a new, powerful and surging urban people's commune movement has arrived."[101] Officials continued to praise party policies and ignored the weakening economy. The chairman of the State Planning Commission reported on the great accomplishments of 1959–60, alleging that the major targets of the Second Five-Year Plan had been fulfilled three years ahead of schedule.[102]

Deputies applauded "the good situation" and the short-lived urban communes at a time when bad weather, the pullout of Soviet advisers, and excessive state procurement of grain were combining to leave many Chinese close to starvation. From 1959 to 1961, the economy was deteriorating and party use of the NPC to drum up support for failed policies could not succeed. At a minimum, mobilization required a tolerant, if not enthusiastic population, and credible, if not immediately popular, policies. By 1960, both conditions were lacking. And using the NPC to promote a lost cause surely diminished its reputation.[103] Who could respect an organ that praised disastrous policies or believe it represented the people's will?

The 1959 session was delayed five months, presumably while China's leaders decided how the Leap would proceed and how to present it to the people. In 1961, leadership divisions went deeper, and the year passed without an NPC session. The leadership wisely chose not to announce retreat through an organization that had trumpeted the Leap long after its demise. Though quiet changes saved face, this violation of constitutional requirements further damaged the NPC's institutional integrity and reemphasized its conditional status in the state apparatus. At a time of rapidly changing policies, local initiative, and leadership dissensus, the NPC was too cumbersome, too national, and too public to be of use.

By 1961, the NPC was not the people's nor the government's spokesman. Lies and exaggerations had undermined its credibility, and it no longer helped a secretive government release information to deputies and ordinary citizens.

Closed sessions and renewed mobilization

In 1962 and 1963, the NPC reconvened, but in secret. In contrast to earlier sessions, the texts of official addresses and deputy's speeches were not published. In 1962, the leadership only released a press communique summarizing Zhou Enlai's government work report; in 1963, only a general press communique was distributed. Nor was there the normal deluge of informal stories and comments that would triple the length of *People's Daily* for several weeks each year in the 1950s. *People's Daily* printed one editorial in 1962 and a single, short account and picture of the 1963 Congress.[104]

Available evidence suggests a subdued atmosphere at both Congresses. Liu Shaoqi and Zhou Enlai presided over the sessions and their speeches focused on economic recovery. Although the 1962 communique still spoke of "tremendous achievements" of the Leap, Chinese leaders admitted "considerable difficulties in the national economy" and "shortcomings and mistakes in practical work."[105] Reports at the session emphasized agriculture, production of consumer goods, and improving living standards, and downplayed heavy industry. Marcus Green attributes the sessions' relative sobriety to a "thankfulness for perils surmounted, as well as the fact that such improvement as had been achieved was not enough to boast about."[106]

The strict secrecy is more difficult to explain. Perhaps the regime wished to conceal disappointing statistics from all eyes except those of the deputies; perhaps closed meetings were held to ensure privacy to permit free discussion by those present.[107] George Yu notes that small-group discussions grew in importance in 1962 and 1963, with approximately 60% of the session time devoted to provincial groups and 40% to plenary sittings. Though no transcripts or excerpts of these discussions exist, Yu surmises that in small groups, deputies may have gone beyond approving the party line to discuss controversial issues of national importance.[108]

Absence of detailed information on these two sessions makes it impossible to evaluate Yu's conjectures. Perhaps meaningful discussions took place that later affected policy. More likely it was already too late to resuscitate the legislature and to reactivate its representational and supervisory roles.[109]

The 1963 and year-end 1964–5 sessions cast soberness aside in favor of bounding optimism. Talk of consolidating the united front returned,[110] but without the respect for diversity seen in the mid-1950s. The 1964 session in particular resembled those of 1958–60. Just as the earlier congresses had attempted to rally public opinion behind the Leap, the 1964 NPC publicized the Socialist Education Movement and foreshadowed the Cultural Revolution. Although *People's Daily* (January 5, 1965) claimed that officials listened to deputy criticisms and proposals and answered questions, knowledgeable Hong Kong journalists believe that questioning of officials had become empty.[111] As in 1958–60, mobilization and policy dissemination predominated and the NPC was used to assist Mao in his efforts to launch a political campaign, with deputies singing the praises of the "Study Mao Zedong Thought Movement."[112] Any vestige of NPC autonomy had vanished. People's deputies stood ready to publicize and build support for whatever movement unfolded next.

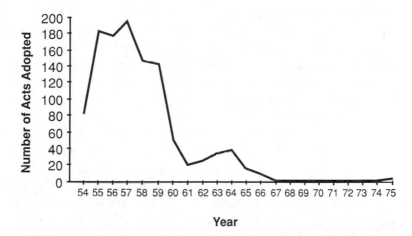

Figure 3.1 Number of legislative acts adopted by the State Council and the National People's Congress or its Standing Committee, 1954–75. Source: Wu Daying, Liu Han, Chen Chunlong, Xin Chunying, and Zhou Xinming, *Zhongguo Shehuizhuyi Lifa Wenti* [Problems in Chinese Socialist Legislation] (Beijing: Qunzhong Chubanshe, 1984), p. 241. The figures exclude local regulations for the entire period and State Council regulations for the years 1964–6.

The NPC by 1966

On the eve of the Cultural Revolution, the viability of the people's congress system was in question. Local congress elections in most places had ended in 1963 and party committees had taken over their duties. The NPC had shown itself unable to resist external pressures, including those that undermined its position. The NPCSC had not actively used its powers of legal interpretation and enforcement and patently unconstitutional party interference in state affairs had not drawn its attention. Legal nihilism was rampant and existing laws were widely ignored. NPC participation in law making had disappeared with hardly a trace. From 1949–66, more than 1500 laws, decrees, and administrative measures were enacted by state bodies,[113] but very few after 1959, and none at all for nine years after 1966 (Figure 3.1).

Some important laws were discussed for years, but never reached the NPC for final passage. Two drafts of a criminal law were completed before the NPC was established. In the First NPCSC report to the NPC in 1955, Peng Zhen said that the NPCSC was collecting additional materials to draft criminal and civil laws. A year later, one major report to the NPC was entitled "We Hope that a Criminal and Civil Law will be Elaborated Soon." On November 24, 1956, *Guangming Ribao* revealed that the thirteenth draft of the criminal law had been completed and that it had 261 articles and two parts. The draft was then reviewed by the Central Committee and revised by the Party Secretariat. Over the next several months, the NPC Motions Committee made revisions and the twenty-second draft was submitted to the 1957 NPC for further opinions and revisions. In June 1957, the Minister of Justice said she hoped the criminal law would be promulgated within a year and that relevant departments were drawing up civil- and criminal-prosecution laws. For six years, work continued, albeit at a slower pace, until Mao and the Politburo Standing Committee examined the thirty-third draft of the criminal law in 1963 and urged speedy enactment. Yet nothing emerged; no laws were submitted to the NPC. Political movements, beginning with the Anti-Rightist Campaign and Great Leap Forward and ending with the Four Cleanups, prevented promulgation.[114] By 1966, despite occasional protests to the contrary, the party had forsaken rule by law in favor of rule by leadership decree.

Chinese scholars now acknowledge this era of lawlessness and its effect on the people's congress system. They admit that the NPC's decline predated the Cultural Revolution and had roots deep in Chinese society and traditional leadership techniques. Xu Chongde and He Huahui ascribe NPC enfeeblement to remnants of feudal thinking, including "autocracy, patriarchalism, bureaucratism and special privilege thinking." These, they say, remained in people's minds and were out of tune with the people's congress system.[115] Wu Daying et al. look to the history of the international communist movement and "unresolved deviations in the relationship between leaders and the party," implying that Stalin's disregard for constitutions and law sanctioned a similar attitude within China's political elite.[116] Wu Jialin directly blames Chinese leaders and their work style:

Even during the period of its normal activities [i.e., before 1966], I'm afraid the NPC was not really the highest organ of state power. This is a systemic problem, and also one of knowledge and work style.... Some leading cadres had a weak democratic viewpoint and lacked democratic work style; this hindered the NPC from playing the role it should have in the nation's political life.[117]

These explanations encircle but fail to pinpoint the underlying cause of NPC marginality: namely, party control of the legislature's agenda, jurisdiction, and personnel, and uncertainty about what a legislature should do. Bound by an ideology that calls for popular sovereignty and pieties about the people as masters, Chinese scholars cannot discuss the unpromising historical and institutional context into which the NPC was thrust. For the Communists, even more than their predecessors, *chose* to have a legislature; it was not an institutional response to societal pressures or a development brought on after acknowledging citizens' rights. The legislature was created by the grace of the party and enjoyed whatever latitude the party bestowed on it. Constitutional provisions notwithstanding, the NPC had only a qualified right to question, resist, or act independently – lest it endanger its privilege to exist. Constitutional powers and functions were controversial; symbolic activities, socialization, and propaganda were not. In such circumstances, "remnants of feudal thinking," "looking down on the constitution," and "a weak democratic viewpoint" were predictable and continuing obstacles to legislative development. Only with a thorough rethinking of party–state and party–society relations could a legislature become an intrinsic part of the Chinese political system and a significant contributor to governing and systemic legitimacy.

By 1966, the NPC had not found its niche. It did not legitimize party rule or legalize party policy; it did not supervise state organs for the people or the party; its potential role as a mediator between the people and the leaders had not developed; its attention to form interfered with a direct relationship between leaders and led; its mobilization, propaganda, and socialization work could have been carried out by other more reliable organizations or the party itself. The promise of the constitution had not been fulfilled. Instead, the leadership had narrowed the NPC's mandate back to its essential core. Because the NPC contributed little to party rule, it was vulnerable to attack.

The NPC and the Cultural Revolution

Though crippled by the early 1960s, the NPC limped on until 1965. Then, a session was not held in late 1965 or 1966, nor for the next nine years. The last meeting of the NPCSC convened April 26, 1966. After that date, the NPCSC "attempted nothing and accomplished nothing" and "NPC existence became a mere formality."[118]

The NPC could have continued as an instrument of mobilization, propaganda, and socialization, striving to unify the populace behind the party – but it was cast aside. To understand why, we must understand China's rising radical leaders and their view of law and other impediments to revolution.

To the radicals, law was "something we might take or leave, all would be well as long as we had the party's policies."[119] The constitution lacked binding force and could be suspended when it ran counter to the policy of the day.[120] With Mao's support, the radicals intended to continue movement away from legal rule toward a de-institutionalized system based on party decrees and direct links between masses and central elites. They downplayed intermediary bodies and the united front and emphasized class divisions – priorities exactly opposed to those of the NPC. In their view, NPC attention to formal rules and procedures limited leadership flexibility and hid class conflict behind a facade of national unity. A symbol of legal rule and unity of all the people, the NPC could not easily be remade into a tool of class struggle and continuing the revolution. Ideologically, it was tainted by association with bourgeois parliaments and Soviet revisionism. To the radicals, the legislature, like all symbols of rational, impersonal authority, stood in the way of the revolution. From their vantage point, the NPC did not strengthen the state or popularize Communist rule; it was an unnecessary and mistaken concession to the enemies of socialism.

The radicals thus encouraged the people to destroy state legal organs and branded the NPC an "old government" in contradiction with the new Cultural Revolution. At the height of their power, the radicals' theorist Zhang Chunqiao, remarked: "We don't want the NPC."[121] Elected NPC deputies were overthrown or pushed to the side and new elections were not held.[122] Sixty of the 115 members of the NPCSC were charged with being spies, traitors, counterrevolutionaries, capitalist roaders, or corrupt elements.[123] Some deputies were arrested and imprisoned and a great majority were "stifled and depressed" (*zhixi chenmen*).[124]

For ten years, decrees were enacted that violated the constitution; "laws were produced in many places, leadership organs made laws without authorization, and leaders' utterances became law."[125] The constitution was abrogated without any announcement and party organs appropriated NPC powers and resorted to mass movements to implement policy. Relying on movements, however, disrupted economic construction and reopened wounds that had already been closed.[126] Techniques used to gain power, when used by a party in power, produced disorder rather than development. To discard post-1949 institutions in favor of personal power and charisma did not continue the revolution to its end, but sidetracked it into its past.

An incident involving the state chairman illustrates the extent of de-institutionalization that occurred during the Cultural Revolution. On August 5, 1967, Kang Sheng criticized and denounced State Chairman Liu Shaoqi in the leadership compound at Zhongnanhai and sent two envoys to insult Liu and detain him in his office. Though weary, the Chairman pulled a copy of the constitution from his desk and said, "How you treated me is of no consequence. But I am the Chairman of the People's Republic of China and must be given the respect due to a chairman. Who can remove the Chairman?

I must be tried and the decision must be passed by the NPC. Acting as you do insults our country."[127] Though a sound argument, these remarks likely struck the envoys as absurd. Liu's jailers derived their authority from the Cultural Revolution Small Group and Mao himself; they would certainly brook no interference from a body unseen for nearly three years. Ultimately, on the basis of "one large character poster and one party meeting [in October 1968], the State Chairman was overthrown, relieved of his duties and imprisoned."[128] The NPC was not consulted and no protests from deputies were heard.

From 1966–75, the NPC had no real or symbolic role in the political system. Formal provisions on NPC competence and jurisdiction had long been ignored and few informal routines had developed. A small clique in the party discarded the constitution and NPC with impunity. The Cultural Revolution and various minicampaigns were carried out without soliciting the opinion of the people or obtaining the approval of the NPC. Channels of information, socialization, and influence were closed, and deputies, like most citizens, "often did not even know what kind of movement was going on."[129]

The future of the NPC depended on the progress of elite power struggles; leaders considered convening the NPC if they desired publicity for their policies or official imprimatur for their position. The Fourth NPC was heralded at party meetings in August 1970 and August 1973, and included in the party's administrative program in the New Year's editorials of 1971, 1972, and 1974, but it did not reappear.

Power struggle and the 1975 NPC

The Fourth NPC finally convened in January 1975. Like the 1962 and 1963 sessions, the country at large did not learn that the NPC had met until after it had dispersed. And like the 1957 session, a long preparatory meeting preceded the session: in this case, at seven days, longer than the five-day session itself.

The session agenda contained only three items, with the main business being to pass a new constitution. The draft submitted closely followed an aborted 1970 draft, which had been discussed at Central Committee meetings, distributed outside China, but never promulgated. It had thirty clauses (compared to 106 in 1954), with most of the reduction in sections dealing with the NPC and the state structure. Hsin-chi Kuan has called the 1975 constitution a revolutionary constitution because class struggle was at its center. Unlike most constitutions, it emphasized future policies and paid marginal attention to protection of citizen's rights and political institution-alization.[130] It reflected ten years of conscious deinstitutionalization and le-galized and expanded and expandable role for the party in state affairs.

The constitution might have clarified party–state relations, but instead it created confusion. According to a team of Chinese constitutional scholars: "its provisions on powers and duties of state organs were very unclear. It had unspecified legal scope and the sloganeering style of a political manifesto, making it difficult to implement."[131] Chinese also often comment on its "illogical provision" that "the NPC is the highest organ of state power under the leadership of the Communist Party of China." They observe that this article effectively made the party a state organ above the NPC and ask "if the NPC is highest how can it be led?"[132]

Besides ambiguities, a number of omissions undermined the NPC's po-sition. The explicit powers and functions granted the NPC fell from fourteen to six, and those of the NPCSC from nineteen to seven. Absent were the NPC's right to decide on questions of war and peace, to supervise enforce-ment of the constitution, to address questions to the State Council, and to appoint commissions of inquiry. The NPCSC lost its authorization to su-pervise work of the State Council, the Courts, and the Procuracy, to revise or annul State Council decisions, and to decide on questions of war and peace when the NPC was not in session.

The constitution gave formal command of the nation's armed forces and certain NPC nomination powers to the party Central Committee. It dropped clauses on NPC deputy immunities and made no mention of permanent NPC committees.[133] The radicals, as shown in the constitution they crafted, valued flexibility above all else. They promulgated a constitution but did not believe in constitutionalism. Their NPC owed little to Soviet, liberal, or earlier Chinese Communist national assemblies. It was simply a meeting: an epiphenomenon without independent significance.

The 1975 NPC was the shortest and most perfunctory in party history. Deputies' speeches disappeared, along with criticism or questioning of of-ficials. Although Zhou Enlai spoke of the four modernizations in his gov-ernment work report, his 5,000 words hardly touched on the changes in government work since 1964. A full deputy name list was never released, nor any economic data, and the session documents filled one slim, sixty-page volume. (This contrasts with 1,700 pages of materials released on the 1957 session.) In the eyes of a Hong Kong-based observer, just as the 1964 NPC seemed anemic compared to the First NPC (1954–8), the 1975 NPC did not measure up to 1964.[134] After a ten-year interruption, the NPC was revived, but showed few signs of its early liveliness.

Despite listless sittings, the 1975 session was a significant political event and unveiled a new use of the NPC. Unlike earlier sessions summoned to approve the policies of well-entrenched rulers, the 1975 NPC took place when the distribution of power was uncertain.[135] The radicals retained Mao's favor, but their opponents were in ascendance. The radicals planned to use the NPC to solidify their gains since 1966 and to redistribute formal power and to organize a cabinet.[136] Instead of smashing the state apparatus, they now sought to control it. But Mao had made Zhou Enlai responsible for the session and State Council personnel decisions and he had assigned Deng Xiaoping to assist Zhou with drafting the government work report. Armed with Mao's endorsement, Zhou and Deng frustrated the radicals' plans and launched an internal struggle against them that continued until late 1975.[137]

The swirl of factional activities around the 1975 NPC did not yield a clear victor. Although the radicals did not take over the government and Mao criticized Jiang Qing for her "wild ambition," the Zhou–Deng forces also failed to untrack the radicals and could only draw hope from what in retrospect was assessed as an "important round in the struggle against the Gang of Four."[138]

The NPC was a clear loser, however. In the power struggle unfolding at the end of Mao's life, it had become a stage for plots and counterplots to run their course in two Chinese observers' words, "a political shell through which the Gang of Four tried to achieve their counterrevolutionary goals."[139] The NPC had no institutional presence in the political system and served whoever convened it and whoever wrote the reports. Its very existence depended on the immediate needs of whichever faction controlled the party and state.

By the end of Mao's life, belief in continuous revolution had replaced support for political development and legal construction. The NPC's creator had turned against it and he had repudiated stable, legalized rule and class accommodation. Post-1949 events one by one closed off avenues of legislative development: representation and supervision after 1957; law making in the Great Leap Forward; mobilization, socialization, and even propaganda work in the Cultural Revolution. By 1975, China's leaders did not value what a national legislature could offer.

The Fourth NPC, like the Third NPC, met briefly and then was never heard from again.[140]

The NPC by 1976

When Mao died in September 1976 and the radicals fell, the NPC was a battered shell. Though we lack public opinion data, domestic scholars attest to the NPC's low repute. Typical remarks include: "for a long time the NPC's prestige has declined and it has not received respect; it is a mere formality that the people mock as a rubber stamp; in the people's eyes the people's congress system exists in name only; people regard the NPC as a phony organ of idle talk."[141] Popular esteem for the NPC had to be low. No local, direct elections had been held since 1963; millions of citizens over 30 years old had never voted and teenagers had never seen an election.

China's leaders did not support the NPC after the mid-1950s. Instead, they interfered with its development and systematically appropriated its powers and functions: real and potential, substantive and symbolic. It's no wonder ordinary citizens lost interest in the NPC: it did little other than speak for vanguard elements, the party, and ultimately a small, unpopular clique.

Political winds explain much but not all of the NPC's first quarter century. The structure of the NPC also channeled legislative development. Before looking at the system in which the NPC operated and before considering post-1976 reforms, we turn to the NPC's internal organization. For though China's leaders promise history will not recur and the NPC appears secure, its structure, if unchanged, will again inhibit legislative development. For the NPC, history is not decisive, but structure may be.

4

Structural features

Although declining elite support was an important factor in the NPC's demise, it was not the only one. Structural features and a divided mandate also circumscribed legislative development. On the one hand, the NPC was set up to build support and enhance stability – to mobilize and socialize subnational elites, to disseminate policy, and to gather information from the provinces. On the other hand, the NPC was also set up to undertake policy making (law making, supervision) and representative tasks. Though these roles were not necessarily incompatible, in practice, structural facilitators for support activities acted as structural constraints on policy activities. Four organizational attributes, embedded at the NPC's founding, inclined the legislature toward support and stabilizing functions and away from decision making and representation: (1) party control of deputy selection, (2) large chamber size, (3) brief, annual sessions, and (4) underdeveloped committees.

Elections and deputy quality

From the beginning, Chinese leaders understood that control of the NPC hinged on control of its personnel. Thus, when setting up the legislature, the Constitutional Drafting Committee reinstituted the four-stage election process first used in Jiangxi and the pre-1936 Soviet Union. Under this system, voters directly elected basic-level congresses, which then elected county congresses, which then elected provincial congresses, which then elected the NPC.

In 1953, Deng Xiaoping explained that so long as most voters were largely unfamiliar with national policies and the names of state leaders, indirect elections would be necessary. Other commentators, then and more recently, noted high levels of illiteracy, low mass political consciousness and cultural level, and large areas where communications and travel were still difficult. Several years of economic development and political education, it was said, would prepare the population for political participation and, as soon as conditions ripened, would allow direct elections at the county level and above.[1] Despite frequent proposals for reform, systemwide direct elections failed to appear between 1954 and 1966. Every four years, local people's congresses elected the next higher-level congress.

The reasons for delay are not hard to find. The 1954 electoral law did not stipulate electoral procedures at every stage and stepwise elections gave party committees a strong hand in deputy selection. Beginning at the basic level, local party committees controlled nomination lists and election committees, as they had since Jiangxi. All candidates ran unopposed, and this was defended on grounds that the debate preceding nomination and the representativeness of the final result was more important than electoral form.[2] Candidate lists were produced through joint consultation of party committees, democratic parties, and mass organizations, and "took into account" (*zhaogu*) minorities, national capitalists, and others who, it was claimed, might not be chosen in open elections.[3] A single list of candidates ensured balance and allegedly prevented prestigious party members from winning most seats.[4]

By relegating choice in local people's congress elections to the Chinese equivalent of smoke-filled rooms, the party prevailed on controversial decisions, or at least retained veto power. In the absence of formal rules and procedures, the weak had few means to challenge the powerful. Outsiders were excluded and voting was primarily an exercise in political education, communication, and mobilization that formalized decisions made elsewhere. Casting one's ballot had little to do with selecting leaders or formulating public policy and much to do with providing a guaranteed and unanimous vote of confidence in the party. Elections, like those in other socialist states, demonstrated the regime's political control and organizational effectiveness: they were trumpeted in extensive media campaigns, drew citizens into pre-election meetings and culminated in a legitimizing civic ritual of participation and commitment.[5]

Above the basic level, we know little about deputy selection procedures. Most likely, overt coaching was unnecessary, as political savvy alone led deputies to elect reliable colleagues to the next-higher congress. Sometimes, leaders ignored appearances and designated deputies or supplied nomination lists themselves. We do know that all NPCSC and legislative committee leaders fell on the Central Committee nomenklatura list, and, unlike the Soviet Union, even some ordinary deputies (e.g., "patriotic personages") were covered.[6] From 1954 to 1966, party committees undoubtedly exploited ambiguities and gaps in the electoral laws and vague constitutional provisions to handpick many legislators.

For the 1975 NPC, the leadership did not reestablish provincial people's congresses and abandoned all pretense of elections. The 1975 constitution replaced indirect elections with selection by "democratic consultation." Recent Chinese authors condemn both this method and its results. A Special Commentator in *Guangming Ribao* wrote that deputies produced by democratic consultation in 1975 "did not necessarily accord with the broad masses' opinions and hopes, and this practice turned elections into an empty exercise of leadership selection by one or a few persons after gathering opinions."[7] Most important to Chinese critics, democratic consultation allowed a small group of radical leaders to "monopolize everything" (*bachi baoban*), to "arbitrarily replace NPC deputies elected by law," and to "infiltrate their mainstays into organs of political power."[8] Beijing- and Shanghai-based radicals presumably recognized the limits of their control at the basic level and bypassed local nominating committees in favor of selection by reliable provincial and central officials. This enabled them to fashion an NPC to their liking, including individuals such as the notorious blank examination paper hero, who had gained fame several years before by turning in an unopened entrance exam to show his dissatisfaction with the inegalitarian educational system.

But even before 1975, deputy quality was open to question. Indirect, uncontested elections produced an NPC composed chiefly of two kinds of deputies. Honorary deputies were chosen due to united-front considerations (i.e., breadth, representativeness, and progressiveness) and regarded selection as a "political favor."[9] This group had three subtypes. The first included democratic party members, intellectuals, members of minority groups, and former capitalists. These deputies were well represented, especially in the First NPC (1954–8), and were largely responsible for the liveliness of the mid-1950s – but they paid a heavy price afterwards. The second subtype overlapped with the first and contained long-time allies of the regime rewarded for their years of service. Believed to be politically reliable, and often enfeebled by age, these deputies gained a measure of prestige in exchange for support of party policy. The third subtype included "meritorious members," "labor heroes," and "advanced models." These deputies were elevated to the NPC to promote new policies and to publicize ongoing campaigns. Usually younger and more vigorous than the other honorary deputies, examples such as the revolutionary art workers in 1964 and the worker–peasant–soldier deputies in 1975 were handicapped by low educational levels and limited political experience. Moreover, they typically rotated through the NPC quickly, as one movement gave way to the next.[10]

None of the honorary deputies offered much potential for independence from the party or input into the policy process. Many had no regular involvement in state affairs and lacked specialized knowledge about government work. The bold were aging and cautious after 1957; the vigorous were inexperienced and reliably acquiescent. Such deputies could not form the core of a body partly devoted to government oversight. In the words of one commentator: "it was difficult for these deputies to express their opinions or to serve as people's representatives."[11]

The regime's top political figures comprised the second group of deputies. These official–deputies were elected by their home provincial congress, their work unit, or place of origin, or, in some cases, were even assigned to delegations at random.[12] Such practices, when combined with electoral norms that favored urban over rural residents 8:1, filled the NPC with Beijing-based officials and provincial leaders. At the 1964 NPC, for example, sixteen vice premiers, sixty-three heads of seventy-one ministries and commissions, and twenty-six of twenty-seven governors of provinces and mayors of provincial-level cities were included among the deputies.[13] Though these officials had indisputable power, they had little incentive to take part in NPC affairs. Most had less say in the NPC than in the bureaucracy or region they headed. Furthermore, the electoral law, by allowing state officials to serve on the NPC, NPCSC, and permanent committees, assigned state officials to supervise themselves. Diligence could hardly be expected.

All in all, NPC composition facilitated party control of the legislature and encouraged use of it as a united-front organ. Timid, coopted honorary deputies and uninspired official–deputies sat beside a united bloc of Communist Party officials. Moreover, nonparty members were consistently outnumbered. From 1954–8, 54.48% of NPC deputies were CCP members. After the Anti-Rightist Campaign, party representation increased to 67% at the Second NPC (1958–63), and 85% at the Third NPC (1964).[14]

Deputies also regularly chose party stalwarts to lead the NPC. The chairman of the NPCSC was always a veteran party cadre (e.g., Liu Shaoqi, Zhu De), and approximately half of the vice chairmen were central party officials.[15] A typical 254-member Presidium, which collectively guided NPC work at individual sessions and resolved procedural questions, included all 26 members of the Politburo, 25 of 29 provincial party first secretaries, 8 of 11 military region commanders, 6 ministers or deputy ministers, and 74 additional members or alternate members of the Central Committee.[16] Members of the party center always presided over the Presidium and held the post of NPC secretary-general, whose incumbent determined the session's style and pace, oversaw the proposal of motions and news releases, and guaranteed that all went according to plan.[17]

The party, through the Presidium, also controlled the NPC Credentials Committee. Central Committee members always served on the Credentials Committee and kept watch for troublemakers who had escaped detection at earlier stages in the electoral process.[18] Given party involvement in deputy selection and certification, and its domination of NPC seats and leadership positions, "there wasn't any need to say much about NPC control of itself. . . . The party had all-around and consistent control of the NPC."[19]

The structure of the NPC did not ensure citizenship or local congress control over the selection of the people's representatives; instead, it left open numerous avenues for the party to manipulate the legislature's composition. Despite laws that treated the NPC and state system as self-contained and high-sounding words about the people as masters of the state, NPC deputies had stronger ties to the party apparatus than to their constituents. Some would risk their position and speak against the party or its policies, but not many. The constitution and electoral laws proclaimed people's control of NPC deputies, in fact, deputies did not gain or lose their position because of constituents' actions or feelings – they served at the party's discretion and did what party leaders asked. They were an arm of the party rather than representatives of the people.

NPC size and physical setting

According to Chinese authors, China warranted a large national legislature because of its "huge population, vast extent, and complicated conditions."[20] From 1954 to 1963, the NPC had 1,226 deputies. In 1964, the Congress was enlarged to 3,040 members. This made the NPC the largest unicameral legislature in the world, by a considerable margin. Gu Angran, a prominent legal scholar, justified legislative expansion on grounds of increased population and a need to better reflect working-class leadership and to include superior people of all sorts and all nationalities.[21] Several foreign analysts agreed that expansion might broaden and strengthen the mass foundation of the polity, and also emphasized improved mobilizational and representative capabilities: it might help members serve as the eyes and ears of the government and make the NPC a more effective transmitter of mass opinion.[22]

Augmenting the number of deputies might have aided mobilization and other support activities, but its effect on representation was more complicated. Gu Angran said that workers in new and expanded cities deserved more representation. He also argued, however, that peasants, scientific and technical workers, minorities, and even democratic party members deserved increases.[23] Gu implied that each group would gain in representation, when, in reality, different rates of increase diluted the position of some. Statistics on the 1964 expansion suggest that the proportion of party, Communist Youth League, model worker and peasant, and scientific and technical deputies increased, while that of democratic party members fell.[24] New, more docile deputies surrounded those who had caused the uproar in 1956 and 1957.

Expansion not only provided an occasion to adjust group proportions, it also reduced deputy participation in session activities. Many deputies arrived too late to speak at sessions and those who arrived on time had few opportunities to make their voices heard. "Only the Great Hall of the People in Beijing could accommodate the deputies and, besides reading proclamations, deputies could not rise to speak because it was impossible to conduct discussions there."[25] Deputies sat auditorium-style in long rows, facing the rostrum of government leaders. Long speeches, often read in a high-speed monotone without a single change, echoed throughout the cavernous main auditorium as deputies perused printed copies of the text – the only noise arising from the simultaneous turning of pages and the shuffling of briefcases.[26] Convening sessions (after 1959) in the Great Hall of the People (instead of the smaller Huairentang in the Zhongnanhai leadership compound) and expanding the size of the legislature meant that deputies attended sessions to listen, rather than to talk.

The size and physical setting of the NPC contributed to legislative formalism and made it difficult for the NPC to exercise powers that relied on debate, discussion, and interaction. Expansion, proposed as a means to improve representation, actually circumscribed it and accentuated the legislature's ceremonial and united-front functions. With 3,000 deputies crowded in one hall, leaders dominated sessions, applause swept the chamber in great waves, and the lively plenary forums of the mid-1950s disappeared.

Brief, yearly sessions and unanimous votes

NPC session length ranged from twenty-six days in 1955 to five days in 1975. Most sessions lasted about two weeks, and no two occurred in a calendar year. In 1955, Qian Duansheng, a western-trained political scientist, NPC deputy, and head of the Beijing College of Politics and Law, explained why the NPC had brief, annual sessions:

Deputies are all actively engaged in various types of work, and do not give up their jobs on being elected. It is through their work that they keep in contact with the people, their needs and opinions. . . . It is held that if the deputies gave up their own work even for their period of office, they could quickly lose their representative character and become professional politicians.[27]

Qian's explanation echoed Marx's reasoning in "The Civil War in France," but strained credibility. Deputies could stay in touch with their constituents if they lived at home fewer than fifty weeks each year, and the time freed for legislative work would benefit, not harm, the NPC's representative character.

Brief sessions more likely originated because NPC leaders and other of-ficial–deputies had to attend to their work as state and party functionaries. The CCP regards state power as unitary and rejects formal separation of powers. It supports legislative oversight in principle, but, at least in the 1950s and 1960s, saw no need to forbid "double-hatting." Thus, members of executive organs who served in the NPC also had other, more important work to return to after their stint as legislator ended. NPC sessions had to be brief and procedures simple. Legislators could not be full-time politicians or engage in "complex maneuvers such as filibustering, which can do so much to delay public business."[28] If the NPC was to initiate and revise little, but required the attendance of China's political elite, it could not drag on for months.

Accordingly, floor activities were conducted with remarkable dispatch. In its first quarter century, few bills were challenged, and the NPC did not reject any nominated officials nor remove any on its own initiative. Deputies always passed the government work report unanimously, and rarely voted against any measure.

During the Hundred Flowers interregnum, some legal scholars criticized habitual unanimous passage as undemocratic. After the crackdown, other legal scholars sought to reconcile unanimous votes and democracy. They claimed that deputies of different strata might have different opinions, but all had a common "political base," and so could achieve unanimity after discussion. In an extreme variant of this argument, unanimous votes were considered to be evidence of the NPC's democratic nature, that is, proof of adequate discussion before voting.[29] More recently, however, Chinese com-mentators have criticized "voting-machine" deputies and have suggested that brief sessions make it impossible to review legal drafts adequately, suggest amendments, or vote intelligently.[30]

To ask 1,000 or more deputies to make decisions on diverse and highly specialized subjects in two weeks invited superficial deliberation. And then to assert that spontaneous unanimity arose defied belief. Complete consensus could not be a normal outcome for a shifting group of individuals, over many years, on every issue.

Even so, routine unanimity was not the cause of the NPC's machinelike proceedings, but rather a symptom. Party control of the agenda drew the life out of NPC sessions. Party plenums or central work conferences customarily preceded NPC sessions, passed the main reports, and instructed the NPC how to act on important matters. Although decisions of the central party organs only had the status of suggestions, it is widely acknowledged that they were treated as orders. The Central Committee had the final say on most issues, and deputies only conducted perfunctory discussions before assenting to the "imperial edict."[31] According to Wu Jialin:

For many years we have been accustomed to regarding "raising proposals" as "taking orders" and "deliberation and passage" as "passage as usual.". . . Motions submitted to the NPC, in reality had more often than not been passed by the Central Committee and already had legal effectiveness.[32]

The NPC thus not only lacked power to decide or revise, but also gave its stamp of approval after policies were implemented. This led "the people to believe that what the party says goes on important questions in state life, and that the NPC must simply go through the motions and unanimously pass motions."[33] Brief, ceremonial sessions sufficed, with minimal debate on specific measures and thirty minutes of hand raising at the final sitting.

Meanwhile, off-the-floor activities provided some opportunity for discussion. From its inception, the NPC devoted a sizable proportion of each session to small-group meetings of deputies, organized by province or electoral unit and held in rooms gaily decorated with regional arts and crafts motifs, depicting scenes of local history or natural beauty. Afternoon plenary sittings typically alternated with morning group meetings. Chinese leaders introduced small-group discussions to counteract the drawbacks of brief sessions and a large assembly, and to give a greater number of deputies a chance to speak and to exchange ideas.

In the 1980s, small-group discussions have developed greatly and have become the innovation they were once hailed as. In most of the NPC's first generation, however, their potential remained hidden. After 1957, division into groups physically separated democratic party members and preempted divisions along party or factional lines. In the 1960s, small-group meetings increased in size from an average of 40 deputies each to over 100 – with a corresponding decrease in liveliness and domination by governors, first party secretaries, ministers, mayors, and their like. Although more deputies spoke, small groups isolated malcontents and smothered sectarian tendencies. Meetings took place simultaneously in rooms ringing the Great Hall that separated deputies with common background or interests and discouraged the expression of functional or group demands: this was especially important because plenary sittings were tightly scripted and provincial delegations were housed in different hotels scattered around Beijing.[34]

The composition of small groups did abet the articulation of regional interests but they remained inherently more private than plenary debate and reports of their discussions often did not circulate within the Congress or beyond. Through small groups, deputies could consult with leaders and make suggestions, but without publicity or the ability to marshal public or congress opinion, they could easily be ignored. Though small groups provided an opportunity for informal input that might flourish given elite support, in the late 1950s and 1960s, that support was rarely forthcoming.

In sum, brief, yearly sessions disposed the NPC to focus on tasks associated with explaining and defending government policies, and forced the NPC into practices that deprived much of its policy making and representative work of meaning. Brevity encouraged perfunctory deliberation and unanimous votes and led to routine approval of party-inspired decisions. In small-group discussions, deputies could at most prick government leaders. In just two weeks per year, deputies could not be partners in rule.

Legislative committees

Given the NPC's size and brief sessions, legislative participation in policy making hinged on the assembly's standing organs. But the structure of the NPC did not lend itself to meaningful between-session activity. The needed follow-up to the burst of institution building in the early 1950s never occurred.

The Nationalities and Bills committees were elected through 1964, though reports on their activities dwindled after 1959. In 1979, Xu Chongde and He Huahui ascribed committee inaction to weak organization. They wrote: "for many years the role of legislative committees has not really been brought out because they only had specified tasks, but not any work order."[35] Without clear guidelines, procedures, or customary practices, committees existed, but did little.

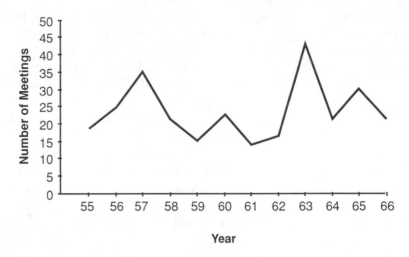

Figure 4.1 Number of National People's Congress Standing Committee Meetings, 1954–66. Source: Adapted from Kenneth Lieberthal, *A Research Guide to Central Party and Government Meetings in China 1949–1975* (White Plains, NY: International Arts and Sciences Press, 1976), p. 306. The years run from July through June of the year shown, except for 1955, which begins at the NPC's founding in September 1954.

Unlike the Nationalities and Bills committees, the Standing Committee of the NPC appeared strong and active. In the 1950s, it organized investigatory committees to look into issues such as self-rule in areas where national minorities were concentrated.[36] As prescribed in the NPC organic law, the NPCSC averaged two sessions/month, and year-to-year variations showed no particular pattern (Figure 4.1).

Even as meetings continued, however, NPCSC output declined. The NPCSC Bulletin recorded all NPCSC decisions after 1957 and the number of bulletins published each year roughly measures NPCSC activity. Figure 4.2 shows an unmistakable drop in NPCSC output from 1957–66, with the exception of 1965, which had an increase associated with electing and convening a new Congress.[37]

Why did the NPCSC become less active? Elite disruption certainly caused much of the decline, but persistent organizational obstacles also impeded the NPCSC. First, as in the NPC itself, "a considerable proportion of the members were elected on the basis of their 'representativeness' or their 'honor,' and their primary functions were to appear at the sessions of the

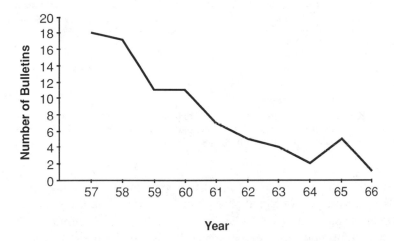

Figure 4.2 Number of National People's Congress Standing Committee Bulletins, 1957–66. Source: *Zhonghua Renmin Gongheguo Quanguo Renmin Daibiao Dahui Changwu Weiyuanhui Gongbao* [Bulletin of the Chinese National People's Congress Standing Committee], Reports Nos. 1 81 (1957–66). Reports for 1959 and 1960 were incomplete, though continuous numbering confirms that twenty-two were issued. I have estimated that eleven were published in each year.

NPCSC and observe the proceedings."[38] Important party members, of course, served on the NPCSC; but they also met in other closed settings more conducive to decision making. Thus, as in its parent, personnel composition enervated the NPCSC. Some members lacked power; others, motivation.

Second, the NPCSC had grown from its original 80 members to 114 in 1964 to 167 in 1975. Meetings became cumbersome and increasingly old, inexperienced and less educated members (see Table 4.1) found it difficult to participate in state affairs.

After enlargement in 1964, "the NPCSC had many 'titular members,' who held other full-time jobs, and only came to meetings, listened to reports, discussed opinions, made proposals and raised their hands. . . . They could not really manage affairs or do NPCSC work well."[39] Many Standing Committee members did not live in Beijing and could not regularly attend meetings. Some were not even on the NPCSC mailing list and did not stand by for work.[40] Weak structure and haphazard staffing, combined with neglect, frustrated NPCSC development.

Table 4.1. *Age, turnover, and educational level of NPCSC members*

NPCSC term	Mean age	Turnover (%)	Tertiary education (%)
1954–9	58	—	71
1959–64	63	27	72
1964–75	64	48	67
1975–8	68	70	40

Source: Hsin-Yi Ou-Yang, "From Proletarian Dictatorship to People's Democratic Dictatorship: Elite Transition in the National People's Congress, People's Republic of China," master's thesis, Ohio State University, 1984, pp. 80, 82, 88.

Inadequate support also limited the NPC and its standing organs. Legislative staff levels declined precipitously after 1957 to the point where the NPC lacked the ability to compete with the Central Committee's Political-Legal Group and other party organs.[41] Nor did the legislature have established ties with China's intellectual community, or access to informed opinion therein. The NPC thus had few sources of independent information and less ability to generate it itself. It could act, but only at the bidding of individuals or organizations that gathered and processed information elsewhere.

In theory, the NPC was the centerpiece of the state structure – an organ with significant policy-making and oversight roles; in practice, structural ambiguities and unclear jurisdiction allowed opponents of legislative growth to minimize NPC influence merely by preventing its strengthening. At the same time, those who might have sought a stronger policy and representative role for the NPC could only try to mobilize support to upgrade the NPC, a difficult and risky task after the Anti-Rightist Campaign in 1957. Few, if any, took the chance, and acceptance of the status quo channeled legislative activities toward noncontroversial work gaining compliance and generating and maintaining support for leaders and their policies.

Over time, we can surmise, a consensus among the political elite emerged in favor of a tame, predictable NPC. With the exception of 1975, the leadership spoke as one at NPC sessions and suppressed ongoing disputes. Factional and policy differences were generally hashed out beforehand in other forums, though on occasion Mao or other party leaders may have gone further in an NPC speech than had been agreed upon.

Despite claims to the contrary, the Chinese leadership set up a weak legislative system and did not strengthen it. They spoke of a working organ of people's power but constructed a cheerleader for party rule. They mocked liberal democratic legislatures, but built an alternative that was little more than a conventional united-front organ. By the early 1960s, the NPC and NPCSC were meetings rather than organizations. For most of each year, the NPC had no institutional presence.

5

The NPC in the political system

For much of its first generation, the NPC operated in an inhospitable environment enfeebled by an ineffectual structure. External pressures and internal constraints circumscribed legislative development and ultimately caused legislative decline. This chapter draws on both Chinese and western legislative theory to assess the consequences of decline on four activities commonly associated with legislatures – law making, supervision, representation, and regime support. By determining what the NPC contributed to the political system, I summarize the findings to this point and establish a baseline against which post-Mao changes can be measured.

Law making and influence over policy

In theory, legislatures legislate. Nelson Polsby writes: "legislative activity at its core refers to a process of law making, to a pattern of actions which regularly results in the promulgation of general rules having application to some specified population."[1] Students of nonwestern legislatures have long known, however, that many legislatures seldom make rules and often are excluded from important political decisions. With several notable exceptions, the influence of legislatures pales before that of executives.[2] Popular assemblies generally pass executive proposals with minimal change or opposition; few regularly make political decisions or allocate values.

The NPC from 1954 to 1976 was not among these few. Deputies "did not enjoy and exercise the right to decide on laws."[3] Laws were infrequently submitted and less frequently amended. Before convening, NPC and NPCSC members did not know what proposals they would see, and at the end, they could do little more than raise their hands in agreement.[4] Deputies rarely initiated policy changes and never exercised power through voting.

Even so, voting behavior is far from the only indicator of influence over rule making. Recent research in developing countries suggests that legislative involvement in decision making falls along a continuum: it is not a dichotomous variable.[5] Both Blondel and Mezey explain that although legislators may be unable to initiate legislation or reject proposals, they may use more subtle techniques to resist an executive. Scholars now focus on constraints – either those placed on the legislature or those that the legislature can place on the executive – and suggest that the influence of legislatures and individual legislators may be greater before and after voting.[6] Prior consultation may result in a change to a legislative proposal or a decision not to submit. Influence may be exerted during implementation rather than in formulation or decision making. Power may be more apparent on certain classes of issues: namely, narrow, practical matters rather than major policy decisions. Or it may arise in particular settings: closed arenas such as caucuses or committees rather than public debates and votes.[7] In short, influence over law making (and other decisions) may occur lespite unanimous votes and minimal legislative initiative.

Without candid interviews[8] or access to internal documents, this line of argument is difficult to test for the early NPC. We know that committees were largely inactive and that NPCSC meetings were poorly attended. Other restricted arenas, most notably small-group discussions and secret sessions in 1962 and 1963, provided opportunities for influence, though with unknown results. Available evidence suggests that consultation with honorary deputies declined after 1957 and changes made at the behest of official–deputies occurred because of their position and power in the state or party apparatus, not because of their status as an NPC deputy. Few narrow, practical matters were raised in short, fast-paced sessions and most major policy decisions sailed through with little evidence of viscosity. As in the early years of the Supreme Soviet, deputies were not inclined to introduce private bills or to propose amendments on questions more important than wording.[9] Laws, budgets, plans, and reports were enacted after brief debate and perfunctory informal consultation.

After passing a decision, implementation provided an occasion for deputy influence, but increasingly nonchalant inspection tours, undeveloped feedback loops, and outside full-time employment diminished the opportunities for real impact. Though it is an overstatement to say that NPC deputies had *no* decision-making power or influence, they probably fell near the low end of the continuum.

The reasons for this are not limited to historical and organizational factors discussed in earlier chapters. Long-standing systemic and ideological considerations also played a part. For one, powerful usurpers of legislative authority encircled the NPC. Although the legislature had sole authority to make, revise, and annul laws, executive organs decided which laws it would discuss. The NPC lacked sufficient staff and effective powers of legislative initiative, and so relied on the State Council to prepare and submit bills.[10] The State Council and its departments and commissions also issued legal norms of their own – administrative measures, administrative regulations, decisions, directives, and orders. In some respects, the State Council was more of a legislature than the NPC; many of its acts did not require NPC sanction, and legislative approval, when sought, was given without delay.[11]

The State Council, of course, was not the NPC's only or main rival. Rule making ordinarily began in the central organs of the party. Especially after 1957, commentators advocated "party leadership in all levels of people's congresses" and "party proposal of all NPC laws and decisions." In a *People's Daily* article otherwise strongly critical of China's legislative history, Zhou Xinming and Chen Weidian outlined "correct practices" and "useful experiences" accumulated since 1949:

Important legal drafts first pass through party investigation and research in practical work. Experience is then summarized and a draft written. It is examined and approved by the center, then submitted to the NPC or NPCSC for discussion, revision, passage and proclamation. That the party is the leadership core and guides legislative work is entirely necessary.[12]

Typically, before any bill reached the NPC, the Central Committee's Political-Legal Group or special drafting committees conducted research and made revisions and then reported the bill to the Central Committee. After further revisions, the legislature simply "boiled raw rice into cooked rice."[13]

An ideological justification for low deputy participation in law making lay behind the historical, organizational, and systemic causes. Chinese Communist constructs on the people's democratic dictatorship marked a symbolic break from Soviet-style dictatorship of the proletariat, but did not imply a truly different state form or a heightened decision-making role for representative institutions. The laws reviewed by deputies were an expression of party policy – a means to concretize and enforce the party's will. Nonparty deputies took part in the NPC to be educated to party policy, not to bargain with CCP deputies or to coax them into accepting new views. Deputies were gathered together to show support for Central Committee decisions; constraining the executive fell outside their mandate.

As a rule, few opportunities arose to resist the executive before, during, or after voting. Chinese claims had a measure of truth: power was unified and legislation and administration were combined – but in the executive rather than the legislature. Deputies *qua* deputies did not exercise power; it was exercised on them.

Supervision

In one sense, supervision is a component of legislative decision-making power – a form of power exercised during policy implementation and over executive and judicial personnel. In another sense, however, government oversight deserves consideration on its own as an activity found in some legislatures in which most forms of decision-making power are absent. In an era of strong executives, supervision, scrutiny, and surveillance are reasonable expectations for a legislature. Legislatures may be more able to illuminate problems than to provide specific solutions in the form of law.[14]

From 1954–77, the NPC did not actively supervise the state organs accountable to it. Few investigatory committees were set up after the mid-1950s and recall and appointment of top state officials took place at party initiative, sometimes without the formality of NPC voting.[15] The NPC always passed the NPCSC, Supreme Court, and Procurator's reports unchanged and never revoked a decision made by the supreme state executive organ, the State Council.[16] As far as we know, on no occasion did the NPC or its committees have a formal, open disagreement with, or attempt to force its will on, any subordinate body. As an organization, the NPC made few efforts to illuminate problems in other state organs.

Individual deputies also rarely called ministers and state officials to account. The frequency and depth of deputy investigations declined through the 1950s and questioning of officials at plenary sessions fell. Deputies' right to inquiry, which "originally was an important means to supervise the government," evaporated because "concrete procedures were not laid out."[17] No rules required officials to respond to deputies' inquiries or criticisms in a set period of time and, in an increasingly chilly political climate, challenges seldom arose and were easily deflected. After the flurry of comments made to Zhou Enlai and Chen Yun in 1956, significant exchanges between ministry officials and deputies did not reappear until 1980. The few criticisms that emerged were directed at corrupt, local officials who violated laws or discipline and, as in the Soviet Union of the 1950s, served primarily to warn other wayward middle-level bureaucrats.[18] By and large, deputies were unfamiliar with government work and lacked sufficient data to draw conclusions.[19] The only well-informed deputies were typically administrators themselves, who had little incentive to open their agencies to legislative scrutiny. High officials could act as they pleased and were immune from deputy criticism.[20] High-handedness, illegal actions, and constitutional violations frequently went unsanctioned. The conclusion of a Chinese legal specialist rings true:

> The system was not sufficiently sound. In theory the NPC was the highest organ of state power, but in practice it did not control state power; it was unable to supervise the enforcement of the constitution or to exercise its extensive powers of supervision.[21]

Lackluster supervision was not a foregone conclusion once a Soviet-style legislature was established. Even before Gorbachev's rise and the upheaval of 1989, legislative oversight and investigation of government bureaucracies was growing in much of Eastern Europe and the Soviet Union. In particular, these nations increased the number and power of standing committees. According to Stephen White, committees monitored observance of laws by government bodies and required ministers and state officials to provide information on questions of the legislature's choosing. Of course, these committees did not challenge party rule, but rather were a means by which the party, via party deputies, legally intervened in state affairs and checked government performance and conformity to party policy.[22] Legislative committees acted as the party's agent in the state apparatus, overseeing state organs as they took on new responsibilities in the course of economic development.

Roderick MacFarquhar suggests that the proposal by Liu Shaoqi and Peng Zhen in 1956 to strengthen NPC committees and the NPCSC had a similar aim. It "may have represented an attempt by Liu to assert himself as Chairman of the NPC [and a high party leader] to oversee the activities of Zhou's government apparatus."[23] But nothing came of it. Weak, unspecialized committees remained incapable of meaningful government oversight.

Why did supervision of executive organs and lower-level policy implementation falter after promising first steps from 1954–7? Most obviously, beginning in the late 1950s, the party intervened directly in state affairs and commanded or supplanted state administrative organs. The potential usefulness of legislative supervision thus disappeared. The party, through personnel overlap and dual rule, controlled the state from the inside; it did not need legislative committees to watch over state officials. For many years in China, party and state were virtually indistinguishable.

CCP leaders could have used people's congresses to oversee policy implementation and to ensure control, but they chose not to. In the wake of the Hundred Flowers, central leaders apparently concluded that vigorous people's congresses were a disruptive influence. Although legislative supervision could have been contained and targets selected from above, oversight entailed certain risks – risks deemed excessive in light of the alternative of direct party pressure and supervision by party and ministry hierarchies. After the mid-1950s, supervision declined as policies were formulated, implemented, and reviewed by party/state executive organs without notable legislative involvement.

From its inception, the NPC lacked the organizational muscle to tell the State Council, ministries, or courts what to do. Prevailing political theories placed the NPC at the apex of the state structure, but at the same time, delegitimized its supervisory role. Theory accorded the NPC formal supremacy and a mandate to be involved in administrative work, yet this meant little in a system in which all state organs were considered to be simultaneously legislative and executive and the party enjoyed unclear and ever-changing legal status.[24] The result was a maze of overlapping jurisdiction and numerous opportunities for party committees, powerful individuals, or subordinate state bodies to make and carry out policy in house, outside the purview of the NPC. Constitutional provisions notwithstanding, rejection of checks and balances in favor of unified power put legislative supervision on unsure footing and freed the hand of party/state executive organs.

Representation

Since their early years, the Chinese Communists have advocated popular sovereignty and political representation within a centralized state. In 1937 Mao said:

There is no impossible gulf between democracy and centralism, both of which are essential for China. On the one hand, the government we want must be truly representative of the popular will; it must have the support of the broad masses throughout the country and the people must be free to support it and have every opportunity to influence its policies. This is the meaning of democracy. On the other hand, the centralization of administrative power is also necessary.[25]

Mao saw at least six divisions in Chinese society that merited representation in the political process: those arising from differences in class, organizational affiliation, region, age, gender, and ethnicity.[26] People's congresses were set up partly to complement direct mass-line participation, to give these groupings a voice in state affairs, and to legitimize party rule.

Many western theorists dismiss Chinese claims of representation out of hand and hold that representation cannot exist with unfree elections and routine unanimous votes. Hanna Pitkin argues that representative government requires institutional machinery for the represented to express their wishes and leaders who respond to these wishes unless there are good reasons to the contrary.[27] These conditions did not hold in Mao's China. Some deputies had ties to their electors; some had influence within the political elite; few spanned the distance from voter to decision maker. The connection between constituency policy preferences, official behavior of deputies, and high-level policy decisions was tenuous at best.

Be that as it may, representation in legislatures, like decision-making influence, is not as clear-cut as it first appears. Eulau and Karps advance a view of representation that allows for representation even when policy responsiveness is low. They stress deputy role orientations rather than the relationship between decision-making, roll-call voting, and constituency views. Instead of exclusive focus on policy responsiveness, they draw attention to other components of representation, namely, "service responsiveness" and "allocation responsiveness." Service responsiveness refers to advantages and benefits that representatives obtain for particular constituents, including response to letters, case work, errand-boy functions, and actions undertaken as an advocate for special interests against bureaucracies. Allocation responsiveness refers to more generalized benefits, which accrue to a representative's district as a whole.[28] An example of allocation responsiveness would be haggling over a constituency's share of the state budget. Service and allocation responsiveness complement policy responsiveness in strong legislatures and comprise the bulk of representative activities in weaker legislatures.

According to Michael Mezey, allocation responsiveness appears to be a concern for all legislators everywhere and particularized constituency demands are a common feature of Third-World legislatures.[29] In socialist legislatures, Stephen White has identified bargaining over budgetary allocations in the Supreme Soviet and Vanneman and Nelson have commented on constituency services and a nascent ombudsman function before the Gorbachev era.[30]

Chinese legislative practice up to 1976 showed little evidence of deputy policy, allocation, or service responsiveness. After the mid-1950s, pressure for unity undermined allocation responsiveness and limited sectoral bargaining. Honorary deputies spoke infrequently and official–deputies spoke only to support party policy in their area. Though deputies occasionally requested more funds for sectors such as transportation (1958) or education (1960), they rarely drew attention to particular needs of their locality. Over time, vague calls to set up new organizations and to improve planning supplanted the funding requests for local projects seen in the mid-1950s. From their speeches, votes, and comments in small groups, delegates from coal-mining areas could hardly be distinguished from those from agricultural areas, who acted much like their urban colleagues. All advocated the center's policies and accepted central priorities.

Indirect elections made service responsiveness unlikely. According to *Guangming Ribao,* since deputies were not produced by real elections, they often had a "weak outlook" on responsibility to electors. Few deputies served as a bridge between the masses and the leadership and many were not even known in the district they represented.[31] According to the vice president of the party school, "the people at large were not in a position to supervise the deputies and leaders they elected, to say nothing of exercising the right to remove them from office."[32] In the view of one Hong Kong-based author:

Since the NPC representatives were not really elected by the people but decided on by votes on leadership-provided candidate lists, these "imperial ordered" representatives lacked the courage and character to plead on behalf of the people and the people were indifferent toward them and their activities.[33]

At certain times and places, deputies met with constituents and encouraged letters and visits. Undoubtedly, deputy motions at the end of a Congress sometimes arose from formal or informal contact with constituents. But lack of staff support, pay, and electoral sanctions discouraged service responsiveness and the potential readiness to respond that Pitkin argues lies at the heart of representation.[34]

The best hope for service responsiveness lay with inspection tours. Tours were designed to increase contact between deputies and constituents and to inform deputies of mass opinions and needs. For several years, inspections may have had their desired effect, but problems soon arose. For one, it was reported that deputies often lacked a plan of inquiry and visited too many units, "penetrating deeply into the situation in none." In some units, delegates did not seek contact with the masses and instead spent all their time closeted with leaders; in others, leaders did not arrange the inspectors' agenda or ignored suggestions. Problems brought to the attention of concerned ministries or departments were not always handled conscientiously or promptly and some suggestions were declared inappropriate without explanation.[35] Inspections could have provided a means for the represented to express their preferences, but without sufficient publicity or institutionalization, their effect dwindled. Through inspections, deputies learned of specific problems at lower levels, but inadequate follow-up and coordination allowed entrenched patterns of rule to stand.

All in all, NPC deputies had few reasons to devote their energy to constituency service and minimal effect when they did. More often than not, deputies brought the government to the people rather than the people to the government. From 1954–66, the NPC chiefly performed what Packenham calls a safety-valve or tension-release function. Heavy press coverage allowed release of tensions both by legislators and various layers of the attentive public who read about activities and gained symbolic reassurance that the government was democratic and vital.[36] Quasirepresentative activities connected the citizenry to the government, but did not involve significant interest articulation or conveyance of demands. Like many socialist legislatures of the time, deputies were neither trustees nor delegates; the arrangement resembled the British Parliament before the seventeenth century, where the symbolic contact of subjects and court was most important.[37]

Chinese theorists based claims of NPC representation not on popular elections, deputy votes, or services provided, but on what might be called representation in a sociological sense.[38] Quotas ensured that minorities and soldiers had suitable representation, and nomination committees "took into consideration" members of other groupings (e.g., women, youth, former capitalists, intellectuals), who might not be elected in appropriate numbers in the normal course of events.[39] Legislative representation thus rested on the social background of deputies, which typically mirrored the population reasonably well.[40] Focus on demographic doubling, however, discouraged development of institutional machinery and countenanced minimal interaction between deputies and constituents. With representation mainly a question of a legislature's composition, communication with constituents was hardly necessary. Representation could exist on a symbolic plane with virtually no tangible consequences for deputies, constituents, or the political system.

Chinese theories of representation struggled to reconcile responsiveness with distance from constituents and placid plenary sessions. To accomplish this, theorists highlighted certain aspects of representation and downplayed others. First, they underscored a deputy's role in governing the nation. They held that the NPC embodied the will of all Chinese, and that deputies worked together to clarify this will and to resolve differences in the name of the greater good. They denied irreconcilable conflicts or partial interests and deemphasized deputy–elector contact. By 1959, commentators no longer stressed "maintaining close ties with the people" and "bringing into play local activism" and instead hammered home the importance of using people's congresses "to foster unity and guarantee national centralization" (*guojia de jizhong*).[41] Deputies, at root, were not seen to be agents of a locality.[42] As one member of the Party Policy Research Office explained:

Some have argued that peasant associations are not necessary because the NPC and LPCs already represent the peasants. But the NPC and LPC are not representative organs of the peasants; they represent the whole people, i.e., the people of all strata.[43]

Deputies from rural areas did not represent peasants; the whole NPC represented the whole people. In this view, NPC representation did not entail an interpersonal relationship between deputy and constituent, but instead an intercollectivity relationship between the assembly and the political community. In a society characterized by ethnic and regional diversity, this outlook encouraged a largely symbolic approach to representation and a focus on national unity at the expense of group and individual interests.

Second, theorists adopted a highly deductive definition of interests that allowed deputies to serve their constituents without consulting them. Deputies were frequently reminded to abide by the objective will and needs of the masses and to avoid following their every whim.[44] Since the party was the vanguard of the masses, this formulation in effect reduced representation to following the party's lead. In Gu Angran's words, "the party's policy is simply the working classes' will, is simply the people's will."[45] Party-drafted bills were always accepted because "in every instance the proposals were based on the will and interests of the people."[46] Representation did not entail deputy participation "in racket like that made in bourgeois legislatures,"[47] but cooperation with party deputies and other NPC members. Representation and party leadership were bound together and following the people's will meant accepting party guidance. As two Chinese commentators explained in 1959, "party leadership is not in conflict with the principle of 'the people as masters,' but actually guarantees it."[48] This meant that the NPC did not represent the diversity of the people, but rather their objective interest in party rule.

Representation is an inherently more abstract concept than law making or supervision and has both symbolic and tangible features. To assess it from afar, without public opinion data, is not easy. Conceptual and linguistic ambiguities also allow for many interpretations of what representation is and how it is manifested. According to certain Chinese formulations, sociological representation of objective, national interests took place in the NPC from 1954 to 1976. Most westerners would reject this claim, or at least express suspicion about an argument that hinges on legislative composition and cannot be disconfirmed on other grounds. It seems clear to this author that representation was not pursued in the NPC after 1957 (and only on scattered occasions before that). Responsiveness to non-elites occurred face to face in noninstitutionalized settings, in the interstices of the system where central power did not reach or where leaders truly followed the mass line. The NPC was not an important channel for indirect mass participation in political affairs. Most constituents did not have the means or inclination to pressure deputies to act on their behalf and most deputies did not take on allocation or service responsibilities on their own.

Legitimacy, integration, mobilization – regime-support activities

According to Michael Mezey, many assemblies in Third World and socialist nations conform to the specifications of a system-maintenance model of legislatures. Though often powerless and weakly representative, so-called minimal legislatures contribute to regime support and promote stability and political integration. These legislatures, weak as they are, recruit and socialize elites, gather and dispense information, and provide an institutional setting to manage conflict – activities all designed to ensure that policies meet public needs and are acceptable to those affected.[49]

Though Chinese leaders and legislative analysts rarely speak in the language of western political science, their attention to sociological representation and the united front suggests a strong interest in pursuing legitimacy, integration, and mobilization through the NPC. Party elites have always expected the NPC to organize societal interests, to defuse conflict, and to prove the high esteem in which the party is held. Deputies, like legislators elsewhere, have explained and defended government policies in an attempt to mobilize consent; they have acted as buffers, softening demands and shielding policy makers from discontent.[50]

In the 1950s, the party used the NPC to appeal to social groups that fell outside their reach because of outlook and background (e.g., intellectuals), occupation (e.g., capitalists), or region and ethnicity (e.g., minorities). As in Jiangxi and Yanan, leaders expected the legislature to serve as a united-front organization with symbolic, if not always substantive, inclusion of various classes and strata. Policies, such as the socialization of industrial assets, were discussed by former capitalists who then explained to others why the policy was necessary and patriotic. Attendance at plenary sessions and committee meetings facilitated intraelite integration and helped deputies understand central elites' concerns. Without necessarily sharing power, the party was building a cadre of socially prestigious propagandists who symbolized how people of different occupations, ethnic groups, and educational levels could work together for socialism.[51]

Through NPC deputies, the party sought to penetrate primary, occupational, or geographical groups with a broader national identity and to imprint party concerns in the minds of the public and lower-level elites. Seats were apportioned among individuals who had ties to parochial groups and elections served as a vote of confidence in party rule. For the majority of people who lacked political power, the visibility and operation of the NPC helped maintain and perhaps strengthened the acceptability of the political system.[52] In these early years, "elections were important for uniting and transforming upper-level minority personages and national capitalist deputies, and for consolidating and developing the united front."[53] In 1954, *People's Daily* could, with some accuracy, write of "the high degree of unity and solidarity among the deputies, and their unanimous praise for achievements in the past five years and for the correct and efficient leadership of the CCP."[54] For several years, the NPC provided citizens with the sense they were being represented, even if in fact they were not.[55] Like other legislatures, "simply by meeting regularly and uninterruptedly . . . (it produced) a wider and deeper sense of the government's moral right to rule than otherwise would have obtained."[56]

As with many other functions of the NPC, use as a vehicle for integration and legitimacy peaked in the mid-1950s and gradually declined thereafter. After the Hundred Flowers wilted, deep rifts between the party and nonparty elite became evident and the CCP leadership grew suspicious of the NPC. Meaningful discussions ceased and it became impossible for the NPC to credibly symbolize a united political community or unanimous acceptance of one-party rule.[57] NPC sessions became a get-together of current power holders and model individuals convened to show which political groups were in favor.[58] Deputies were missionaries rather than intermediaries; they sought to build support for the party by actively changing people's views to those of the leadership. Instead of creating the impression that socialism incorporated all interests and embraced all views, deputies demanded integration on the party's terms, without real or symbolic compromises. Even the most mild dissent disappeared and that part of integrative responsibilities assigned to the NPC shifted to party channels, where communist ideology could be taught undiluted and charismatic appeals to Mao's authority unified the people more surely than a legislature bound by a two-edged mandate to pursure both representation and the united front.

As the perceived value of democratic party members, legal professionals, intellectuals, scientists and technicians, and worker–peasant–soldiers swung wildly, the NPC could hardly be an effective symbol of citizen–party unity, unless that meant support for whatever and whomever the party supported. By 1975, the consensus manufactured at the NPC was artificial and transitory; it could not help integrate the political community. It seems unlikely that many Chinese felt included in 1975, just as many were left out in 1958–60 and 1964–5. Recognition of diversity in the NPC's first three years disrupted harmony, and the unity imposed afterwards excluded the people that the NPC was designed to attract. For most of its first two decades, the NPC did not effectively penetrate society or build legitimacy among the unconverted.

If the NPC seldom performed its legislative functions or regime-support activities, why did it exist?[59] The short answer is that for thirteen of its first twenty-four years, NPC sessions were not held, and in other years, it was dormant for long stretches of time. It appeared on the political stage mostly to mobilize cadres and mass activists to take part in implementation of new policies and to gather feedback on developing problems, especially in times of difficulty. Supplementing cadre mass-line activities, deputies served as the eyes and ears of the government, reporting to it local feelings and transmitting government policy to the governed.[60] The basis of integration and legitimation rested on mobilization and propaganda blitzes rather than on representation. Inspection work, for example, "made the government more responsive to the opinions of individuals who government personnel ordinarily are not aware of or neglect," but, more importantly, it "corrected shortcomings quickly so that the government could improve relations and mobilize all positive factors for socialist construction."[61] Deputies gathered opinions to smooth policy implementation; representation and overtures to the disenchanted took a back seat to mobilizing the forces needed to continue the revolution.

NPC sessions also provided an opportunity to relax habitual secrecy and to announce changes to the attentive public. (Of course, this was also done through other means.) Although people did not think highly of the NPC, they paid attention to what policy makers said at its sessions. At a minimum, partial policy consensus was necessary to hold a congress and, especially when sessions were put off, the ensuing reports and leadership appearances were eagerly awaited.[62]

In one sense, congresses were a significant political event. Policies were announced and high-level disputes and coverups were revealed – if not openly, by implication. Though the NPC carried out its formally prescribed functions negligibly or not at all, it was an important political show. It had a new script every year and several different directors, some of whom disagreed on fundamental points. Occasionally, actors forgot their lines or said them with an inflection that reversed their meaning. The audience never knew what would happen next, but were well advised to listen closely for new information hidden in speeches and asides. Reading between the lines yielded even more. Educative, informational, and mobilizational functions were most important. In a time of rapidly changing policies and a society where rule required the dissemination of doctrine, the NPC was one of many means to demonstrate to citizens the aims and concerns of the leadership.

Eventually, however, China's leaders chose to base claims to popular rule on a direct relationship with the masses. Revolution replaced modernization as the highest priority and guerrilla work style and mass mobilization took the place of legal rule. With limited costs, communications and mobilization functions were performed outside the NPC, through local cadres or the media. The CCP controlled policy making and mobilization, dispensed with representation, and staked its legitimacy on correct policies. In the final years of Mao's rule, institutional symbols of popular sovereignty became superfluous.

PART III
The NPC under Deng

6
Plenary sessions
and policy discussions

Although some Chinese commentators felt that the Gang of Four had damaged the people's congress system beyond repair,[1] in February 1978, sixteen months after the fall of the radicals and three years after the last NPC, the legislature reconvened. In the 1980s, plenary sessions were held each year and legislative activity surpassed that at any time from 1954 to 1976. None of this was remarkably surprising. Radical political winds blew away the NPC; moderate winds brought it back. In the late 1970s and early 1980s, a shift in the balance of power toward Deng Xiaoping and fellow victims of the Cultural Revolution led to a reversal of leftist policies and efforts to institutionalize and regularize the exercise of power. The party reassessed its history and set out to correct leftist "mistakes," including many that had crippled the legislature.

Undoing mistakes and changing long-standing policies was not without controversy, however, nor was it as speedy as some had sought. At times it was difficult to reach agreement on the distinction between "leftism" and "fine party traditions" on the one hand, and "bourgeois liberalization" and "socialist democracy" on the other. Tensions also arose between those seeking institutional reform and those wishing to return the People's Republic to its golden age (placed in the early to mid-1950s), before Mao launched his leftist experiments. In this environment, the NPC acted as a forum on de-Maoization and reflected disputes over how far it should proceed. The NPC became a barometer of the political climate and an indicator of the extent to which competing leadership groups rejected or clung to Mao's (and Lenin's) legacy. Recent sessions highlighted both the broad sea changes taking place in Chinese politics and the opposition and uncertainty present at every step.

Over a decade after Mao's death, and in the aftermath of the Tiananmen suppression, yet another succession crisis loomed, and the credibility of China's transitional leadership was shaken. Use of military force against civilians weakened the party's ability to address national problems and leadership instability was rife. Policy makers vowed to continue restructuring the economy and the political system, but suggested many reforms would be reevaluated and perhaps slowed or reversed. Although party leaders controlled policy making and continued to speak of reform, they had yet to build a stable, postrevolutionary state or to reconstitute the political system they inherited.

One unresolved question concerned the role of the NPC itself. Throughout the 1980s, all agreed that the ultraleftism of the Cultural Revolution had to be excised – for the legislature, this meant reviving united-front legitimation, socialization, and mobilization work. Most agreed that the Third Plenum's call to improve socialist democracy and to begin legislative work entailed rethinking the relationship between party policy and state law and rejecting the legal nihilism spawned by the Great Leap Forward. More controversial, a small group of intellectuals and deputies posed questions about representation and supervision first raised during the Hundred Flowers Movement. A very few proposed truly liberal reforms that challenged one-party rule.

The following three chapters consider legislative rejuvenation under Deng from three different vantage points – history, structure, and system – paralleling the earlier treatment of legislative decline. This chapter chronicles recent legislative activity largely through analysis of small-group discussions and the changing atmosphere at NPC sessions. The next chapter focuses on organizational reforms, especially those that concern the obstacles to legislative development outlined in Chapter 4. The concluding chapter assesses recent law-making, supervision, representation, and regime-support activities in order to provide a second snapshot of the legislature, against which the one developed in Chapter 5 can be compared and systemic implications considered.

The 1978 NPC: Two parts continuity, one part change

When the NPC met in early 1978, the nation was in the midst of the third campaign against the "counterrevolutionary line of the Gang of Four." The press vilified the Gang almost daily and held them responsible, in one way or another, for most of China's ills. Criticism at this time, however, centered on the four ringleaders personally and excluded Mao and the broader political system. The long-term political and economic implications of ousting the Gang had not yet crystallized, nor was it clear in what new direction China would head. Consensus on anything save opposition to the Gang was elusive and leftists of various shades remained in power – under pressure, but far from beaten.

The 1978 NPC was not an historic turning point or an occasion to evaluate the past – that would come nine months later at the party's Third Plenum. The session convened too early either to clarify the future or to resolve the ongoing power struggle and was merely one episode in a continuing succession crisis. Occurring just before Deng Xiaoping achieved a decisive edge, its message to the Chinese people and the outside world was ambiguous, even contradictory.

For one, the Congress denounced Cultural Revolution political priorities yet approved a left-leaning economic program. Premier Hua Guofeng's report spoke of developing light industry and agriculture, but stressed heavy industry and capital construction – typical foci in radical phases of communist rule. Government reports and deputy speeches praised the Maoist developmental models of Dazhai and Daqing and emphasized grain and steel production, while deputies approved a Ten-Year Economic Development Plan, first drafted under radical leadership, that foresaw exceptionally swift growth and achieving industrialization by the year 2000.[2]

Yet all was not warmed-over radicalism. Hua discussed market principles as well as central planning and devoted far more attention to science, technology, and education than had been seen in years. The goal of economic construction was placed at a level rivaling that of class struggle and continuing the revolution, and Hua spoke of rebuilding socialist democracy, improving the legal system, reviving local state and mass organizations, and "giving full scope to the abilities of intellectuals" – ideas inconceivable under the Gang. Hua condemned those who maligned education and deemed intellectuals a "force to be united with."[3]

Hua denounced ultraleftism yet upheld its Maoist inspiration. His report at the Congress was a hodgepodge of conflicting views, presented alongside each other with little effort at reconciliation.

Constitutional and personnel changes also strained to satisfy different constituencies. According to Jerome Cohen, the new constitution was a "halfway house" between the 1954 and 1975 constitutions that restored some but not all the institutional restraints on the exercise of power.[4] It reestablished the Procurator and enlarged NPC powers, but also preserved a fundamentally radical approach to property relations, individual rights, and dictatorship of the proletariat.[5] The 1978 constitution was a transitional, compromise document that spoke to a number of constituencies in a number of voices. It promised a legal revival and a strengthening of state organs, but contained few meaningful restraints on leadership discretion.

Given the vitriolic criticism of the Gang, the Congress brought fewer personnel changes than had been expected. Hua Guofeng, a Mao loyalist, was reelected premier. More than half of the 1975 NPCSC was returned, including eighteen of twenty-one living vice chairmen. Even several disgraced or soon-to-be disgraced vice chairmen retained their posts.[6] Deng Xiaoping did not yet have the power to alter the state system or to carry out a wholesale purge of Cultural Revolution beneficiaries. Especially at the top, many who had served under the Gang or who had close ties to Mao remained untouchable.

Lower in the state hierarchy, however, Deng was more successful. Many veteran cadres were appointed to administrative positions, including individuals long associated with Deng. According to a Taiwanese source, only three of thirteen vice premiers could be considered remnants of the radical faction and Deng's rehabilitated cadres controlled most of the ministries and state commissions.[7] Among NPCSC members, intellectuals, democratic party members, minority representatives, and pre-1966 deputies reappeared, as the leadership sought to improve relations with social groups it had persecuted. Selection to the NPCSC reassured and honored respected nonparty elites and symbolized an end to officially sanctioned discrimination. It returned scores of prominent Cultural Revolution victims to the political stage and welcomed their participation in modernization. Though legislative representation did not accord these groups the status of a legitimate social force in a pluralist setting, it strengthened their hand against local radicals and carried a promise of better working conditions and less interference.[8] In 1978, through NPC personnel policies, the leadership was expanding the united front.

In retrospect, the 1978 NPC provided an occasion for moderate leftists to promote their economic policies and for rehabilitated cadres to maneuver their forces into position. The Congress did not announce major policy changes or cement a decisive victory in the post-Mao power struggle. Deng's position was improving, but he lacked the power to make a clean break with the past. The new was mixed in with the old and dissensus was obvious though not admitted or explored. Conflict rumbled below the surface, but deputy speeches were singularly uninteresting, full of fulsome praise, reminiscent of the 1960 and 1964 sessions. The 1978 NPC was a mobilization congress in the tradition of those earlier gatherings. The goals were not the same, but the use of the legislature was. In a transition era, the NPC was not an independent force, nor a tool of particular leaders, nor a broom to sweep away opponents. It had returned to its informational and mobilizational role: it stirred up hatred of the Gang of Four and support for a mixed bag of policies.

Legislative supervision and the 1979 NPC

Throughout 1978, and especially at the Third Plenum, new slogans appeared – "practice is the sole criterion of truth," "seek truth from facts," "emancipate the mind" – that questioned Mao's infallibility and rejected ready-made solutions to China's problems. Although Mao himself remained off limits, the tide had begun to turn against Hua Guofeng and other Mao loyalists. At the Third Plenum in December 1978, many rehabilitated cadres won positions on the Politburo and Central Committee, and by early 1979, the leadership had scrapped the Ten-Year Economic Development Program and reduced the scale of capital construction, shifted investment toward agriculture and light industry, and begun to stress consumption. The battle against the left was turning, though not yet won.

The NPC reconvened in June 1979. The session followed a stormy Enlarged Politburo Meeting at which Hua and his rivals vied for power.[9] Although Hua kept his posts and exacted several compromises, the anti-Hua forces emerged strengthened and well positioned to consolidate their gains. On the eve of the session, well-known rehabilitated cadres (Peng Zhen, Bo Yibo, An Ziwen, Tao Xijin, Lin Huijia) were nominated to fill NPC vacancies and the press abounded with calls to preserve and strengthen the Third Plenum spirit.[10]

Reports at the Congress focused on adjusting the economy and strengthening democracy and legal system – topics high on the antileft agenda. Even Hua Guofeng's government work report took up these issues and offered concessions to his opponents. If on the one hand Hua emphasized democratic centralism and the dangers of anarchy, on the other he downgraded class struggle and acknowledged the need to institutionalize socialist democracy and to enact laws. He admitted that democracy had never been publicized nor practiced sufficiently and that this had encouraged the spread of autocracy, bureaucracy, and love of privilege. Hua deemed political democracy essential to the four modernizations and reminded officials to accept the supervision of people's congresses. He added that it was "absolutely impermissible to conceal information from people's deputies or to lie to them."[11]

To the surprise of many, the leadership acted upon Hua's words and conducted a more open Congress than any since 1957. The economic reports submitted in 1979 were comparatively sober and detailed and included statistics on production, expenditures, and revenues.[12] Small- group discussions were lively and wide-ranging and penetrating criticism appeared with unprecedented frequency. Even the official press commended deputies for "taking ranking cadres to task ... for privilege-seeking, under-the-counter dealings, and suppressing people's democratic rights."[13] In the words of one observer from Hong Kong, "a democratic wind entered the august Great Hall of the People that challenged special privileges, bureaucratism and autocracy."[14]

As might have been expected, Cultural Revolution-era atrocities were the prime targets of deputy censure. NPC delegates advocated trying the Gang of Four publicly and bringing to justice the murderers of Zhang Zhixin – a young party functionary who was tortured and shot under the Gang. Some deputies also favored reversing the verdicts of Liu Shaoqi and former Shanghai Deputy Mayor Pan Hannian.[15] Many urged the government to clear the names of the innocent and to assign responsibility to the guilty. They proposed thorough and speedy inquiries into Cultural Revolution crimes and encouraged the authorities to pursue investigations wherever they might lead.

Reviewing the recent past inevitably ensnared individuals who remained in power, including Politburo member and long-time Mao associate, Wang Dongxing. Deputies scored him for opposing the Third Plenum spirit and for using his position for personal gain. He apparently had built a 6,000 square meter mansion in Zhongnanhai, whose construction costs rivaled those of major state projects. NPC deputies scolded him for "defying the toils and poverty of the nation" and forced him to make a self-criticism. They also found fault with Politburo member Ji Dengkui and Vice Premier Chen Yonggui, one a veteran internal security official and the other the head of the soon-to-be discredited Dazhai brigade.[16] Though these leaders still held high positions, the attacks were not unexpected. By June 1979, their influence was dwindling and their removal was near.

More surprising, deputies also asked several rising stars to improve their work style and to forsake special privileges. For example, Liao Chengzhi, an NPCSC vice chairman and leader of the 1979 Chinese Friendship Mission to Japan, was held responsible for allowing many of the mission's 606 members to gain admission through "backdoor connections."[17] NPC deputies also criticized personal use of VIP airplanes by high officials, especially an incident involving Chen Muhua, a vice premier and minister of economic relations with foreign countries. On the day she was planning to return from a trip to Romania, a delegation of Chinese athletes was preparing to take the same route home. Several members were ill and needed treatment urgently. In order to save foreign exchange and to expedite the trip, the delegation's leaders suggested sharing Chen's plane. The Chinese embassy agreed and sent the athletes to the plane, but when Chen arrived she demanded they leave. They complied, and since they had already cleared customs and checked out of their hotel, they spent the night in the airport. While waiting, the athletes were shocked to see crates of West German furniture being loaded onto the plane, and after returning home, they reported Chen's behavior to officials in the Physical Culture and Sports Commission. Shortly before the NPC met, Chen discovered she was under suspicion and instructed an underling in her ministry to telephone the Sports Commission to explain that a secretary was responsible for the incident and that Chen had not known about it. She also asked that the athletes cease discussing the matter. The Commission official refused to listen to her request and, instead, encouraged deputies from sports circles to reveal everything at the NPC, including the attempted coverup. The deputies told their story at the Congress and, according to some reports, Chen offered a sincere self-criticism.[18] What is interesting is that both Liao and Chen remained in power after their reprimands; this was an auspicious sign for the NPC. Deputies had some say over officials on the way up as well as those on the way down.

At the 1979 NPC, legislative supervision was resurrected. Deputies exposed high-level wrongdoings and warned officials to discontinue corrupt practices. Deputies served no single leader, or perhaps several competing ones. They confirmed rumors, spoke out on abuses discussed on every street corner, and were not labeled antiparty or antisocialist for their remarks. Although domestic reports carried only elliptical references to criticisms covered more fully in the Hong Kong press, information undoubtedly trickled out. The Congress allowed citizens (through their representatives) to let off steam and to feel that some of the high and mighty had received just punishment. Through the legislature, the leadership defused embarrassing incidents and displayed a new, sophisticated approach to reviving the party's reputation and relegitimizing CCP rule.

Admittedly, the NPC did not topple powerholders or interrupt promising careers. Its reach was far more limited. Disclosures aimed to reinvigorate party traditions and to reinstill internal checks on wayward leaders. In 1979, deputies could only admonish dishonest and unethical leaders; not until 1980 would they criticize wrongheaded and incompetent officials and their policies.

The 1980 NPC: Frank discussions and power struggle

The 1980 NPC was the most open and lively legislative session in the history of the People's Republic.[19] Changes in appearance and atmosphere were apparent from the outset. Gone were the processions of NPC leaders and rounds of seemingly endless applause; gone were slogan-laden banners and large portraits of Mao and Hua. In their place was a businesslike approach to legislative responsibilities that stressed equality of deputies and attention to "democratic form." Secret ballots were used in elections of state leaders, resulting in several votes against new Premier Zhao Ziyang and hundreds against NPCSC vice chairmen.[20] Many ranking officials participated fully and frequently in group discussions, unlike past sessions where they only "came down to meet fellow deputies" or "to give instructions."[21] Ordinary deputies leveled criticisms of a sort unseen since 1957 and exercised, for the first time, their right to summon ministers to answer questions. Perhaps most significantly, the leadership invited the public at large to review the proceedings and to assess government performance: throughout the session, *People's Daily* published extensive excerpts of small-group discussions that revealed previously unknown blunders and deepening divisions within the post-Mao leadership. Attentive audiences saw rival leaders in deep disagreement, struggling to achieve preeminence.

In the fall of 1980, the anti-Hua coalition was victorious but splintering. Three distinct tendencies were appearing, advocated by separate but loose and unstable opinion groups. Farthest to the left stood the conservers or restoration faction. Centered in the ministries responsible for energy production and machine building, these individuals had prospered from 1949 to 1966 and emerged from the Cultural Revolution intact, if not unscathed. They by and large denied the need for fundamental change and sought to restore the political and economic system to its pre-1966 (or perhaps pre-1957) state. They accordingly stressed party strengthening and revival of Leninist norms. In economics, they supported heavy industry over light industry and agriculture, planning over market principles, and accumulation over improved living standards.[22]

A second group, called the practice faction or the reformers, endorsed a more thorough overhaul of the political system and a reversal of conserver economic priorities. Led by Deng Xiaoping, their byword was systemic reform; they favored bold departures from the past, including separation of party and state, institutional limitation of power, and increased autonomy and self-management in economic subsystems.[23]

A third opinion group, the adjusters, fell between the conservers and the reformers. Often associated with Chen Yun, they accepted the traditional preference for planning over market controls and centralization over decentralization, but shared the reformers' belief in measured growth and investment in light industry and agriculture. More than either rival group, adjusters were concerned with deficits and inflation.[24]

The 1980 NPC convened just after Deng's August 18 speech at an Enlarged Politburo Meeting – a speech that signaled a high point in the fortunes of the reformers. Reform was riding high, but readjustment was the official policy and conservers refused to concede defeat.[25] At the NPC, all three groups gained a hearing and jockeyed for position: a reform/adjustment coalition drew attention to conserver subjectivism, mistaken priorities, and waste. Provincial-based conservers rallied support for coal interests and domestic machinery producers. Adjusters highlighted deficits, inflation, and other unforeseen consequences of reform. More so than in the past, "the NPC acted as a forum for hashing out significant differences – for evaluating recent economic performance, for responding to political feedback that appeared in the press in preceding months, and possibly for garnering the support of particular social constituencies."[26]

The financial reports delivered by State Planning Commission Minister Yao Yilin and Finance Minister Wang Bingqian were detailed and forthcoming.[27] Most surprising, after several rounds of discussion by the Central Committee, Premier Zhao Ziyang and Vice Premier Wan Li, both reformers, prevailed on their colleagues to reveal a 17 billion yuan 1979 deficit and projected smaller, yet substantial, deficits for 1980 and 1981. They persuaded their colleagues that avoiding the issue or fabricating statistics (as had been done as recently as 1979) was unnecessary because the reasons for the deficit were tenable.[28] Zhao and Wan admitted that the deficit had been caused by higher agricultural procurement prices, increased investment in agriculture and light industry, wage adjustments, increased financial powers for localities, and backpay for rehabilitated cadres, but argued that the benefits of running a deficit exceeded the costs.

Some deputies accepted the reformers' argument. Several commended leaders for living up to their obligations to the people and for forsaking "false, pompous, meaningless reports" that "pretend everything is all right and nothing wrong."[29] Some deputies, however, noted that the reports were still incomplete. One pointed out statistical discrepancies; others found the explanations of the budget deficit inadequate. Several adjusters assailed the principle of deficit financing. They argued against taking deficits lightly, or said they were excusable for 1979 and 1980, but not in the future. Some deputies found Finance Minister Wang Bingqian's plan to reduce the red ink wanting and proposed additional cuts. Shanshi deputy Chen Xiyue recommended relying on bank loans to finance the deficit only as a last resort and said that Wang should have given a precise date when deficits would be eliminated. Feng Xijia asked: "Will inflation result after a succession of yearly deficits? Why can't we eliminate our financial deficit within 1980–1?"[30]

Inflation, like the deficit, provided an opening for adjusters to check the reformers. Deputies noted marked and unpopular price fluctuations and said the masses feared further increases. They observed that Yao Yilin's report failed to mention inflation and Wang Bingqian's report had only one sentence about it. Deputies criticized "the lukewarm effort to curb price hikes" and called for effective measures to stop indiscriminate and disguised price increases. Deputy Liu Bangwen asked why prices had been going up and how they were being controlled, saying that the people were disappointed that these questions had not been addressed in the reports.[31] On deficits and inflation, adjusters spoke as the guardians of public welfare and the voice of fiscal responsibility.

The 1980 wage adjustment also elicited complaints about reform. Some deputies said that increasing wages for only 40% of state workers caused grumbling and dampened spirits; managers were forced to alienate subordinates and State Council rules rewarded good work attitude, high skills, and contribution, but neglected the "real state of affairs" and were "hard to implement." Several deputies said local cadres treated the wage increase like another movement, which caused tension and disrupted stability and unity. Two Shaanxi deputies recommended increasing everybody's wages, with slightly larger increments for the best workers.[32] In 1980, appeals to fairness or egalitarianism could not be ignored and many conservers still associated monetary incentives with capitalism.

To allay deputy concerns about prices and wages, Liu Zhangfu, Director of the State Price Bureau, and Yu Guanghan, Deputy Director of the State Labor Bureau, appeared before the Sichuan delegation to answer questions. Liu and Yu acknowledged price increases for many daily necessities, problems in the price-control process, padding of bonuses by enterprises, and irrational wage scales and adjustments.[33]

Honesty and reform had costs; candidness could relieve pressure or it could intensify it. At the 1980 NPC, the reformers scrambled to defend their policies and took the brunt of criticism on deficits, inflation, and the wage adjustment.

On other issues, however, the conservers suffered far more than the reformers. Conserver attempts to defend heavy industry foundered when adjusters and reformers extended criticism of the left to include many officials formerly considered centrists. Deputies assembled information that cast conservers in an unflattering light – and a sympathetic editorial staff at *People's Daily* published it. Though some of the news was not new, splashing detailed exposés in the press reinforced its impact and humiliated officials responsible for embarrassing mistakes.

In July 1980, the public learned that the Bohai No. 2 oil rig had sunk in November 1979 with the loss of 72 lives. On August 25, 1980, a few days before the NPC convened, the State Council announced its decision to remove the Minister of the Petroleum Industry and to put a demerit on the record of the concerned vice premier for allowing the incident and then evading responsibility. On September 2, four ministry staff members, including the head of a department, received prison sentences. The timing of these actions emboldened NPC deputies and sanctioned discussion of the disaster and the coverup. It encouraged deputies to publicize widespread "losses in economic construction . . . due to bureaucracy, gross irresponsibility and arbitrary and impracticable orders."[34] Deputies discussed whether higher Petroleum Ministry officials should face trial for their actions and criticized their distortion of Mao's maxim "to fear neither suffering nor death."[35] Petroleum Ministry officials were said to be ready to ignore natural laws and worker safety for increased output.

Reformist deputies also strove to reduce pressure from adjusters by blaming the budget deficit on conservers. In particular, they focused on waste in heavy industry. Yao's and Wang's reports had announced dramatic cutbacks in capital construction (28%), but deputies asked for much more. They singled out ministers responsible for large, often unfinished projects, publicly lambasted them, and, in some cases, sought to assign criminal or economic responsibility.

The half-built Baoshan Iron and Steel Complex near Shanghai received the most attention. Work had begun in 1978 shortly after signing an agreement with Japanese businessmen and securing large loans. Approved personally by Hua Guofeng and constituting an integral part of the Ten-Year Development Program, Baoshan was to be completed by June 1980.[36] But cost overruns and delays plagued the project from the start. As early as the 1979 NPC, Yu Guangyuan questioned a fellow deputy and vice minister about "careless planning" at Baoshan. The vice minister defended the project's economic viability and spoke of the need to pay "school fees" for a lesson. Yu pointed out that the fees were so high they could be paid only once.[37]

In 1980, outlays mounted, and by July, Vice Premier Bo Yibo told a visiting

Japanese delegation that Baoshan was no longer a model but a "heavy burden."[38] In September, NPC deputies came forward with questions and charges. In an unprecedented event, a group of Beijing deputies summoned the Minister of Metallurgy, Tang Ke, to answer inquiries on progress at Baoshan. Caught unprepared, Tang requested a three-day postponement.[39] On the morning of September 4, Tang and two vice ministers finally appeared. Four of the 170 deputies present began the questioning, focusing on the project's total costs, investment recovery rate, site choice, quality of engineering, natural resource supply, foreign loans, and completion date. Qinghua University President Liu Da accused the ministry of "idealizing everything" and favored remodeling existing enterprises rather than building new ones. He also asked why the ministry had imported state-of-the-art technology in a nation with abundant labor and low wages and noted that many people felt Baoshan would become a financial "bottomless pit." Tang and his subordinates admitted they had neglected to study the project's feasibility sufficiently, that equipment had been imported unnecesarily, and that building on soft ground had increased foundation costs. But they insisted "work was going well and fast" and defended building domestic plants over importing iron and steel. They also provided figures that showed total investment would be recovered within thirteen years.[40]

Press coverage of this interpellation led to further discussions and letters from the public showing support and providing new information.[41] Several deputies expressed dissatisfaction with the ministry's account. They pointed out that Tang had avoided the key question of waste and that expected returns would pay off the interest on the loan but not the principal.[42] On September 6, Tang and his vice ministers were again summoned – this time before 150 members of the Shanghai delegation. Yu Guangyuan and sixteen others fired questions at the ministry officials on the total investment in Baoshan, the wisdom of relying on foreign ores, the pollution consequences for Shanghai, the economic value of the project, and the lessons the ministry had learned. Yu noted that Tang had evaded questions on economic rationality and instead had focused on a different issue, that is, the need to increase domestic iron and steel production. Ministry officials, as before, admitted mistakes but downplayed their consequences. They acknowledged that a study of the environmental impact and final cost estimates were still in preparation, but assured the deputies that Shanghai would be safeguarded and total costs would not exceed 30 to 40 billion yuan. Some deputies still found these remarks overoptimistic and recommended setting up an independent commission to investigative ministry statistics, to inspect Baoshan, and to find ways to reduce losses to a minimum.[43] They firmly rejected the view that "mistakes and losses were inevitable."[44]

Public exposure of the Metallurgy Ministry induced reform-minded deputies to join with adjusters to identify other overambitious and wasteful construction projects. Reformers and adjusters alike emphasized reducing capital construction and ending unneeded imports. Deputies cited iron and steel projects in Ningxia and Xinjiang, an oil refinery in Urumqi, and the Wan'an Hydro-electric Plant, all of which had consumed hundreds of millions of yuan but were not operational.[45] They questioned importing 100 sets of comprehensive coal-mining equipment for 25 million yuan each and called the Minister of Chemical Industry to answer questions about unfinished ethylene projects in Nanjing and Shandong at which expensive imported equipment was lying idle. Anticonserver deputies rejected shifting blame to the Gang of Four for these losses and instead saw a pattern of post-Mao mistakes that extended throughout industrial ministries. They cited incompetent, unscientific officials and a personalized political system that gave individuals excessive power. Systemic reform was needed, beginning with legislation and better oversight, "so that no one responsible for big wastes could get away with it."[46] Liu Da suggested:

When it comes to major construction projects, it should not be decided alone by one minister or one vice premier. If they do not have to report to the NPC and do not want to hear everyone's opinion, then we are still operating under the old system wherein one person or a few individuals have the say. If so, what do we need the NPC for? Let them go and institute a dictatorship![47]

In this view, the NPC existed to limit the personal power of state officials, especially those unconcerned with efficiency. Legislative oversight would trim losses and check officials who had a penchant for capital construction. Through the NPC, reformers and adjusters would restrict the influence of the conservers.

Opponents of the left questioned officials responsible for misguided decisions and long-standing development priorities. Deputy Wu Lengxi noted that Yao Yilin's report dealt with heavy industry at great length, but only devoted one brief sentence to agricultural and light industry development. He asked, "In which position has agriculture been placed?" and said it was "dangerous" if "the State Planning Commission puts the stress on heavy industry, light industry and agriculture in that order."[48] Many rural deputies argued that expenditures for agriculture were too small and called for larger appropriations[49]; others recounted experiences in areas where agricultural reform had begun and asked for guidance. One deputy mentioned that peasants in Hubei had requested returning to individual farming, but cadres had hesitated, pending clear-cut instructions from the Central Committee.[50] Changes were brewing in the countryside; rural deputies came to the Congress to advocate reform and to learn how far it would proceed.

NPC members also probed and prodded officials on social welfare issues. Many welcomed double-digit increases in the education budget for 1980 and 1981, but felt they were still insufficient. One deputy criticized the lack of attention to adult education in Yao's report; others called for enlarged enrollments in higher education and for setting up part-time universities.[51]

Pollution also gained a prominent place in discussions. Three Shanghai deputies pointed out that the financial reports by Yao and Wang slighted household interests in the name of production, especially in regard to pollution of the Shanghai water supply. They noted the "niggardly" amount spent on purifying water compared to the billions wasted on Baoshan and "strongly demand(ed) that the control of the Huangpu River in Shanghai be incorporated in the national plans."[52] Others cited similar pollution problems in Beijing and Guilin.[53]

Through followers in the NPC, reformers, adjusters, and conservers addressed and mobilized supporters, made known differences in approach,[54] attacked each other's vulnerabilities, and engaged popular opinion to discredit their opponents. The NPC had become a political event; rivals competed for support by discussing their policies and priorities and highlighting their opponents' mistakes. Right, center, and left were not equally matched, however. The reformers suffered some criticism, the adjusters very little; both gave out far more than they received. With the far left (represented by the Gang) eliminated, the middle left was most vulnerable. Reformers and adjusters had an advantage and they used the NPC to press it.

At the 1980 NPC, legislative supervision expanded and quasirepresentational activities appeared, albeit in the service of a continuing power struggle. At this remarkable session, top–down manipulation declined as legislators spoke for leaders, but also for economic or regional interests and the public at large.[55] Deputies took advantage of an opening provided by elite conflict to reflect public opinion on issues (e.g., prices, wages, pollution) that concerned the whole nation and rarely received an open hearing. They endeavored to give meaning to the concept of representation in a one-party state.

The 1981 NPC: The consequences of reform

The Fourth Session of the Fifth NPC met from November 30 to December 13, 1981. Many Hong Kong-based observers were disappointed with the Congress, judging it "dull" or "lackluster," bereft both of news and lively debate. Indeed, comparatively few deputy speeches appeared in the domestic press and none criticized specific individuals or events. According to some, democracy had come and gone; deputies had "lost last year's brave spirit" and "did not reflect mass opinions as much as at the last two congresses."[56]

It is true that the 1981 NPC was not as open as those that preceded it. Changing elite priorities and political needs prompted deputy restraint. After a number of strikes and protests in 1980, misgivings about political and social pluralism resurfaced and inspired the leadership to round up mass democracy activists and to crack down on literary dissent. By December, a movement against bourgeois liberalization was in full swing and the political climate was tense; the time for deputy outspokenness had passed.[57] Also, after the final fall of Hua Guofeng in July 1981, there was no obvious target for legislative pressure.[58] In 1981, consolidating political power and reasserting party control took precedence over personnel shifts and restructuring the political system. Many potentially contentious questions of high politics were shelved or resolved behind closed doors. This did not mean, however, that conflict disappeared or that all NPC discussions were dull and inconsequential. Debate simply returned to less glamorous but important economic policy disputes.

In late 1980 and early 1981, the leadership tightened central controls and limited enterprise autonomy to reduce deficits and control inflation. Announced reforms were postponed and readjustment again moved to the top of the agenda. Then, in the late spring of 1981, Zhao Ziyang reintroduced the theme of economic reform and conservers began to agitate for greater attention to heavy industry. Behind the united political front, controversy over China's economic future deepened. In the period between the 1980 and 1981, NPC "disagreement was rife over the question of centralization versus autonomy for the lower levels; over using mainly administrative versus economic methods; on the subjects of speedy growth and the place of heavy industry; and over how much weight to give to inflation, deficits, and profits."[59]

Zhao's government work report leaned toward reform. He agreed that readjustment had been necessary and should continue for five more years, but recommended relaxing centralized controls to rejuvenate reform. He emphasized extending enterprise autonomy and rural reform, arousing worker initiative and increasing reliance on the market.[60] Most deputies praised Zhao's report but only a handful came forth with new initiatives. Few followed the Vice Governor of Heilongjiang, Chen Jiafei, in advocating "revolutionary" rather than "improving" reforms. Nor did many echo Wang Ruoshui, a deputy editor at *People's Daily,* who faulted Zhao for discussing organization and discipline but neglecting socialist democracy.[61] Deputy support for reform was "unanimous" but restrained, almost perfunctory. As the leadership looked to accelerate reform, deputies reminded them that adjustment was not yet complete. Sharp criticism emerged only from adjusters.

Adjusters first questioned statistics on the decline in the deficit in 1980 and 1981. According to a Hong Kong journalist stationed in Beijing, pleasant surprise turned to consternation when deputies realized that official figures took into account internal but not foreign debt. After rebalancing the books, it became clear that much, if not all, of the supposed deficit reduction was illusory. Deputies were distressed by this news and several proposed new legislation to control state finances.[62]

Persistent inflation also drew concern. Zhu Benhong, a deputy from Shandong, supported price increases that lightened the burden of state subsidies, but most deputies disagreed and favored price stabilization. Many adjusters questioned Zhao's claim that basic price stability had been achieved.[63] Representatives from Beijing, Guangdong, Sichuan, and Gansu noted numerous price increases, some of which had occurred quite recently. They charged that the government had promised to limit increases to several dozen agricultural goods, but instead hundreds had gone up, causing anxiety among the masses. They cited especially unpopular hikes in the cost of furniture, pans and bowls, cigarettes, and liquor and urged the authorities to make price control a high priority.[64]

Jia Tangshan, a deputy who also served as Third Party Secretary of Beijing, responded on behalf of the reformers. He explained that reducing subsidies to loss-making enterprises had necessitated the price increases, and admitted that inadequate public relations had caused a strong negative reaction. He acknowledged continuing rumors about further increases and asked deputies to assure the masses they were unfounded.[65] But some legislators remained unconvinced. Even as the session closed, they hedged their support for Zhao's report. The final NPC resolution approved the speech and indicated "satisfaction" with the State Council's work, but reiterated concern over deficits and inflation.[66]

In 1981, deputies also pointed to undesired social and cultural consequences of reform policies. Many criticized artistic works that did not provide "spiritual nourishment" and newspapers and journals that "encourage bourgeois liberalism."[67] One PLA deputy reportedly endorsed intensifying "antibourgeois liberalization efforts . . . because the intellectuals have again become cocky." This remark is said to have spread quickly inside and outside the NPC, and caused quite a stir. Opposition arose, and some deputies suggested the problem was not the arrogance of intellectuals, but that the policy toward intellectuals had not been carried out sufficiently. Debate swirled, yet no authoritative source stepped forward to refute the remark.[68]

The 1981 NPC was a dull congress only for those who expected dramatic policy or personnel changes. Nothing of this nature occurred. But economic disputes continued to be aired: disputes that reflected elite cleavages and a growing awareness that the dislocations of reform could not be ignored. The session enabled adjusters to advance their views even as reformers regrouped and prepared to move forward. If deputies urged reform when many leaders were skeptical, they urged caution when confidence returned. If the NPC helped peel away layers of leftists, it also restrained the right. Deputies were beginning to speak as the voice of patience and experience, tempering their support of reform initiatives with reminders of the difficulties ahead and the perils of blitzkrieg-style rule. More than displaying an ideological disposition, they were seeking to minimize risk and to avoid even short-term dislocation, to slow the pendulum swings of change, to break from campaign-style policy implementation and reliance on revolutionary enthusiasm and charisma.

The 1982 and 1983 sessions

In 1982 and 1983, agricultural reform deepened, family farming became the norm, and political reform gained a new life. Deng and his colleagues reorganized the State Council, reduced the number of ministries and commissions, and pressed administrative simplification as the party's "number one task." The economy rebounded from a sharp recession and an upturn in state revenues encouraged relaxation of some of the more draconian adjustment policies. Reform-minded leaders spoke often of market regulation, commodity circulation, and price reform, and they advocated potentially expensive policies, such as enterprise tax reform and improving productivity.[69] Yet the lessons of 1979–81 were by no means forgotten. Adjusters and reformers alike upheld price stability and central control over finances and investment. Most agreed that markets should only supplement planning and that limited enterprise flexibility did not entail abrogating tight control over fiscal policy or large deficits.[70] In 1982 and 1983, reform gained ground, but not at the expense of adjustment.

NPC sessions were held in December 1982 and June 1983. Official speeches both years reflected a centrist approach to macroeconomic policy that blended reform and readjustment. In 1982, Zhao Ziyang said that "reform of the current price system is imperative," but added that "we cannot afford the least rashness in this matter." A year later he advocated structural reform of the economy and changes in enterprise profit retention, but then criticized the "incorrect and harmful" view that "reform simply means decentralization."[71] Slow and measured steps to restructure the economy would not disrupt production: efficiency and output would increase partly through market reforms, partly through improved bureaucratic performance.

Deputies at the 1982 and 1983 NPCs, by and large, accepted this mix of reform and readjustment without objection. Clear-cut pro-reform or pro-adjustment statements were rare and even Chinese reports emphasized the "warm" rather than "lively" atmosphere. Most deputies agreed with Zhao's focus on economic results and found the goals he offered "realistic" and "inspiring."[72] Typical deputy speeches elaborated official policy, often via colorful local stories, and brimmed with praise for the progress since 1978. Building on the broadest consensus since Mao's death, the leadership used the NPC to take stock and to affirm achievements. Deputies and officials minimized differences, recounted successes, and looked with confidence to the future.

In this sea of applause and self-congratulation, only minor reservations appeared. In 1982, some deputies questioned the goal of quadrupling total output by the year 2000, and warned of unforeseen developments and the danger of "wild slogans."[73] In 1983, several deputies pointed out that the leadership could take pride in improvements in rural life, but cautioned against "blind optimism." Li Xing, a Prefectural First Secretary in Hebei, in particular, reminded the government that peasants needed help in resolving supply problems for diesel oil and agricultural production materials, including fertilizer, insecticides, feed, trace elements, and plant hormones.[74]

Some deputies also challenged complacency over cadre "economic crimes," including, graft, embezzlement, bribery, speculation, and swindling. Zhao Ziyang, in his 1982 government report, had denied that "we are only swatting flies, not hitting big tigers." He explained:

Of the total of over one hundred thousand criminal cases uncovered so far in the economic sphere, only a very small number involve, to varying degrees, senior leading cadres. Some were taken in by the actual offenders due to serious bureaucratism, others were not strict enough with their children, and still others have been tainted with unhealthy tendencies. These cases have been or are being dealt with in all seriousness. However, until now we have not found any senior leading cadre should himself be held accountable for any serious irregularities in economic matters.[75]

Several deputies doubted the thoroughness of investigations of leading cadres and one, Li Wenjie, said all offenders should face legal as well as party sanction and that it was premature to conclude none were guilty. Many agreed that conscientious treatment of this problem was necessary to improve party performance and party prestige.[76]

Scattered criticisms aside, deputies in 1982 and 1983 accepted policies they were asked to review; a few called for humility and sobriety, none questioned basic programs or priorities. Pressure for unity, after five years of turbulence, quieted obstreperous deputies and produced agendas with few openings for commentary. The leadership position on the major agenda items – the Sixth Five-Year Plan, a new constitution, a new state leadership slate – had been hammered out in party councils months before NPC sessions and deputies were not invited to disturb a carefully constructed consensus.[77] Public discord did not serve any active leader or opinion group and, without high-level patrons, only the most venturesome deputies spoke out. The 1982 and 1983 Congresses thus were quiet sessions that promoted unity and publicized centrist economic policies. Legislative liveliness awaited new conflicts and leaders who saw an advantage in publicizing their disputes.

The 1984 NPC: The path to reform

1984 was a watershed year for China's market reformers. In the wake of an aborted and counterproductive campaign against spiritual pollution, reformers pressed ahead on several fronts. In the rural sector, they loosened restrictions on trade, peasant mobility, and acquisition of the means of production and hiring assistants, and they encouraged peasant households to specialize in sideline industries and nongrain crops. Press reports almost daily extolled entrepreneurship and praised peasants who through hard work and initiative prospered.[78]

As reform deepened, it also spread. After five years of focus on the countryside, reformers turned to the cities: they promoted responsibility systems that specified industrial workers' tasks and tied wages to output, and the use of contracts in industrial enterprises, commerce, and capital construction. They convened conferences to assess urban experiments and even toyed with price reform and narrowing the scope of the state plan. A major party decision in October 1984 envisioned quasi-independent industrial enterprises empowered to plan and market their output, to hire and fire workers, and to set wages and prices – within certain limits. For all but the largest enterprises, reform would involve less government interference and more discretion over after-tax profits.[79] In the cities, as in the countryside, it promised expanded decision-making powers for lower levels and incentive systems that would unleash worker initiative.

The NPC reconvened in May 1984, just as the momentum behind reform was building. Premier Zhao Ziyang's report to the Congress commended "heartening progress on all fronts" and spoke of continuing problems (low economic efficiency, burdensome subsidies, and an irrational price system) that only reform could resolve. Zhao particularly emphasized the need to restructure the economy and to open to the outside world. Invigorating the economy, in his view, depended on closing inefficient enterprises, importing advanced technologies, unclogging trade channels, and expanding use of material incentives.[80]

Deputies warmly received Zhao's report and few raised the usual arguments against reform (cost, loss of control) or warned of the financial implications of downplaying readjustment. Instead, deputies championed reform as never before, only pausing to point out the obstacles lying ahead.

Far more than Zhao Ziyang, deputies at the 1984 NPC underscored the depth of local opposition to urban reform and the need to protect reformers. Wang Maolin, a deputy and Mayor of Taiyuan, reproached local officials who punished or crushed reform pioneers guilty of minor, honest mistakes.[81] Liu Zheng, the Governor of Hunan, cited an electronics institute praised by Zhao for using contracts to reduce dependency on the state treasury, which had been continually criticized and obstructed by local cadres. Liu explained how leftist ideas, selfish departmentalism, egalitarianism, and outdated and unreasonable regulations restricted people's thinking and fostered overconcentration of power.[82] Wang Maolin joined Liu in calling for further discussion of how leftist ideology and "conventional forces" impeded reform. Both men suggested removing uncooperative cadres and renewing central pressure via directives requiring local departments to draw up concrete reform measures within a specified time.[83] Neither man called for dramatic new policies; both aimed to ensure policy implementation and to guarantee the feasibility of change by urging reformers to translate daring words into action and to persist in the face of opposition.

Other deputies drew attention to difficulties in carrying out party policy toward intellectuals. Zhao, in his report, had reaffirmed the importance of knowledge and intellectuals and had urged rapid promotion of young and middle-aged scientists and technicians. To back up this policy, he endorsed stern treatment, including removal, of cadres who discriminated against intellectuals.[84] Many better-educated deputies echoed these remarks and detailed the problems that intellectuals encountered, ranging from lingering contempt for knowledge to local leaders who preferred sycophants to innovators. They welcomed Zhao's pledge to dismiss antiintellectual cadres and cited numerous examples, some from personal experience, in which removal of such leaders had decisive and beneficial consequences.[85]

At the 1984 NPC, deputies and officials alike swung behind reform. It was not a year for highly technical discussion of economic policy, nor did intraelite disputes or power struggles spill into legislative debates. Discussions instead centered on topics that touched deputies personally and were easily understood by nonspecialists: obstacles to reform and policy toward intellectuals. Deputies did not attempt to restrain leaders, as in other years, but rather goaded them to carry out announced policies and reminded them that high-sounding words required concrete confirmation. They cited examples of local opposition and challenged the leadership to overcome it. Less a voice of caution or moderation than one of reason and experience, deputies supported bold initiatives, but stressed the difficulties ahead and the dangers of overoptimism.

The 1985 NPC: Socialist renewal and the costs of reform

Late 1984 and early 1985 brought dizzying changes followed by a pause to evaluate and reconsider. Urban reform carried China into uncharted territory as a leading party theoretician proclaimed, "there are no Marxist quotations for what we are doing now," and Deng Xiaoping assured top party leaders that China need not fear "a little capitalist stuff." Spurred by market reforms and relaxed controls, the economy boomed and growth rates soared. Yet fiscal and monetary imbalances remained. Enlivening the economy had led to a precipitous decline in foreign currency reserves, expansion of the deficit, resurgent inflationary pressures and an enormous overissue of currency and credit. By the time the NPC met in March 1985, the economy was seriously overheated and reform was partly to blame.

Official reports at the NPC acknowledge "conspicuous problems" but struggled to defend reform. Premier Zhao, for example, noted "drastic increases" in loans and credit (up 29%) and in wages and bonuses (up 19%) in 1984, yet stressed the need to be "steadfast" in upholding "correct concepts and policy decisions for restructuring our economy."[86] Even as he admitted mistakes arising from inexperience, Zhao emphasized technical problems (e.g., too loose fiscal policy) that could be rectified and avoided in the future. Like other reformers, Zhao resisted the suggestion that sectoral imbalances or loss of control were inevitable consequences of reform.

Some deputies joined Zhao and hewed the reform line. One representative from Henan commended the leadership for discovering problems early, disclosing them, and adopting correctives; others spoke of "the generally good situation" or argued that abandoning reform would be the most serious error.[87] Deputies of this mind admitted problems that could not be denied but staunchly defended the overall thrust of the reform program.

Some legislators took a different tack. They showed "a new willingness . . . to air critical views, (and exploited) a new readiness in the party to listen."[88] Many condemned the get-rich-quick mentality that had swept the country with reform. They pointed to an unhealthy tendency to "look toward money" (*xiang qian kan*) and to press reports that glorified consumption and downplayed thrift. They questioned the direction Chinese society was heading and suggested that there be no more talk of prosperity without mention of hard work and increased productivity.[89]

Their immediate targets were officials who were milking reform for personal gain. Although one deputy said his dictionary did not include the words "speculation" or "profiteering," and held that the first was merely "information" and the second "enlivening the economy,"[90] most deputies were dismayed by official misdoings. In fact, according to one Hong Kong commentator, high-level corruption became the "hot issue" (*remen*) of the session.[91] Deputies censured children of high cadres for using connections to set up companies and scorned cadres who demanded large fees to process forms. They criticized illegal importing of pornographic videotapes and music, and agreed with Zhao that indiscriminately issuing bonuses and subsidies, randomly hiking prices to make high profits, taking advantage of power to buy and resell commodities in short supply, hosting banquets, sending gifts, and engaging in bribery and smuggling all tarnished reform and impeded its progress.[92]

All speakers at the Congress opposed "unhealthy practices," but two contrary cures were prescribed. Some deputies accepted the reform diagnosis that financial fine-tuning, such as tightening the money supply and restricting credit, would clear up the problem. They argued that cadre abuses were not a by-product of reform and were "nothing to be panic-stricken by." Ji Xianlin, for example, said that small-group discussions dispelled his anxieties on this subject and made him confident it would soon be resolved.[93] Deputies who shared Ji's view opposed allowing a minor problem to interfere with the growing momentum of reform.

A second group of deputies was less sanguine. They saw significant, far-reaching corruption and half-hearted efforts to combat it. One Jiangsu deputy said that correcting unhealthy practices must begin at the center – after the top leads, he said, the bottom will follow. Several deputies from Beijing urged serious punishment of cadre children who were guilty of unhealthy practices, and remarked that the light fines dispensed would not resolve anything.[94] To prevent abuse of position and power, these deputies demanded measures more severe than tightened controls over credit and currency (which would soon be imposed): they advocated renewed attention to socialist culture and ideology. Beijing deputy Bai Shouyi reproached state propaganda organs (and Deng by implication) for urging people to pursue wealth, saying it caused ideological confusion. He added: "In recent years we have encountered some bad social conduct. I think the lack of attention paid to socialist ideology is partly responsible. I don't think Zhao's report expounded the lofty ideals nearly enough."[95]

Henan's Zhao Wenfu likewise stressed the importance of inculcating "high ideals and a high sense of discipline" – and not only for officials. Newly rich peasants also had obligations under socialism. One deputy from rural Hubei noted: "those people who have become affluent should help others become affluent. . . . When somebody becomes affluent, he must think of other people and not himself alone, much less should he benefit himself at the expense of others."[96] Profiteering and unfairness were powerful, impeccably socialist, charges to level against reform. And who could question the cures? The reformers were hard-pressed to disassociate themselves from examples of selfishness, corruption, and immorality that accompanied their initiatives. Whatever the benefits of reform, in the Chinese context, they were vulnerable.

Even Deng's showcases – the special economic zones and the countryside – were not immune from criticism. After several years of strong support for foreign-investment zones, the disclosure of extensive, illegal activities had caused second thoughts. Foreign-exchange laundering, fraudulent bank loans, excessive wage and bonus payments, smuggling, gambling, prostitution, and pornography had heightened fears of bourgeois liberalization and had revived memories of nineteenth-century foreign concessions.[97] NPC deputies joined in the patriotic swell: they questioned favorable accounts of foreign investment enclaves given by high-ranking officials, and said the largest one, Shenzhen, contrary to some claims, was "not a perfect example for the country's other regions," because of rampant corruption and widespread unhealthy practices.[98] Deputies decried currency blackmarkets and called for cutting back imports to save money and to protect domestic manufacturing.[99] Opposition to the open policy was coming out in public: according to some deputies, dealing with capitalists contaminated Chinese and brought the problems of the West to China.

Legislators even exposed the underside of the much-vaunted agricultural reform. Qin Hezhen, the Chairman of the Shandong Provincial People's Congress, noted that average peasant incomes, though increasing, were still low. He cited a representative county in Shandong in which 15% of the households only had enough for food and other necessities (150 yuan/year), while a miniscule 0.08% had an income of 10,000 yuan or more.[100] A survey by a young Hubei deputy found even greater poverty – about 35% of the households inspected.[101] And some areas were worse. Deputies from outlying provinces spoke of remote, often mountainous villages, where reform had yet to penetrate and the economy remained remarkably backward. A Yunnan deputy noted that some people in mountainous areas of Yunnan had an income as low as any in the world.[102] Deputies from Jilin, Hunan, Shaanxi, and Beijing reminded leaders that the decline in the 1984 grain harvest left many peasants with little grain on hand and that there had been no breakthrough in food production, but only "holding ground" and "uneven progress." One pointed out (in a refrain heard throughout the late 1980s) that ignoring grain production "is extremely dangerous, with consequences that can't be imagined."[103] This line of argument challenged the breadth of reform and its emphasis on cash crops. Deputies plaintively asked: Would reform ever touch poor, subsistence farmers and what did it offer them?

These deputies had no patience with leaders who "loved to hear good things and engage in exaggeration" and disputed the belief that agricultural reform was already a success.[104] Wen Mingrui, for one, reacted strongly against Zhao's "excessive" and "complacent" claim that "we can generally guarantee basic clothing and food for the people, leaving a little surplus," and Song Ping's promise "to guarantee an ample supply of goods in the off-season and to have more goods in the peak period." He said these remarks did not correspond with reality in poor areas and should not be made. Other deputies recalled the exaggeration common during the Great Leap Forward and recommended "sober-mindedness" and a realistic appraisal of peasant poverty.[105]

Deputies particularly warned that overenthusiasm and weakening central controls encouraged local cadres to make excessive monetary demands on peasants. They criticized cadres who demanded a contribution of up to one-third of a peasant's yearly income (50 yuan) for public construction projects.[106] In their speeches, NPC delegates stood up for peasants against government extraction and sought to protect the poorest of the poor from unreasonable local officials.

To improve life for China's rural poor, a few deputies advocated more reform; most emphasized expanding government welfare expenditures. Ma Qingnian, the Chairman of the Ningxia People's Congress, agreed that development must be based on reform and self-reliance, but stressed outside support for poor and isolated areas. Lin Xingwu praised plans to improve forestry and agriculture in underdeveloped counties, but still saw a need for outright aid to backward, mountainous regions. Even in prosperous areas, deputies suggested reform would not solve everything. Yang Jinshan, from rural Hebei, pointed out that disaster or insufficient labor created poor households in the wealthiest villages. He called for government support of those in straitened circumstances.[107]

It is probably incorrect to see the 1985 NPC as a return of the left, or a Maoist revival. Instead, we should speak of a backlash, perhaps inevitable, against smugness and policies that favored the well-off. Deputies urged realism and concern for the people who reform had passed by. They denounced commercialism, profiteering, and corruption and called for ideological vigilance to eliminate bourgeois contamination. They pressed for a socialist renewal, starting with attention to values that had been neglected in the rush to get rich. They argued that China must not lose sight of the strong points of prereform socialism – that reform (though still essential) was going too far too fast, or was too narrowly based.

The 1986 and 1987 sessions

In the two years following the 1985 NPC, China entered a period of consolidation, retrenchment, and compromise. Elite conflict centered on agenda setting and rival leaders were unable to implement their programs fully. After Vice Premier Chen Yun's chilling speech at a party conference in September 1985 spotlighted misgivings about the open-door policy, falling grain production, and increasing corruption and consumerism, the leadership set out to cool the overheated economy and to combat ideological laxity. They met with only mixed success. While an overly high growth rate was reduced, deficits reemerged and inflation approached double digits. Grain output remained below the record 1984 harvest, the balance of trade worsened, and foreign-exchange reserves fell. Accounts of corruption in the special economic zones and on Hainan Island continued to appear, and a widely trumpeted effort to reduce unhealthy tendencies brought warnings to cadres engaged in illegal money-making schemes but little action against the "big tigers" or their children. Finally, just as the reformers seemed to be gaining a second wind, nationwide student protests ended discussions of political structural reform, led to the ouster of General Secretary Hu Yaobang, and precipitated a new campaign against bourgeois liberalization.[108]

Throughout the system, the political costs of failure or miscalculation were increasing. Politics was becoming more fluid and politicians more vulnerable. In this environment, the NPC sessions held in the spring of 1986 and 1987 were occasions to build consensus rather than to exploit political advantage. Zhao Ziyang's government work reports reflected bargaining, compromise, and efforts to balance competing views: Zhao stressed economic development but also socialist ideology and culture; he tempered satisfaction with economic progress with concern over sectoral imbalances, inflation, and macroeconomic mismanagement; he called for increased grain production, but said it was "impossible to bring about radical changes in a short time"; he pledged to struggle against bourgeois liberalization, yet dwelt on the dangers of resurgent leftism and the need to restrict the campaign to party members and urban areas; he applauded improving living standards, but implored people not to "sacrifice their pioneering spirit to a love of luxury." Implicitly in 1986 and explicitly the following year, Zhao's reports sought a middle ground between overeager reformers (who were insufficiently "clear-headed") and overcautious conservatives (who were sufficiently "emancipated").[109]

Deputy small-group speeches contributed to Zhao's balancing act, with the sharpest comments inveighing against imbalances created by reform. As in 1985, agriculture (especially grain production) drew special attention. Deputies from rural constituencies stood up for grain farmers and criticized low prices, "grudging" investment, and shortages of inputs. They demanded inexpensive and reliable supplies of fertilizer, seeds, fuel, pesticides, plastics, and machinery and fresh measures to stabilize grain production.[110] Li Zhen, a deputy from Shandong, pointed out that his province lost cultivated land equivalent to a medium-sized county each year and natural disasters occurred because of inattention to water conservancy projects and irrigation facilities.[111] A number of deputies argued that Zhao's measures for solving agricultural problems were "not forceful enough" and they criticized reductions in agricultural investment from 11% of total capital investment in 1978 to 3 or 4% in 1987.[112] In response to these entreaties, passages were added to Zhao's reports promising greater outlays and sufficient acreage for grain production.[113]

Deputies were particularly concerned with life in the hinterlands. A Gansu representative noted the widening gap between Gansu and coastal areas and requested large capital allocations lest greater amounts be needed in the future.[114] Calls for aid to Ningxia, Gansu, and other inland provinces were common, especially for primary and secondary schools, which were said to be deteriorating because most new educational funds went to support and increase the enrollment of colleges and universities. What money was left for the countryside was earmarked for teacher salaries, leaving too little for construction and renovation of classroom space and few opportunities for rural students to gain access to higher education.[115] Zhao's revised report in 1986 addressed these concerns (in part) by offering additional funds, materials, and technical assistance for underdeveloped regions.[116]

Lastly, deputies stressed ideological and political work. They spoke of "the spirit of self-reliance and arduous struggle" and "one-sided" propaganda work that confused young people and undermined stability and unity. Concerned deputies deplored weak cultural leadership and declining study of Marx and Lenin and advocated increasing the quantity and quality of political education to deter student protests. Many legislators defended party leadership, socialism, and the use of Marxism to solve social problems.[117] Several Hong Kong deputies went against the tide and called for increasing freedoms for students and intellectuals, but their remarks were drowned in a sea of calls to maintain stability and unity. In response to deputies' comments, Zhao's revised 1986 report urged the nation's theoreticians and social workers to devote themselves to promoting socialist ethics; in 1987, nearly a quarter of Zhao's report focused on the antibourgeois liberalization drive and a statement was added criticizing consumerism and praising socialist China's "fine tradition of building the country through diligence, thrift, and hard work."[118]

In 1986 and 1987 Zhao's middle-of-the-road reports received middle-of-the road criticisms. Neither strongly conservative nor strongly reformist in tone or content, deputies refrained from disturbing a carefully constructed (and illusory) consensus. On balance, deputy speeches erred on the side of soberness and moderation. The sessions provided opportunities to examine the unexpected consequences of reform and to urge caution and concern for all sectors and regions. Small-group meetings elicited demands for protection from the market and western influences and gave semiretired central elites, regional leaders, and mass representatives an outlet to question the transformation of priorities underway under Deng.

Transparency and the 1988 NPC

The NPC session convened in the spring of 1988 was noteworthy for its openness and "transparency" (*toumingdu*). Unlike past sessions, barbed comments were not dulled by the NPC Press Bureau or circulated primarily in restricted journals; nor did an ad hoc censorship group select speeches for publication. Instead, stenographers recorded all deputy views, and Chinese, Hong Kong, Taiwanese, and western journalists were permitted to witness, record, and disseminate discussions – excluding those concerned with personnel decisions. Two hundred fifty foreign and 400 Chinese reporters covered the session and many attended a dozen or more small-group meetings. Party and state leaders held seven press conferences that were broadcast live on radio and television and rebroadcast nightly following the evening news.[119]

The media offered the Chinese people an intimate view of a changing legislature. "Slang, grievances, and even cynical remarks from ordinary people could be heard at the group discussion meetings."[120] Personal anecdotes and jokes abounded, and interruptions and rejoinders added an element of real debate. Provincial and local leaders eschewed formal language and deputies from grass-roots units spoke often and at length. Even young PLA soldiers overcame their usual reticence and commented without waiting for their superiors.[121] A number of deputies asked central leaders to observe small-group deliberations (with one remarking, "if ministers do not attend our panel discussions, how can they hear what we say?") and over thirty ministers and vice ministers heeded their advice.[122] Politburo Standing Committee Members also attended provincial discussions, made speeches, and listened to comments: Li Peng joined the Jilin delegation, Hu Qili the Tianjin delegation, Qiao Shi the Shanghai delegation, and Zhao Ziyang the Beijing delegation.

Premier Li Peng's government work report contained few surprises and little on new reforms. Instead, it paralleled Zhao Ziyang's remarks at the Thirteenth Party Congress and focused on economic development, inflation, price ceilings, and agriculture. Many deputy speeches also tread well-worn ground. A third consecutive below-target grain harvest produced a chorus of complaints over declining farmland, irrational prices, and increasing costs of agricultural inputs. One deputy archly asked why foreign currency had been spent on luxury automobiles for officials rather than chemical fertilizer and plastic film for farmers. Another noted that "farmers who produce the most grain sometimes lose the most money."[123] Deputies called for more investment in agriculture and contended that the planned 15% increase was "fine, but not enough," since a large proportion of investment funds were used for subsidies or diverted to rural industry.[124] Dozens of legislators found the report's comments on agriculture insufficiently thorough, concrete, or detailed, and many warned Premier Li that the nation had already received a "dangerous signal."[125] For the third consecutive year, the report was amended to allay concerns that the central government was neglecting agriculture.[126]

Zhao Ziyang's coastal development strategy also generated charges of favoritism and skewed national priorities. Legislators from inland provinces again questioned policies that intentionally gave seaboard provinces an edge in attracting foreign funds and technology and expanding foreign trade. They argued that market-oriented, export-led growth would leave the interior untouched. Song Ruixiang, the governor of Qinghai, said his province would fall further behind as coastal areas developed and recommended the State Council formulate a policy encouraging cooperation between eastern and western China that transferred funds, technology, and trained technicians inland. Others noted that the flow of talented people to the coastal areas had already begun. Tibetan deputies criticized "insensitive" national economic policies that ignored the problems of minority regions, and the chairman of the Tibetan people's government said it was unfair to expect backward areas to compete with economically developed areas. The vice chairman of Xinjiang's people's government summed up the views of many deputies when he asked: "If the coastal policies only look to exports, how are we in the western areas going to be able to modernize?"[127]

Lobbying for leadership attention and budget reallocation also occurred along occupational lines. In his government work report on March 25, Li Peng suggested that intellectuals "gear their professional work to economic development" and "offer their services to society." Five days later, at a small-group meeting of the Beijing delegation, General Secretary Zhao Ziyang argued that it was "necessary and possible" for researchers and professors to take second jobs to supplement their incomes. These remarks were not well received. Although the press and public opinion supported the policy, the majority of legislators did not.[128] A few deputies acknowledged that moonlighting (as a temporary expedient) would help balance school budgets and improve compensation, but most criticized its effect on teaching, research, and student training. University professors and administrators offered the strongest resistance. In Zhao's presence, deputies from educational circles openly questioned introducing market forces into education, and Mei Zuyan, a professor at Qinghua University, claimed some teachers already neglected their jobs because they were too involved in other work. The president of Nanjing Polytechnical Institute strenuously opposed spare-time employment on grounds that it diverted the attention and energy of scientists, endangered key research projects, and improved intellectuals' life in the short term at the expense of long-term national interests. Tianjin

University President Wu Yongshi and Nankai University President Wu Guo-
guang insisted that efforts by schools to earn money would impair teaching
by giving teachers less time to prepare their lectures.[129]

Several dozen Beijing college students expressed their views on part-time
employment by congregating outside the Great Hall of the People, posting
wall posters, and staging two demonstrations and a sit-in to protest party
treatment of intellectuals and misguided educational policies. One group
sarcastically offered to shine the shoes of NPC deputies.[130]

Deputies opposed second jobs for intellectuals, but not higher salaries. A
Beijing representative said the position of intellectuals at the bottom of the
income ladder was abnormal. Qian Jiaju, a long-time campaigner for raising
teacher's salaries and educational standards, disputed a remark by Zhao
Ziyang and maintained that the purchasing power of teachers' salaries had
declined to one-tenth of its level fifty years ago.[131] Ding Shisun, president
of Beijing University, blamed student discontent on corruption and low
salaries rather than ineffective ideological work. He noted that many students
looked at their teachers, saw thirty years of hard work, and pay of only 160
yuan/month (US$43), and renounced academia and went to work for a private
company. On students abroad, he added: "We should not criticize them for
not coming back. As things stand now, conditions are not very attractive for
them." He said that leaders who say young people are only concerned about
fame and prosperity should examine their consciences and "those who fail
to pay attention to education and the treatment of intellectuals will stand
condemned for a thousand ages" (*qiangu zuiren*).[132]

Although the majority of deputy speeches in 1988 supported leadership
policies, and there was virtually no controversy on issues such as creating a
new province, quelling Tibetan disturbances, and amending the constitution,
the most newsworthy remarks centered on the neglected: neglected sectors,
neglected regions, neglected social groups. High-ranking regional officials,
educational leaders, and ordinary deputies exploited expanded media coverage to publicize opposition to policies that exacerbated, rather than reduced, social and economic cleavages. For many deputies, policy debates
were becoming more textured: it was no longer a question of extending
reform throughout the country, but one of assessing and choosing between
the painful trade-offs that preferential policies presented.

Austerity and elite conflict at the 1989 NPC

Expectations were low when the NPC convened in March 1989. Since the
previous session, the economy had deteriorated and the leadership had

stopped discussing rapid transition to a market-oriented economic system. Inflation exceeded 30% in most cities, goods were in short supply, the crime rate was on the rise, and the public was growing angry with corruption and nepotism. Bank runs and panic buying had occurred in the summer of 1988 and falling real income was a reality for one-third of urban residents. Price and ownership reform had been indefinitely postponed and experiments in stock markets had been curtailed. In the weeks before the legislature met, leadership expectations were made very clear: deputies were to show patience and unity; the focus of the session would be on stability and damage control rather than on new reforms.[133]

To ensure harmony, controls over deputies and media coverage were tightened. Domestic journalists were instructed to display restraint and discretion and to limit their questions at press conferences. Reporters from China's most outspoken newspaper, *Shijie Jingji Daobao*, were banned from the Great Hall, though they were allowed to cover the session from their offices in Shanghai. Foreign journalists were again invited to observe the proceedings, and leaders answered their questions before live radio and television audiences, but diplomats and scholars had difficulties gaining access to small-group meetings and a portion of the meetings were declared off limits. High-level warnings discouraged informal, unapproved interviews with deputies, which had been quite common and informative in the past.[134]

Premier Li's sober government work report underscored the prevailing tone of caution and discipline. Instead of "deepening reform," he focused on austerity and belt tightening; his talk brimmed with references to recentralization and restoration of government control over the economy, and he highlighted the urgency of cooling the overheated economy and taming inflation. Li spoke of price increases "beyond the endurance of the masses" and declining public confidence in reform. In a thinly veiled rebuke of Zhao Ziyang, Li noted "shortcomings and mistakes in our guidance," a "tendency to be too impatient for quick results," and inattention to limits imposed by China's huge population and meager resources. Though cast as self-criticism and acceptance of collective responsibility, it was clear to the assembled that remarks such as "we often lacked a full understanding of the arduousness and complexity of reform" and "we failed to take firm action and effective measures to stabilize finance and control prices when inflation was already rather conspicuous" were directed at Zhao, who had been responsible for economic policy making until August 1988.[135]

By acknowledging elite conflict, Li disrupted the atmosphere of unity and stability he had sought to create. On one side, deputies echoed Li on Zhao's error of "overeagerness to get quick results" and linked it to inflation and excessive monetary expansion. They criticized the May 1988 price-reform decision because it was made without legislative consultation and they were dismayed that a request from deputies to stabilize the economy and prices had been replaced by a risky initiative originated by several officials. The mayor of Shenyang found this style of decision making unscientific and undemocratic, while a deputy from Zhejiang likened government policy changes under Zhao to "four tunes for four seasons."[136]

On the other side, however, reform-minded deputies parried attacks on Zhao with feints toward Li Peng. "Angry" deputies upbraided Li (by name) for his failure to explain policy mistakes and 270 legislators submitted a motion proposing delay of a US$10 billion hydroelectric project on the Yangtze. Li had championed the dam when he was vice premier responsible for energy and a State Council-sponsored commission of 500 experts had just concluded that technical problems could be overcome. Opponents in the NPC disagreed. Deputies suggested that the project's scale of investment, its evacuation of a million people, and its environmental effects would weaken the national economy and harm social order; they called for further geological and seismological studies and investigation of the sand and mud situation. Two days after the motion was submitted, Politburo Standing Committee member Yao Yilin announced (in Li Peng's presence) that the government had reconsidered its decision: both supporters and opponents of the project had strong arguments, further studies were needed, and the project would not be included in the upcoming five-year plan.[137]

Signs of a collapsing consensus also appeared in discussions on implementing austerity. Most deputies acknowledged that economizing was necessary, but felt the costs of higher taxes, declining enterprise funding, diminished loans, and foreign-trade autonomy should be borne elsewhere. Yao Yilin's appeal for "certain parts" (*mouxie jubu*) to accept "temporary sacrifices" and to relinquish "vested interests" was largely ignored.[138] Deputies from booming, coastal provinces defended special policies; deputies from lagging, inland provinces demanded exemptions from cutbacks. Wagging fingers and shouting, inland deputies said they had already suffered under a policy emphasizing development of coastal cities and "the austerity measures should not be applied to us who are already falling behind."[139] Li Gui said the economy in Inner Mongolia was far from heated up and did not require cooling down; he called for preferential policies to encourage self-reliance. Many inland deputies defined their interests explicitly in opposition to coastal areas. "Look at all these big buildings in Beijing," said one delegate from rural Yunnan. "Stop one of those hotels and you'd be able to help thousands of my people in the countryside." Or even more vividly:

"to the coastal areas the retrenchment is like taking a knife to the tail of an ox, but to us poor districts, it's like hitting him on the head with a brick."[140]

Deputies from coastal areas and their patrons did not accept challenges to their special status without comment. Zhao ally and Politburo Standing Committee member Tian Jiyun defended preferential treatment on grounds that uniformity would erode the benefits of ten years of openness. The governor of Guangdong stoutly supported policies that produced a provincial growth rate of 25%, denied that his province was "colonizing" inland neighbors, and asked that Guangdong be treated differently because it was "special." Beijing's mayor pointed out that Beijing needed help to build power stations and had to be protected because "China has only one capital." A deputy from prospering Fujian told a journalist that China should let its rich coastal areas develop and wait to help the impoverished interior.[141] Throughout the 1980s, defenders of aggrieved poor areas had used the NPC as a platform to express their views; by 1989, with the onset of austerity, defenders of (potentially) aggrieved rich areas were beginning to act similarly.

From 1978 to 1989, the NPC participated, on all sides, in the debate over how to manage and restructure China's economy. At a time of shifting alliances and swift reversals, deputies spoke for leaders, opinion groups, and the public at large. When the leadership demanded unity, they usually complied; when changes were brewing, they prepared the way by disclosing blunders and discussing alternatives. Deputies spoke out most boldly in favor of purging the left and, later, restraining the right. Their most newsworthy remarks appeared on the side of caution and against corruption and inequities. In this period, the NPC increasingly filled a role it never had in Mao's China: as a forum in which, couched in general approval of this year's line, regional leaders and mass representatives expressed minority opinions and sought to moderate policy changes.

Small-group discussions revealed an NPC neither predictably conservative nor predictably reformist. At times, deputies praised innovation; at times, they pointed out the virtues of continuity and stability. Not reliable opponents (or defenders) of market reforms, legislators instead stood for rationalizing and legalizing policy making and for guaranteeing policy implementation; they weighed in most often on the side of planned change and manageable risks, and against sloganeering and personalized, unaccountable rule.

But is talk really influence in China? A socialist legislature may preempt or defuse pressures, without having any influence over policy. Lively debates may only be a smokescreen that disguise continued domination of political decision making by a small elite. All the clamor may only indicate a belated realization that long-term legitimacy requires recognition of, though not necessarily responsiveness to, outside opinions.

Under Mao, deputies had few means to translate talk into action or policy-making influence – but this has shown signs of change. Structural reform of the legislature accompanied the de facto upgrading evident in small-group discussions. After 1979, reformers sought to expand and institutionalize channels of legislative influence and to strengthen ties between deputies and constituents.

7
Structural reforms

When the NPC reemerged in 1978, China was at a crossroads. The Third Plenum was nine months away and Deng Xiaoping had yet to consolidate his power. The first post-Mao constitution accurately reflected the unsettled political situation: it both praised the Cultural Revolution and promised a return to predictable, nondisruptive patterns of rule; it granted the NPC more powers than it had in 1975, but fewer than it had from 1954 to 1966.[1] Two years after Mao's death, the NPC resembled the mobilization congresses of the late 1950s. The organizational obstacles to legislative development – indirect elections; brief, infrequent sessions; large size; weak committees – remained in place.

As 1978 progressed, Deng's power increased. By the end of the year, he was able to control the agenda of the party's Third Plenum and to initiate a decisive break with the policies of the Cultural Revolution. Although Deng was in ascendance, his power was far from absolute. Hua Guofeng reigned as Mao's handpicked successor and beneficiaries of the Cultural Revolution held key positions throughout the nation. Often outmanned in leadership councils, Deng turned to allies on the fringe of power (typically academics and advisers in theory, planning, and propaganda) to publicize and build support for his policies.[2] Through the press, he put pressure on his political opponents and aligned himself with the forces of reform. From 1979 to 1982, a loose coalition of reformist intellectuals drew support from Deng and published scores of articles elaborating his ideas. These policy analysts and academics accepted Deng's diagnosis of China's systemic problems and pre-scribed radical cures; they generated hundreds of policy proposals and chal-lenged Deng to follow through with the reforms he had begun.[3]

As regards the NPC, Liao Gailong, a research fellow in the Policy Research Office of the Central Committee Secretariat, and Feng Wenbin, the Vice President of the Central Party School, took the lead in urging reform. In a speech to the party school in October 1980, Liao interpreted and expanded ideas first raised by Deng two months before at an enlarged Politburo meeting. Of particular interest, Liao transformed a recommendation to upgrade the legislature into a penetrating critique of the NPC's past ineffectiveness. Soon after Liao's speech, Feng Wenbin gave legislative reform a prominent place in a two-part *People's Daily* article on socialist democracy.[4] Other legal scholars, often writing in *Guangming Ribao,* chimed in with specific proposals to strengthen the NPC.[5] Deputies at the 1980 People's Congress reviewed the history of the NPC and submitted "detailed proposals for correcting current organizational shortcomings."[6] The autumn of 1980 saw a debate launched that would continue for two years, finally culminating in a new constitution and a new NPC organic law.

Why did interest in legislative reform grow after years of neglect? Amid many possible reasons, four motives stand out. First, and most important, reformers aimed to enhance regime acceptance by devising a validating formula that combined institutionalized legitimacy with legitimacy based on performance and ideology. Reformers sought to redraw the party's compact with society and to reduce reliance on charismatic leaders and campaign-style politics. They hoped to absorb antisystemic demands, to direct political energies toward approved channels, and to reinvigorate institutional symbols of mass–elite linkage. Relegitimation was particularly pressing in the face of continuing ideological flux and the deep crisis of faith that emerged following Mao's death.

Second, the reformers sought to create political conditions conducive to economic development. They felt that an active, lively legislature would heighten enthusiasm and encourage cooperation of groups needed for modernization. Institutionalized political participation would inspire production and complement increased reliance on material incentives. Institutional recognition of social diversity would boost legitimacy and help party leaders implement their economic program.[7] Rebuilding the legislature would expand the united front; it would help win over intellectuals, technicians, merchants, former industrialists, and others who were crucial to the nation's future, but who were slow to accept socialism because of their essentially bourgeois nature.

Third, commentators linked legislative reform to heightened government efficiency and improved information gathering. In Deng's China, the party would not monopolize state organs, but would attend to its own tasks. Pathologies resulting from overconcentration of power would disappear and a rational division of labor would free leadership cadres from the need to be experts at everything. Ideas would percolate from below, state organs would be responsible and accountable to each other, and a stronger legislature would help realize party policy. Clarified jurisdiction would enhance government capabilities and strengthen party leadership.[8] An able NPC would rationalize and popularize authority and regularize one-party rule.

Lastly, and most speculative, a strengthened legislature would guarantee reform and contribute to political stability. Reformers would secure their position by building institutions whose functions and members promoted reform. Fully aware of the importance of personal power in China and the protracted nature of institutionalization, reformers sought to create a counterweight to inner-party coups. A national assembly that lived up to its name would check defiant leftists and mobilize public pressure behind reform. In Gao Gongyou's words: "During the Cultural Revolution the people had no way to dismiss the Gang of Four from the political stage; only with systemic guarantees and strengthening of the NPC system can we prevent restoration of counterrevolutionary schemers and careerists."[9]

This was the vision guiding legislative reform – ambitious and controversial in itself, revolutionary if fully implemented. The NPC had served regime legitimacy and the united front in the mid-1950s and was beginning to do so again by the late 1970s; using a legislature to rationalize authority and gather information had been a goal of imperial reformers and had reached the agenda of the Eighth Party Congress in 1956, but had never been fully implemented; legislative influence over leaders and policies had been suggested during the Hundred Flowers Movement, but had been quickly dismissed. How far would Deng go in repudiating the past? Would he countenance removing the structural obstacles that sapped legislative vitality and limited the NPC's contribution to legitimacy, development, efficiency, and stability? Systemic reform entailed more than speeches and articles; it required organizational confirmation – in the case of the NPC, changes in deputy selection procedures, membership size, session conduct, and committee structure.

Electoral reform and deputy quality

A new electoral law, passed in 1979, took an important step toward contested, popular election of state leaders. It introduced direct elections for county people's congresses and provided that voters at all levels were to have a choice among candidates. For county and commune congresses, the law stipulated one and one-half to two times as many candidates as positions; for provincial congresses and the NPC, it required 20 to 50% more candidates.[10] The law stopped short of fully enfranchising China's citizens, however, county and provincial deputies, in a series of stepwise elections, were to continue choosing members of higher congresses. Universal, popular elections awaited "the passage of considerable time and work."[11]

In 1980, the timetable suddenly changed and electoral reform became a matter of some urgency. Liao Gailong's speech did not mention NPC selection procedures, but Feng Wenbin did. Feng derided those who thought direct county elections signified a great stride toward democracy. He wrote: "Our electoral system still leaves much to be desired. . . . Measures should be taken step by step to elect people's deputies at all levels by direct popular vote."[12] Reform-minded academics immediately adopted Feng's argument and explored its implications. Wu Jialin suggested drawing up election zones and conducting nationwide NPC elections as soon as possible.[13] Wu and Feng both linked direct election of NPC deputies to improved accountability and challenged the back-room politics inherent in indirect elections.

Other reformers were more guarded; they conceded the unlikelihood of organizational change and emphasized opportunities within the existing structure. The 1979 electoral law granted NPC electors a choice – moderate reformers implored them to use it. Shen Baoxiang advised deputies in local congresses to review candidate lists for higher-level congresses carefully, including deputies recommended from above, and to turn down candidates who did not comply with the job specification or who did not conform with the people's interests.[14] Cao Siyuan urged that votes against party members should not be feared or criticized and suggested that even if party candidates were occasionally defeated by nonparty individuals, there was "no reason for panic."[15] A confident leadership, moderate reformers argued, should allow provincial electors to weed out unpopular or unqualified NPC candidates. Choice, within limits, need not produce chaos.

Several reformers recognized that meaningful indirect elections required informed voters as well as conscientious (and brave) ones. Cao Siyuan suggested periodic publication of NPC document collections "to give the electorate a clear understanding of the legislative activities and proposals of each deputy."[16] Wu Jialin, more boldly, argued that campaigning went hand in hand with contested elections and was the key to supervising deputies and ensuring their sense of responsibility. Campaigning, he said, was especially important in indirect elections and for deputies allotted by the center, who did not participate in election congresses and often were not known to voters. He believed that candidates should openly express their views to electors, clearly indicate why they want to be a deputy, and explain what they would do after they were elected. Campaigns would enable provincial electors to see if NPC deputies were keeping their promises and help electors make a decision at the next election.[17] In Wu's view, if direct elections could not be used to supervise NPC deputies, perhaps provincial delegates could.

The revised 1982 electoral law failed to include many of the proposed reforms. Direct, contested NPC elections were again consigned to the future on grounds they were inefficient, embarrassing for losers, and "would cause considerable difficulties and chaos."[18] Unpleasant surprises in the 1980–1 county elections, including the appearance of non-Marxist candidates, precipitated restrictions on campaigning. The revised electoral law prescribed that candidates be introduced by others at nominating meetings rather than be "publicized" through "various methods."[19] Commentators defended party manipulation of NPC candidate lists and enjoined electoral units to accept party supplements and quotas. In both the 1983 and 1988 NPC elections, more than a few candidates were "determined undemocratically" and "were unknown to the people."[20]

Although the 1980–1 proposals were rejected, it appears that the 1979 reforms were implemented. According to NPC Credentials Committee Reports, in all recent elections, the number of candidates was greater than the deputies to be selected. Provincial tallies in both 1983 and 1988 indicated that deputies discussed nomination lists at some length and party nominees, including the president of the Guangdong provincial people's court, were defeated.[21]

Prevailing practices and norms continued, however, to favor party-sponsored nominees. Candidates proposed by the party and mass organizations were discussed before an election and a vast majority were elected, whereas nominees proposed by groups of deputies were introduced on the spot, discussed in isolated small-group meetings, and few were elected. The process of compiling the party-approved list remained extremely secret: it was hidden from the public, deputies, and even individuals engaged in election work. In some elections, approved candidates were listed first on the ballot and efforts were made to intimidate or bribe others to renounce their nomination.[22] In one notorious case, the election of nearly one-third of Ningxia's NPC deputies was nullified after irregularities in the provincial election.[23]

As for NPCSC elections, Party General Secretary Hu Yaobang convened a "democratic consultation meeting" before the 1983 Congress and accepted several changes in the candidate list for NPCSC members and vice chairmen.[24] In 1988, the first contested NPCSC elections were held. Votes were cast against every candidate for NPCSC vice chairman (see Table 7.1) and nine of 144 candidates for the full NPCSC were defeated. Defeated candidates, whose names were not officially released, were said to be primarily

Table 7.1. *Number of votes NPCSC chairman and vice chairmen received, 1988*

Name	For	Against	Abstained
Wan Li	2,808	64	11
Chen Muhua	2,525	313	45
Wei Guoqing	2,653	206	24
Yan Jici	2,638	200	45
Zhou Gucheng	2,323	164	96
Ni Zhifu	2,740	119	24
Chu Xuefan	2,773	95	15
Lei Jieqiong	2,764	93	26
Ye Fei	2,786	88	9
Ulanhu	2,788	79	16
Xi Zhongxun	2,829	46	8
Wang Hanbin	2,831	44	8
Fei Xiaotong	2,836	40	7
Panchen Lama	2,846	31	6
Sun Qimeng	2,848	26	9
Seypidin Aze	2,852	24	7
Liao Hansheng	2,858	22	3
Ngapoi Ngawang Jigme	2,856	19	8
Rong Yiren	2,865	15	3
Peng Chong	2,866	14	3

Sources: Yau Shing-mu, "Paper on Voting for President, Vice Chairmen," *FBIS* 70 (April 12, 1988): 26–7, from *Hong Kong Standard*, April 9, 1988, pp. 1, 6. Antonio Kamiya, "KYODO Reviews Dissenting Votes in Elections," *FBIS* 69 (April 11, 1988): 21–2, from Tokyo KYODO, April 9, 1988.

older, middle-ranking party members and military officers with mediocre records.[25]

NPC electoral reform, all in all, was quite modest. Changes made in 1979 were maintained, but not extended. Early support for universal, direct elections or invigorated, indirect elections proved thin and then quickly dissipated. The potential gains from a more open process were outweighed by the gains in certainty under prevailing, murky procedures; despite frequent proposals to increase accountability and reform nomination procedures, talk of combining contested elections with open campaigning remained both an "old forbidden zone" and a "new forbidden zone." Soviet or East European-like electoral reforms, for China, were both "sensitive" and "complicated" and political figures from Foreign Minister Qian Qichen and Premier Li Peng to reformers in the Chinese Academy of Social Sciences continued to stress China's differences with the Soviet Union and the impossibility of "mechanically copying another country's reforms."[26] In recent years, only dissidents, like Yan Jiaqi, dared call for a complete overhaul of electoral procedures.[27]

After 1981, the debate turned from how deputies were selected to who was selected. Procedural reform took a back seat to improving deputy quality as a means to enhance NPC capabilities.

Attention came to rest on the number of "honorary deputies." Reformers disdained united-front appointments and emphasized the need for deputies with "political and organizational abilities."[28] They criticized excessive concern with broad representation and noted that scholars, scientists, and model workers may excel at what they do, but often were not good politicians. They reminded the leadership that united-front organs honored exemplary individuals and the NPC was an "organ of strategic decisions," whose members should have political experience, know-how, and resourcefulness.[29] With the right people, however chosen, the legislature could fulfill its constitutional duties and serve as a counterweight to other institutions. Reformers saw the contradiction between a united-front organ and an organ of state power, and they opted for power.

They started by criticizing the escalating age of NPC leaders. Liao Gailong noted that the members of the Fifth NPCSC (1978–83) were 70 or 80 years old and many had difficulty walking, needed attendants, and were unable to attend meetings.[30] Other commentators were unsparing in their criticism of doddering legislators, some of whom they claimed were senile.[31] The solution reformers offered was simple: remove the dead wood. Zhang Shixin argued that the NPCSC should not be an "old folks home" and that its members should be young and spirited, capable of full participation in state affairs.[32] Liao Gailong and Cao Siyuan said future NPCSC members should be in their prime and able to work eight hours each day: "any who because of deteriorating health cannot attend NPCSC meetings for 60 or more days each year, should resign."[33]

Reformers were aware that reducing the number of "honorary deputies" and "old comrades" on the NPCSC was politically sensitive, yet they felt it was essential. Zhang Shixin argued:

Those old cadres who have much merit, are healthy and capable of carrying out work ought to have considerable representation on the NPCSC. Those old comrades who are not capable of performing their duties ought to retire, but they can always make suggestions to the party or state leadership organs and when necessary could be invited to attend the relevant conferences and discuss major national plans.[34]

Cao Siyuan, mindful of likely opposition, sugar-coated the pill even more:

Not to have those highly respected and venerated deputies who are of failing health participate in routine work is a most appropriate show of consideration and a most reasonable arrangement. It must be clear that a deputy's political status remains the same whether he is a member of the Standing Committee or not.[35]

Honor, access to central documents, and the right to give speeches had always been important perquisites for NPCSC members. Transition from a united-front organ to a working legislature would disappoint recently rehabilitated allies of Deng Xiaoping, who felt they deserved recognition and a soft job in the capital. But old friends and retired cadres could be placated without enfeebling the standing committee of an important organ of state power.

Elections in the 1980s altered the composition of the NPC substantially, if not entirely in the fashion reformers envisioned. Beginning in 1983, representation became more closely proportionate to population, as the number of deputies from Beijing, Tianjin, and Shanghai was cut by nearly two-thirds. The armed forces' representation was halved and party representation declined 10% to 62.5%.[36] The educational background of deputies improved dramatically, with 44.5% said to be of university level and 41.5% engaged in professional or technical work.[37] Of the deputies, 76.5% were freshmen and their average age at election was 53.[38] By 1988, 76% of deputies were under 60 years old and their average age was "less than 53," party representation increased slightly to 66.8%, and army representation remained unchanged. Newcomers made up 71% of the deputies, 23.4% were said to be intellectuals, and 56% were educated in colleges or universities.[39]

Selecting younger deputies, boosting the number of intellectuals, and reducing the number of special deputies suggested an earnest effort to enhance deputy quality. But this did not mean traditional selection considerations were discarded. Peng Chong's 1983 report and Liao Hansheng's 1988 report on deputy credentials emphasized the number of trailblazers in modernization and reform and detailed the usual mix of labor models, young shock workers, star athletes, heroic soldiers, playwrights, poets, opera singers, inventors, chefs, sportscasters, and so on.[40] In some respects, the NPCs of the 1980s had many new faces but much the old complexion. The young and middle-aged, including the intellectuals, were not noteworthy for their political skills, legal knowledge, or experience. Many labored at two or more jobs and those with specialized skills, such as scientists and researchers, often were "unwilling to contribute" or were "not interested in deputy work."[41] They may have "embodied the spirit of reform and strengthened NPC vitality,"[42] but they lacked the wherewithal to transform the legislature into an effective political actor. This depended on the legislature's leading core – its Standing Committee.

Personnel changes on the 1983 NPCSC were pronounced and potentially significant. Two-thirds of its members were new, and the representation of non-Communists and intellectuals increased considerably. Eleven of twenty NPCSC vice chairmen were newcomers, only ten of twenty were Communists, and the number of democratic party members doubled to eight.[43]

The age problem was not addressed, however. In a speech at the democratic consultation meeting preceding the 1983 NPC, Hu Yaobang emphasized the need to groom a new generation of leaders, the "third echelon," but excluded the NPC and its Standing Committee, publicly asking esteemed "old friends" to stay in their leading posts.[44] The 1983 NPCSC consequently averaged 69.3 years old and the twenty vice chairmen approached 74. NPCSC Chairman Peng Zhen was healthy and capable, but 81 years old at the time of his election.

Observers were disappointed with the 1983 Standing Committee. A Taiwanese source judged its members to be "elderly party, government, or army cadres who have been eliminated by competition and are retiring to the second line." Usually sympathetic Hong Kong sources saw an effort to remove obstacles to reform and to pacify old, first-line cadres with status and position. A Chinese commentator noted a large number of cadres in their last post before retirement and suggested this was incompatible with the NPC's status as the supreme organ of state power.[45]

These assessments were correct but incomplete. The 1983 NPCSC had potential and went some distance in developing it. Three of its leaders (Peng Zhen, Chen Pixian, and Xi Zhongxun) were also Politburo members who used the legislature and its committees as a base to augment their power. (Peng Zhen, in particular, brought prestige and powerful connections to the legislature.) As NPCSC chairman, Peng more than once used the Standing Committee to oppose Deng Xiaoping on the pace and scope of reform – most notably from 1986 to 1988 when the NPCSC repeatedly remanded drafts of the bankruptcy law, the state-owned enterprise law, and the villagers' committee law.

On the bankruptcy law, opposition to hardening budget constraints and making factories responsible for their losses arose at three consecutive NPCSC sessions and centered on the unfairness of punishing enterprises whose directors had little control over costs and profits and whose workers were administratively selected and had no welfare system to depend on if fired. NPCSC members pointed out that "the way it is now, an enterprise could fail for many reasons having nothing to do with bad management, such as government price controls and tax policies," and they advocated prior formulation of six complementary laws – an industrial enterprise law, a joint-venture enterprise law, a state-owned enterprise law, a collectively owned enterprise law, a labor service law, and a social insurance law.[46]

From June to November 1986, successive drafts of the bankruptcy law were prepared, clauses on the placement of staff members of bankrupt enterprises were clarified, and separate regulations were passed by the State Council governing the authority of plant managers, labor contracting, hiring and firing workers, and unemployment insurance.[47] Throughout the summer and fall of 1986, a media campaign promoting the bankruptcy law was launched and articles in *People's Daily* and other outlets made it clear that timely passage was expected. Just before the start of the August NPCSC session, the NPC Law Committee held four meetings to discuss comments of NPCSC members and central and local government officials, and a number of compromise amendments were proposed. In the late fall, the NPCSC conducted further investigations in several cities and concerned officials were invited to an eight-day symposium in Beijing. Finally, in December 1986, two years after drafting began and two months after nationally televised and highly contentious NPCSC debates in which ten of fourteen NPCSC members spoke against the law, the NPCSC passed a trial bankruptcy law. But even then, the Committee postponed implementing the law until the state-owned enterprise law went into effect – something that did not occur until late 1988.

On the state-owned enterprise law, NPCSC deliberations focused on the autonomy granted managers vis-à-vis party secretaries and concerns that the law would weaken party control over the economy. In five deliberations from January 1985 to March 1988, NPCSC members acknowledged the need for enterprise reform and for expanding the responsibilities of factory directors, but many members were troubled by the implications of reform for the party committee in each factory, a body whose functions would be narrowed and whose role might become "unclear." Legislators also felt the law might have an adverse effect on ideological and political work and on the "socialist orientation of enterprises."[48]

In an unusual step, in March 1987, after a series of provincial investigations, the NPCSC debated two "completely different" (*jieran butongde*) draft proposals on the factory director's role – one favored by party and trade-union cadres, which gave the factory director responsibility for production and management of the factory, and the second favored by most factory directors, which gave directors "the central position" in all activities in the enterprise. After intense debate, the bill was tabled pending further revisions. Finally, in January 1988, an acceptable compromise was reached that specified grass-roots party organizations in enterprises would supervise the implementation of party policies and support factory directors in exercising their powers, while factory directors would be granted overall responsibility and the central position in enterprise management.[49] After a month of national discussions on the law, a final draft was adopted by the full NPC in April 1988.

On the organic law of villagers' committees, some NPCSC members judged the responsibilities of the village committees to be "too heavy" and sought to reduce the committees' autonomy and include them within the state hierarchy under the jurisdiction of town and township governments.[50] After NPCSC consensus proved elusive, a draft law was submitted to the 1987 NPC for further deliberation. NPC deputies expressed doubts over the relationship of the committees, a form of mass organization, to grass-roots party organizations and township governments, and critics pointed out that in some places they were already illegally performing tasks for which they lacked authorization. Many deputies feared that self-governing villager committees would ignore state interests or defy township instructions and noted that this might make it difficult to carry out rural conscription, family planning, public security work, and grain procurement.[51] In light of continuing "sharply differing opinions," the Presidium of the 1987 NPC decided it was "improper to force the draft law through the legislative procedure," and proposed instead that deputies approve the law in principle and authorize the NPCSC to make further revisions, before promulgating it on a trial basis.[52] This motion was accepted and eight months later, in November 1987, after further "heated debate" and over the opposition of NPCSC members who felt the law was premature given the prevailing educational and scientific level of peasants,[53] the trial villagers' committee law was passed.

For each of these three laws the NPCSC, with Peng Zhen at its head, stood in the way of key planks in the reform program designed to redefine the party's role in society, to devolve decision-making authority, and to empower nonparty institutions and individuals. Even official Chinese sources, usually unwilling to acknowledge elite conflict, admitted that NPCSC activities led some people to "believe that... the NPC Standing Committee (was) abusing its power of legislation and obstructing the economic structural reform."[54]

Contrary to the reformers' expectations that a revitalized NPC would be a political club to wield against opponents, NPCSC sessions provided opportunities to question the unforeseen consequences of reform and to urge greater caution before surging ahead. Legislative discussions brought into the open demands to protect administrators, factory managers, workers, peasants, and consumers from the market and from the uncertainties of political change.

It appears that the old tigers retired to the NPC still had some teeth, especially an active NPCSC chairman and those given chairmanships of committees. They might have been second-line leaders, past the peak of careers essentially made outside the legislature, but they retained considerable power and had a stake in building up nonparty political institutions. (Wan Li, the chairman of the NPCSC elected in 1988 and a former Zhao associate, bears watching in this regard.) Although overall leadership control was secure, a standing committee comprised of prominent pensioned-off opponents, former allies of Zhao Ziyang, seasoned democratic party members, aging intellectuals, and minority representatives has proved to be a far more interesting place than first imagined.

It may be remembered that the (unmet) hopes for revocation of martial law and restoration of Zhao Ziyang in May 1989 rested with NPCSC petitioners and Wan Li, who aborted a trip to the United States and was said to be returning to China to convene a special session of the legislature. Moreover, even after the military crackdown derailed an emergency meeting, the NPCSC gave beleaguered journalist and Standing Committee member Hu Jiwei an opportunity to defend himself and to assert his "sacred duty and right" to gather signatures to call the NPCSC into session. Though most of his NPCSC colleagues abandoned Hu and denied participation in the incident by July 1989, and some of Hu's supporters were excluded from subsequent NPCSC meetings, it appears likely that as many as thirty-eight legislators had signed Hu's motion in May.

Within limits, plain speaking by Standing Committee members may continue to be heard. Although Hu Jiwei and several colleagues were expelled from the NPCSC in early 1990, other outspoken Standing Committee members and Wan Li survived the initial, post-Tiananmen shakeups. Among ordinary deputies, exiled dissident Yan Jiaqi was removed, but massive purges did not occur, as they did during the Anti-Rightist Movement and the Cultural Revolution. In the wake of reforms in the Soviet Union and the unraveling of Eastern Europe, law was seen by many to be an alternative to arbitrary rule and bloodshed. Chinese lawmakers may once again endeavor to revise laws, reject drafts, and confront smug and distant leaders – if it does not bring about disgrace, removal, or imprisonment.

Moreover, the leadership has recognized that most legislators continue to suffer from excessive age or inadequate experience. NPC deputies themselves have commented on the dearth of "third-echelon" individuals in the NPCSC and have called for adjustments and supplements to include them.[55] At this time, it is impossible to say whether these recommendations will be heeded, or whether the traditional united-front, old-age-home atmosphere will be maintained indefinitely. For the time being, indirect elections appear secure and symbolic recognition of important individuals and social groups has taken precedence over devolution of power. But this may change. The current arrangements are transitional; a revised election law and a new people's deputies' law are on the legislative calendar.[56] After the old revolutionaries die, new means may be discovered to retire leaders gracefully without enfeebling the NPCSC. Future NPCs may be stocked with young up-and-comers selected by the party or with nonparty influentials elected through more open election procedures. Improving the quality of legislators will require organizational reform, however. China's future leaders will not be asked to assume leading posts in the legislature (some of which require full-time attention), unless the NPC is granted additional powers. Serving as an NPCSC vice chairman or chairman must be a step up rather than a retreat from real politics.

NPC size and bicameralism

Decreasing the size of the NPC was a linchpin in the legislative reform program. Reformers considered it an essential first step in transforming the NPC into a working body that combined discussion and action. The legislature's size had always inhibited deputy interaction and had encouraged a casual attitude toward session preparation. With fewer deputies, the NPC could meet longer and more frequently, and deputies would play a larger role in law making, supervision, and representation.

Support for a smaller NPC originated high in the leadership. In September 1980, *People's Daily* reported that a deputy at the NPC had argued for a smaller legislature – one of 600 members or fewer. A month later, Liao Gailong broached the subject in his speech to the Central Party School. He indicated that "a reduction in the number of deputies was under consideration, perhaps to 1,000."[57] Press reports quickly corroborated Liao's words, and a parade of commentators called for "some reduction" or accepted Liao's number of 1,000.[58] Just one month before the draft constitution was published in April 1982, Dong Chengmei observed that only the English (including the House of Lords) and Soviet parliaments had more than 1,000 legislators, and suggested a "small number of keen and capable deputies" for China – about 1,500, with further "gradual reduction" to come.[59]

For several of these authors, size reduction was only a beginning. Liao Gailong wrote that "1,000 is still quite a big number" and Xu Chongde concluded that 1,000 deputies "crowded together in one hall will hardly be able to solve problems." Liao, Xu, and others thus offered a more radical proposal: divide the NPC into two chambers.[60] Novel though it was, reformers presented bicameralism as a compromise:

Reducing the number further to a few hundred, we are afraid cannot be done. What can be done? We may only have to struggle to reduce the delegates to 1,000 and some, and then have them meet in two separate chambers. This is a feasible proposal and would satisfy both sides.[61]

Political realities demanded careful packaging. A bicameral legislature would satisfy those who demanded a large number of deputies (for demographic representation), yet it would also increase the legislature's capacity for work.

Most supporters of bicameralism agreed that the lower house would be elected on the basis of population and would "represent the common interests and will of the whole people."[62] But they differed on the composition and powers of the upper chamber. Song Richang resurrected the Hundred Flowers-era proposal to turn the People's Political Consultative Conference into an upper house.[63] Others suggested a Chamber of Nationalities Affairs (as in the pre-Gorbachev Soviet Union) or a Chamber of Senior Statesmen.[64] Xu Chongde and Liao Gailong opted for functional representation in a Chamber of Social Professions and Occupations. Liao suggested a 300-member Regional Chamber and a 700-member Social Chamber that shared powers of initiative and legislation and jointly supervised government work. Xu was uncertain whether the two houses should have equal powers or whether one should be dominant and have tasks formally divided. Xu called for further research on election procedures, committee organization, oversight responsibilities, and procedures for resolving conflicts.[65] Numerous plans circulated, but all shared a common vision: increased legislative influence through heightened efficiency and clearer norms of representation in a smaller, divided national assembly.

Proposals to reduce the size of the NPC and to introduce bicameralism challenged long-standing Chinese legislative practices. Some reformers cast away conciliatory language and drew contrasts sharply. Liu Chuanchen, for example, criticized the NPC enlargement in 1964 on grounds that it filled the legislature with deputies who lacked "political abilities" and led to empty talk and inadequate legislative supervision. Liu mocked "paying attention to targets" and stopped just short of calling demographic doubling, as the main basis for representation, a fraud.[66] Xu Chongde, more subtly questioned "mechanical" views of representation that equated more deputies with more democracy.[67] What he neglected to say was that this mechanical way of thinking had been the de facto official line since 1964, if not earlier.

Unsurprisingly, bicameralism met opposition on theoretical, historical, and practical grounds. The vice president of the East China Political Legal Institute, Pan Nianzhi, noted that capitalist bicameral legislatures arose as a concession to the landed nobility in nations where revolutions were incomplete and in federal, multistate systems. He explained that neither of these conditions applied in China, where the revolution was complete and state power unified.[68] Dong Chengmei pointed to two thousand years of Chinese history as a unitary, multinational state and declared it inappropriate to use two chambers to resolve the problem of too many deputies or to improve representation.[69]

Opponents also found fault with the proposed structure of the second chamber. To upgrade the People's Political Consultative Conference, it was said, would destroy the integrity of the state system by changing a united-front organ into an organ of state power.[70] Some commentators also argued that China did not need a second chamber to represent ethnic minorities: the NPC and NPCSC had minority deputies and the Nationalities Committee looked after their interests. A separate Nationalities Chamber might fan divisiveness.[71] According to these authors, a broad united front did not require an upper chamber, new representational norms, or steps toward federalism. Ethnic and social tensions could be resolved within a unicameral legislature.

Some defenders of the status quo argued that dividing the NPC would further weaken it. In 1980, Liao Gailong had suggested that two legislative chambers would "check and constrain each other. . . . If one makes a wrong decision, the other may still correct it."[72] In all likelihood, Liao simply sought to reassure skeptics that reform would not strengthen the NPC unduly against the party. Instead, he heightened fears that bicameralism would enervate the legislature. Pan Nianzhi, for example, argued: "Up to now the NPC has not completely exercised its authority to its limits, its powers are not too great and there is no need to institute a restrictive balance."[73] In this view, bicameralism was only sham strengthening, or a sincere attempt that would backfire.

Pan's concern, though probably genuine, appears misguided. A second house, however organized, would add access points for non-elites and would institutionally acknowledge diversity. It would legitimize partial interests and free deputies from single-minded attention to "objective, national interests." It might foster bargaining and compromise, careful review and the

elusive, constructive, yet democratic, atmosphere Chinese leaders have always sought. And even if insistence on broad representation resulted in an
upper chamber largely composed of powerless representative individuals,
bicameralism offered a chance to segregate symbolic tasks and real work. It
is conceivable that a large Social House could handle sociological representation and political mobilization, thus freeing the 300-member Regional
House to take on day-to-day political tasks.

But downsizing the legislature failed to win sufficient support. The 1982
constitution retained a large, unicameral assembly. The 1982 electoral law
(art. 13) limited the NPC to 3,500 deputies and a 1986 revision reduced this
number to 3,000. But nothing was said of large decreases or bicameralism.
Constitutional scholars mysteriously spoke of "altered plans," "conventions
that are not easy to change," and "difficulties in implementation,"[74] and
NPCSC Chairman Peng Zhen rehashed arguments that justified a sizable
NPC because China was a large and populous country, with more than 2,000
counties and 55 nationalities.[75] Reforms that appeared virtually certain in
early 1981 were dismissed in a sentence or two in late 1982. Although some
NPC deputies and legal researchers continued to advocate size reduction
throughout the 1980s, the issue lost its prominence and its high-level support.[76] Views highlighting the importance of broad representation and implying that "[deputy] quantity can be used to accumulate [deputy] quality"
reappeared.[77] In both 1983 and 1988, 2,978 deputies were elected to the
NPC.

After three years, the debate had circled back to its starting point. The
size of the legislature was not negotiable. Though this was a defeat for
reformers, it also redirected them toward more promising avenues. Unable
to reduce the size of the NPC, they redoubled their efforts to make sessions
more meaningful and to strengthen legislative committees.

Upgrading plenary sessions

The Great Hall of the People has been the seat of the Chinese government
and the home of the NPC since 1959. In the 1980s, plenary sittings, small-
group discussions, Standing Committee meetings, and press conferences all
convened in the Great Hall. On days when the full congress was in session,
Tiananmen Square became a corridor for incoming traffic and its western
edge a parking lot for buses and cars (mostly Mercedes, Toyotas, and Nissans)
of deputies, national leaders, reporters, and foreign guests. Deputies typically arrived early and passed time in an outer ballroom, where they drank

tea, renewed friendships, and bought commemorative stamps and postcards. Security was tight and every attendee wore a badge. As the opening gavel approached, most of the chatting stopped, deputies were given copies of the day's speeches and they filed into the main auditorium. In the auditorium, they sat by province in long rows that reached the length of the room, with special sections reserved for army representatives and state ministers. Behind a speaker's podium at the front of the stage, there were rows of NPCSC vice chairmen, party and state leaders, and members of the NPC Presidium. Speeches, once they began, were rarely interrupted. When the agenda was completed, provided there were no small-group meetings scheduled, deputies returned to their hotels and guesthouses (no longer Beijing's most luxurious) to go shopping, eating, or sightseeing.[78]

Despite manipulated elections and unwieldy size, the NPC could become a significant force if its deputies displayed initiative during plenary sessions. Via either speeches or votes, active legislators could present minority views, scrutinize government actions, and prod leaders toward accountability. Deputies have always had a right to information and access to China's leaders; what they lacked was time to express their opinions, procedures to exercise their rights, and guarantees that outspokenness would not be punished.

Time

Beginning in the autumn of 1980, indications appeared that changes in session duration and frequency were under consideration. Several reformers, including an NPCSC vice chairman, suggested professionalizing the legislature by increasing the length of NPC sessions and holding two sessions each year.[79] For the first time in many years, Chinese commentators acknowledged an important structural constraint to legislative development – part-time representatives – and asked if change was possible.

Although the idea of longer legislative sessions undoubtedly originated in top party councils, it quickly encountered opposition. Spokesmen rediscovered traditional arguments against "professional politicians who stand above the masses" and deemed extended sessions "inappropriate."[80] In the 1980s, as in the past, the only professional politicians among NPC deputies were full-time party or state functionaries who could not be drawn away from their regular posts for long. Legislative sessions continued to be brief, annual events, typically two or three weeks in duration, and deputies were not paid for their efforts, though subsidies for transportation, lodging, food, and entertainment reached 100 yuan (US$27) per day.[81]

Courage

Unable to increase session duration or frequency, reformers turned to making short sessions more meaningful. Many traced the source of legislative weakness to passive, fearful legislators and advocated activating NPC veto powers. They criticized "voting-machine" deputies, decried cursory examination and approval of reports, and called for constitutional provisions granting the NPC the right to veto, amend, or table any government report, bill, or proposal.[82] These critics accepted outside powers of initiative, but dreamed of a legislature able to check government actions and to prevent "typhoon-like movements." Legislative consideration of "all strategic decisions," and the real possibility of rejection, would frustrate "schemers" and improve the "correctness" of laws. It would restrain party and state leaders and reveal impractical decisions before they were implemented.[83]

Although the 1982 constitution reaffirmed the NPC's supreme power, it did not increase the significance of NPC voting. In fact, explanations of the constitution cautioned deputies to "seek truth from facts" and reminded party members that party discipline demanded support for leadership policy and opposition to "mistaken things" proposed by nonparty colleagues.[84] Many party members felt the NPC should not reject documents submitted by the party or the government. They charged that such activity would amount to "putting on a rival show."[85] Some officials even defended routine unanimity, with Zhou Gucheng, an 88-year-old NPCSC deputy secretary-general, arguing that 3,000 votes to 0 was much "more convincing" and "more democratic" than 50 votes to 49.[86]

Zhou's curious notion of democracy notwithstanding, the custom of NPC unanimity progressively lost support. Li Zuxing opposed the view that "unanimous votes were necessary to uphold leadership authority and to demonstrate national stability and unity," and pointed out that "many of the documents unanimously passed from 1954 to 1985 were not perfectly correct and in accordance with the people's wishes."[87] Zi Mu noted that even party deputies were elected by the people, not by other party members, and they should be able to talk freely about disagreements with the party at the NPC.[88] Pu Xingzu reminded proponents of unanimity that a party proposal to the NPC did not have legal force and could not be regarded as a formal decision until it was adopted by the legislature. A proposal, Pu argued, should be turned down if it was inappropriate or poorly explained.[89]

In practice, deputies began exercising their right to oppose party and state proposals: nay votes were cast at the 1986 NPC against the Supreme Court and Supreme Procurator's Report and against two aged Standing Committee

Table 7.2. *Number of votes state leaders received, 1988*

Position	Name	For	Against	Abstained
President	Yang Shangkun	2,725	124	34
Vice President	Wang Zhen	2,594	212	77
CMC Chairman	Deng Xiaoping	2,850	25	8
Premier	Li Peng	2,854	18	5
Vice Premier	Yao Yilin	2,811	43	5
	Tian Jiyun	2,725	122	12
	Wu Xueqian	2,723	123	13
State Councillor	Li Tieying	2,620	229	10
	Qin Jiwei	2,803	53	3
	Wang Bingqian	2,615	225	19
	Song Jian	2,777	76	6
	Wang Fang	2,641	204	14
	Zou Jiahua	2,811	42	6
	Li Guixian	2,426	404	29
	Chen Xitong	2,733	118	8
	Chen Junsheng	2,786	72	1

Sources: "Hong Kong Paper Gives State Council Vote Tally," *FBIS* 71 (April 13, 1988): 27–8, from *Hong Kong Standard*, April 13, 1988, p. 6. Yau Shing-mu, "Paper on Voting for President, Vice Chairmen," *FBIS* 70 (April 12, 1988): 26–7, from *Hong Kong Standard*, April 9, 1988, pp. 1, 6. Antonio Kamiya, "KYODO Reviews Dissenting Votes in Elections," *FBIS* 69 (April 11, 1988): 21–2, from Tokyo KYODO, April 9, 1988.

nominees[90]; candidates for state leadership positions received hundreds of dissenting votes and abstentions in 1988 (see Table 7.2), and for the first time in NPC history, not a single legislative committee was elected unanimously[91]; in 1989, every government report faced opposition and 40% of NPC deputies opposed or abstained on a State Council proposal to delegate law-making power to the Shenzhen special economic zone's people's congress.[92]

Yet voting against a party or government proposal remained an extraordinary and newsworthy event. Efforts may continue to make voting more significant, but in the 1980s, most reports and legislative drafts were accepted without thorough deliberation and near unanimity was often achieved. After interjections by several deputies in 1988 and 1989 (including a call for a vote recount), impromptu speeches were made subject to Presidium approval and all remarks from the floor were limited in duration (10 minutes) and frequency (two per member).[93] Votes and speeches in the full NPC challenged, but they rarely altered, major policy or personnel decisions.

Before a proposal reached the floor, however, deputies appeared to gain a measure of influence. Consultation with deputies before the 1983 NPC led to changes in the state-leadership candidate lists: a scientist was added as NPCSC vice chairman, two minority representatives were added to the NPCSC, and one elderly minister was dropped.[94] Though the party did the preparatory work and the Politburo confirmed all changes, deputies had input at the margin.

Efforts were also made to give legislators timely notice of policy initiatives. At the 1980 NPC, many deputies suggested fixing the NPC's meeting date and allowing deputies sufficient time to review and discuss drafts. NPC deputy and Vice President of the Chinese Academy of Social Sciences Yu Guangyuan suggested distributing documents to deputies three months before convening a Congress.[95] Wu Jialin concurred:

> Draft resolutions to be examined and approved by the Congress should be sent to deputies before each session. Deputies have the duty to find out opinions of voters and voting zones from which they are elected. They should have the opinions well prepared before going to the session.[96]

Although the 1982 NPC organic law (art. 4) did not go as far as Wu or Yu suggested, it clarified the duties of provincial-level delegations and enjoined delegation leaders to schedule preparatory meetings before each Congress. In the 1980s, deputies typically received draft government work reports several days before convening; beginning in 1990, they were to receive all draft laws, personnel name lists, and the session's date and agenda one month before convening.[97] With improved preparation, it was hoped deputies would become more effective participants in substantive discussions.

Lively debate requires knowledge and preparation; it also requires participants unafraid of repercussions. In order to "dispel deputies' political misgivings" the constitution (art. 74, 75) and organic law (art. 43, 44) restored deputy immunities granted in 1954, forbade arrest or trial of NPC deputies without permission of the NPCSC, and guaranteed that deputies would not be called to legal account for plenary speeches or votes. These clauses "drew on the serious lessons learned from the expansion of the 1957 Anti-Rightist Movement in which not a few deputies suffered censure and punishment" and were designed to prevent further "illegal usurpations of deputy rights." Strengthened immunities would "encourage deputies to show initiative in representing the people, to speak out freely, to air their own views, and to discuss national affairs and give advice."[98] Commentators were confident that most deputies would reject "inappropriate" opinions, should they arise, and they promised that "even if what is said goes too far, or criticism of certain government officials is excessive, it will not be legally investigated."[99]

At the same time, deputies were warned not to abuse their rights and were reminded that immunity from prosecution did not license irresponsibility. These warnings appeared hardly necessary. Deputies preferred to be too responsible; they avoided confrontation and "there was too much making one's position known and too little debating substance."[100] On paper, deputies enjoy privileges other Chinese citizens lack; whether they will develop the courage to exercise their rights and whether the post-Zhao leadership will tolerate outside criticism remain to be seen.

Procedures

If deputies speak more often and more knowledgeably, and with fewer inhibitions, it will probably occur in small-group discussions. In small groups, deputies discuss items on the agenda, and if they are so inclined, summon officials to answer questions. Past constitutions granted a right to interpellation – that is, formal questioning of ministers – but it had not been used prior to 1980. After sharp exchanges over the Baoshan construction project, several reformers advocated expanding and institutionalizing NPC interpellations. Liu Chuanchen, in particular, pointed to obscurities in existing laws and called for procedures that would transform "addressing inquiries" (*zhixun*) into "holding to account" (*zhiwen*). Liu explained that a simple requirement to respond to interpellations was not sufficient:

(Without) a legally set time limit, or if deputies are unsatisfied, what can they do next? And then, if through whatever procedures, they are able to submit the problem to the whole NPC for deliberation, and if the NPC judges the government organ to be in the wrong, how can the legislature investigate and affix legal responsibility? Finally, there are no clear provisions on whether a vote is necessary to give an interpellation the force of law.[101]

Liu, in effect, asked if interpellation was to evolve into a regular, institutional form of supervision, or if it was to remain an occasional lever to topple factional opponents.

The 1982 organic law (art. 16, 17), the constitution (art. 73), and the NPC rules of procedure partially addressed Liu's questions. These documents affirmed the right of deputies to address inquiries to the State Council and its ministries and commissions and required either written or oral responses. Those receiving inquiries were instructed to answer questions in a responsible manner (constitution, art. 73) and to respect deputies' rights. Although time limits and punishments were not specified, if questioners were not satisfied with a reply, they were permitted to submit another inquiry and the department questioned was required, if instructed by the Presidium, to give another reply. Written replies were to be signed by the head of the organ questioned and, at the Presidium's discretion, were to be printed for distribution at the session. All inquiries had to be written (presumably to deter spontaneous, embarrassing questions) and they were to be presented by full delegations or groups of thirty or more deputies – "to guarantee that the inquiries had a definite mass base."[102]

As with deputy immunities, commentators continued to emphasize responsibility. Deputies were given carte blanche to "seek information" (*xunwen*) from administrative departments, but were requested to show restraint when tendering criticisms, suggestions, and opinions. Reformers had used deputy interpellations to their advantage in 1980, but were clearly hesitant to institutionalize a mechanism that could be turned against them. Especially under Peng Zhen, reform enthusiasts and their proposals might have suffered from extensive use of legislative interpellation. Under the 1982 constitution, deputies could ask informational questions, but could "hold leaders to account" only with the consent of national leaders – including the head of a provincial delegation and the Presidium, which accepted or rejected an inquiry and passed it on.

Leadership ambivalence also characterized new provisions on legislative bills, proposals, criticisms, and opinions. On the one hand, for the first time, delegations and groups of thirty or more deputies gained the right to submit legislative bills to the NPC and NPCSC (organic law, art. 10; constitution, art. 72). But the new laws also made a distinction between legislative bills and common opinions and suggestions. Opinions and suggestions, it was said, involved considerable effort, expense, and time, and many concerned matters outside the jurisdiction of the NPC or NPCSC. Piles of them were printed and issued at each session, but few were read or decided upon. In the name of simplified procedures, the 1982 organic law (art. 21) and the 1989 rules of procedure stipulated that proposals, criticisms, and opinions would no longer be presented in the form of bills, but would be submitted to the General Office of the NPCSC, which would refer them to concerned departments. This would "reduce the amount of work at each session, and enable the session to devote its primary energies to important matters on the agenda, so strengthening session efficiency and raising the quality of work."[103] The NPC would also dispense with reports on how proposals were handled, freeing time for legislative work and eliminating an "unnecessary, trivial task."[104] To ensure attention, concerned departments were directed to respond to proposals within six months, and if deputies were not satisfied, they could resubmit their motion to be handled anew.[105]

It is too early to judge the effect of reformed procedures for handling proposals, criticisms, and opinions. In the past, they often went "through a long journey only to return to the deputies who made them," and problems were often ignored after they were discussed.[106] Nevertheless, proposals, criticisms, and opinions always provided a channel for NPC deputies to bring local concerns to the attention of central authorities and usually reflected important issues. From June 1983 to April 1988, NPC committees and government departments handled 14,215 deputy suggestions, criticisms, and opinions.[107] Consigning these to the NPCSC may have had no effect or may even have improved referral to decision makers, but it also may have decreased their visibility, thus allowing state officials to ignore them more easily.

The final scorecard on strengthening NPC sessions was mixed. The leadership flirted with truly liberal reform (longer, more frequent sessions; professional deputies; meaningful votes), but then pulled away. Several moderate reforms were adopted, but not without accompanying explanations or countermeasures that reduced their effect. The problems of inadequate session time, timid deputies, and undeveloped procedures were not fully addressed. Efforts to encourage liveliness were offset by measures to ensure that sessions ran smoothly. In normal circumstances, deputies continued to act as a group rather than as individuals and offered consent rather than questions. They rarely demanded explanations and avoided embarrassing government departments or individual officials. Lively panel discussions arose over the ecological impact of the Three Gorges Dam Project and the wisdom of the bankruptcy and enterprise autonomy laws, but not without behind-the-scenes prodding and Presidium support. Realizing the potential for policy influence inherent in voting or in speeches protected by expanded immunities and new powers of interpellation awaited openings provided by leadership dissensus or additional organizational strengthening.

Support for radical session and size reform peaked during a wave of reform in late 1980, but faded within a year. Perhaps a change of heart occurred; more likely, comparatively liberal academics and advisers went beyond their patrons or their patrons were outflanked by factional opponents. Exactly what happened is impossible to say; the real players failed to explain their reasoning and the ranks quickly closed behind the official line.[108] What is certain is that as interest in NPC plenary reform declined, attention shifted to upgrading the NPCSC and creating a working committee structure. If the NPC could not be made into a working body, perhaps its committees could.

Strengthening committees

As the constitutional revision debate progressed, it became clear that the full NPC, even after reform, could not address the backlog of legislative work that had accumulated since the 1950s. Plenary sessions remained crowded, brief affairs where leaders spoke and deputies listened. An assembly of 3,000 deputies could ratify decisions and legitimize rule, but had minimal ability to initiate or revise. By early 1982, anything approaching a Gorbachev-style Supreme Soviet was probably out of the question, but using the legislature to legalize and regularize party power remained possible. If the NPC was to rationalize rule and increase government efficiency, however, it needed specialized organs and trained personnel.

To enhance legislative capabilities reformers looked first to the NPCSC. Expanding Standing Committee powers was an ideal strategy – neither excessively controversial nor without import. It did not involve changing the mission of the full NPC, but rather strengthening its working core. It did not challenge party control, but simply rejuvenated a nonparty organ that was small enough to meet regularly and to conduct meaningful discussions.[109] Given the failure of radical plenary reform, reformers suggested a division of labor: the full NPC for discussion, information gathering, and symbolic tasks, the NPCSC for law making and supervision.

After some debate, the leadership accepted this compromise and set out to transform the Standing Committee into a legislature within a legislature.[110] The 1982 constitution (art. 67) granted the NPCSC the power to enact and amend laws (as well as decrees), with the exception of basic laws concerning criminal offenses, civil affairs, and the structure of the state. The NPCSC also gained the right to adjust the state plan and budget between NPC sessions, "because in the course of socialist modernization unexpected situations often occur."[111] As China's second law-making body, the NPCSC was to discuss and pass statutes that could not wait for NPC deliberation.[112] Standing Committee members were to be kept informed of the legislative agenda (organic law, art. 2) and to participate in legal drafting and supervision. NPCSC members could address inquiries to state officials and organize and take part in nationwide inspections. They were to work diligently at and between sessions and to gather information from all quarters, in order to reduce mistakes in law making and policy implementation.[113] To ensure that these reforms were carried out, the leadership strengthened NPCSC organization and redefined deputy responsibilities in six ways.

First, the size of the Standing Committee was reduced from 196 to 155 members. This 21% decrease (one and one-half times that of the full NPC) was designed to improve attendance and to allow frequent and lengthy meetings. A smaller NPCSC, it was hoped, would elicit greater participation from each member and a more conscientious approach to legislative work.[114] Fewer members would sit in each of the NPCSC's small groups and four medium-sized joint meetings (a 1980s' innovation) would be held to discuss controversial issues, aggregate opinions, provide explanations, and supplement reports.[115]

Second, the leadership acknowledged the need for a core of full-time legislators who engaged in NPCSC work year-round. Under Mao, members had no responsibilities beyond attending meetings, and some found it difficult to do that. The NPCSC met only several days bimonthly and most members had other jobs.[116] The 1982 organic law (art. 23) sought to change this. It prohibited NPCSC members from holding state administrative, judicial, or procuratorial posts in order to give them more time and energy for legislative work and the independence essential for government oversight.[117]

Available evidence suggests progress in professionalizing the NPCSC.[118] Prior to the 1983 elections, commentators claimed that "a portion of NPC deputies" would be "half or fully released from their regular work," or that a "considerable number" of NPCSC members would devote all their energies to deputy work. As NPCSC personnel decisions were made, the number of full-time members increased to "quite a number" or "most of them."[119] Interviews in 1989 suggested that each NPCSC vice chairman maintained a residence in the capital, most had no other job, and at least several reported to the Great Hall every day. Furthermore, 60% to 80% of ordinary NPCSC members lived in Beijing and were available for Standing Committee work. Some Standing Committee members, however, continued to hold state posts illegally, and many held responsible party, mass organization, or enterprise positions (none of which were forbidden); all received salaries from their original unit, even if they worked for the legislature full time.[120] Amateurism, overlapping memberships, and self-supervision were reduced in the 1980s but not eliminated.

A third organizational reform established a chairmanship group composed of the NPCSC chairman, vice chairmen, and secretary-general. With 20 to 25 members, the chairmanship group handled regular NPC work and guaranteed continuity and implementation of NPC decisions. Its formal tasks included scheduling and drafting the agenda of NPCSC meetings, referring bills and inquiries to the NPCSC and the committees, and coordinating day-to-day work. The chairmanship group met before every NPCSC session, had the right to initiate bills, and scheduled votes and interpellations.[121] As the prime organizational base of the NPCSC chairman, it was authoritative and the source of the chair's power over deputies and state officials.[122] If the NPCSC was a legislature within a legislature, the chairmanship group was the working organ of the working organ.

A fourth structural reform sprang from the realization that the NPCSC alone could not clear up the crowded legislative calendar. As early as January 1979, a *People's Daily* article suggested establishing additional permanent committees and enlarging committee duties to include examining and drawing up legislative bills.[123] Committees had existed intermittently since 1954, but without great effect. The Budget Committee, for example, met only during sessions to examine the state budget, plans, and final accounts. It did no preparatory work beforehand and had no authority to conduct investigations afterward. Committee members could not thoroughly and rigorously examine financial matters, nor did they take part in drafting legislation or oversight.[124]

In February 1979, the NPC set up a Legislative Affairs Commission, with Peng Zhen at its head. Later that year, the Nationalities Committee was reestablished and several meetings were convened. Reports suggest that the Nationalities Committee participated in drafting the law on regional autonomy and the Legislative Affairs Commission proposed twelve of the thirteen laws passed by the NPC from 1979 to 1981.[125]

These activities heartened reformers and augured further changes. In 1980 and 1981, reformers suggested establishing fifteen or more permanent committees.[126] They supported committee participation in legal drafting and committee discussion and investigation of all matters within NPC competence. They envisioned functionally specific committees examining each legislative proposal and a Law Committee determining whether to submit bills to the NPC or NPCSC for deliberation. They argued that deputies taking part in committee work, like NPCSC members, should be released from other duties and outside experts should be invited to offer advice.[127]

The leadership adopted most of these proposals. The constitution (art. 70) set up six permanent committees – Law; Nationalities; Finance and Economics; Education, Science, Culture, and Public Health; Foreign Affairs; and Overseas Chinese – and commentators promised further additions after a period of gathering experience.[128] (In 1988, an Internal Judicial Affairs Committee was formed.) Legislative committees worked under the NPC when the Congress was in session and under the NPCSC when it was not. They were not given full law-making powers (as committees in some countries enjoy), but virtually every other function just cited. Committees drafted legislative proposals and examined bills and inquiries referred by the NPC or NPCSC (including administrative measures considered potentially un-constitutional). They also had the authority to investigate and study any issue that fell within the scope of NPC or NPCSC powers. "To help maintain the uniformity of the legal system and (to) avoid contradictions," the organic law and NPCSC proceedings regulations provided that all bills be examined by the Law Committee before submission to the NPC or NPCSC. Although all committee members were selected from the NPC, the committees, through the NPCSC, were encouraged to appoint outside specialists to serve as part-time or full-time advisers.[129]

Committee chairmen were typically former party leaders (e.g., Peng Chong, Wang Renzhong, Geng Biao, Xi Zhongxun, and Chen Muhua) who served concurrently as NPCSC vice chairmen (and thus were members of the chairmanship group). Throughout the 1980s, many committee members were old and in poor health, but in the latter half of the decade, efforts to improve committee composition and structure appeared. In 1988, each com-mittee formulated working procedures to guide its activities. In several stages, beginning in 1986, the size of each committee was enlarged from a dozen or so individuals to seventeen to thirty members. By 1988, 63% of NPCSC members served on committees; by 1989, 74% did.[130]

Though committee sessions were rarely disclosed, and some committees met less than once each month, the most active committee, the Law Com-mittee, met on 35 occasions from April 1988 to April 1989. Committee chairmen and vice chairmen were said to assemble considerably more often than full committees.[131] Members were assigned to committees according to their expertise and many were specialists with considerable experience in relevant fields. A high proportion were well-educated and many had the background and skills needed to carry out careful investigations and to make worthwhile suggestions on legislative proposals.[132] If, in the future, equally distinguished, but younger, experts are chosen for committee assignments, committees could become a political force.

A fifth organizational reform increased NPC staff support.[133] Legislative committees in 1989 had 30 to 45 staff members and a coordinating office (*bangongshi*) responsible for logistics and document distribution. At least three committees had permanent research offices, which employed from several to ten staff members – though the Education, Science, Culture, and Public Health contingent was somewhat larger. These research offices carried out investigations, compiled documents, and studied committee legal drafts.

Staff members who worked directly under the Standing Committee were divided into two departments: the General Office (*bangongting*) and the Legislative Affairs Commission. The General Office had nine bureaus and the following (1989) staff levels: secretariat (60–70); research office (70); liaison bureau (20–30); press bureau (12); foreign affairs bureau (40); letters and visits bureau (20–30); personnel bureau (20–30); administrative management bureau (40–50); Great Hall management (approximately 1,000, mostly workers).

The Legislative Affairs Commission (*fazhi gongzuo weiyuanhui*), though under the NPCSC, was in many senses the working staff of the Law Committee. It was the descendant of the similarly named organization (*fazhi weiyuanhui*) set up by Peng Zhen in 1979, and, more distantly, of the Law Office that existed in the 1950s. It had 180 staff members, all of whom were full-time employees and most of whom worked in the Great Hall of the People. Twenty of its employees played support roles (e.g., drivers, secretaries), and the remaining 160 were professionals, largely college graduates and holders of advanced degrees from law departments and law schools.

The Legislative Affairs Commission (LAC) was divided into six offices. The forty-member coordinating office (*bangongshi*) was responsible for routine work, including convening meetings, day-to-day affairs, and issuing and distributing documents. The two dozen workers in the LAC research office were professional researchers. One group studied comparative law and foreign laws, including the codes of the United States, West Germany, Britain, and Japan. Several members of this group were language experts who carried out translations. A second group focused on Chinese law, including its history and theory. Employees in a subordinate materials office compiled laws of other nations (including the U.S. Code and the New York State Code) and distributed materials to four specialized offices under the Legislative Affairs Commission: the criminal law office; the civil law office; the state and administrative law office; and the economic law office. These offices had fifteen to thirty staff members and research offices in various stages of formation. Members arranged provincial investigations, solicited opinions from concerned officials, convened conferences of scholars and officials, and wrote reports for the NPCSC and the Law Committee. They were responsible for ensuring that draft laws were consistent with existing laws and for drafting amendments under the guidance of the Law Committee.[134] They also formulated basic, criminal, and organic laws that were not drafted under the State Council Legislative Affairs Bureau and polished laws recommended by the State Council before transmitting them to the Law Committee.

The NPC's ability to draft laws and oversee the government rested with its staff. In the late 1980s, calls for increased support were common and comparisons to the well-endowed U.S. Congress were heard. The size of the Legislative Affairs Commission was increased sixfold after 1979; in 1988, it was reported that NPC staff levels would be increased a further 40% at a time when other government organs were being streamlined.[135] Much more is needed if deputies are to legislate and supervise as well as to advise.

A sixth structural reform concerned the long-term viability of the NPC itself. Legislative strengthening clearly meant little if the constitution could be suspended or ignored with impunity. How to handle constitutional enforcement was the subject of much debate.

Past constitutions charged the full NPC with constitutional supervision, but left procedures and methods unspecified. Deputies lacked both time and courage to identify unconstitutional behavior and machinery to punish offenders. Unenforced, the constitution quickly lost its normative force and leaders ruled free from its restraint.[136]

From 1979 to 1982, reformers looked to other nations' experiences for methods to guarantee enforcement of the constitution.[137] Some suggested creating permanent special organs solely responsible for constitutional supervision and legal interpretation. Possibilities included a system of constitutional courts, modeled after the United States or Yugoslavia, or special constitutional committees, such as those in France.[138] A judicial organ would have a clear mandate and adequate time to investigate unconstitutional actions. Wholly separate from the NPC, it would also eliminate legislative review of legislative decisions.

Other reformers advocated keeping constitutional supervision within the NPC, but delegating it to the Standing Committee. Pan Nianzhi believed that the NPC should check and handle constitutional violations with the assistance of a Committee on Constitutional Questions.[139] Kang Damin envisioned a hybrid system, in which the NPCSC would carry out general supervision, such as guaranteeing the legality of laws and constitutional interpretation, while a judicial organ would handle constitutional violations.[140]

The 1982 constitution granted the NPCSC primary responsibility for constitutional enforcement. No new judicial organs were established. Constitutional analysts defended this decision primarily on theoretical grounds, explaining that in China's unified state system, the scope of legislative supervision was greater than that of judicial supervision because NPC powers were greater than that of any judicial organ.[141] In this view, rejection of checks and balances and commitment to legislative supremacy dictated an NPC-based supervisory system. More practically, legislative supervision was also said to be prompt (the NPCSC could review any decision without waiting for a case) and decisive (NPC decisions were final). Commentators admitted that if the NPCSC violated the constitution problems would arise, but expressed confidence that the full NPC would correct any mistakes.[142]

Publication of the draft constitution did not end the debate on constitutional enforcement. During nationwide discussions of the draft, criticisms of the new supervisory system were common. Yu Haocheng, then the editor of *Faxue Zazhi,* and more recently a prominent government critic, wrote that "some people" felt the draft was very vague and lacked detailed provisions on how to handle unconstitutional behavior; Yu advocated establishing a special legislative or judicial organ, or at least a new NPC committee.[143] Cui Min and Yu Chi suggested adding explicit provisions that explained under what conditions and in what ways the NPCSC could investigate unconstitutional actions, including measures on rescinding laws, edicts, and regulations and procedures to prosecute and punish offenders.[144]

After 1982, efforts to enforce the constitution began. The 1986 NPCSC Work Report addressed constitutional issues in some detail and admitted continuing problems in unconstitutional transfers and appointments and violation of electoral procedures.[145] The NPCSC's 1988–92 Work Outline instructed NPC committees to examine local statutes and to report unconstitutional measures to the Standing Committee.[146] Efforts were initiated to decide whether the NPCSC should supervise the party in addition to state organs: advocates spoke of an "onlooker seeing the game best"; opponents saw Standing Committee supervision of party committees as "yet another mother-in-law."[147]

That constitutional enforcement remained imperfect was widely acknowledged. Proposals regularly appeared to establish special organs and to absorb the benefits of judicial and committee systems. Commentators often spoke of multitrack (*yiyuan duogui*) supervision, with a constitutional court or committee subordinate to the NPC and a prescribed division of labor.[148] Further reform is nearly certain and a new constitution committee or a reorganized Law Committee is a distinct possibility.[149] Reform of the NPC committee structure has yet to conclude.

Conclusion

The legislative reforms adopted in 1982 did not give the Chinese people or their representatives remarkably more say over important matters of state. Decision-making power remained closely guarded, limited to a comparative handful. Outside control of leaders and regular influence over policy became rallying points for several years, but lacked the elite support to become policy. Other than in a simple demographic sense, the NPC was not a more popular body than it was in the past. Deputies may have spoken for the people, but not because the people controlled their fate. Leaders may have listened to deputies, but not because deputies had an established and essential place in policy making. Reform did not recast the NPC into a liberal democratic legislature; those who foresaw such a development had forgotten the realities of one-party rule, the lessons of 1957, and indeed the entire history of Chinese legislatures.

But the post-Mao NPC did offer the possibility of drawing in some who in the past were excluded. It enlarged the united front and signified official recognition of social diversity. Individuals, outside the normal leadership hierarchy, some of whom represent minority views, were selected to the chairmanship group and committees; such individuals gained the right and resources to participate in a wide range of political decisions. On specialized matters, the seven committees granted access to experts who otherwise had limited say in policy making. The NPC thus served as an olive branch – offered less to ordinary citizens or disenchanted students than to estranged social elites on the fringe of power. It offered minority factions and coopted individuals from key social groups a presence in policy making in exchange for support of party rule.

Beyond inclusion, structural reforms suggested changing party–state relations and a desire to recast party power: to establish a more indirect pattern of rule in which law and state organs played a larger part. Thirty-five years of "winding and tortuous development" brought Chinese legal thinking full circle – the words of the 1956 Eighth Party Congress gained new relevance as did nearly forgotten proposals to establish permanent standing committees and a nationwide supervisory system.

As for the NPC, the committees are key. Work capacity must be translated into actual work if potential participation is to become real. What was given in 1982 can easily be taken away or ignored. To be maintained, organizational reforms must be confirmed again and again, and this is uncertain – just as uncertain as the party's commitment to self-restraint, law, and a "rational division of labor."

Nearly a decade has passed since the constitution was promulgated. Movement toward rationalization has been arrested in the wake of the Tiananmen supression and the return of gerontocracy and personal rule. The leadership has once again denounced liberalization and increased the level of loyalty demanded for inclusion.

Whether the events of 1989 and increased personalism unhinge the NPC remains to be seen. The NPC does not stand for stability by dictate or heroic, party rule by "old revolutionaries." Nor can it function properly if laws are cast aside, mass movements sweep the nation, and speech is tightly controlled. The next chapter considers what has changed and what has endured in the last four decades by investigating recent legislative activities and comparing the role of the NPC in the 1980s with that it played under Mao.

8

The NPC and systemic change

Legislative development from 1978 to 1989 paralleled development of the political system; changes were fitful and uneven, unexpected and incomplete. For each lively NPC session, there was a lifeless one, and for each significant reform, there was a rejected proposal or failed experiment. Political and legal institutionalization failed to take hold, and legislative strengthening continued to hinge on party initiative and forbearance. At times of crisis, the leadership was willing to use violence and psychological pressure to gain obedience and to abandon efforts to win popular consent. Reminiscent of the late 1950s, the party center, by the end of the 1980s, opposed all signs of political pluralism and silenced intellectuals and advisers who promoted procedural succession and parliamentarianism. In a matter of days, the full propaganda apparatus of the state was turned against purported advocates of "total westernization," deputies were removed, and forums to discuss democratic reform were crushed.

One might conclude that the NPC and the Chinese political system closely resembled their predecessors under Mao. This would be mistaken. A review of legislative activities in the 1980s shows that the NPC came to occupy a new position in China and the political system, *though still illiberal,* was not unchanged by reform.

The last two chapters reviewed NPC plenary sessions and structural reforms and highlighted the process of change – its advocates and opponents, its chronology, and its scope. This chapter concludes the analysis by focusing on the results of change – what the NPC did from 1978 to 1989 and where it and the Chinese political system may be heading. Mirroring Chapter 6, I examine NPC involvement in four legislative activities (law making, supervision, representation, regime support) and consider the relationship of the legislature to other organizations engaged in these tasks. Tracking the role of a legislature, we explore efforts to maintain the legitimacy and efficacy of one-party rule in a society undergoing social and economic transformation.

By focusing on one political institution and one set of political functions, we trace the path of Chinese political development.

Law making

After a lapse of two full decades, legal drafting resumed in 1979. From 1979 to 1989, the NPC and its Standing Committee passed eighty-eight laws, amended and revised twenty laws, and made forty-five legal decisions. Legislative planners indicated that an additional 117 laws were scheduled to be drafted or revised by 1993.[1] Following twenty years of near lawlessness, the beginnings of a legal code was emerging.

The Chinese leadership turned to law for a number of reasons. In the early post-Mao years, they sought to dispel lingering fears and to mobilize society for modernization. Law was seen as a means to curtail abuses of power and to ensure stability; recourse to law implied a rejection of class struggle and safeguards against arbitrary behavior. Rule by law would protect elites and reassure an uneasy and untrusting populace. It would help the leadership undertake ambitious modernization plans and gradually transform suspicion into active support.[2]

As time passed and China reopened to the outside world, the leadership relied on law to generate international support for modernization. A steady stream of laws appeared – in areas such as taxation, joint ventures, contracts, patents, and trademarks – designed to portray China as a stable and orderly society, a reliable trading partner, and a safe haven for foreign investment. Foreign investors and traders demanded a network of rules and regulations to settle disputes and to protect capital and technology, and the Chinese were anxious to provide assurances. Legal codes, for Chinese and foreigners alike, promised stability and a predictable framework of relations.

As economic reform deepened, law was used to confirm policy and regulate change. With domestic economic and social relations becoming more complicated and market influences infiltrating a planned economy, the leadership encouraged observance of laws that regulated production and relationships among productive units, codified rights and obligations, and provided guidelines for economic activities. Specific, legal norms were designed to enable enterprises to plan their work efficiently and to help mobilize societal resources.[3] In an era of controlled decentralization, laws aimed to reduce the need for central planning and direct control, to institutionalize reform, to prevent misunderstandings, and to enliven the economy.

Legal codes also promised to ensure (and perhaps tighten) social control. The explicit, detailed provisions found in laws would be "easier" than party pronouncements "to observe strictly and implement conscientiously"[4] and would serve as a reminder that the freewheeling days when Mao said "to rebel is justified" were over. Local political and economic decision makers were expected to observe laws and to find it more difficult to purposefully misinterpret party policies or frustrate central control. In this way, laws were designed to anchor decentralization and limit prerogative.

The intentions of the leadership were clear. But China had functioned without law for many years, with party policy replacing it at every level. For the legal revival to succeed, law needed to regain a legitimate and secure place next to policy.

"Policies," as defined by Wang Shuwen, the director of the Law Research Institute of the Chinese Academy of Social Sciences, were "principles formulated by the party and state, which guided political, economic and cultural life and all other work. The implementation of policies mainly depended on the consciousness of the people, without compulsion."[5] Laws, though guided by party policies, differed from policy in extent, maturity, and binding force. Some party policies only applied to party members; laws applied to all citizens. Policies were to some extent only principles; laws were rigorously standardized and explicitly and concretely stipulated what people could and could not do. While policies were flexible and ever-changing, laws were relatively stable. Reforms were first implemented through policies, and only later were "actively" but "prudently" transformed into law.[6] Laws thus did not restrict reform, but stabilized it and protected it with the coercive power of the state.[7] Laws, in short, followed, elaborated, and clarified policies, and provided an organizational framework for implementation.

Law had a purpose and a place in Deng's China, but institutionalized drafting procedures were still lacking. Twenty years of lawlessness left the nation with a handful of outdated codes, an enormous backlog of work, and few institutions experienced in legal drafting. Several organizations were mobilized into law making, at various stages with varying degrees of influence. In particular, four separate hierarchies were assigned a role in translating broad programmatic decisions of the party leadership into specific legal norms.

First, was the Communist Party itself. Direct party involvement in law making in the 1980s occurred primarily at the earliest stage of drafting – determining if an issue was ripe for legislation – and near the end – reviewing and approving a bill.[8] Legal journals closely scrutinized every utterance by party officials responsible for legal affairs, and it is likely that editorials published in *People's Daily* or speeches by figures such as Peng Zhen, Chen Pixian, Zhang Youyu, and Wang Hanbin initiated legal drafting. Months (or even years) later, the Central Committee considered completed bills. In the interim, however, the CCP turned responsibility for drafting over to other organizations and indirectly controlled the process through party members in nonparty settings who reported legal principles (but not detailed provisions) to the Central Committee. Interviews with legal drafters suggest that participation in law making by the Central Committee Political-Legal Committee declined throughout the decade and state-employed professionals attended Political-Legal Committee meetings to advise rather than to be advised. Available evidence suggests that party committees set the law-making process in motion and checked the results; state organs did most of the actual work.[9]

The State Council headed a second bureaucratic complex involved in law making. The role of administrative bodies in drafting and enacting laws grew rapidly in the decade after 1979. The State Council's Legislative Affairs Bureau became a prime force in legal drafting, and ministries drafted such measures as the fisheries law, the forestry law, the accounting law, the mining resources law, and the environmental protection law.[10] Legal scholars quietly abandoned the fiction of unified legislative authority along with "the conventional view that the NPC and NPCSC were the only two legislative organs," and some went so far as to argue that "legislative authority was an important function of administrative organs," or that "administrative organs primarily bore the burden of legislative work."[11] In the past, the State Council had the power to draft administrative regulations; in the 1980s, it gained the authority to enact "empowered legislation" (*shouquan lifa*). On three occasions in 1984 and 1985, the NPCSC authorized the State Council to pass legislation on issues (retirement policy, tax reform, economic restructuring, and open-door policy) "beyond the realm of administrative regulations." By empowering the State Council to make "quasi-laws" (*zhun falü*), the leadership aimed to improve legislative continuity, comprehensiveness, and speed and to lay a groundwork for NPC action.[12]

Provincial-level people's congresses comprised the third set of law-making bodies. Although most Chinese commentators continued to reject federalism, the evolving legislative system exhibited a strong, relatively autonomous, local component. Legal scholars argued that China's size and diversity made it impossible for the NPC and NPCSC to pass all necessary laws, and suggested that delegating power accorded with the spirit of reform, reducing overconcentration of power, and bringing into play local activism.[13] While debate continued over whether China had a one-level (NPC and NPCSC), two-level (NPC and provincial congresses), or multilevel (NPC, provincial congresses, State Council, ministries) legislative system, the issue was resolved in practice.[14] Dispersed legislative capabilities proliferated and were accepted even by those who favored the one-level notion.[15] From 1983–9, provincial-level congresses and their standing committees passed over 1,000 local laws on topics ranging from regional minority affairs to provincewide political, economic, and cultural life and constitutional enforcement.[16] Provincial legislatures under Mao simply enforced laws; under Deng, they enacted them.

Legislative authority in the 1980s came to be shared across systems and within the legislative system. But what of the NPC and its committees – the fourth leg in the legislative complex? Did the NPC take part in making laws? According to a deputy director of the Law Institute of the Academy of Social Sciences, "legislation has become the key task of the NPC and its Standing Committee."[17] Through the NPCSC's Legislative Affairs Commission, the NPC "plays a very active role in each stage of the legislative process, including the drafting task force, investigation in different cities and provinces, solicitation of opinion from government officials, and conferences of scholars and officials."[18] By 1989, professionals in the Legislative Affairs Commission maintained regular contact with their counterparts in the State Council Legislative Affairs Commission and staff from the Economic Law Office were often sent to participate in State Council Legislative Affairs Commission deliberations, inspections, and field studies. Likewise, members of the State Council Legislative Affairs Commission frequently telephoned or visited NPC offices in the Great Hall of the People to explain and justify legislative initiatives.[19]

NPC formal involvement in law making began with "legislative forecasting" (*lifa yuce*) and "legislative planning" (*lifa guihua*). Legislative forecasting entailed anticipating the social results of laws, determining which laws were to be revised or repealed, setting up drafting timetables, and evaluating trends in law making. Nongovernment academics and advisers carried out the bulk of forecasting in the 1980s, but the NPC (through its Law Committee) provided guidance and was responsible for incorporating forecasts into policy.[20]

Legislative planning entailed using the information gained from forecasting to lay out specific legislative measures and goals. Forecasting was a precondition for planning and planning gave meaning to forecasting.[21] Although forecasting was irregular and incomplete under Deng, the State Council Legal Research Center drew up a legislative plan for 1982–6, including names of regulations, proposers, issuing organizations, and drafting conditions, and the NPCSC produced a work outline that provided a list of priorities and laws to be enacted.[22]

After laws were promulgated, the NPCSC was responsible for legislative interpretation (*lifa jieshi*) and legal coordination (*falü xietiao*). Legislative interpretation encompassed explaining a law's wording, scope, and methods of implementation. It occurred most often in response to a question from localities and government departments, and it took the form of notices issued by the NPCSC General Office to provincial people's congresses (e.g., concerning deputy quotas for the armed police in 1983), of interviews with NPCSC or Legislative Affairs Commission members (e.g., concerning local elections in 1984), and revision of laws.[23] Pending implementation of reforms that draw the Law Committee and the full NPCSC into legislative interpretation, the NPCSC Legislative Affairs Commission assumed responsibility for this task and replied to "numerous" questions from local people's congresses on legal enforcement, legal procedures, and "other matters."[24] It also added provisions to the criminal and pharmaceutical laws to clarify their intent and eliminate contradictions.[25]

If interpretation was needed for individual laws, it was also needed for the legal code as a whole. According to a vice chairman of the NPC Law Committee, since the Supreme Court did not enjoy such powers, the Law Committee "seems to be responsible for legal coordination" – for seeing that laws tally with the constitution, accord with party policies, are reasonable, and are not in conflict with each other.[26] As the number of laws multiplied, commentators argued that the NPC and its committees should "adjust laws via feedback" (*fankui tiaojie*) in the name of centralization and unity.[27] Suggestions for reform abounded, but consensus proved difficult to achieve. One popular proposal envisioned a National Legal Construction Coordination Control Center under the NPCSC with offices in each provincial people's congress, empowered to conduct research, collect information and feedback, and transmit directives on legal coordination.[28]

As a component of legal coordination, the NPC was charged with organizing legal education. Beginning in the mid-1980s, the NPCSC General Office distributed a work newsletter "to transmit cases of illegal local activities, to ensure implementation of law, and to reinforce legal knowledge."[29] It also published a bimonthly bulletin and prepared comprehensive compendia of laws and regulations. Throughout the decade, the NPCSC regularly arranged discussions on popularizing legal knowledge and improving local legislative work and it convened meetings and lectures for government officials and legal specialists to discuss new laws. In December 1985, for example, 180 legal experts and local officials took part in a seven-day joint NPCSC–NPC Law Committee conference on the draft civil code and exchanged opinions on how to ensure implementation.[30]

The constitution granted the NPC exclusive domain over certain areas (e.g., criminal laws and matters of state organization) and other areas, such as economic laws, became the focus of its work.[31] Deputies at each session from 1978 to 1989 introduced dozens of motions advocating new laws, NPC committees included experts from administrative organs and research institutes who assisted in drafting laws and carrying out legislative planning, and, in some cases (e.g., the regional autonomy law, the inheritance law, the Hong Kong basic law), NPC committees actually wrote bills (or parts of them).[32]

Even for those 70% of NPC and NPCSC laws drafted by the State Council,[33] legislative viscosity, at times, was considerable. Party leaders encouraged legislative deliberation of legal drafts and decreed that when major articles of a draft were "rather controversial" and "many Standing Committee members held different opinions," voting should be postponed and no effort should be made "to try to force the bill through."[34] The NPCSC, accordingly, on several occasions returned draft bills received from the State Council or Central Committee. Most notably, in 1986, Standing Committee members spoke on national television against a draft of the bankruptcy law and remanded the bill to the Law Committee for further revisions. The state-owned enterprise law went through multiple drafts over three years and was debated four times by the NPCSC before it was released for public discussion and finally passed by the NPC in April 1988. A law concerning villagers' committees was tabled twice in 1987 after "heated debate" and the expression of "sharply differing opinions" in both the NPC and NPCSC.[35]

Finally, the NPC's Law Committee revised and edited *all* bills submitted to the legislature – sometimes substantially. In three noteworthy cases, the Law Committee extended the coverage of the patent law from inventions to new models and exterior designs and required collective enterprises to share patents, it altered provisions of the inheritance law concerning widow's rights and heirs who did not support bequeathers, and it added several sets of compromise amendments to the bankruptcy law.[36]

In sum, the NPC of the 1980s, and its committees, occasionally drafted legislation often revised and edited it, and always oversaw the drafting process. As in most legislatures, deputies in plenary sessions did not greatly alter drafts. Changes were made in smaller, working sessions – typically, joint or group meetings of the NPCSC or sessions of the NPCSC Legislative Affairs Commission or the Law Committee. The NPC occupied a position at the center of a horizontally and vertically integrated legislative system, linked sideways to the State Council, ministries, and party, and downwards to regions via local congresses. Although its mandate narrowed (because law-making powers were shared with the State Council and provincial legislatures), its activities grew. In its role as law maker, the legislature occasionally resisted central initiatives and provided a forum for bargaining and negotiating. It also, as a matter of course, served to clarify and elaborate general directives and to coordinate a law-making process that involved individuals and groups scattered across a number of organizations. The NPC thus both expanded the policy-making process to include selected elites and legalized and regularized rule making. It served as both an agent of inclusion and of rationalization.

Supervision

Increasing focus in the 1980s on economic construction and efforts to reduce functional duplication brought new responsibilities to state organs and less party involvement in day-to-day administration. Party committees retained ultimate control, of course, but major political decisions often passed through formal, legal procedures before implementation by a separate state agency. Greater State Council, ministry, and local government participation in policy making aimed to enhance efficiency and to allow the party to attend to its own tasks, but it also introduced uncertainties. To ensure that its directives were faithfully carried out and to prevent inclusion from evolving into liberalization, the party reestablished long-unused, indirect channels of control over state organs. One such channel involved the NPC. Through representatives in the NPC, party leaders monitored state bureaucrats to ensure they were implementing policies and observing party principles. In this sense, the legislature became a proxy for the party – an alter ego embedded in the state apparatus. The rejection of liberalizing constitutional reforms at the turn of the 1980s (and the crushing of student movements in 1987 and 1989) cast doubt on the ability of the NPC to limit party power on behalf of "the people"; it did not, however, preclude party efforts to rationalize authority, to define the political system, and to exert institutional leverage over non-party organs.[37]

Legislative supervision may be conducted by the full NPC, its committees, or individual deputies, and it may be directed at state functionaries or the institutions they head. Supervision may be personal and sporadic or it may be institutional and regular. In the 1980s, three forms of supervision in three different settings came to the fore – (1) criticism of ministry or State Council officials by deputies in small-group meetings, (2) inspection of local government organs and economic enterprises by groups of NPCSC or NPC deputies, and (3) institutional oversight of subordinate administrative agencies by NPC committees.

Incisive interpellations and angry deputy speeches became a common occurrence at NPC sessions in the decade after 1979. In one instance, deputies at the 1988 convening criticized Premier Li Peng's suggestion that intellectuals moonlight to supplement their incomes, saying it was an "improper measure" that would interfere with teaching and research and "damage long-term national interests," and several bluntly disagreed (in his presence) with General Secretary Zhao Ziyang's assessment that such a policy was "necessary and possible."[38] More generally, deputies in small-group meetings at plenary sessions in 1979, 1980, 1981, 1985, 1987, and 1988 took exception to passages in the premier's government work report and criticized state officials for immorality, incompetence, and mistaken priorities. Deputies publicly admonished both powerful and faltering national leaders and questioned established policies as well as ones soon to be abandoned. Through publicity, if not binding sanctions, deputies mocked sloganeering, exposed dishonesty and waste, tempered overoptimism, encouraged the removal of officials, and hastened the reversal of unpopular policies. Speeches (and votes) usually served whichever leadership group was dominant, but at times, legislators joined with temporarily outmaneuvered elites to embarrass those on top.

These activities did not resemble legislative supervision in a parliamentary democracy, but in a weakly institutionalized system with a very strong executive, they served similar ends. Individuals outside the power structure subjected selected decision makers to scrutiny and sought explanations for official misconduct and ill-fated decisions.[39] Particularly when the leadership was divided, deputies, with the support of influential backers, seized popular positions or the moral high ground and used their mandate for supervision to grill factional or policy opponents. Their opponents defended their policies or admitted mistakes and compromised. At such moments, the NPC became an arena for leadership conflict and review of official reports became an occasion for sharp attacks. At times of leadership dissensus, deputies spoke for all sides and against party leaders as well as state officials, and pressures for accommodation built. The likely motive was power struggle and the hope was complete victory, but the outcome was restraint, a tendency to move toward the center, and unfavorable publicity for arbitrary or extreme behavior.[40]

Legislative supervision, of a more conventional sort, took place after a plenary session closed. Beginning in 1980, the NPCSC organized its members to carry out annual inspections of local units. Inspection tours lasted up to several weeks and covered a different topic each year, usually related to the implementation of laws or recent initiatives in economic or educational policy. Inspectors uncovered problems in a sector or region and gathered information on a cross-section of geographically dispersed and economically diverse units. By investigating "good, middle, and poor" and then submitting a statement on findings to the NPCSC, legislators provided central authorities with a flash report on policy implementation and advice concerning potential adjustments.[41]

Following complaints that deputies were "swarming like troops" (*dadui renma yiyong*) and "treating inspections like pleasure trips" (*youshan wanshui*), and that inspected units were lavishing deputies with banquets and gifts and ignoring investigators' requests for materials,[42] efforts were made to institutionalize and regularize deputy inspections. In 1985, NPC leaders revived the process of sending ordinary deputies as well as NPCSC members on inspection tours. In 1986 and 1987, the General Office of the NPCSC issued decisions that reduced the size of inspection groups and gave legislators the right to conduct unannounced spot checks.[43] In recent years, over 50% of deputies visited schools, factories, and government offices in all thirty provinces to investigate "questions pertaining to the state plan and budget and economic structural reform." One hundred twenty legislators toured more than 1,700 units in fifty-one counties and cities in Heilongjiang, and several hundred deputies investigated over 400 government departments in Beijing. Many joined State Council departments to inspect the implementation of the compulsory education law, the nationality autonomy law, the cultural relics protection law, the medicine management law, the food sanitation law, the administrative appeals law, and the environmental protection law. After returning, they wrote reports suggesting solutions to problems with fake and inferior pharmaceuticals, toxic food, and brand-name infringement.[44] Inspections channeled information to decision makers and were designed to help them refine their directives and ensure local compliance. Well-conducted tours aimed to uncover evasion, end it, and warn others of the consequences of continued resistance.

Until recently, inadequate staff support (essentially a small office responsible for visits and letters)[45] and unclear procedures hamstrung legislative efforts to conduct regular, institutional supervision of local people's congresses, the State Council, the Supreme Procurator, and the Supreme Court. A 60% increase (40 members) in the size of the seven specialized NPC committees and new NPCSC Proceedings Regulations eased the problem somewhat by drawing substantive experts into legislative work, liberalizing interpellation rules, and institutionalizing NPCSC joint meetings (*lianzu huiyi*) and small-group meetings (*fenzu huiyi*) as forms in which scrutiny of reports could take place and responsible officials from subordinate organs were required to appear.[46] The NPCSC's work outline for 1988–92 called for legislative committees to redouble their efforts to examine and revoke unconstitutional local statutes, State Council regulations, and autonomous region regulations. Toward this end, deputies in 1989 criticized errors in implementing the national economic plan (particularly unapproved price reforms and excessive growth in money supply and capital investment) and applauded a decision to submit the state plan and state budget to the NPC Finance and Economics Committee a month before each NPC session for review and plenary deliberation.[47]

Institutional supervision in the 1980s remained limited, however, due to uncertainty over how the NPC could supervise judicial and administrative organs without supervising party committees, and because state organs and provincial-level congresses did not report all legal decisions (especially ones jointly issued with the party) to the NPC General Office.[48] Nonetheless, highly circumscribed oversight began, as offenders were "reminded and criticized," several unconstitutional elections, appointments, and transfers at the local level were annulled, and a plan to merge three ministries into a new Ministry of Transportation was blocked.[49]

Institutional supervision increased in the 1980s, but it remained unlikely that the jurisdiction of the NPC (or any other state body) would be extended to party committees or be allowed to greatly impinge on party autonomy. Party cadres observed laws and the constitution, if they did, because of education, moral suasion, and party discipline – not because they were subject to external checks.[50] The advent of limited legal and constitutional supervision did not diminish the importance of party self-restraint. What it endeavored to do was to cement a framework of public rules regulating state officials and to work to ensure that all state administrative, judicial, and procuratorial decisions accorded with party policies.

Inspections and institutional supervision, like law making, involved the NPC with an array of state and party institutions, some of which had considerably more power than the legislature. The NPC's role thus was primarily that of a clearinghouse that gathered information on local officials and central departments that were not implementing policy and that defined and supervised handling of unconstitutional and illegal behavior. The anomaly of influence by a formerly powerless and still weak institution arose because of the legislature's powerful patron – the Communist Party. As Stephen White concluded at the end of a volume on socialist legislatures:

A vigorous legislative body may be quite "functional" to the rule of a single dominant party, providing it with a means of checking upon the performance of government and its conformity to party policy as well as a legal basis, through its representatives, for its intervention in affairs of state.[51]

The third major form of NPC supervision (i.e., that by deputies in small-group meetings) was less frequently found in other pre-Gorbachev socialist legislatures, where ordinary deputies had few opportunities to speak and elite disputes were rarely aired. In China, recurring power struggles and steps toward openness invigorated legislative debate and enabled deputies to palpably, albeit irregularly, restrain leadership discretion.

Representation

For Hanna Pitkin, representation entails regular, institutionalized responsiveness and can only be discussed in reference to the overall structure and functioning of a political system.[52] Seen in this light, the Chinese polity of the 1980s was profoundly unrepresentative. NPC deputies, as in the past, were elected indirectly by lower-level legislators, through a series of stepwise elections, and local, provincial, and central party committees controlled nomination lists and election committees. Ethnic, gender, party, and occupational quotas existed and some deputies were selected and sent by "higher levels."[53] Campaigning was prohibited in most elections, all candidates ran on the same program, and, until recently, all candidates ran unopposed. Most likely, overt coaching was rarely necessary in choosing national legislators as political savvy alone led deputies to elect reliable colleagues to the next higher congress.

Beyond the essentially undemocratic structure of the electoral system, Confucian assumptions of a "natural harmony of interests," and a Leninist conception of the political party encouraged national leaders to equate the party's interest with the people's interest, and justified shaping and manipulating public opinion and silencing inconvenient popular demands. Generations of party leaders took it upon themselves to define the "people's will" and responded to outside opinions as a matter of choice and tactics, not out of obligation or because they feared removal. The party learned from the masses, but, more importantly, it educated them to their own interests. When the people of their representatives were mistaken, the party was within its rights to ignore them. Ideology and decades of communist rule dictated that the people informed the leadership, they did not control it. Formal means of accountability were of secondary importance in a system that was innately elitist and (at times) intentionally unresponsive.

Yet, within this basically unrepresentative system, acts of response did

occur. Communist representation, though circumscribed and fragile, was
not an oxymoron. Despite continued leadership hostility toward institutionalized representation and electoral sanctions, and despite Deng's belief that
direct, popular elections for the NPC were at least fifty years away,[54] activities
by deputies on behalf of constituents, regions, social groups, and the whole
nation appeared throughout the 1980s and had an effect on political
outcomes.

Efforts by deputies to obtain advantages and benefits for particular constituents, that is, "service responsiveness," were infrequent in the NPC's
first generation.[55] This began to change after 1978. Consider the story of a
39-year-old factory worker and deputy from Beijing, Chen Lunfen. Chen
was well-known for pressing local bureaucrats to resolve constituents' problems and for persisting in the face of opposition. Before the 1985 Spring
Festival, several families in Chen's district had a dispute over housing allocations and there was much grumbling about food supplies. A group of
local residents went to the head of the district, who referred them to Chen.
Chen listened to their complaints, found them reasonable, and paid a call
on the district official responsible for food and housing. Upon her arrival,
this official, who had dealt with her many times before, glumly commented:
"Whenever you come to raise suggestions, we get criticized." Chen launched
into an impassioned speech about her constitutional duty to reflect the people's views and concluded with the words, "if you don't resolve these problems, who will?" The official acknowledged his responsibility and undertook
to improve supplies.[56] Though Chen's devotion to constituency work was
undoubtedly extraordinary, it was considered praiseworthy. If other deputies
followed her example, citizens might increasingly turn to their representatives to gain the attention of haughty or negligent bureaucrats who ignored
legitimate grievances.

Chen Lunfen was a model for her conscientious behavior, but also for her
restraint. She transmitted complaints and demanded attention, yet allowed
the concerned official to make the final decision. In recent years, this was
not always the case. NPC Law Committee Vice Chairman Zhang Youyu
reported:

Some deputies are dissatisfied with the status quo on work outside meetings . . . and
would like to do even more. They ask to intervene directly in government, judicial,
and procuratorial work, or to directly handle mass appeals, complaints, and
proposals.[57]

Zhang found this request "understandable" but "inappropriate" – based on
a mistaken view of an NPC deputy's authority. As Zhang and several other
NPC leaders pointed out, although individual deputies uncovered problems

between congresses, they did not have the authority to resolve disputes outside their jurisdiction. Deputies reflected the local situation and raised suggestions to state organs, but were forbidden to "meddle" in government and judicial work, for this would lead to delays and mistakes when deputy views were incorrect, incomplete, biased, based on a misunderstanding of the law, or when they were in conflict with each other. Deputies took part in the work of other systems (*xitong*) but did not supplant them. In no circumstances were they, in the name of representation, permitted to bypass state functionaries or to force them to act.[58]

In addition to conveying private demands, NPC deputies also spoke for regions or occupational groups and pressed for "allocation responsiveness," that is, redistribution of resources.[59] At recent plenary sessions, deputies championed disadvantaged sectors (e.g., heavy industry in 1980, backward and mountainous areas in 1985, inland provinces and grain-producing areas in 1988) as well as groups and sectors (e.g., entrepreneurs, exporters, education, light industry) that were prospering.[60] For the disadvantaged, they sought fairer treatment – that is, greater resources for heavy industry and inland areas and higher prices, greater agricultural investment, and more plentiful inputs for grain farmers.[61] For the advantaged, they requested additional benefits and unflinching policy implementation. Deputies rarely demanded immediate, specific changes (making allocation responsiveness difficult to measure), but instead they publicized and drew leadership attention to territorial and functional claims and attempted to nudge policies in a desired direction.

Yet, well-developed and efficacious allocation responsiveness, like service responsiveness, clashed with the traditional role of NPC deputies and with the traditional bias against representation of special interests. According to Zhang Youyu, deputies were free to do as they pleased in their speeches and votes as long as they "sought truth from facts" and served the public interest.[62] Serving the public interest, however, involved forsaking other special interests. The public or national interest was still regarded to be objective and in some respects deductive; it was not simply a confluence of private, regional, and functional interests. Deputies thus were expected not to overrepresent their own constituency or to construe their responsibilities narrowly in terms of maintaining ties with electors or avoiding recall:[63]

NPC deputies consider important matters that involve the whole people and the whole nation; although they are elected by a certain district and certain voters, they represent the people of the whole nation and must think about the interests of the nation, not just their own district. . . . Individual and partial interests follow the whole. Deputies must pay attention to their district but not fall prey to localism or departmentalism.[64]

Election districts existed primarily to select deputies and representatives were chosen for their maturity and wisdom in recognizing the nation's highest interests; what this meant was that, at times, deputies were expected to execute decisions that conflicted with their district's interests[65] and allocation responsiveness was permissible primarily to request increased funding or on controversial issues for which no national interest had been determined. Well-timed deputy pressure might affect decisions when changes were under consideration, but once a leadership position was established and announced, vigorous lobbying for subnational interests was regarded to be divisive, even unpatriotic. At the 1988 NPC, for example, deputies requested increased agricultural investment, improvements in intellectuals' living conditions, and attention to the development of backward, inland areas, but there was no real disagreement on establishing a new province, opening coastal regions to the outside world, resolving Tibetan unrest, or passing two constitutional amendments.[66] Quite clearly, the party was only willing to partially legitimize partial interests. Despite efforts to reconcile interests of different groups, service and allocation responsiveness continued to occupy a gray area between orthodoxy and "bourgeois liberalization."

More intriguing, and revolutionary if carried out, was the possibility that legislative representation might actually come to serve the purpose that was nominally intended for it – representation of the whole people. In the past, this formulation simply justified party domination of the legislature and ensured the definitional identity of the people's and the party's will. But in a time of reform and experimentation, with the leadership less certain of the national interest on every issue, this formerly empty concept gained new meaning. Perhaps deputies' comments on wages, prices, railway safety, pollution, and equity should be seen as efforts to reflect public opinion and to identify where the people's interest and party policy diverged. More generally, the NPC's institutional preference for moderation might be seen as representation of all those who feared rapid change and valued stability.[67] In this view, political jockeying was not the only motive for deputies to champion popular, minority opinions. Emboldened by the opportunity to reflect "true" public opinion, some deputies took the party at its word, stood up for the people as a whole, and presented policy options that they believed would further societal welfare.

A certain level of legislative responsiveness was functional to party rule, just as were sharing law making and legislative supervision. But representation involved more than rationalizing power and disappeared in the presence of manipulation. It is difficult to imagine effective representation of the whole when national leaders resorted to widespread repression, muzzling the press, forced political education, and mass jailings of dissidents. Representation may threaten established authorities, and without institutional machinery to ensure it, party forbearance and duty-bound deputies were crucial. For representation of the whole people to be both significant and representative, party leaders had to acknowledge that at times they were out of step with the "people's interest," and deputies had to voluntarily and with some accuracy gauge what the citizenry in a large and varied country wanted. It should be no surprise that meaningful representation in a fundamentally unrepresentative system was precarious, inexact, and occasional.

Regime support

By the late 1970s, the party had spent much of its political capital and it faced a population exhausted by decades of upheaval. In the wake of the Cultural Revolution, many Chinese were wary of mass movements, grand plans, and optimistic predictions. Mao's death had deprived the nation of its symbol of rectitude and the reversal of his policies left many people normatively adrift, unsure what socialism meant and unconvinced it had value. Without a charismatic leader of Mao's stature, or indeed any credible base of legitimation, a deep "crisis of faith, confidence, and trust" spread – especially among the young. Party leaders responded, in part, by freeing individual initiative and increasing production of consumer goods, that is, attacking cynicism with measures that quickly and dramatically improved living standards. For almost a decade, healthy growth rates brought the party good will and undoubtedly helped relegitimize it in the eyes of many. The party promised a better life and, for many, it delivered. But, in an era where leaders proclaimed "to get rich is glorious," ever-increasing prosperity became both an elevated expectation and a promise, and it was potentially destabilizing because the market reforms on which it was based tended to undermine the rationale for the party's monopoly of power.

Ultimately, dissatisfaction with party rule, high inflation, and austerity generated a wave of nationwide protest and opposition that severely diminished the party's ability to rule. Military suppression and bloodshed only heightened discontent, compounded legitimacy drain, and increased popular contempt for the leadership, while demonstrating the regime's inability to defuse destabilizing pressures. Furthermore, groups (e.g., students and ethnic minorities) still largely unaffected by economic reform but mobilized during the Cultural Revolution or the upheaval of 1989[68] may again return to the streets, thereby presenting the leadership with a most distasteful choice: tolerance and loss of control or suppression and further loss of legitimacy.

The use of the NPC from 1978 to 1989 suggested that the reformers at least dimly perceived these dangers and intended to establish party legitimacy on a sounder footing. Institutionalized legislative legitimacy was designed to supplement legitimacy based on performance and ideology. To deflect challenges and provide alternatives to autonomous, unsponsored participation, Deng and his associates were seeking to build up the NPC as a nonparty organization composed of socially prestigious individuals who expressed support for party policy and worked for its implementation. Through the NPC (as well as local congresses, consultative organs, and mass organizations), the party was seeking to integrate the polity and to organize it around the principle of one-party rule.[69]

In the 1950s and to a lesser extent in the early 1960s, NPC deputies engaged in activities designed to increase regime support. Change along this dimension was thus in many respects simply revival. What was new, however, was an increasingly subtle approach to building a united front, based on a revised understanding of who the main targets were and what was needed to draw them in.

After the 1957 Anti-Rightist Movement, the thrust of NPC mobilization efforts shifted from untrustworthy "bourgeois elements" back to the party's original constituency of young idealists and worker–peasant–soldiers. The united front narrowed and the party concentrated its appeal on people it had already converted. Special skills and education were regarded as less important than loyalty and commitment to socialism. At the NPC, political activists were revered as models and ordinary people were hailed as the backbone of the revolution.

Under Deng, for most of the 1980s, the strata of society that received the bulk of leadership attention showed unmistakable signs of change. The reformers' modernization program entailed cooperation with precisely those people who were discarded in the 1950s and who were most alienated from communist rule – intellectuals, scientists and technicians, risk takers.[70] Old-style model deputies were still elected to the NPC, but they were given much less attention than democratic party members and scholars, technical experts, and former "tails of capitalism." Industrialists, like Rong Yiren, were invited to serve in the NPCSC next to party bureaucrats, like Wang Hanbin. Minorities and nonparty individuals were given unprecedented representation in NPC committees. Through the legislature, the leadership was appealing to the agents of modernization and urging them "to accept party leadership voluntarily."[71] By allowing social and economic elites to meet with high cadres and to express their opinions, the party was seeking to show it could incorporate a range of interests – that the united front included all loyal citizens and that benefits were available to supporters of socialism and party rule.

The NPC was no longer expected to symbolize a perfectly united political community or unanimous acclaim for one-party dictatorship. Political integration was seen to be a process that required time and compromises. The party aimed first to win back the trust of the unconverted (through coopted colleagues and respected symbols of modernization) and then to gain active support. NPC deputies were portrayed to be mobilizers in a postmobilization regime, opinion leaders who had ties to key social groups. They were entrepreneurs, path-breaking scientists, and millionaire peasants – pioneers in reform who were willing to extol communist leadership and defend socialism. In the NPC, the party was attempting to create a corps of activists and propagandists – models of post-Maoist success who were willing to endorse one-party rule.

The leadership offered limited inclusion to soften demands and to preserve an illiberal state. Party prerogative was not affected in important ways. The party "does not bow to opinions that renounce our principles or diminish our alliance. Democratic consultation is a method that positively influences and attracts other members to the united front and induces them to accept party principles."[72] Through the NPC, the leadership was aiming to undercut mass-based pressures for change and to signal which societal demands it was willing to meet. In some years (1979, 1980, 1985, 1988), a democratic atmosphere was encouraged to defuse embarrassing events, to show party openness, and to mobilize consent. In other years (1982, 1983, 1986), a heavy-handed emphasis on unity was evident, with deputies primarily disseminating official policy. At all times, after decisions were announced, deputies were expected to gather feedback and to smooth implementation. In exchange for the right to question national leaders and articulate group interests, deputies were charged with penetrating society, building legitimacy among doubters, and contributing to system maintenance.[73] The NPC was becoming a more sophisticated tool of mobilization, directed at a more skeptical audience.

The contribution the NPC makes to future system maintenance remains to be seen. In the first few months after Zhao Ziyang's fall, hardline leaders stifled NPCSC debate, excluded legislators from a Standing Committee meeting, and emphasized stability, order, and unity at every opportunity. More recently, discussions of multiclass cooperation and whispers of legislative deliberation and contention have appeared, as national leaders recognized that regaining legitimacy and steering popular demands toward approved channels were urgent tasks. It is likely that Chinese leaders will again attempt to deflect pressures to liberalize partly by rebuilding the NPC's regime-support capacity; it is less likely that credible representatives of disaffected social, ethnic, and economic groups will take up this charge, or that their appeals will meet with the desired societal response.

China's post-Tiananmen leaders face unprecedented opposition from alienated intellectuals, students, and ordinary citizens. Self-limiting reforms designed to enhance legitimacy, rebuild the united front, and "perfect socialism" may not successfully defuse societal pressures. Should pressures mount without sufficient release, dissatisfaction with incremental changes, with the whole notion of top–down reform, could further diminish the political capability of central elites and endanger the continuation of party rule.

Systemic change and the NPC

The decade preceding Zhao Ziyang's removal will be remembered for tentative steps away from revolutionary socialism and a comprehensive reevaluation of Mao Zedong. From the economy to ideology, Maoist priorities and precepts were reviewed and were subject to frequent reinterpretation. Beginning in 1978, the reform coalition opened to the West, privatized agriculture, renounced mass mobilization, and demoted class struggle from its position as the principal contradiction. They rejected egalitarianism, removed class labels, and declared the "turbulent" and "large-scale" class struggles of the past "basically resolved."[74] When faced with opposition, they were more apt to see "nonantagonistic contradictions among the people" than "resurgent enemies." In politics as in economics, Deng and his associates showed signs of discarding the Maoist development strategy, along with the bifurcated view of society at its root, and of reexamining the foundations of communist rule.

The Chinese polity certainly evolved, but toward what and how fast? The NPC, a latecomer to Chinese politics and a fifth wheel in the Maoist era, served as an indicator and an embodiment of the direction and speed of political change. As a representative and mobilizational organ, the NPC reflected shifting approaches to party–society relations; as the nation's law maker and chief supervisory organ, it prospered or suffered with changing attitudes toward legalizing and regularizing party rule. Throughout its history, the NPC witnessed debates over China's economic and political development, and the content of these debates and extent of NPC participation in resolving them shed light on three alternatives to Mao's class-based, illiberal, charismatic style of rule – namely, inclusion, liberalization, and rationalization – alternatives that offered paths out of revolutionary socialism and options for the post-Mao leadership.

The decision to increase the system's inclusiveness was made in the late 1970s. China entered a stage where:

> the locus of political uncertainty has shifted from protecting the precarious values of a newly established revolutionary regime with charismatic qualities to insuring that the social products of its developmental efforts identify themselves in terms that are consistent with the party's ideological self-image and organizational definition.[75]

In this environment, recurring revolutions from above threatened rather than bolstered party legitimacy: surges of class struggle promised only to slow economic growth and to alienate the population.[76] Aware of these perils, party leaders, particularly Zhao Ziyang and Hu Yaobang, sought to cement their position by acknowledging the legitimacy of social (if not political) diversity, by relying on manipulation rather than domination and procedural and empirical modes of action rather than arbitrary and dogmatic modes. They aimed to head off a "plurality of political-ideological definitions" less by command and elite-directed disruption, and more by coaxing support from a variety of social forces.[77] As articulate audiences of the sort found in industrialized nations appeared (especially in China's cities), the reform coalition strove to manage the political consequences of social differentiation and to govern a nation whose modern history brimmed with popular and regional challenges to central authority. Until the explosion of popular protest in 1989 decisively tipped the balance toward repression, the leadership sought to navigate between perceived equally unpalatable alternatives of full responsiveness to citizen demands and hard-line suppression of legitimate impulses and grievances.

Although national leaders periodically identified and criticized enemies on the left or the right – alleged anarchists in 1979 and carriers of bourgeois liberalization and spiritual pollution in 1981, 1983, and 1987 – the Zhao-Hu leadership by and large resisted the impulse to redichotomize society and to reinvigorate societywide terror. Efforts to cleanse the body politic generally ended when reformers chose to coopt the impure rather than exclude them.[78] After years of insulation, party leaders appeared to be seeking reconciliation with newly trusted members of society and were willing to open the system somewhat to achieve it.

In the legislature, we saw this tilt toward inclusion in efforts to broaden the united front and to institutionalize legitimacy. Through the NPC, the party was displaying its readiness to bring professional groups, such as economists and scientists, into the decision-making process and its desire to win over fencesitters to reform-style socialism. The party granted former enemies status as valued and trustworthy members of society and encouraged them to speak out. The leadership allowed lively legislative debate in exchange for consent to one-party rule and active propagation of party policy. Confident that modernization was a widely held goal, party leaders aired their proposals in the NPC, asked for comments, and made concessions to gain support.

Although the political system exhibited increasing inclusiveness for much of the 1980s, it remained illiberal and authoritarian.[79] Recognition of the need to obtain information, advice, and support from key sectors of the population did not diminish the party's commitment to suppress dissent and maintain political power. Even before the Tiananmen suppression, the leadership denied individuals the right to form and join groups that expressed dissatisfaction with party rule: independent student and worker associations were forbidden and satellite parties, trade unions, and mass organizations were all expected to accept the leadership of the Communist Party and the party's political program.

Brief interludes of liberalization, whether initiated from above or below, typically ended quickly and did not legitimize collective political participation or create autonomous interest groups. The designations "antiparty" and "antisocialist" remained available for individuals deemed disloyal or for those accused of promoting "bourgeois liberalization" or fomenting "counterrevolution." Limited inclusion did not guarantee equal rights for all citizens or even equal rights for all members of upgraded social groups. Influence was granted only when it was broadly supportive and the price demanded for inclusion ranged from as little as skeptical tolerance of party leadership to as much as unflinching backing of all party policies and willingness to denounce one's associates and friends.

In the NPC, structural reforms, such as free elections, campaigning, longer sessions, and meaningful votes, were rejected several times and legislative checks and balances were discussed but never adopted.[80] The legislature, even at its strongest, was never more than a helpmate to the party, whose correct leadership was the "key" to successful NPC operation.[81] Legislators discussed improving one-party rule; very few suggested ending it. Criticism of party leaders and policies arose most often when leadership dissensus was high and out-of-favor elites desired publicity for their views. A legislator's ability to press minority positions or to agitate for individual, group, or sectional interests hinged on leadership sufferance, and party leaders continued to oppose meaningful political competition and institutionalized responsiveness.

Over time, popular pressures and experience with inclusiveness may encourage party leaders to consider reforms that entail formal restraint as well as informal consultation, and they may grant the NPC some autonomy from party control, but this is highly improbable without leadership turnover, structural reform, and a thorough reassessment of state–society relations. For now, reform means limited inclusion, and limited inclusion is a substitute for liberalization, not a sign of it.

The leadership's commitment to rationalization wavered throughout the 1980s. For much of the decade, in the face of considerable opposition, reformers sought to reduce the capriciousness that had characterized policy making under Mao. Deng and his lieutenants turned toward procedural regularity to promote modernization and to improve government efficiency. They restructured the organizational machinery of the party and state and reassigned responsibilities. They advocated such rationalizing principles as creation of a civil service, recruitment based on merit, increased specialization, procedural regularity, and reliance on chains of command. They appeared to be trying to build a political order free from Maoist excesses and aberrations – a state in which one-party rule was effective, stable, and predictable. Until the events of 1989, they were ostensibly striving to create a less personalized system that did not need the intervention of "party veterans" – a system in which authority flowed from the party rather than from personal prestige.

In the legislature, this rationalizing tendency was seen in clarified spheres of jurisdiction, emphasis on expertise in personnel decisions, and concern with internal efficiency. The leadership was beginning to use the NPC to oversee the bureaucracy and to ensure that party policies were standardized and carried out. The resulting system need not have been more decentralized or liberal, but it would have inhibited recourse to charisma and chiliastic ideology. Rationalization aimed to protect the nation from rule by fiat and to clear away layers of dogma that impeded creativity. It promised order and control along with flexibility and adaptation. It amounted to an attempt to limit discretion through organizational, intraelite means: to build a system in which power inhered in roles and party rule was secure.

Reconstituting the polity in this fashion, however, met enormous obstacles. Deng Xiaoping, the architect of the rationalization strategy and one of its earliest promoters, ultimately sacrificed a decade of gains to protect what he perceived to be the integrity of the revolution. In the weeks before the crackdown, party elders, who typically lacked formal position but maintained powerful factional networks, were again invited to join policy-making forums and to shape policy decisions. Although a measure of procedural normalcy returned in ensuing months, and laws continued to be drafted, and supervision of lower-level cadres promoted, it was once again clear that the handful of men who ruled China (and their protégés) were beyond the reach of fixed procedures, and intended to remain that way. Rationalization at the beginning of the 1990s affected only middle- and lower-level bureaucrats, and applied primarily to policy implementation rather than personnel; there was little evidence of procedural regularity and predictability when central authorities decided issues of national importance.

In May and June 1989, the limits of rationalization were graphically displayed when NPCSC petitioners and NPCSC Chairman Wan Li proved unable to convene a special session of the legislature to revoke martial law and instead gave their blessing to the Tiananmen suppression, the return of the party elders, and the official line on the "counterrevolutionary rebellion." Though China's leadership may continue to advocate improved legislative oversight and "perfecting the systems and procedures of democratic decision making and democratic supervision," at times of crisis, they showed themselves willing to sacrifice rationalization and to rely on party veterans "who have experienced many storms and have a thorough understanding of things."[82]

Reforms that increase inclusion and rationalization, though less far-reaching than liberalization, limit leadership discretion and make it more difficult to change policies. Efforts to separate party and state and to involve nonparty forces in policy making can easily run aground if they interfere with elite preferences, factional struggles, or succession politics. Indirect channels of control are less certain than direct ones; reforms threaten to give power to those who oppose reform – as well as to those who want more reform than incumbent leaders condone. If political reform (let alone liberalization) is to proceed, leaders must be willing to accept the consequences of consultation and procedural regularity: namely, delay, compromise, and occasional opposition. They must be willing to stand firm against hastiness and arbitrariness, even when they are the ones who wish to act quickly and decisively. Deng and his followers have renounced many of Mao's policies; now they are asked to renounce his methods. To repudiate a long history of authoritarianism and heroic, personal rule is a daunting challenge – and the party's success in meeting this challenge will determine how far China's reforms go, how stable party rule is, and what role the NPC is allowed to play.

Abbreviations

AAPSS   *Annals of the Academy of Political and Social Science*
CB   *Current Background*
CCP   Chinese Communist Party
CNA   *China News Analysis*
CPPCC   Chinese People's Political Consultative Conference
CR:PSM   *China Report: Political, Sociological, and Military Affairs*
CR:RF   *China Report: Red Flag*
FBIS   *Foreign Broadcast Information Service, Daily Report: China*
NPC   National People's Congress
NPCSC   Standing Committee of the National People's Congress
PLA   People's Liberation Army
SCMP   *Survey of China Mainland Press*
SWB   *Summary of World Broadcasts, Part III: The Far East*

Notes

Chapter 1. Chinese legislatures and political change

1. Xu Chongde and He Huahui, "Renmin daibiao dahui zhidu de xin fazhan" [New developments of the people's congress system], *Zhengzhi yu Falü*, no. 1 (June 1982): 29.

2. Xu Chongde and He Huahui, *Xianfa yu Minzhu Zhidu* [The Constitution and Democratic System] (Hubei: Hubei Renmin Chubanshe, 1982), pp. 59–60; Wang Xiangming, *Xianfa Ruogan Lilun Wenti de Yanjiu* [Research on Certain Theoretical Questions on Constitutions] (Beijing: Zhongguo Renmin Daxue Chubanshe, 1983), p. 119; Wu Jialin, "Zenyang fahui quanguo renda zuowei zuigao guojia quanli jiguan de zuoyong" [How to bring into play the NPC as the highest organ of state power], *Xinhua Wenzhai*, no. 12 (December 1980): 48, from *Guangming Ribao*, October 30, 1980.

3. For informative treatments of the components and evolution of political reform, see Harry Harding, *China's Second Revolution* (Washington, D.C.: Brookings Institution, 1987), pp. 40–95, 172–236; Benedict Stavis, *China's Political Reforms* (New York: Praeger, 1988); Victor C. Falkenheim, "The Limits of Political Reform," *Current History* 86 (September 1987): 261–5, 279–81; Brantly Womack, "Modernization and Democratic Reform in China," *The Journal of Asian Studies* 44 (May 1984): 417–39; Victor C. Falkenheim, "Political Reform in China," *Current History* 81 (September 1982): 259–63, 280–1. Over the years, western scholars have produced only a handful of articles on the NPC, with most tending toward narrowly drawn constitutional studies or straightforward accounts of events at an individual session. For representative examples, see Donald Gasper, "The Chinese National People's Congress," in *Communist Legislatures in Comparative Perspective*, eds. Daniel Nelson and Stephen White (London: Macmillan Press, 1982), pp. 160–90; George T. Yu, "The 1962 and 1963 Sessions of the National People's Congress of Communist China," *Asian Survey* 4 (August 1964): 981–90. A thoughtful analysis of four NPC sessions can be found in Dorothy J. Solinger, "The Fifth National People's Congress and the Process of Policy-Making: Reform, Readjustment and Opposition," *Asian Survey* 22 (December 1982): 1238–75. See also, Ta-kuang Chang, "The Making of the Chinese Bankruptcy Law: A Study in the Chinese Legislative Practice," *Harvard International Law Journal* 28:2 (Spring 1987): 333–72. A description of the Chinese state structure is available in Lowell Dittmer, "The Formal Structure of Central Chinese Political Institutions," in *Organizational Behavior in Chinese Society*, eds. Sidney L. Greenblatt, Richard W. Wilson, and Amy Auerbacher Wilson (New York: Praeger, 1981), pp. 47–76.

4. For the seminal discussion of political change, see Samuel P. Huntington, "The

Change to Change," *Comparative Politics* 3 (April 1971): 283–322. On the lack of attention by students of systemic political change to the role and significance of legislatures, see Chong Lim Kim, Joel D. Barkan, Ilter Turan, and Malcolm E. Jewell, *The Legislative Connection: The Politics of Representation in Kenya, Korea, and Turkey* (Durham, NC: Duke University Press, 1984), p. 3.

5. For a similar argument, see Daniel N. Nelson, "Editor's Introduction: Communist Legislatures and Communist Politics," *Legislative Studies Quarterly* 5 (May 1980): 165–7.

6. Peng Zhen, the NPC Chairman from 1983–8, for example, has long favored rationalizing the polity. See Pitman Potter, "Peng Zhen: Evolving Views on Party Organization and Law," in *China's Establishment Intellectuals*, eds. Carol Lee Hamrin and Timothy Cheek (Armonk, NY: M. E. Sharpe, 1986), pp. 21–50. Recent efforts to define the political structure and restore constitutional and legal order described in Womack, pp. 422–4, are also expressions of this impulse, as are efforts to regularize the role of the state, to restaff party and state bureaucracies, to redefine organizational roles and relationships, and to arrange the succession. See Harding, pp. 172–91, 202–36.

7. United-front policy involves the "wavering allies" of communist rule – patriotic intellectuals, bureaucrats, professional and technical workers, merchants and industrialists, and overseas Chinese – who must be united with to further the revolution but struggled against to transform their bourgeois character. For a discussion of the united front, see James R. Townsend, *Political Participation in Communist China* (Berkeley: University of California Press, 1967), pp. 146–8.

8. The concept of inclusion is defined and applied in Kenneth Jowitt, "Inclusion and Mobilization in European Leninist Regimes," *World Politics* 28 (October 1975): 69–96. For applications to China, see Richard Baum, "Modernization and Legal Reform in Post-Mao China: The Rebirth of Socialist Legality," *Studies in Comparative Communism* 19 (Summer 1986): 94–5; Hsin-chi Kuan, "New Departures in China's Constitution," *Studies in Comparative Communism* 17 (Spring 1984): 53–68; Thomas B. Gold, "After Comradeship: Personal Relations in China Since the Cultural Revolution," *China Quarterly*, no. 104 (December 1985): 674–5.

9. Deng, as Paul Cohen has provocatively argued, may best be seen as a socially conservative, authoritarian reformer in the tradition of the Dowager Empress, Yuan Shikai, and Chiang Kaishek – a reformer above all committed to order, stability, and central power and one with "great antipathy" toward Maoist mass mobilization as well as pluralism and power sharing. Paul A. Cohen, "The Post-Mao Reforms in Historical Perspective," *Journal of Asian Studies* 47 (August 1988): 518–40.

10. On the "limited repertoire of social roles and values" available to individuals, the costs and difficulty of change, and the importance of context, see Stephen D. Krasner, "Sovereignty: An Institutionalist Approach," *Comparative Political Studies* 21 (April 1988): 73–4; Stephen D. Krasner, "Approaches to the State: Alternative Conceptions and Historical Dynamics," *Comparative Politics* 16 (January 1984): 240.

11. Nelson W. Polsby, "Legislatures," in *Handbook of Political Science, Vol. 5*, eds. Fred I. Greenstein and Nelson W. Polsby (Reading, MA: Addison-Wesley, 1975), pp. 258–9.

12. William A. Welsh, "The Status of Research on Representative Institutions in Eastern Europe," *Legislative Studies Quarterly* 5 (May 1980): 302.

13. Michel Crozier, *The Bureaucratic Phenomenon* (Chicago: The University of Chicago Press, 1964), pp. 294–5.

14. Crozier, p. 295.

15. For a discussion of the importance of "nonissues," see Steven Lukes, *Power – A Radical View* (London: Macmillan Press, 1974), pp. 21–55. On the lack of at-

tention to history in legislative research, a leading specialist has written: "Historical research as well as interpretations and reinterpretations of historical works force us to ask why institutions are what they are, but this is a question rarely confronted in current empirical research." Heinz Eulau, "Introduction: Legislative Research in Historical Perspective," in *Handbook of Legislative Research*, eds. Gerhard Loewenberg, Samuel C. Patterson, and Malcolm E. Jewell (Cambridge, MA: Harvard University Press, 1985), p. 7.

16. The idea that history follows a branching pattern and that once a fork is chosen it is difficult to return to a rejected path is a central theme in new institutional and statist approaches to politics. See Krasner, "Approaches to the State," p. 225. It should also be noted that some nonstatist, behavioral social scientists also use the branching model of historical development. See Gabriel Almond, "The Return to the State," *American Political Science Review* 82 (September 1988): 871.

17. For a general statement on the inefficiencies of history and the possibility that a unique equilibrium does not exist or is suboptimal, see James G. March and Johan P. Olsen, "The New Institutionalism: Organizational Factors in Political Life," *American Political Science Review* 78 (September 1984): 737, 740–3.

18. On the value of treating legislative processes as independent variables, as well as dependent variables, see Kim et al., p. 4; March and Olsen, p. 739, have also written: "Political institutions affect the distribution of resources, which in turn affects the power of political actors, and thereby affects political institutions."

19. On institutions outliving the functional needs that created them, see Krasner, "Approaches to the State," p. 240.

Chapter 2. Origins of the NPC

1. On the relationship between crisis and institutional change, see Stephen Skowronek, *Building a New American State* (Cambridge: Cambridge University Press, 1982); Stephen D. Krasner, "Approaches to the State," *Comparative Politics* 16 (January 1984): 234–8.

2. For discussions of the Republican era as a contribution, rather than an interruption, to state building, see Robert E. Bedeski, *State-Building in Modern China: The Kuomintang in the Prewar Period*, China Research Monograph, No. 18 (Berkeley: Berkeley Center for Chinese Studies, 1981), pp. 169–71; Paul A. Cohen, "The Post-Mao Reforms in Historical Perspective," *The Journal of Asian Studies* 47 (August 1988): 525.

3. James E. Sheridan, *China in Disintegration* (New York: The Free Press, 1975), p. 110.

4. Cited in Andrew J. Nathan, *Peking Politics, 1918–1923* (Berkeley: University of California Press, 1976), p. 4.

5. John H. Fincher, *Chinese Democracy: The Self-Government Movement in Local, Provincial and National Politics 1905–1914* (London: Croon Helm, 1981), p. 67.

6. Fincher, p. 60.

7. Cited in Nathan, p. 4.

8. Fincher, p. 80.

9. William L. Tung, *The Political Institutions of Modern China* (The Hague, Netherlands: Martinus Nijhoff, 1964), p. 7; Cohen, p. 525.

10. Geng Yunzhi, "The Movement for a Parliament in the Last Years of the Qing Dynasty," *Social Sciences in China* 1 (September 1980): 117.

11. Sheridan, p. 113.

12. Geng, pp. 123–4.

13. Fincher, pp. 16, 175.
14. See Tung, p. 8.
15. Ernest P. Young, *The Presidency of Yuan Shih-k'ai* (Ann Arbor: University of Michigan Press, 1977), pp. 76–81.
16. The analysis here follows Edward Friedman, *Backward Toward Revolution* (Berkeley: University of California Press, 1974), pp. 29–34.
17. Nathan, p. 25.
18. Nathan, pp. 68–9, 25–6. On Yuan's actions, see Young, pp. 122–3.
19. Argument follows Friedman, pp. 46–69, 167–8, 174, 178.
20. Nathan, p. 220.
21. Fincher, p. 252.
22. Fincher, pp. 15–16, 22–3, 270, passim.
23. Nathan, pp. 2, 58, 224.
24. Ch'ien Tuan-sheng [Qian Duansheng], *The Government and Politics of China* (Cambridge, MA: Harvard University Press, 1950), p. 70.
25. Cited in Friedman, p. 46.
26. Cited in Stuart R. Schram, "Introduction: The Cultural Revolution in Historical Perspective," in *Authority, Participation and Cultural Change in China*, ed. Stuart R. Schram (Cambridge, England: Cambridge University Press, 1973), p. 4.
27. Friedman, p. 210.
28. On this theme, see Joseph Fewsmith, *Party, State and Local Elites in Republican China* (Honolulu: University of Hawaii Press, 1985), pp. 172–5; Lloyd E. Eastman, *The Abortive Revolution* (Cambridge, MA: Harvard University Press, 1974), p. 157.
29. Ch'ien Tuan-sheng (Qian Duansheng), *The Government and Politics of China*, p. 114.
30. "Yuan" is an untranslatable word that roughly means "public body" or "council." The five yuans included the Executive Yuan, the Legislative Yuan, the Judicial Yuan, the Examination Yuan, and the Control Yuan.
31. Ch'ien Tuan-sheng (Qian Duansheng), p. 152.
32. Hung-mao Tien, *Government and Politics of Kuomintang China 1927–1937* (Stanford: Stanford University Press, 1972), p. 18.
33. Ch'ien Tuan-sheng (Qian Duansheng), pp. 192, 196, 198.
34. Ch'ien Tuan-sheng (Qian Duansheng), pp. 281, 288–92.
35. See Ch'ien Tuan-sheng (Qian Duansheng), pp. 191–205, 278–95. Many of his criticisms of Guomindang representative and legislative institutions could have been repeated twenty years later about the NPC.
36. Stuart Schram reminds us that this conflict should not be overdrawn: Mao may well have favored orthodox revolutionary tactics after four years of making revolution in one of the most remote backwaters of China. Though Schram denies an "abyss" between Mao and the Returned Students, he still sees "a very clear psychological and political line" dividing the two camps. See Stuart R. Schram, "The Chinese Soviet Republic: Some Introductory Reflections," in *The Legal System of the Chinese Soviet Republic 1931–1934*, ed. W. E. Butler (Dobbs Ferry, NY: Transnational Publishers, 1983), pp. 7–11.
37. Ilpyong J. Kim, *The Politics of Chinese Communism: Kiangsi Under the Soviets* (Berkeley: University of California Press, 1973), pp. 55–6, 87–8.
38. Schram, "The Chinese Soviet Republic: Some Introductory Reflections," p. 8.
39. William B. Simons, "Reflections on State Administration in the Chinese Soviet Republic and the Soviet Union," in *The Legal System of the Chinese Soviet Republic 1931–1934*, ed. W. E. Butler (Dobbs Ferry, NY: Transnational Publishers, 1983), p. 48. The 1934 constitution did not reflect Mao's belief in the equality of peasants

and industrial workers. See Kim, p. 6. One reason may be that Mao's influence declined from 1932 to 1934; first he lost leadership of the Red Army, then the chairmanship of the Council of People's Commissars. By 1934, even if he had contrary ideas, he probably had no choice but to accept Russian legal constructions and inegalitarian representative norms. On Mao's declining influence, see Schram, "The Chinese Soviet Republic: Some Introductory Reflections," pp. 7, 18; Derek J. Waller, *The Kiangsi Soviet Republic: Mao and the National Congresses of 1931 and 1934*, China Research Monograph, No. 10 (Berkeley: University of California Center for Chinese Studies, 1973), passim. Of course, after 1949, when Mao's power far exceeded that of any other leader, peasants continued to receive reduced representation in the NPC. Perhaps Marxist doctrine, rather than Mao's reduced influence, best explains the unequal weighting of peasants and workers.

40. Waller, pp. 27, 50, 86, 41.

41. According to John Hazard, the First Congress assembled approximately 300 deputies and 300 observers. The Second Congress brought together some 700 deputies and 1,500 observers. John N. Hazard, "The Experience with Constitutionalism," in *The Legal System of the Chinese Soviet Republic 1931–1934*, ed. W. E. Butler (Dobbs Ferry, NY: Transnational Publishers, 1983), p. 37. Derek Waller writes that 610 delegates attended the First Congress and 693 full delegates, 83 alternates, and 1,500 observers attended the Second Congress. Waller, pp. 30, 85.

42. See Kim, pp. 68–9.

43. Waller, p. 114. Argument follows pp. 25–7, 52, 98–109.

44. On mobilizing peasants, see Kim, pp. 69, 188, 201–2; Waller, p. 113.

45. Mao Zedong, "On New Democracy," in *Selected Works of Mao Tse-tung*, vol. 2 (Peking: Foreign Languages Press, 1975), p. 351.

46. Mao Zedong, "On New Democracy," p. 352.

47. Mao Zedong, "On Coalition Government," in *Selected Works of Mao Tse-tung*, vol. 3 (Peking: Foreign Languages Press, 1967), pp. 234, 270.

48. This paragraph follows Mark Selden, *The Yenan Way in Revolutionary China* (Cambridge, MA: Harvard University Press, 1971), pp. 127–35, 148, 161–71. The quotation is found on page 135.

49. Mao Zedong, "On Coalition Government," p. 235.

50. Mao Zedong, "On the People's Democratic Dictatorship," in *Selected Readings from the Works of Mao Tse-tung* (Peking: Foreign Languages Press, 1971), pp. 379–80, 386.

51. As early as a December 1947 central work conference, Mao remarked that people's congresses at all levels would soon be established. In August 1948, the North China Provisional People's Congress first met and was said to be "the prelude and embryo of the National People's Congress." See Liu Tingxiao and Ma Hongru, "Valuable Spiritual Wealth of the Party and the People – Studying Comrade Dong Biwu's Political and Legal Thinking," *China Report: Red Flag* 16 (July 29, 1985): 15, from *Hongqi*, no. 11 (June 1, 1985): 9–12.

52. Maurice Meisner, *Mao's China* (New York: The Free Press, 1977), p. 70.

53. For discussions of what the NPC stands for ideologically, the principle of "combining legislation and administration" and their relationship to the Paris Commune, early Soviet experience, and the first twenty-five years of the NPC, see Xiong Xiyuan, "Renmin daibiao dahui shi yixing heyi de guojia quanli jiguan" [The NPC is a state power organ that combines legislation with discussion], *Renwen Kexue Zazhi (Yunnan Daxue)*, no. 1 (January 1958): 19–28; Shi Xiaozhong, "Jianquan guojia zhengzhi zhidu wenti dangyi" [Current discussion on perfecting the nation's political system], *Minzhu yu Fazhi*, no. 10 (October 1981): 6–7; Wu Jialin, "Yixing heyi" [Combination of legislative and executive powers], in *Zhongguo Dabai Kequan Shu*

(Faxue), ed. Zhang Youyu (Beijing: Zhongguo Dabai Kequan Shu Chubanshe, 1984), pp. 702–3. Xiong Xiyuan, p. 19, refers to bourgeois assemblies as "centers of idle talk." On the origins of the Russian soviets, see Peter Vanneman, *The Supreme Soviet: Politics and the Legislative Process in the Soviet Political System* (Durham, NC: Duke University Press, 1977), pp. 22–6. For an excellent selection of writings that underpin these arguments, see Karl Marx, Friedrich Engels, and V. I. Lenin, *On Democracy-Bourgeois and Socialist* (Moscow: Progress Publishers, 1988).

54. This analogy, of course, should not be overstated. Much developed in Jiangxi was carried over to Yanan and certain elements of the Jiangxi Congresses (e.g., contested elections) were not found in the NPC.

55. Dong Biwu, *Dong Biwu Xuanji* [The Selected Works of Dong Biwu] (Beijing: Renmin Chubanshe, 1985), p. 58.

Chapter 3. Development, doubts, and decline

1. Translations of the 1954 constitution and NPC organic law can be found in National People's Congress of the People's Republic of China, *Documents of the First Session of the First National People's Congress of the People's Republic of China* (Peking: Foreign Languages Press, 1955). For a discussion of the "striking resemblance" of the 1954 Chinese constitution to the 1936 Soviet constitution, see Hari Mohain Jain, "Some Aspects of the Chinese Constitution," *India Quarterly* 14 (October–December 1958): 373–9; Shao-chuan Leng and Hungdah Chiu, *Criminal Justice in Post-Mao China* (Albany, NY: State University of New York Press, 1985), pp. 13–14.

2. Franklin W. Houn, "Communist China's New Constitution," *Western Political Quarterly* 8 (June 1955): 213.

3. For early and prominent support of this position, see Dong Biwu, "Zai junshi jianchayuan jianchazhang, junshi fayuanzhang huiyishang de jianghua" [Speech at the congress of chief military procurators and chief military justices], March 18, 1957, in *Dong Biwu Xuanji* [The Selected Works of Dong Biwu] (Beijing: Renmin Chubanshe, 1985), pp. 447–62.

4. For the status of the debate on the relationship of policy to law, see You Junyi, "Jinnian lai faxuejie dui ruogan zhongda lilun wenti de zhengyi" [Recent controversies in jurisprudence circles over certain theoretical questions], *Faxue*, no. 11 (November 1985): 6–7.

5. The communist view of law is drawn from Leng and Chiu, pp. 9–10; John N. Hazard, *Communists and Their Law* (Chicago: University of Chicago Press, 1969), pp. 69–72; Arthur Stahnke, "The Background and Evolution of Party Policy on the Drafting of Legal Codes in Communist China," *American Journal of Comparative Law* 15 (1967): 508–10; Shao-chuan Leng, "The Role of Law in the People's Republic of China as Reflecting Mao Tse-tung's Influence," *Journal of Criminal Law and Criminology* 68 (September 1977): 366.

6. For a thorough discussion of antilaw views, see Li Qi, "Strive to Strengthen the People's Democratic Legislative System of China," *SCMP* 1425 (December 6, 1956): 3–12, from *Renmin Ribao*, November 6, 1956.

7. Interview (April 3, 1989) with a leading member of the NPCSC General Office, who had served in a junior position in the General Office in the 1950s. See also, Quanguo Renda Changweihui Bangongting Yanjiushi, *Quanguo Renda Jiqi Changweihui Dashiji* [A Chronology of the NPC and its Standing Committee] (Beijing: Falü Chubanshe, 1987), pp. 9, 49–50.

8. George Ginsburgs, "Theory and Practice of Parliamentary Procedure in Com-

munist China: Organizational and Institutional Principles," *University of Toronto Law Journal* 15 (1) (1963): 39.

9. The 1954 constitution established three layers of regional congresses below the NPC, with powers and functions in their own jurisdiction that paralleled those of the NPC over the nation. Local people's congresses (LPCs), however, were structurally weaker than the NPC. Basic level, county, and provincial congresses lacked standing organs and formal law-making powers. LPCs existed to ensure that laws were observed and executed, to examine and approve local budgets and plans, and to elect the next higher-level people's congress. LPCs are not systematically considered in this study, and only enter the story when their activities affect those of the NPC.

10. *Renmin Shouce 1955* (Peking: Da Gongbaoshe, 1955), p. 219, gives the following information on the 39 proposals: 8 were on water conservancy, 7 on industry and mining, 7 on labor issues, 7 on medicine and sanitation, 4 on transportation, 3 on agriculture, and 3 on culture and education.

11. "A Milestone in the Historical Development of the People's Republic of China," *SCMP* 899 (September 30, 1954): 1, from *Renmin Ribao*, September 29, 1954.

12. For an example, see Wu Jialin, "Some Questions Concerning Socialist Democracy," *Beijing Review* 22 (June 15, 1979): 11–12.

13. Zeng Lin, "Renmin daibiao dahui zhidu shi wo guojia de jiben zhidu" [The people's congress system is our country's fundamental system], *Faxue Yanjiu*, no. 4 (August 1980): 2.

14. Chen Shouyi, Liu Shengping, and Zhao Zhenjiang, "Thirty Years of the Building up of Our Country's Legal System," *CR.PSM* 70 (March 25, 1980): 26–7, from *Faxue Yanjiu*, no. 4 (October 1979).

15. Kenneth Lieberthal, *A Research Guide to Central Party and Government Meetings in China 1949–1975* (White Plains, NY: International Arts and Science Press, 1976), p. 306. Quanguo Renda Changweihui Bangongting Yanjiushi, pp. 7, 35–111. The NPCSC, at its own discretion, also convened "expanded meetings" (*kuoda huiyi*) "to listen to investigation reports on government ministries and give ministry officials an opportunity to reply to questions." The frequency of these meetings is not known, though one source points to "over 10" in the first four months of 1957. See Xiong Xiyuan, "Renmin daibiao dahui shi yixing heyi de guojia quanli jiguan" [The NPC is a state power organ that combines legislation with discussion], *Renwen Kexue Zazhi (Yunnan Daxue)*, no. 1 (January 1958): 21.

16. "The Structure of the State in China," *CNA* 107 (November 4, 1955): 6. An explanation of this decision can be found in Wu Daying et al., *Zhongguo Shehuizhuyi Lifa Wenti* [Problems in Chinese Socialist Legislation] (Beijing: Qunzhong Chubanshe, 1984), p. 45.

17. Wu Kejian, "Renmin daibiao de guancha gongzuo" [Inspection work of people's deputies], in *Renmin Shouce 1957* (Peking: Da Gongbaoshe, 1957), pp. 309–10.

18. See Ginsburgs, pp. 4–5, 18–19. Chinese sources explain that NPC deputies receive no compensation because they are not high officials, but servants of the people (*qinwuyuan*); moreover, while fulfilling official duties, they continue to draw a salary from their original unit. Xu Chongde and Pi Chunxie, *Xuanju Zhidu Wenda* [Questions and Answers on the Electoral System] (Beijing: Qunzhong Chubanshe, 1982), p. 143. In interviews with Wang Shuwen, March 17, 1989, and with a leading member of the NPCSC Legislative Affairs Commission, April 3, 1989, it was explained that even NPCSC members engaged in full-time legislative work for many years continue to receive their salary (and appropriate raises) from their home unit.

19. Wu Kejian, pp. 309–10.

20. See Sun Tianfu, "Tantan shicha gongzuo zhong de jige wenti" [Discussing several problems in inspection work], *Guangming Ribao*, April 1, 1957, p. 3.

21. Wu Kejian, p. 309. Sun Tianfu, p. 3, also writes that after inspections, "deputies better reflected the masses' will in the NPC and made better proposals on government work." The importance of inspection tours (past and present) in giving deputies "grounds" (*yiju*) to speak at a session was emphasized by a leading member of the NPCSC General Office in an interview conducted April 3, 1989.

22. Mu Fu, "Zhongguo renda de zhiheng zuoyong" [The NPC's system-balancing role], *Qishi Niandai*, no. 162 (July 1983): 23.

23. Zhang Yanjie, "Quanguo renmin daibiao dahui shouquan changwu weiyuanhui zhiding danxing fagui shi hefa" [The NPC's authorization of the NPCSC to enact special regulations is legal], *Faxue*, no. 3 (March 1958): 16.

24. In an interview (March 17, 1989), Professor Wang Shuwen, a member of the NPC Law Committee and vice president of the China Law Society, emphasized that these provisions constituted a major break with Soviet practices and demonstrated China's attention to its own particular conditions and national characteristics. See also Sun Chenggu, *Lifa Quan yu Lifa Chengxu* [Legislative Power and Legislative Procedures] (Beijing: Renmin Chubanshe, 1983), p. 101.

25. Ginsburgs, p. 34.

26. Gu Angran, "Fensui youpai fenzi gongji quanguo renmin daibiao dahui shi 'xingshi' de miulun" [On denouncing the absurd statement of the rightist elements that the NPC is only a "formality"], *Zhengfa Yanjiu*, no. 6 (December 1957): 33.

27. For Zhou's report, see *Renmin Shouce 1956* (Peking: Da Gongbaoshe, 1956), p. 242.

28. "July 1955 Session of the First National People's Congress," *CB* 346 (August 18, 1955): 1, 15–16. At the 1955 NPC, deputies made 214 legislative proposals, with 33% on industry and transportation; 21% on agriculture, forestry, and water conservancy; 21% on culture, education, and health; 18% on political-legal matters; and 7% on finance and trade. From *Renmin Shouce 1956*, p. 240.

29. Chen Yun, "On Commercial Work and Industrial–Commercial Relations," and Zhou Enlai, "Premier Zhou Enlai on Government Work at Concluding Session of NPC, June 30," both in *CB* 398 (July 12, 1956): 1–10.

30. For an insightful and timely analysis of Mao's rejection of Soviet interpretations of the dictatorship of the proletariat, see Benjamin Schwartz's 1957 essay "Communist Ideology and the Sino–Soviet Alliance," most readily available in his *Communism in China: Ideology in Flux*, (Cambridge, MA: Harvard University Press, 1968), pp. 66–98.

31. Gu Angran, *Zhengfa Yanjiu*, no. 6 (December 1957): 33.

32. For example, in 1955 and 1956, the NPC and NPCSC discussed the "Sufan" (Elimination of Counterrevolutionaries) policy, with some deputies arguing that a mass movement had not been an appropriate form to carry it out. This did not change what had happened, but perhaps made it easier to swallow. See Gu Angran, *Zhengfa Yanjiu*, no. 6 (December 1957): 33.

33. Mu Fu, p. 23.

34. Central Committee of Communist Party of China, *Eighth National Congress of the Communist Party of China (Documents)* (hereafter Eighth Congress Documents) (Peking: Foreign Languages Press, 1956; reprint 1981), p. 133.

35. Dong Biwu, "Jinyibu jiaqiang renmin minzhu fazhi, baozhang shehuizhuyi jianshe shiye" [Further strengthen the people's democratic legal system and ensure socialist construction], in *Dong Biwu Lun Shehuizhuyi Minzhu he Fazhi* (Beijing: Renmin Chubanshe, 1979), p. 132.

36. From 1954–6, NPC committees met briefly and infrequently. Although the Nationalities Committee offered 89 corrections to a bill on regional autonomy and 239 comments on policy, the Budget Committee came and went with each NPC session, and the two permanent committees (Nationalities and Bills) had little regular or lasting impact on policies. On early committee activities, see Donald Gasper, "The Chinese National People's Congress," in *Communist Legislatures in Comparative Perspective*, eds. Daniel Nelson and Stephen White (London: Macmillan Press, 1982), pp. 178–81.

37. Roderick MacFarquhar, *The Origins of the Cultural Revolution, Vol. 1: Contradictions Among the People* (hereafter MacFarquhar, 1974) (New York: Columbia University Press, 1974), p. 115; Quanguo Renda Changweihui Bangongting Yanjiushi, p. 10.

38. Harry Harding, *Organizing China* (Stanford, CA: Stanford University Press, 1981), p. 122.

39. Zhang's remark echoed and enlarged on Liu Shaoqi's November 1956 description of the CPPCC as "in a sense" the upper house of the NPC.

40. See MacFarquhar, 1974, pp. 274–7; Harding, pp. 124–5.

41. Roderick MacFarquhar, *The Hundred Flowers Campaign and the Chinese Intellectuals* (hereafter MacFarquhar, 1960) (New York: Praeger, 1960), pp. 264–5.

42. Eighth Congress Documents, p. 196.

43. The Guomindang Revolutionary Committee is one of the seven major "democratic parties," and is comprised mainly of individuals who shifted their support from the Guomindang to the communists before 1949. In the 1950s, the democratic parties included many of the most prominent noncommunists who remained in China after communist victory. The following remarks by Shao Lizi, Wang Kunlun, Huang Shaohong, and Tan Tiwu are excerpted from MacFarquhar, 1960, pp. 41–3, 46–7, 108–18, 226–7.

44. See "The Ministries from Within," *CNA* 184 (June 7, 1957): 6. Wang Jixin reportedly praised Wu's comments as "well said" and "sound." See Zhang Limen, "Buxu youpai fenzi Wang Jixin xiang renmin minzhu fazhi jingong" [Rightist Wang Jixin's attack on the people's democratic legal system is not allowed], *Zhengfa Yanjiu*, no. 2 (April 1958): 69. For readings of the constitution that justify delegation of partial law-making powers and NPCSC involvement in territorial-administrative changes, see Zhang Yanjie, pp. 15–16, 25; Gu Angran and Li Jianfei, "Bochi Wu Jialin weixie zuigao guojia quanli jiguan weifa fazhi de miulun" [Refuting Wu Jialin's slanderous falsehood that the highest state organs violated the law], *Renmin Ribao*, September 24, 1957, p. 3.

45. The charges and what amounted to an official response can be found in a flood of articles published in late 1957 and 1958. For representative examples, see Li Youyi, "Lun woguo de xuanju zhidu" [On our country's electoral system], *Renmin Ribao*, November 29, 1957, p. 7; Zhang Dapeng, "Wo guo xuanju zhidu shi zhenzheng minzhu de xuanju zhidu" [Our country's electoral system is a truly democratic electoral system], *Faxue*, no. 6 (December 1957): 37–9; Gu Angran, *Zhengfa Yanjiu*, no. 6 (December 1957): 31–4; Luo Shiying, "Bochi youpai fenzi dui wo guo xuanju zhidu de weixie" [Denouncing and refuting the rightists' slander of our country's electoral system], *Zhengfa Yanjiu*, no. 6 (December 1957): 27–30; Hua Guoquan, "Bochi youpai dui lianhe timing he deng'e xuanju de wuxie" [Denouncing and refuting rightist slander of joint nomination and equal quota elections], *Faxue*, no. 5 (May 1958): 40–3.

46. Cited in MacFarquhar, 1960, pp. 108–9.

47. See Schram, "Introduction: The Cultural Revolution in Historical Perspective," pp. 47–8; Dennis J. Doolin, "Chinese Communist Policies Toward the Chinese

Intelligentsia: 1949–1963," (Ph.D. dissertation, Stanford University, 1964), pp. 36–9, 58.

48. Terminology and concepts discussed in Kenneth Jowitt, "Inclusion and Mobilization in European Leninist Regimes," *World Politics* 28 (October 1975): 69–96.

49. Gordon White, "The Post-Revolutionary State," in *State and Society in Contemporary China*, eds. Victor Nee and David Mozingo (Ithaca, NY: Cornell University Press, 1983), p. 47.

50. Chen Shouyi, "A Review of New China's Law Research During the Past Thirty Years," *CR:PSM* 100 (July 18, 1980): 38, from *Faxue Yanjiu*, no. 1 (February 1980).

51. MacFarquhar, 1960, p. 261; MacFarquhar, 1974, p. 274.

52. MacFarquhar, 1974, p. 274.

53. "Current Session of National People's Congress," *SCMP* 1566 (July 10, 1957): 9, from *Renmin Ribao*, June 26, 1957.

54. "Current Session of National People's Congress," p. 10.

55. MacFarquhar, 1974, p. 275.

56. Cited in "China Goes to the Polls," *CNA* 245 (September 19, 1958): 5, from *Renmin Ribao*, July 5, 1957, p. 2.

57. Yan Yi, "Wo mudu neici kepa de renda huiyi" [I saw with my own eyes that frightful NPC], *Zhengming*, no. 36 (October 1980): 34–5.

58. Yan Yi, p. 35.

59. "The 1957 Session of National People's Congress (VIII) – The Rightists Surrender: Comment," *CB* 470 (July 26, 1957): 1.

60. "A Great Victory Against the Rightists," *SCMP* 1578 (July 26, 1957): 1, from *Renmin Ribao*, July 16, 1957.

61. For representative examples, see Yan Yi, p. 35, and MacFarquhar, 1974, p. 274.

62. For typical comments, see Zeng Lin, p. 2; Chen Shouyi, Liu Shengping, and Zhao Zhenjiang, pp. 25–40; Wang Xiangming, *Xianfa Ruogan Lilun Wenti de Yanjiu* [Research on Certain Theoretical Questions on the Constitution] (Beijing: Zhongguo Renmin Daxue Chubanshe, 1983), pp. 118–19; Quanguo Renda Changweihui Bangongting Yanjiushi, pp. 2–3, 12–18.

63. Mu Fu, p. 23; Yan Yi, p. 35.

64. Luo Bing, "Paohuang nüfu zongli shijian ji qita" [The incident of bombarding the woman vice-premier and others], *Zhengming*, no. 22 (August 1979): 8.

65. Gao Chongmin, "The Sole Outlet for Bourgeois Intellectuals is to Transform Their Political Stand and Take the Road of Socialism," *CB* 503 (April 10, 1958): 12.

66. *Renmin Shouce 1958* (Peking: Da Gongbaoshe, 1958), p. 323; Ginsburgs, pp. 7–8.

67. Asserted in Gu Angran, *Zhengfa Yanjiu*, no. 6 (December 1957): 34.

68. See Zhang Dapeng, pp. 37–8; Gu Angran, *Zhengfa Yanjiu*, no. 6 (December 1957): 31; Hua Guoquan, pp. 40–3; Zhang Yanjie, pp. 15–16, 25; Gu Angran and Li Jianfei, p. 3; Liu Renxian and Gu Angran, "Renmin daibiao dahui zhidu shi gonggu wuchan jieji zhuanzheng, jinxing shehuizhuyi jianshe de youli wuqi" [The people's congress system is a powerful weapon to consolidate the dictatorship of the proletariat to realize socialist construction], *Zhengfa Yanjiu*, no. 3 (June 1959): 10.

69. Gu Angran and Li Jianfei, p. 3.

70. See *Renmin Shouce 1958*, p. 330; "China Goes to the Polls," p. 6; "China, November 1957," *CNA* 207 (November 29, 1957): 5.

71. Ginsburgs, p. 5.

72. Zhao Binglin, "Jianshe gaodu minzhu de shehuizhuyi zhengzhi zhidu" [Construct a highly democratic socialist political system], *Minzhu yu Fazhi*, no. 7 (July 1981): 9; Chen Shouyi, Liu Shengping, and Zhao Zhenjiang, p. 25.

73. Franz Michael, "The Role of Law in Traditional, National and Communist China," *China Quarterly*, no. 9 (January–March 1962): 146.

74. Liao Gailong, "Historical Experiences and our Road of Development (Part II)" (hereafter Liao Gailong, Part II), *Issues and Studies* 17 (November 1981): 93.

75. Shi Xiaozhong, "Jianquan guojia zhengzhi zhidu wenti dangyi" [Current discussion on perfecting the nation's political system], *Minzhu yu Fazhi*, no. 10 (October 1981): 7. (Also available in *CR:PSM* 261.)

76. Chen Shouyi, Liu Shengping, and Zhao Zhenjiang, p. 27. See also Lin Hsintao, "Supreme Paramount Power – How the NPC Can Be Really Worthy of its Name, Part 1," *CR:PSM* 148 (December 15, 1980): 26, from *Wen Wei Po* (Hong Kong), November 9, 1980, p. 3; Wu Jialin, "Zenyang fahui quanguo renda zuowei zuigao guojia jiguan de zuoyong" [How to bring into play the NPC as the highest organ of state power] (hereafter Wu Jialin, *Xinhua Wenzhai*), *Xinhua Wenzhai*, no. 12 (December 1980): 48. Gordon White, p. 39, also writes of a "virtual fusion of political and administrative roles," and the party assuming "greater direct administrative and managerial responsibilities, especially after the extension of dual rule in the late 1950s."

77. Liu and Gu, pp. 11–13.

78. Cited in John Bryan Starr, *Continuing the Revolution: The Political Thought of Mao* (Princeton: Princeton University Press, 1979), pp. 204–5.

79. Cited in Jerome A. Cohen, "China's Changing Constitution," *China Quarterly*, no. 76 (December 1978): 800. On the failure to consult the NPC on the creation of communes, see Quanguo Renda Changweihui Bangongting Yanjiushi, p. 12.

80. "Legal Principles and Practice," *CNA* 284 (July 10, 1959): 1. On the declining attention to law, see also Benkan Bianjibu [editors], "Zai gaige zhong tabu qianjin" [A big step forward in reform], *Zhengzhi yu Falü*, no. 5 (October 1984): 2.

81. Chen Shouyi, Liu Shengping, and Zhao Zhenjiang, p. 27.

82. Zhao Binglin, pp. 9–10.

83. See Wu Daying and Ren Yunzheng, *Lifa Zhidu Bijiao Yanjiu* [Comparative Research on Legislative Systems] (Beijing: Falü Chubanshe, 1981), p. 147; Wu Jialin, "Some Questions Concerning Socialist Democracy," p. 11.

84. For an explanation of the forces aligned against legislative development, see Li Qi, pp. 3–12.

85. Argument follows Michael, pp. 146–7; Stahnke, pp. 510, 524.

86. Victor H. Li, "The Evolution and Development of the Chinese Legal System," in *China: Management of a Revolutionary Society*, ed. John M. H. Lindbeck (Seattle: University of Washington Press, 1971), p. 239.

87. Wu Daying et al., p. 59.

88. Chen Shouyi, p. 39.

89. Tao-tai Hsia, "Chinese Legal Publications: An Appraisal," in *Contemporary Chinese Law*, ed. Jerome A. Cohen (Cambridge, MA: Harvard University Press, 1970), p. 54.

90. See Stahnke, pp. 507, 524.

91. Zhongguo Renmin Daxue Falüxi "Zhengfa Gongzuo" Yanjiu Xiaozu, "Woguo renmin minzhu fazhi de jige wenti" [Several questions about our country's people's democratic legal system], *Zhengfa Yanjiu*, no. 2 (April 1959): 5.

92. Quanguo Renda Changweihui Bangongting Yanjiushi, p. 15.

93. Merle Fainsod, *How Russia is Ruled*, revised ed. (Cambridge, MA: Harvard University Press, 1963), p. 384.

94. Ginsburgs, p. 27. For example, in 1960, the NPC enacted the Twelve-Year Agricultural Program, with no substantial changes from the revised 1957 version. References to Advanced Producer Cooperatives remained intact even though they

had been supplanted by communes in late 1958. Parris Chang concludes that this "legislative sloppiness" strongly suggests NPC irrelevance to the policy process during the Great Leap Forward. See Parris H. Chang, *Power and Policy in China* (University Park, PA: Pennsylvania State University Press, 1975), p. 124.

95. "A Congress Session that Strives for a Leap Forward," *CB* 496 (March 7, 1958): 15, from *Renmin Ribao*, February 12, 1958.

96. Chen Shutong, "Industrial and Commercial Circles Must Be Fully Determined to Reform Themselves," *CB* 502 (April 7, 1958): 3. Chen was a vice chairman of the NPCSC whose legislative experience began in the 1912 National Assembly.

97. "The Middle Class in 1960," *CNA* 321 (April 29, 1960): 2.

98. Cited in "Ts'ao Ts'ao on the Stage," *CNA* 274 (May 1, 1959): 5–6.

99. See *CB* 573–7.

100. Parris Chang believes that the Central Committee was divided at the time of the 1959 NPC (Chang, p. 108), which suggests the possibility that Mao used the Congress to put pressure on hesitant colleagues and to build support for the second stage of the Leap. Inadequate information on NPC personnel, factional alliances, and party meetings limit this line of thought to speculation.

101. From *Renmin Ribao*, April 11, 1960, reprinted in National People's Congress of the People's Republic of China, *Second Session of the Second National People's Congress of the People's Republic of China (Documents)* (hereafter Second Documents) (Peking: Foreign Languages Press, 1960), p. 174.

102. Second Documents, p. 1.

103. The NPC perhaps suffered more loss of public esteem than other state and party organs because of the publicity accorded its work and the gushing enthusiasm displayed by deputies, who were not involved in practical work and not responsible for policy implementation.

104. The official document collections for the 1956, 1957, and 1958 NPC sessions totaled over 3,000 pages (in Chinese). In 1962 and 1963, less than ten pages were released.

105. Cited in George T. Yu, "The 1962 and 1963 Sessions of the National People's Congress of Communist China," *Asian Survey* 4 (August 1964): 983.

106. Marcus Green, "The National People's Congress," *China Quarterly*, no. 17 (January–March 1964): 248.

107. A. M. Halpern, "Between Plenums: A Second Look at the 1962 National People's Congress in China," *Asian Survey* 2 (November 1962): 2.

108. Yu, pp. 989–90.

109. Mu Fu, p. 23.

110. National People's Congress of the People's Republic of China, *Main Documents of the First Session of the Third National People's Congress* (Peking: Foreign Languages Press, 1965), p. 90.

111. See Tao Jin, "Tan wujie wuci renda" [Discussing the Fifth NPC Fifth Session], *Zhengming*, no. 62 (December 1982): 46; Mu Fu, p. 23.

112. Mu Fu, p. 23.

113. See Wang Hanbin, "Wo guo lifa gongzuo sanshiwu nian lai de chengjiu he dangqian de renwu" [Achievements and current tasks in thirty-five years of our country's legislative work], *Falü yu Shenghuo*, no. 10 (October 1984): 4; Benkan Bianjibu [Editors], *Zhengzhi yu Falü*, p. 2.

114. This account of the drafting process is pieced together from a number of sources. For a fairly complete version in English, see Stahnke, pp. 519–21. A comprehensive, Chinese account can be found in Wu Daying et al., pp. 57–8. For other odds and ends, see "The Structure of the State in China," *CNA* 107 (November 4, 1955): 5; Sun Chenggu, pp. 107–8; Benkan Bianjibu [Editors], *Zhengzhi yu Falü*,

p. 2; Wang Xiaotang, "Wei 'renda changweihui' heyi she fazhi weiyuanhui?" [Why has the NPCSC created a legal commission?], *Zhonggong Yanjiu* 13 (March 1979): 78; "The Judiciary (I)," *CNA* 140 (July 20, 1956): 2.

115. Xu Chongde and He Huahui, *Xianfa yu Minzhu Zhidu* [The Constitution and Democratic System] (Hubei: Hubei Renmin Chubanshe, 1982), pp. 58–9.

116. Wu Daying et al., pp. 61–2.

117. Wu Jialin, *Xinhua Wenzhai*, p. 48.

118. Shi Xiaozhong, p. 6; Yu Haocheng, "Xin xianfa fazhanle shehuizhuyi minzhu" [The new constitution develops socialist democracy], in *Wo Guo de Minzhu Zhengzhi yu Fazhi Jianshe*, ed. Yu Haocheng (Taiyuan: Shanxi Renmin Chubanshe, 1983), p. 151. Latter also available in *Renmin Ribao*, December 20, 1982.

119. Chen Shouyi, Liu Shengping, and Zhao Zhenjiang, p. 30.

120. See Wang Bixuan et al., *Xin Xianfa Wenda* [Questions and Answers on the New Constitution] (Taiyuan: Shanxi Renmin Chubanshe, 1983), p. 142; Hsin-chi Kuan, "New Departures in China's Constitution," *Studies in Comparative Communism* 17 (Spring 1984): 63.

121. Cited in Wang Shuwen, "Lun xuanju" [On elections], *Faxue Yanjiu*, no. 1 (April 1979): 8.

122. See Xu Chongde and Pi Chunxie, p. 33; Shi Xiaozhong, p. 7; Xu Chongde and He Huahui, *Xianfa yu Minzhu Zhidu*, p. 58.

123. Quanguo Renda Changweihui Bangongting Yanjiushi, p. 18.

124. Xu Chongde and Pi Chunxie, pp. 138–9; Teyue Pinglunyuan (Special Commentator), "Dangqian lifa gongzuo zhong de yixie wenti" [Several problems in current legislative work], *Guangming Ribao*, December 22, 1978, p. 3; Wang Guangmei, "Shishi xin xianfa de baozheng" [Carry out the guarantees of the new constitution], *Faxue Zazhi*, no. 1 (February 1983): 5.

125. Zhou Xinming and Chen Weidian, "Dui lifa chengxu wenti de yixie kanfa" [Some views on the issue of legislative procedures], *Renmin Ribao*, January 5, 1979, p. 3.

126. Wu Daying et al., p. 61.

127. Cited in Yu Haocheng, "Yige jiqi zhongyao de jianyi" [An extremely important proposal], *Faxue Zazhi*, no. 4 (August 1982): 24.

128. Pu Zengyuan, "Guanyu xiugai xianfa de wenti" [Questions concerning revising the constitution], *Minzhu yu Fazhi*, no. 11 (November 1980): 15.

129. Cao Siyuan, "Ten Proposals for Revising the Constitution," *CR:PSM* 201 (June 30, 1981): 6, from *Minzhu yu Fazhi*, no. 2 (February 1981): 11–12.

130. Kuan, p. 53.

131. Wang Bixuan et al., p. 4.

132. Wu Jialin, *Xinhua Wenzhai*, p. 48. See also Zhang Youyu, cited in Kuan, p. 67n.

133. For a side-by-side comparison of the 1954 and 1975 constitutions, see "Chronicle and Quarterly Documentation," *China Quarterly*, no. 62 (June 1975): 386–406.

134. "The People's Congress, Part 1," *CNA* 989 (February 7, 1975): 2.

135. For a contemporary analysis, see "The People's Congress, Part 2," *CNA* 990 (February 14, 1975): 2.

136. See Xu Chongde and He Huahui, *Xianfa yu Minzhu Zhidu*, p. 58; Xu Chongde and Pi Chunxie, p. 34.

137. Cited in National People's Congress of the People's Republic of China, *Documents of the First Session of the Fifth National People's Congress of the People's Republic of China* (hereafter *Fifth NPC First Session Documents*) (Peking: Foreign Languages Press, 1978), pp. 6–7.

138. *Fifth NPC First Session Documents*, p. 5.

139. Xu Chongde and He Huahui, *Xianfa yu Minzhu Zhidu*, p. 58.

140. The Fourth NPCSC did meet on four occasions: January 20, 1975, March 18–19, 1975, November 30-December 2, 1976, and October 23–4, 1977. The sessions in general were not newsworthy, except for the third, at which some of the early post-Cultural Revolution personnel changes were announced.

141. Xu Chongde and He Huahui, *Xianfa yu Minzhu Zhidu*, pp. 59, 60; Wang Xiangming, p. 119; Wu Jialin, *Xinhua Wenzhai*, p. 48.

Chapter 4. Structural features

1. For remarks by Deng, see Franklin W. Houn, "Communist China's New Constitution," *Western Political Science Quarterly* 8 (June 1955): 205. For similar comments by Liu Shaoqi and Zhou Enlai, see National People's Congress of the People's Republic of China, *Documents of the First Session of the First National People's Congress of the People's Republic of China* (Peking: Foreign Languages Press, 1955), p. 43; Ch'ien Tuan-sheng (Qian Duansheng), "Our New State Structure," *China Reconstructs* 4 (February 1955): 2; Xu Chongde and Pi Chunxie, *Xuanju Zhidu Wenda* [Questions and Answers on the Electoral System] (Beijing: Qunzhong Chubanshe, 1982), p. 58. On the advantages of indirect elections (ease, low cost, flexibility, accessibility, and speed of recall), see V. I. Lenin, "The Proletarian Revolution and the Renegade Kautsky," in Karl Marx, Friedrich Engels, and V. I. Lenin, *On Democracy – Bourgeois and Socialist* (Moscow: Progress Publishers, 1988), p. 209.

2. Liu Renxian and Gu Angran, "Renmin daibiao dahui zhidu shi gonggu wuchan jieji zhuanzheng, jinxing shehuizhuyi jianshe de youli wuqi" [The people's congress system is a powerful weapon to consolidate the dictatorship of the proletariat to realize socialist construction], *Zhengfa Yanjiu*, no. 3 (June 1959): 10.

3. For an explanation of nomination procedures and defense of uncontested elections, see Wu Ke-chien (Wu Kejian), "People's Congress – People's Democracy – People's Power," *China Reconstructs* 8 (January 1959): 28; Zhang Dapeng, "Wo guo xuanju shi zhenzheng minzhu de xuanju zhidu" [Our country's electoral system is a truly democratic electoral system], *Faxue*, no. 6 (December 1957): 38; Chen Hefu, *Xuanju Manyu* [Notes on Elections] (Beijing: Qunzhong Chubanshe, 1983), p. 99; Hua Guoquan, "Bochi youpai dui lianhe timing he deng'e xuanju de wuxie" [Denouncing and refuting rightist slander of joint nomination and equal quota elections], *Faxue*, no. 5 (May 1958): 40–3; Luo Shiying, "Bochi youpai fenzi dui woguo xuanju zhidu de weixie" [Denouncing and refuting the rightists' slander of our country's electoral system], *Zhengfa Yanjiu*, no. 5 (December 1957): 29; Li Youyi, "Lun woguo de xuanju zhidu" [On our country's electoral system], *Renmin Ribao*, November 29, 1957, p. 7.

4. See Hua Guoquan, p. 43; Li Youyi, p. 7. Hua and Li both claim that party members at the 1957 NPC proposed instituting contested elections, but were opposed by "rightists" who feared this would diminish the number of non-CCP members in congresses. Though conceivable, more information is needed to assess the motives of those who opposed reform. Perhaps they felt it was only sham democratization since party informal control could easily determine outcomes in contested elections.

5. For electoral functions and an account and typology of plebiscitary and limited-choice elections, see Alex Pravda, "Elections in Communist Party States," available in *Communist Politics: A Reader*, eds. Stephen White and Daniel Nelson (Washington Square, NY: New York University Press, 1986), pp. 27–54. Other information on electoral functions can be found in Theodore H. Friedgut, *Political Participation* *in the USSR* (Princeton: Princeton University Press, 1979), pp. 137–47. On the use of Soviet noncompetitive elections for political mobilization and socialization, as well as feedback and systemic legitimation, see Stephen White, "Non-competitive Elections and National Politics: The USSR Supreme Soviet Elections of 1984," *Electoral Studies* 4 (1985): 215–29. For a thorough discussion of Chinese nomination procedures and basic-level elections in the 1950s, see James R. Townsend, *Political Participation in Communist China* (Berkeley: University of California Press, 1967), pp. 103–37. On basic-level elections in the 1980s, see Brantly Womack, "The 1980 County-Level Elections in China: Experiment in Democratic Modernization," *Asian Survey* 22 (March 1982): 261–77; Andrew J. Nathan, *Chinese Democracy* (Berkeley: University of California Press, 1985), pp. 193–223; Barrett L. McCormick, "Leninist Implementation: The Election Campaign," in *Policy Implementation in Post-Mao China*, ed. David M. Lampton (Berkeley: University of California Press, 1987), pp. 383–413.

6. Interview with three members of the NPCSC staff, April 3, 1989. On designating deputies, see Xu Chongde and He Huahui, *Xianfa yu Minzhu Zhidu* [The Constitution and Democratic System] (Hubei: Hubei Renmin Chubanshe, 1982), p. 60; Wu Jialin, "Zenyang fahui quanguo renda zuowei zuigao guojia quanli jiguan de zuoyong" [How to bring into play the NPC as the highest organ of state power] (hereafter Wu Jialin, *Xinhua Wenzhai*), *Xinhua Wenzhai*, no. 12 (December 1980): 49. On the confusion and opportunities for abuse in a system where deputies were chosen both by election and to meet occupational, gender, or ethnic quotas, see Li Guoxiong, "Woguo renmin daibiaozhi dangyi" [An opinion on the Chinese people's congress system], *Faxue Pinglun*, no. 1 (January 1987): 13–15, 72. For information on recent nomenklatura practices, see John P. Burns, "China's Nomenklatura System," *Problems of Communism* 36 (September–October 1987): 36–51.

7. Teyue Pinglunyuan [Special Commentator], "Dangqian lifa gongzuo zhong de yixie wenti" [Several problems in current legislative work], *Guangming Ribao*, December 22, 1978, p. 3. This article also recounts the story of one NPC deputy who received notice of his selection to the NPC in the mail and became very nervous, wondering if after coming out of the "cowshed" (a makeshift prison) he now had to enter a "study class." The anecdote is used to criticize the excessive mystery and lack of publicity surrounding the 1975 NPC.

8. Xu Chongde and Pi Chunxie, p. 34; Wang Shuwen, "Lun xuanju" [On elections], *Faxue Yanjiu*, no. 1 (April 1979): 9.

9. Pan Nianzhi, "Some Ideas About Revising the Constitution," *CR:PSM* 202 (July 6, 1981): 33, from *Minzhu yu Fazhi*, no. 4 (April 1981); Wu Jialin, *Xinhua Wenzhai*, p. 49; Liu Xia, "Zhengzhi tizhi gaige yu renmin daibiao suzhi" [Political system reform and people's deputy quality], *Fazhi Jianshe*, no. 5 (October 1987): 20.

10. See Li Chiu-yi, "Composition of the Chinese Communist Third National People's Congress," *Issues and Studies* 1 (December 1964): 18.

11. Xu Chongde and He Huahui, *Xianfa yu Minzhu Zhidu*, p. 61.

12. For examples drawn from the 1978 NPC, see Zhao Zong, "Shiping wujie renda" [Evaluating the fifth NPC], *Mingbao Yuekan*, no. 148 (April 1978): 3.

13. Compiled by Yao Meng-hsuan, "Peiping's National Congress and Trends," *Issues and Studies* 1 (February 1965): 13.

14. For the First NPC, see "China Goes to the Polls," p. 5, citation from *Gongren Ribao*, October 19, 1957. For the Second NPC estimate, see George T. Yu, "The 1962 and 1963 Sessions of the National People's Congress of Communist China," *Asian Survey* 4 (August 1964): 988. For Third NPC estimate, see Yao Meng-hsuan, p. 13.

15. For comparison of the Second and Third NPCs' leadership composition, see Chang Ching-wen, "Reshuffles in the Peiping Regime After the First Session of the Third National People's Congress," *Issues and Studies* 1 (February 1965): 24–8.

16. Example drawn from 1978 NPC. See Donald Gasper, "The Chinese National People's Congress," in *Communist Legislatures in Comparative Perspective*, eds. Daniel Nelson and Stephen White (London: Macmillan Press, 1982), p. 177.

17. Mu Fu, "Zhongguo renda de zhiheng zuoyong" [The NPC's system-balancing role], *Qishi Niandai*, no. 162 (July 1983): 22.

18. The removal of 38 deputies on the eve of the 1958 NPC was only the most obvious example of the Credentials Committee effectively overruling the choice of provincial electors. Nearly every year one or more deputies had his or her credentials rescinded.

19. Mu Fu, pp. 22–3.

20. For a typical statement of this position, see Gu Angran, "Fensui youpai fenzi gongji quanguo renmin daibiao dahui shi 'xingshi' de miulun" [On denouncing the absurd statement of the rightist elements that the NPC is only a "formality"], *Zhengfa Yanjiu*, no. 6 (December 1957): 33.

21. Gu Angran, "Disanjie quanguo renmin daibiao dahui kuoda daibiao ming'e shi wo guo zhengzhi shenghuo zhong de yijian dashi" [Enlarging the number of deputies at the Third National People's Congress is a big event in our country's political life], *Zhengfa Yanjiu*, no. 1 (March 1964): 5–6.

22. See Chang Ching-wen, p. 25; Yu, p. 989.

23. Gu Angran, *Zhengfa Yanjiu*, no. 1 (March 1964): 6–7.

24. Chang Ching-wen, pp. 25, 28. The 150% expansion was not fully reflected in the minority quota, which was only doubled. Though this reduced minority representation, minority strength remained above its proportion of the general population. See Gasper, pp. 167–8.

25. Liao Gailong, "Historical Experiences and Our Road of Development, Part III" (hereafter, Liao Gailong, Part III), *Issues and Studies* 17 (December 1981): 86. On late arrivals, see Dong Chengmei, "Shilun xianxing xianfa ruhe xiugai de jige wenti" [Discussion of several issues on how to revise the current constitution], *Minzhu yu Fazhi*, no. 3 (March 1982): 9. For other discussions of the baleful consequences of expansion, see Sun Chenggu, *Lifa Quan yu Lifa Chengxu* [Legislative Power and Legislative Procedures] (Beijing: Renmin Chubanshe, 1983), pp. 100–1; Wang Shuwen, "Jiaqiang shehuizhuyi he fazhi de liangxiang zhongda cuoshi" [Two important measures to strengthen socialist democracy], *Minzhu yu Fazhi*, no. 7 (July 1982): 7. Also available in *CR:PSM* 342; Wang Xiangming, "Xiancao tixianle gexin guojia jigou de jingshen" [The draft constitution embodies the spirit of national reform], *Faxue Jikan*, no. 3 (July 1982): 13.

26. Author's observations at the 1989 NPC, confirmed as essentially unchanged since the 1950s by many long-time observers, including Chang Shao Wei, *Ta Kung Pao* reporter, in an interview March 31, 1989.

27. Ch'ien Tuan-sheng (Qian Duansheng), "Our New State Structure," p. 3. See also Zhang Yanjie, "Quanguo renmin daibiao dahui shouquan changwu weiyuanhui zhiding danxing fagui shi hefa" [The NPC's authorization of the NPCSC to enact special regulations is legal], *Faxue*, no. 3 (March 1958): 16. Xiong Xiyuan also emphasizes that part-time deputies retain "ties to production realities and the masses . . . and so reflect all sorts of problems in socialist construction." Xiong Xiyuan, "Renmin daibiao dahui shi yixing heyi de guojia quanli jiguan" [The NPC is a state power organ that combines legislation with discussion], *Renwen Kexue Zazhi* (*Yunnan Daxue*), no. 1 (January 1958): 22.

28. Ch'ien Tuan-sheng (Qian Duansheng), p. 3.

29. Gu Angran, *Zhengfa Yanjiu*, no. 6 (December 1957): 34. Some Chinese authors continue to defend unanimous votes and argue that brief sessions do not foreclose thorough deliberation: "After deputies fully discuss issues and bring up different opinions, since the NPC represents the people's basic interests, as do the proposals forwarded to the NPC, it is no surprise that the votes are often unanimous." See Li Buyun, "Shehuizhuyi minzhu yu zibenzhuyi minzhu de qubie" [The differences between socialist and capitalist democracy], *Faxue*, no. 12 (December 1983): 16.

30. Wu Jialin, *Xinhua Wenzhai*, p. 49; Zhou Xinming and Chen Weidian, "Dui lifa chengxu wenti de yixie kanfa" [Some views on the issue of legislative procedures], *Renmin Ribao*, January 5, 1979, p. 3.

31. See Lin Hsin-tao, "Supreme Paramount Power – How the NPC Can Really Be Worthy of its Name, Part 1," *CR:PSM* 148 (December 15, 1980): 26–7, from *Wen Wei Po*, November 9, 1980, p. 3; Ma Lu, "How to View the Succession of Zhao Ziyang," *CR:PSM* 143 (December 3, 1980): 17–18, from *Zhengming*, no. 36 (October 1, 1980); Yi Shi, "Jielu zhonggong renda de neimu" [Exposing the inside story of the Chinese Communists NPC], *Dong Xi Fang*, no. 7 (July 1979): 9.

32. Wu Jialin, *Xinhua Wenzhai*, p. 48.

33. Wu Jialin, *Xinhua Wenzhai*, pp. 48, 49; see also, Wu Jialin, "Minzhu santi" [Three problems of democracy], *Minzhu yu Fazhi*, no. 12 (December 1980): 19.

34. Conversation (March 31, 1989) with *Ta Kung Pao* reporter Chang Shao Wei and author's observation of Guangdong and Liaoning small-group meetings, March 31, 1989. On small groups in the 1950s, see Ginsburgs, p. 45.

35. Xu Chongde and He Huahui, *Xianfa yu Minzhu Zhidu*, p. 61.

36. Xiong Xiyuan, p. 21.

37. Part of the decrease can be attributed to less NPC activity in later years, and part, perhaps, to more secret work. Nevertheless, the magnitude of change strongly indicates the NPCSC considered fewer measures in the 1960s than in the 1950s.

38. Zhang Shixin, "Some Views on the Issue of the Position of Head of State in China," *CR:PSM* 263 (January 26, 1982): 51, from *Minzhu yu Fazhi*, no. 9 (September 1981): 8–9.

39. Wu Jialin, *Xinhua Wenzhai*, pp. 49–50; see also Liao Gailong, Part III, pp. 87–8; Zhang Shixin, p. 51.

40. Discussion with NPCSC staff members, April 3, 1989. See also Cao Siyuan, "Ten Proposals for Revising the Constitution," *CR:PSM* 201 (June 30, 1981): 12, from *Minzhu yu Fazhi*, no. 2 (February 1981): 6–10.

41. Quanguo Renda Changweihui Bangongting Yanjiushi, *Quanguo Renda Jiqi Changweihui Dashiji* [A Chronicle of the NPC and its Standing Committee] (Beijing: Falü Chubanshe, 1987), p. 15. For proposals to strengthen the NPC's research capabilities, see Joseph Y. S. Cheng, "How to Strengthen the National People's Congress and Implement Constitutionalism," *Chinese Law and Government* 16 (Summer–Fall 1983): 106–8; Zhou Xinming and Chen Weidian, p. 3.

Chapter 5. *The NPC in the political system*

1. Nelson W. Polsby, "Legislatures," in *Handbook of Political Science*, Vol. 5, eds. Fred I. Greenstein and Nelson W. Polsby (Reading, MA: Addison-Wesley, 1975), p. 258.

2. After a thorough survey, Robert Packenham concluded: "existing knowledge suggests that the principal function of most of the world's legislatures is not a decisional function." Robert A. Packenham, "Legislatures and Political Development," in *Legislatures in Developmental Perspective*, eds. Allan Kornberg and Lloyd D. Musolf (Durham, NC: Duke University Press, 1970), p. 522.

3. Teyue Pinglunyuan [Special Commentator], "Dangqian lifa gongzuo zhong de yixie wenti" [Several problems in current legislative work], *Guangming Ribao*, December 22, 1978, p. 3.

4. Zhou Xinming and Chen Weidian, "Dui lifa chengxu de yixie kanfa" [Some views on the issue of legislative procedures], *Renmin Ribao*, January 5, 1979, p. 3.

5. Michael L. Mezey, "The Functions of Legislatures in the Third World," in *Handbook of Legislative Research*, eds. Gerhard Loewenberg, Samuel C. Patterson, and Malcolm E. Jewell (Cambridge, MA: Harvard University Press, 1985), p. 737.

6. Michael L. Mezey, "Policy and Regime Support Functions: Theory and Research," paper prepared for delivery at the Conference on Parliaments, Policy and Regime Support, Duke University, Durham, NC, December 2–5, 1982, p. 8; see also Jean Blondel, *Comparative Legislatures* (Englewood Cliffs, NJ: Prentice-Hall, 1973), pp. 36–53.

7. Mezey, "The Functions of Legislatures in the Third World," pp. 739–40.

8. Questions on NPC decisional influence in the 1950s and 1960s to three NPCSC staff members, an NPCSC vice chairman, a legal expert employed at the Chinese Academy of Social Science, and several law professors yielded very little useful information. Possible conclusions include: they did not know about or had never researched the topic; they preferred not to talk about historical issues to a foreigner; there was very little NPC participation in policy making.

9. Ch'ien Tuan-sheng (Qian Duansheng), "Our New State Structure," *China Reconstructs* 4 (February 1955): 3. Deputy legislative proposals seldom exceeded one line in length and were quite general. For a list of proposals and responses by the Motions Examination Committee in a year (1958) after the NPC's heyday but before its period of rapid decline, see Quanguo Renmin Daibiao Dahui, *Zhonghua Renmin Gongheguo Diyijie Quanguo Renmin Daibiao Dahui Diwuci Huiyi Huikan, Xia* [Documents of the Fifth Session of the First People's Congress of the People's Republic of China, Vol. 3] (hereafter First NPC Fifth Session Documents) (Peking: Renmin Chubanshe, 1958), pp. 1003–20. On legislative proposals in the Supreme Soviet, see Stephen White, "The USSR Supreme Soviet: a Developmental Perspective," *Legislative Studies Quarterly* 5 (May 1980): 141. In 1957, Gu Angran, a frequent commentator on legal affairs who rarely strayed from the party line, claimed that "deputies' opinions have been paid attention to, not only with changes in wording but with changes in principle and content." Gu, however, only cited two instances where this had happened, thereby weakening his argument and suggesting a contrary conclusion. See Gu Angran, "Fensui youpai fenzi gongji quanguo renmin daibiao dahui shi 'xingshi' de miulun" [On denouncing the absurd statement of the rightist elements that the NPC is only a "formality"], *Zhengfa Yanjiu*, no. 6 (December 1957): 34.

10. See George Ginsburgs, "Theory and Practice of Parliamentary Procedure in Communist China: Organizational and Institutional Principles," *University of Toronto Law Journal* 15 (1) (1963): 42–3; Byron S. J. Weng, "The Role of the State Council," *Chinese Law and Government* 16 (Summer–Fall 1983): 161–2; Liao Gailong, "Historical Experiences and Our Road of Development, Part III" (hereafter, Liao Gailong, Part III), *Issues and Studies* 17 (December 1981): 87.

11. In 1957, deputies, apparently for the first time, initiated changes in the expenditures and revenues proposed in the draft budget submitted by the State Council. See Gu Angran, *Zhengfa Yanjiu*, no. 6 (December 1957): 34. I have found no evidence that this occurred again from 1957–76.

12. Zhou Xinming and Chen Weidian, p. 3.

13. Zhou Xinming and Chen Weidian, p. 3.

14. See Joseph G. LaPalombara, *Politics Within Nations* (Englewood Cliffs, NJ: Prentice-Hall, 1974), p. 161.

15. For example, eight years after the unconstitutional removal of State Chairman Liu Shaoqi, Hua Guofeng was appointed premier without NPC approval.

16. In 1958, Zhang Yanjie reported that the NPC in its first four sessions had been satisfied with NPCSC work and ratified its report without change. In the years after 1958, I found no evidence that the NPC ever criticized, required further research, or demanded revision or repeal of an NPCSC decision. For information on 1954–8 and a discussion of NPC powers vis-à-vis the NPCSC, see Zhang Yanjie, "Quanguo renmin daibiao dahui shouquan changwu weiyuanhui zhiding danxing fagui shi hefa" [The NPC's authorization of the NPCSC to enact special regulations is legal], *Faxue*, no. 3 (March 1958): 25.

17. Xu Chongde and He Huahui, *Xianfa yu Minzhu Zhidu* [The Constitution and Democratic System] (Hubei: Hubei Renmin Chubanshe, 1982), p. 61.

18. Peter Vanneman, *The Supreme Soviet: Politics and the Legislative Process in the Soviet Political System* (Durham, NC: Duke University Press, 1977), p. 88.

19. See Xu Chongde and He Huahui, *Xianfa yu Minzhu Zhidu*, pp. 60–1. On the limited data released to deputies, see Zong Nankai, "Chuping renda huiyi" [First evaluation of the NPC], *Dong Xi Fang*, no. 7 (July 1979): 7.

20. For a discussion in a Hong Kong communist publication of "immunity from criticism" and "forbidden zones," see Jin Zhiming, "Lun Zhongguo minzhu qiantu" [Discussing China's democratic future], *Dong Xi Fang*, no. 22 (October 1980): 27.

21. Shi Xiaozhong, "Jianquan guojia zhengzhi zhidu wenti dangyi" [Current discussion on perfecting the nation's political system], *Minzhu yu Fazhi*, no. 10 (October 1981): 6.

22. Stephen White, "Some Conclusions," in *Communist Legislatures in Comparative Perspective*, eds. Daniel Nelson and Stephen White (London: Macmillan Press, 1982), pp. 192–4.

23. Roderick MacFarquhar, *The Origins of the Cultural Revolution, Vol. 1: Contradictions Among the People* (New York: Columbia University Press, 1974), p. 115.

24. On abolishing the division between legislatures and executives, see Karl Marx, "The Civil War in France," and V. I. Lenin, "The State and Revolution," in Karl Marx, Friedrich Engels, and V. I. Lenin, *On Democracy – Bourgeois and Socialist* (Moscow: Progress Publishers, 1988), pp. 257–60, 195–205. Representative Chinese interpretations of Marx and Lenin on communist legislatures can be found in Shi Xiaozhong, pp. 6–7; Wu Jialin, "Yixing heyi" [Combination of legislative and executive powers], in *Zhongguo Dabai Kequan Shu (Faxue)*, ed. Zhang Youyu (Beijing: Zhongguo Dabai Kequan Shu Chubanshe, 1984), pp. 702–3; Xiong Xiyuan, "Renmin daibiao dahui shi yixing heyi de guojia quanli jiguan" [The NPC is a state power organ that combines legislation and discussion], *Renwen Kexue Zazhi (Yunnan Daxue)*, no. 1 (January 1958): 19–28. For a provocative discussion of the consequences of mixing legislative and executive functions, see Byron Weng, "Some Key Aspects of the 1982 Draft Constitution of the PRC," *China Quarterly*, no. 91 (September 1982): 499–500.

25. Mao Zedong, "Interview with the British Journalist James Bertram," cited in John Bryan Starr, *Continuing the Revolution: The Political Thought of Mao* (Princeton: Princeton University Press, 1979), pp. 215–16.

26. Starr, pp. 216–20.

27. Hanna F. Pitkin, *The Concept of Representation* (Berkeley: University of California Press, 1967), pp. 221–33.

28. Heinz Eulau and P. D. Karps, "The Puzzle of Representation: Specifying

Components of Responsiveness," *Legislative Studies Quarterly* 2 (August 1977): 243–5.

29. Mezey, "The Functions of Legislatures in the Third World," pp. 741–2.

30. See Stephen White, "The Supreme Soviet and Budgetary Politics in the USSR," *British Journal of Political Science* 12 (January 1982): 75–94; Daniel N. Nelson, "Editor's Introduction: Communist Legislatures and Communist Politics," *Legislative Studies Quarterly* 5 (May 1980): 169; Vanneman, p. 167.

31. Teyue Pinglunyuan [Special Commentator], p. 3.

32. Feng Wenbin, "Guanyu shehuizhuyi minzhu wenti" [Problems concerning socialist democracy], *Renmin Ribao*, November 25, 1980, p. 3.

33. Tao Jin, "Poushi liujie renda" [An analysis of the Sixth NPC], *Zhengming*, no. 69 (July 1983): 51.

34. Pitkin, pp. 232–3.

35. Argument follows Sun Tianfu, "Tantan shicha gongzuo zhong de jige wenti" [Discussing several problems in inspection work], *Guangming Ribao*, April 1, 1957, p. 3.

36. Packenham, pp. 529–30.

37. Argument follows Nelson, p. 169.

38. Concept explained in LaPalombara, p. 140.

39. This argument rings true only if the "normal course of events" means party control of nominations. Given the composition of congresses, party members appear to have benefited most from "special consideration"; other groups had much to gain and little to lose from more open nomination procedures. For emphasis on sociological representation and quotas, see Liu Renxian and Gu Angran, "Renmin daibiao dahui zhidu shi gonggu wuchan jieji zhuanzheng, jinxing shehuizhuyi jianshe de youli wuqi" [The people's congress system is a powerful weapon to consolidate the dictatorship of the proletariat to realize socialist construction], *Zhengfa Yanjiu*, no. 3 (June 1959): 10. More recent discussions can be found in Xu Chongde and Pi Chunxie, *Xuanju Zhidu Wenda* [Questions and Answers on the Electoral System] (Beijing: Qunzhong Chubanshe, 1982), pp. 63–7; Sun Chenggu, *Lifa Quan yu Lifa Chengxu* [Legislative Power and Legislative Procedures] (Beijing: Renmin Chubanshe, 1983), p. 120; Ye Ruixian, "Socialist Democracy is the Broadest Form of Democracy," *CR:PSM* 13 (August 29, 1979): 16, from *Nanfang Ribao*, June 27, 1979, p. 3.

40. In a break with equal representation, the Electoral Law affirmed the leading role of the working class and accorded city dwellers eight times the representation of ruralites. Since rural population dwarfed that of the cities, overrepresentation of urban workers, intellectuals, specialists, and party cadres was prescribed to prevent peasant numerical domination of the NPC. According to contemporary Chinese authors, "special proportions" accorded with Soviet practice prior to 1936 and China's "historical conditions," and reflected the people's objective interest in working-class leadership as China industrialized. Democratic essence (*minzhu shizhi*) was placed above democratic form (*minzhu xingzhi*), as balancing the city and countryside took precedence over one man, one vote. See Li Youyi, "Lun woguo de xuanju zhidu" [On our country's electoral system], *Renmin Ribao*, November 29, 1957, p. 7. A strong statement explaining why an "extremely large proportion of peasant deputies" must be avoided can be found in Xu Chongde and Pi Chunxie, pp. 64–5.

41. Liu Renxian and Gu Angran, p. 11.

42. According to William Welsh, the "organic" deputy role is "generally favored by socialist writers": deputies should represent the interests of the whole state, not those of voters in a given constituency. See William A. Welsh, "The Status of Research on Representative Institutions in Eastern Europe," *Legislative Studies Quarterly* 5 (May 1980): 280–1.

43. Liao Gailong, Part III, p. 92.

44. Feng Wenbin, p. 3.

45. Gu Angran, *Zhengfa Yanjiu*, no. 6 (December 1957), p. 31.

46. See Liu Renxian and Gu Angran, pp. 12–13; Wu Ke-chien (Wu Kejian), "People's Congress – People's Democracy – People's Power," *China Reconstructs* 8 (January 1959): 29.

47. Li Buyun, "Shehuizhuyi minzhu yu zibenzhuyi minzhu de qubie" [The differences between socialist and capitalist democracy], *Faxue*, no. 12 (December 1983): 15.

48. Liu Renxian and Gu Angran, p. 12.

49. For an explanation of the "system-maintenance model," see Michael L. Mezey, *Comparative Legislatures* (Durham, NC: Duke University Press, 1979), pp. 11, 18–20, 259–70, 281–2.

50. See Mezey, *Comparative Legislatures*, pp. 18–20.

51. See Nelson, p. 170.

52. See Joseph Y. S. Cheng, "How to Strengthen the National People's Congress and Implement Constitutionalism," *Chinese Law and Government* 16 (Summer–Fall 1983): 95–9.

53. See Chen Hefu, *Xuanju Manyu* [Notes on Elections] (Beijing: Qunzhong Chubanshe, 1983), p. 99; Luo Shiying, "Bochi youpai fenzi dui woguo xuanju zhidu de weixie" [Denouncing and refuting the rightists' slander of our country's electoral system], *Zhengfa Yanjiu*, no. 5 (December 1957): 29.

54. "A Milestone in the Historic Development of the People's Republic of China," *SCMP* 899 (September 30, 1954): 1, from *Renmin Ribao*, September 29, 1954.

55. Argument follows Mezey, "Policy and Regime Support Functions: Theory and Research," p. 24.

56. Packenham developed this persuasive but difficult-to-prove argument in a literature review on world legislatures published in 1970. It is my opinion that it applied to the early NPC. See Packenham, pp. 526–30; for similar remarks on legitimacy and integrative aspects of legislatures in developing and communist nations, see Mezey, "The Functions of Legislatures in the Third World," pp. 746–50; White, "Some Conclusions," p. 193; Nelson, p. 170.

57. According to Nelson, integration in a communist system implies acceptance of party hegemony and a situation in which "all familial units, occupational strata, and national or linguistic ties are less imprinted in the minds of citizens than . . . party concerns." See Nelson, p. 170.

58. Fan Jiahua, "Xin tizhi de lao wenti" [The new system's old problems], *Qishi Niandai*, no. 162 (July 1983): 20.

59. Some scholars downplay domestic legitimacy and stress foreign-propaganda benefits. George Ginsburgs, writing before the Cultural Revolution, believed that the party instituted and maintained the NPC out of "a strong, somewhat strange concern for outward appearance, possibly in the expectation that its public adherence to various procedural techniques associated with the rule of law would further its acceptance . . . abroad." See Ginsburgs, pp. 45–6. Taiwanese assessments of NPC functions typically emphasize foreign-propaganda benefits. Ji Peng writes: "the NPC is a party tool and puppet put on for the benefit of the world to watch." See Ji Peng, "Wei wujie renda dierci huiyi gaikuang" [The general situation at the Fifth NPC Second Session], *Zhonggong Yanjiu* 13 (July 1979): 26. These views have merit, as the regime certainly prefers not to be seen as imposed, but only limited applicability to the period 1954–76. Given Chinese–western estrangement and the propaganda war between the United States and China, it seems unlikely the Chinese expected to improve their democratic reputation through the NPC. Their claims to superiority

rested on differences with the West, not pale imitations of archetypal bourgeois institutions. The Chinese mocked bourgeois parliaments as inferior to the NPC, but few in the West were convinced. Yearly press reports on the NPC invariably called it a "nominal parliament" or "rubber stamp." Of course, unsuccessful propaganda does not signify a lack of trying. But complete failure suggests a minor foreign-propaganda role of the NPC – certainly insufficient to explain the time and expense the legislature entailed. If anything, foreign-propaganda efforts were directed at Third World and, especially, socialist countries, where different expectations for legislatures allowed for Chinese inclusion among the "people's democracies."

60. George T. Yu, "The 1962 and 1963 Sessions of the National People's Congress of Communist China," *Asian Survey* 4 (August 1964): 989.

61. Sun Tianfu, p. 3.

62. Discussions with my driver, hotel staff, numerous reporters, and members of the People's Institute of Foreign Affairs during the 1989 NPC suggest eager interest in the Pekingological aspects of NPC sessions. Who appears, what they wear, who they stand next to, and how they are received are the talk of Beijing (though perhaps not the whole country) for a period of weeks.

Chapter 6. Plenary sessions and policy discussions

1. For this remark, see Zhou Xinming and Chen Weidian, "Dui lifa chengxu wenti de yixia kanfa" [Some views on the issue of legislative procedures], *Renmin Ribao*, January 5, 1979, p. 3.

2. See Hua Guofeng, "Unite and Strive to Build a Modern, Powerful Socialist Country" (hereafter Hua Guofeng's Report at the 1978 NPC) in National People's Congress of the People's Republic of China, *Documents of the First Session of the Fifth National People's Congress of the People's Republic of China* (Peking: Foreign Languages Press, 1978), pp. 17–18, 35–66; "NPC, CPPCC Participants Continue Group Meetings," *FBIS* 41 (March 1, 1978): D1.

3. See "Hua Guofeng's Report at the 1978 NPC," pp. 35–98, especially pp. 77–8, 91–2. For an interpretation of the first four sessions of the Fifth NPC (1978–81) that emphasizes the economic policy debates, see Dorothy J. Solinger, "The Fifth National People's Congress and the Process of Policy-Making: Reform, Readjustment and Opposition," *Asian Survey* 22 (December 1982): 1239–75. Solinger correctly notes that Hua's report was not as leftist as later Chinese assessments would have it.

4. Jerome A. Cohen, "China's Changing Constitution," *China Quarterly*, no. 76 (December 1978): 836, 809–10.

5. I will not discuss the 1978 constitution at length because its import quickly dwindled. Thirty months after it was promulgated, a comprehensive revision began. For discussions of the 1978 constitution, see Cohen, pp. 794–841; Wang Hsiao-t'ang (Wang Xiaotang), "An Evaluation and Analysis of China's Revised Constitution," *Chinese Law and Government* 11 (Summer–Fall 1978): 34–53.

6. Statistics and analyses of the NPC and State Council composition can be found in Chiang Chih-nan, "An Analysis of the Personnel Composition of the Fifth National People's Congress and the State Council," *Chinese Law and Government* 11 (Summer–Fall 1978): 54–83; Ch'i Hsin (Qi Xin), "A Brief Analysis of China's New Personnel Arrangements," *Chinese Law and Government* 11 (Summer–Fall 1978): 84–97; Zhu Wei, "A Look at the General Situation in Communist China," *Translations on People's Republic of China* 429 (May 15, 1978): 7–10, from *Zhengming*, no. 6 (April 1978).

7. See Ch'i Hsin (Qi Xin), pp. 89–94; Chiang Chih-nan, p. 67.

8. On changes in the NPCSC, see Ch'i Hsin (Qi Xin), pp. 89–90.

9. See Long Fei, "Wei wujie 'renda' sanci huiyi dui gaoceng lingdaoren de tiao-zheng" [High-level leadership changes at the Fifth NPC Third Session], *Zhonggong Yanjiu* (Taipei) 14 (October 1980): 33; Stuart Schram, "'Economics in Command?' Ideology and Policy Since the Third Plenum," *China Quarterly*, no. 99 (September 1984): 428.

10. For analyses of the personnel changes at the 1979 NPC and the factional struggle preceding it, see Zong Nankai, "Chuping renda huiyi" [First evaluation of the NPC], *Dong Xi Fang*, no. 7 (July 1979): 6–8; Ji Peng, "Wei wujie renda dierci huiyi gaikuang" [The general situation at the Fifth NPC Second Session], *Zhonggong Yanjiu* (Taipei) 13 (July 1979): 25–7; Yi Shi, "Jielu zhonggong renda de neimu" [Exposing the inside story of the Chinese Communists NPC], *Dong Xi Fang*, no. 7 (July 1979): 9–11.

11. Hua Guofeng, "Report on the Work of the Government," in *Main Documents of the Second Session of the Fifth National People's Congress of the People's Republic of China* (Beijing: Foreign Languages Press, 1979), pp. 18–23, 62–81. Quotation on page 69.

12. See Zong Nankai, pp. 6–8.

13. "NPC: Lively Political Atmosphere," *Beijing Review* 22 (July 13, 1979): 20.

14. Luo Bing, "Paohuang nüfu zongli shijian ji qita" [The incident of bombarding the woman vice premier and others], *Zhengming*, no. 22 (August 1979): 8.

15. Reporters from Hong Kong, some of whom attended the Congress, are the sources for these discussions. See Luo Bing, pp. 6–7; Hong Yuan, "Wujie renda hou de Beijing" [Beijing after the Fifth NPC], *Dongxiang*, no. 10 (July 1979): 4–5; Mu Fu, "Zhongguo renda de zhiheng zuoyong" [The NPC's system-balancing role], *Qishi Niandai*, no. 162 (July 1983): 23–4.

16. My sources for these criticisms are two Hong Kong journalists and an NPC deputy who lives in Hong Kong. See Luo Bing, pp. 6–8; Mu Fu, pp. 23–4; "Kyodo Cites Criticism of PRC Leaders at Recent NPC" (hereafter Kyodo), *FBIS* 159 (August 15, 1979): L26.

17. Kyodo, p. L26; Mu Fu, p. 24.

18. A detailed account of NPC involvement in the Chen Muhua incident can be found in Luo Bing, p. 8; briefer reports are available in Kyodo, p. L26, and Mu Fu, p. 24.

19. This view is shared by both Chinese and foreign commentators. See Peter R. Moody, *Chinese Politics After Mao* (New York: Praeger, 1983), p. 142; Mou Runsun, "Wujie renda sanci dahui hou zhonggong zui zhuyao de gongzuo" [The most important tasks for the Chinese Communists after the Fifth NPC Third Session], *Mingbao Yuekan*, no. 178 (October 1980): 2; Fu Shihui, "Renda sanji" [Random notes on the NPC], *Mingbao Yuekan*, no. 178 (October 1980): 7; Shih Tien-hui, "A Milestone in the Modernization of the Chinese Political System – On Covering the NPC in the Great Hall of the People," *CR:PSM* 128 (October 15, 1980): 48, from *Dongxiang*, no. 24 (September 1980): 4–6; Dong Xi Fang Commentator, "Preliminary Observations on the Third Plenary Session of the Fifth NPC," *CR:PSM* 138 (November 17, 1980): 13–14, from *Dong Xi Fang*, no. 21 (September 1980): 12–13; Tian Sansong, "Democracy in Action, Accent on Reforms," *Beijing Review* 23 (September 29, 1980): 33–7.

20. Tian Sansong, pp. 36–7.

21. Tian Sansong, p. 33; Guo Lihua, "A Letter from a People's Representative," *FBIS* 175 (September 8, 1980): L38; Jin Zhiming, "Lun Zhongguo minzhu qiantu" [Discussing China's democratic future], *Dong Xi Fang*, no. 22 (October 1980): 26.

22. The labels that will be used here – conserver, adjuster, and reformer – and

the idea of three competing economic policy packages come from Solinger, pp. 1239–75. See also various articles in Dorothy J. Solinger, ed., *Three Visions of Chinese Socialism* (Boulder, CO: Westview Press, 1984), pp. 1–143. For the theoretical argument, see Dorothy J. Solinger, *Chinese Business Under Socialism* (Berkeley: University of California Press, 1984), pp. 60–74. Information on the restoration faction can be found in Moody, pp. 122, 131–6; Jiu Zhongyi, "Xin jingjipai doukua shiyoupai" [The new economic faction topples the petroleum faction], *Dongxiang*, no. 24 (September 1980): 9–11. Different analysts conceive divisions differently, often depending on what issues they study. For example, some have identified three main political lines, but these are not entirely consistent with Solinger's economic opinion groups. See Victor C. Falkenheim, "Political Reform in China," *Current History* 81 (September 1982): 259–63, 280–1; Gordon White, "The Post-Revolutionary State," in *State and Society in Contemprary China*, eds. Victor Nee and David Mozingo (Ithaca, NY: Cornell University Press, 1983), pp. 44–7. The following analysis benefits from insights in all these sources.

23. See Falkenheim, pp. 260–1; Jiu Zhongyi, p. 9; Solinger, pp. 1242–3.

24. On the readjustment policy begun in 1979, see Solinger, pp. 1242–3; Nicholas R. Lardy, "China's Economic Readjustment: Recovery or Paralysis," in *China Briefing, 1980*, eds. Robert B. Oxnam and Richard C. Bush (Boulder, CO: Westview Press, 1980), pp. 39–51.

25. For a perceptive analysis of "two-pronged" attention to both readjustment and reform, see Bruce L. Reynolds, "The Chinese Economy in 1980: Death of Reform?" in *China Briefing, 1981*, eds. Robert B. Oxnam and Richard C. Bush (Boulder, CO: Westview Press, 1981), pp. 41–52. My analysis, as might be expected when studying a legislature, emphasizes conflict. Reynolds convincingly explains how reform and readjustment also are, and are seen by Chinese leaders to be, complementary.

26. Solinger, p. 1242. Solinger uses these words to describe all NPC sessions from 1978–81; it is my judgment that they best apply to 1980.

27. The reports can be found in National People's Congress of the People's Republic of China, *Main Documents of the Third Session of the Fifth National People's Congress of the People's Republic of China* (Beijing: Foreign Languages Press, 1980), pp. 5–85.

28. The decision to reveal the deficit is discussed in Shih Tien-hui, p. 47; "Excerpts of Speeches by NPC Deputies at Panel Discussions" (hereafter *People's Daily* Excerpts 2), *FBIS* 179 (September 12, 1980): L5, from *Renmin Ribao*, September 6, 1980, p. 2.

29. See Tian Sansong, p. 33; "NPC Holds Panel Discussions on Yao, Wang Speeches," *FBIS* 171 (September 2, 1980): L23.

30. The quoted text is in *People's Daily* Excerpts 2, p. L11. The other comments can be found in "Excerpts of Speeches by NPC Deputies at Panel Discussions" (hereafter *People's Daily* Excerpts 5), *FBIS* 180 (September 15, 1980): L19, from *Renmin Ribao*, September 9, 1980, p. 2; "NPC Deputies Criticize Waste in Economic Construction," *FBIS* 173 (September 4, 1980): L18; Tian Sansong, p. 34; "Excerpts of Speeches Made by NPC Deputies in Panel Discussions" (hereafter *People's Daily* Excerpts 1), *FBIS* 178 (September 11, 1980): L23, from *Renmin Ribao*, September 5, 1980, p. 2; *Renmin Ribao*, "Excerpts of NPC Deputies' Speeches at Panel Discussions" (hereafter *People's Daily* Excerpts 8), *FBIS* 187 (September 24, 1980): L13, from *Renmin Ribao*, September 15, 1980, p. 4.

31. *People's Daily* Excerpts 5, p. L19; Tian Sansong, p. 34; *People's Daily* Excerpts 8, p. L13.

32. "Excerpts of Speeches by NPC Deputies at Panel Discussions" (hereafter *People's Daily* Excerpts 3), *FBIS* 180 (September 15, 1980): L12–13, from *Renmin*

Ribao, September 7, 1980, p. 2; *People's Daily* Excerpts 2, p. L4; Tian Sansong, p. 34; *People's Daily* Excerpts 5, p. L19.

33. "Sichuan NPC Deputies," *FBIS* 178 (September 11, 1980): L17.

34. "NPC Deputies Criticize Waste in Economic Construction," p. L18.

35. Fu Shihui, p. 7; Jiu Zhongyi, p. 11.

36. For information on the decision to build Baoshan and the early contract negotiations, see Ryosei Kokubun, "The Politics of Foreign Economic Policy-Making in China: The Case of Plant Cancellations with Japan," *China Quarterly*, no. 105 (March 1986): 20–2.

37. "Shanghai Deputies Discuss Issues at NPC Session," *CR:PSM* 1 (July 18, 1979): 25; *People's Daily* Excerpts 5, p. L19.

38. *Asashi Shimbun*, July 4, 1980 (Evening Edition), cited in Kokubun, p. 25.

39. Shih Tien-hui, p. 47.

40. Partial minutes of this question-and-answer session can be found in *People's Daily* Excerpts 5, pp. L7–10; Tian Sansong, p. 35; "NPC Deputies Continue Discussion Group Meetings," *FBIS* 174 (September 15, 1980): L1–2.

41. "A New Beginning," *FBIS* 180 (September 15, 1980): L32.

42. Tian Sansong, p. 35.

43. Reports on this second interpellation can be found in "Excerpts of Speeches by NPC Deputies at Panel Discussions" (hereafter *People's Daily* Excerpts 7), *FBIS* 184 (September 19, 1980): L18–20, from *Renmin Ribao*, September 12, 1980, p. 4; Tian Sansong, p. 35.

44. "NPC Panels End with Discussion of Hua's Speech," *FBIS* 177 (September 10, 1980): L21.

45. "NPC Deputies Criticize Waste in Economic Construction," p. L18; *People's Daily* Excerpts 5, pp. L14, L21; "Excerpts of Speeches by NPC Deputies at Panel Discussions" (hereafter *People's Daily* Excerpts 4), *FBIS* 179 (September 12, 1980): L17–18, from *Renmin Ribao*, September 8, 1980, p. 2; *People's Daily* Excerpts 1, pp. L18, L23; *People's Daily* Excerpts 2, p. L11.

46. Quoted text in Tian Sansong, p. 34. See also *People's Daily* Excerpts 3, p. L10. Information on other wasteful projects can be found in *People's Daily* Excerpts 4, p. L18; "Deputies Criticize Waste in Economic Construction," p. L18; *People's Daily* Excerpts 1, pp. L18, L23; *Renmin Ribao*, "Excerpts of NPC Deputies' Speeches at Panel Discussions" (hereafter *People's Daily* Excerpts 9), *FBIS* 188 (September 25, 1980): L8, from *Renmin Ribao*, September 17, 1980, p. 3; Shih Tien-hui, p. 47.

47. Cited in Bi Kong, "The People Hear the Voices of Their Deputies," *FBIS* 176 (September 9, 1980): L18, from *Renmin Ribao*, September 6, 1980, p. 1.

48. Quoted in *People's Daily* Excerpts 1, p. L21.

49. *People's Daily* Excerpts 2, p. L12.

50. *People's Daily* Excerpts 2, p. L13.

51. "NPC Deputies Continue Group Discussion Meetings," *FBIS* 174 (September 5, 1980): L4–5; *People's Daily* Excerpts 2, p. L13; *People's Daily* Excerpts 3, p. L12.

52. "NPC Deputies Discuss Yao Yilin, Wang Bingqian Reports," *FBIS* 175 (September 8, 1980): L27; *People's Daily* Excerpts 1, p. L24.

53. *People's Daily* Excerpts 4, p. L22; *People's Daily* Excerpts 5, p. L21.

54. This follows Solinger, p. 1241.

55. For a careful discussion that distinguishes deputies' speeches by regional origin, see Solinger, pp. 1257–9.

56. For quotations and commentaries in the Hong Kong left press, see Lan Yanzhi, "Pingdan wushi de jingji huiyi" [A flat, pragmatic, economic congress]," *Qishi Niandai*, no. 144 (January 1982): 44–5; Xu Xing, "Issues Raised by the Fourth Session of the Fifth NPC," *CR:PSM* 279 (March 3, 1982): 72, from *Zhengming*, no. 51 (January

1982): 18–20; Luo Bing, "Behind-the-Scene News at the NPC," *CR:PSM* 275 (March 2, 1982): 67–8, from *Zhengming*, no. 51 (January 1982): 8–10.

57. On the connection between external events and NPC atmosphere, see Solinger, p. 1266, Xu Xing, p. 72, and Lan Yanzhi, p. 45.

58. See Xu Xing, p. 72.

59. Solinger, pp. 1264–5. Solinger explains the main lines of debate in late 1980 and 1981 on pp. 1260–5. On the retreat from reform, see Reynolds, p. 51.

60. See Zhao Ziyang, "The Present Economic Situation and the Principles for Future Economic Construction," *FBIS* 241 (December 16, 1981): K1–2, K6–12, K22–4; Solinger, p. 1265.

61. For Chen and Wang's remarks, see Luo Bing, "Behind-the-Scene News at the NPC," p. 68; Li Tsung-ying, "NPC Deputies Query Phrases Such as 'Basic Price Stability,' Put Forward Stream of Criticisms," *CR:PSM* 261 (January 19, 1982): 81, from *Ta Kung Pao* (December 1981): 1.

62. Luo Bing, "Behind-the-Scene News at the NPC," p. 69.

63. For Zhao's original remark, see Zhao Ziyang, p. K2.

64. For deputy speeches on inflation, see "Deputies Discuss Zhao's Report," *FBIS* 235 (December 8, 1981): K4; Luo Bing, "Behind-the-Scene News at the NPC," pp. 70–2; Lan Yanzhi, p. 44; Wang Xiaotang, "Dui zhonggong zhaokai wujie 'renda sici huiyi' zhi yanxi" [Analysis of the Fourth Session of the Fifth NPC], *Zhonggong Yanjiu* (Taipei) 15 (December 1981): 26.

65. See "Beijing Deputies Speak Out on Price Issues," *FBIS* 242 (December 17, 1981): K7–8.

66. "Resolution of the Fourth Session of the Fifth National People's Congress of the People's Republic of China Concerning the Report 'Present Economic Situation and Principles for Future Economic Construction,'" *CR:PSM* 253 (December 30, 1981): 70–1.

67. For a representative sampling of such speeches, see "Coverage of Fifth NPC, Fifth CPPCC Sessions Continues," *FBIS* 238 (December 11, 1981): K5–6.

68. Luo Bing, "Jun daibiao yujing sizuo" [Army deputy's statement received with raised eyebrows], *Zhengming*, no. 51 (January 1982): 11–13.

69. On China in 1982 and 1983, see Kenneth Lieberthal, "China in 1982: A Middling Course for the Middle Kingdom," *Asian Survey* 23 (January 1983): 26–37; Joyce Kallgren, "China in 1983: The Turmoil of Modernization," *Asian Survey* 24 (January 1984): 60–80; Falkenheim, pp. 262–3; Moody, pp. 156–9. Economic results and tax reform were discussed at both the 1982 and 1983 NPCs. See Zhao Ziyang, "Report on the Sixth Five-Year Plan" (hereafter Zhao's 1982 Report), in *Fifth Session of the Fifth National People's Congress (Main Documents)* (Beijing: Foreign Languages Press, 1983), pp. 114–18, 173; Zhao Ziyang, "Report on the Work of the Government" (hereafter Zhao's 1983 Report), in *The First Session of the Sixth National People's Congress (Main Documents)* (Beijing: Foreign Languages Press, 1983), pp. 31–3, 38.

70. For statements by Zhao Ziyang on the importance of planning and central control, see Zhao's 1983 Report, pp. 33, 43; Zhao's 1982 Report, p. 170. Lieberthal, pp. 34–5, also see concessions by Deng in 1982 on economic policy and a slowing of structural reform.

71. Zhao's 1982 Report, p. 171; Zhao's 1983 Report, pp. 38, 43.

72. For typical deputy remarks, see "First-Stage Agenda Concluded," *FBIS* 114 (June 13, 1983): K25–6.

73. Luo Bing, "Zhao Ziyang baogao shou piping" [Zhao Ziyang's report receives criticism], *Zhengming*, no. 63 (January 1983): 15.

74. See "Deputies Make Suggestions," *FBIS* 114 (June 13, 1983): K12–13; Luo

Bing, "Liujie renda huinei huiwai" [Inside and outside the Sixth NPC], *Zhengming*, no. 69 (July 1983): 11.

75. Zhao's 1982 Report, p. 148.

76. Luo Bing, "Zhao Ziyang baogao shou piping" [Zhao Ziyang's report receives criticism], p. 14.

77. The Sixth Five-Year Plan had been implemented for nearly two years before it was discussed by the NPC; the constitution had already gone through a long process of public discussion and revision before it was submitted to the NPC; party involvement in personnel decisions predated legislative consideration by more than a year. For discussions of the "consolidation" of the "Deng-Hu-Zhao system" and its effect on the 1982 and 1983 NPCs, see, Ming Bao, "Forum of the 1980s – Forum on the Sixth NPC," *CR:PSM* 152 (September 2, 1983): 131, from *Ming Bao*, June 27, 1983, p. 21; Fan Jiahua, "Xin tizhi de lao wenti" [The new system's old problems], *Qishi Niandai*, no. 162 (July 1983): 19; Qi Xin, "Deng Hu Zhao tizhi de xin geju" [The new setup of the Deng-Hu-Zhao system], *Qishi Niandai*, no. 162 (July 1983): 16–17.

78. Spiritual pollution, also translated as cultural contamination, included such deviations as advocacy of Marxist humanism and the idea of socialist alienation, and liberal tendencies in art and literature. For a discussion of the reaction against this campaign, see Thomas P. Bernstein, "Domestic Politics," in *China Briefing, 1984*, ed. Steven M. Goldstein (Boulder, CO: Westview Press, 1985), pp. 1–4. The overall evaluation of 1984 is drawn from Dorothy J. Solinger, "Economic Reform," in *China Briefing, 1984*, ed. Steven M. Goldstein (Boulder, CO: Westview Press, 1985), p. 87. On rural reform in 1984, see Thomas P. Bernstein, "China in 1984," *Asian Survey* 25 (January 1985): 36–8.

79. Discussions of the 1984 urban reform initiatives can be found in Bernstein, "China in 1984," p. 38; Solinger, "Economic Reform," pp. 94–9. On the opposition to reform, see Bernstein, "Domestic Politics," pp. 8–9.

80. For Zhao's comments at the 1984 NPC, see Zhao Ziyang, "Report on the Work of the Government" (hereafter Zhao's 1984 Work Report), *FBIS* 107 (June 1, 1984): K1–20.

81. Duan Cunzhang, "At NPC Panel Discussions, Wang Maolin, Deputy to the NPC and Mayor of Taiyuan City, Adds Three Points to Zhao Ziyang's Government Work Report," *FBIS* 100 (May 22, 1984): K11–12, from *Renmin Ribao*, May 18, 1984, p. 1.

82. Shi Baohua, "Hunan Governor Supports Reforms," *FBIS* 101 (May 23, 1984): K11–12.

83. Duan Cunzhang, p. K12; Shi Baohua, p. K12.

84. Zhao Ziyang's 1984 Work Report, pp. K11–12.

85. For representative remarks, see "Intellectual Issue Discussed," *FBIS* 99 (May 21, 1984): K13–14.

86. Cited in Richard Baum, "China in 1985: The Greening of the Revolution," *Asian Survey* 26 (January 1986): 44. For the full text of Zhao's report to the 1985 NPC, see Zhao Ziyang, "Government Work Report" (hereafter Zhao's 1985 Report), *FBIS* 61 (March 29, 1985): K1–17.

87. See Lin Nian, "Cong dang de houshe kan renda zhengxie huiyi" [Looking at the NPC and CPPCC as the party's tongue], *Zhengming*, no. 91 (May 1985): 47.

88. Many Chinese and foreign sources remarked on the lively atmosphere at the 1985 NPC. See Liang Qian, "Jingji gaige zhong chule shemma wenti?" [What problems are emerging in the economic reform?], *Zhengming*, no. 91 (May 1985): 43; Lin Nian, p. 49; "Children of High-Ranking Cadres, Special Zone Currency," *FBIS* 65 (April 4, 1985): W7, from *Hsin Wan Pao*, April 2, 1985, p. 1; "Session Discusses

Congress Reports," *Beijing Review* 28 (April 8, 1985): 7–8; Han Baocheng, "NPC Sidelights – Taking the Road to Common Prosperity," *Beijing Review* 28 (April 22, 1985): 17–19. The quoted text is from John F. Burns, "Peking's Legislative Forums are Increasingly Feisty," *The New York Times*, April 15, 1985, p. A12. Burns also wrote, "What has caught attention more than anything said by officials is the latitude of debate at the congress. . . . The current meetings are evidence of a broader tolerance than Communist Chinese leaders have customarily shown."

89. See "Session Discusses Congress Reports," p. 7; Burns, p. A12; Liang Qian, p. 46.

90. See Liang Qian, p. 46.

91. Yu Jiwen, "Zhongguo jingji: gaige yu shikong" [Chinese economy: reform out of control], *Jiushi Niandai*, no. 184 (May 1985): 21.

92. Liang Qian, p. 46; Zhao's 1985 Report, p. K16.

93. See Zhao Jin, "From Anxiety to Confidence," *FBIS* 69 (April 10, 1985): K2–4; "Deputies Discuss Reform," *FBIS* 64 (April 3, 1985): K3. According to Liang Qian (p. 46), Party General Secretary Hu Yaobang, in a talk with Hong Kong reporters, denied that reform caused unhealthy practices, and Ren Zhongyi, the First Party Secretary of Guangdong, said the majority of cadres are good and attention must be paid to maintaining cadre and mass support for reform.

94. Liang Qian, p. 46; *Hsin Wan Pao*, p. W7.

95. "Session Discusses Congress Reports," p. 7.

96. "Deputies Discuss Reform," p. K4. For other calls for prosperous peasants to contribute to the public welfare, see Han Baocheng, p. 19.

97. Baum, pp. 42–3.

98. Burns, p. A12.

99. "Deputies on Imports, Exchange," *FBIS* 66 (April 5, 1985): K9; Yu Jiwen, p. 24; Liang Qian, pp. 44–5.

100. Qin's comments received prominent press coverage. Accounts can be found in Han Baocheng, p. 17; Lu Ren and Guo Xiusheng, "Shandong Official Speaks at NPC Session," *CR:PSM* 39 (April 26, 1985): 49; Liang Qian, pp. 43–4.

101. "Deputies Discuss Reform," p. K4.

102. Liang Qian, p. 44.

103. Liang Qian, p. 44.

104. Deng reportedly was one of the (unnamed) targets of these remarks. See Liang Qian, pp. 43–4.

105. For Zhao's remark, see Zhao's 1985 Report, p. K2. The commentary by Wen Mingrui and other deputies can be found in *Hsin Wan Pao*, p. W7; Liang Qian, p. 43.

106. Lu Ren and Guo Xiusheng, p. 49; Liang Qian, p. 44.

107. Han Baocheng, pp. 17–19.

108. For discussions of China in 1985–7, see Baum, pp. 30–53; Stanley Rosen, "China in 1986: A Year of Consolidation," *Asian Survey* 27 (January 1987): 35–55; Stanley Rosen, "China in 1987: The Year of the Thirteenth Party Congress," *Asian Survey* 28 (January 1988): 35–51; Lowell Dittmer, "China in 1986: Domestic Politics," in *China Briefing, 1987*, eds. John S. Major and Anthony Kane (Boulder, CO: Westview Press, 1988); Anthony J. Kane, "1987: Politics Back in Command," in *China Briefing, 1988*, ed. Anthony J. Kane (Boulder, CO: Westview Press, 1988), pp. 1–18.

109. Zhao Ziyang, "Report on the Seventh Five-Year Plan" (hereafter Zhao's 1986 Report), in *The Fourth Session of the Sixth National People's Congress (Main Documents)* (Beijing: Foreign Languages Press, 1986), pp. 1–62; Zhao Ziyang, "Report on the Work of the Government" (hereafter Zhao's 1987 Report), in *The Fifth Session*

of the Sixth National People's Congress (Main Documents) (Beijing: Foreign Languages Press, 1987), pp. 1–52. On the economy, see Zhao's 1986 Report, pp. 14–24, and Zhao's 1987 Report, pp. 12–19. On grain production, see Zhao's 1986 Report, pp. 18, 35–6, and Zhao's 1987 Report, pp. 10–12. On bourgeois liberalization, see Zhao's 1987 Report, pp. 9, 37–46. On living standards, see Zhao's 1986 Report, pp. 33–4, and Zhao's 1987 Report, pp. 14–15. For criticism of those on both his flanks, see Zhao's 1987 Report, p. 40.

110. "Plan Discussion Ends," *FBIS* 63 (April 2, 1986): K11; "Local Leaders Advocate Attention to Agriculture," *FBIS* 61 (March 31, 1986): K10; "Deputies Discuss Premier's Report," *FBIS* 62 (April 1, 1987): K12; "Study of Zhao Report Continues," *FBIS* 61 (March 31, 1987): K6.

111. "Local Leaders Advocate Attention to Agriculture," p. K10.

112. "Study of Zhao Report Continues," p. K6; "Deputies Discuss Premier's Report," p. K12.

113. "NPC Gives Go-Ahead to 5-Year Plan," *Beijing Review* 29 (April 21, 1986): 5; "National People's Congress: A Democratic Session," *Beijing Review* 30 (April 20, 1987): 5.

114. "Poor Areas Want Attention," *FBIS* 62 (April 1, 1987): K9–10.

115. "Discuss Problems in Education," *FBIS* 64 (April 3, 1987): K15–16; "Plan Discussion Ends," *FBIS* 63 (April 2, 1986): K12; "Deputies Discuss Premier's Report," p. K12.

116. "NPC Gives Go-Ahead to 5-Year Plan," p. 6.

117. For representative remarks, see "Ideo-Political Work Stressed," *FBIS* 62 (April 1, 1986): K21–2; Chi Maohua and Zhou Jianfang, "Yunnan Secretary on Liberalism," *FBIS* 64 (April 3, 1987): K12–13; "Crossfire at the Congress," *Asiaweek* 13 (April 12, 1987): 18–23.

118. "NPC Gives Go-Ahead to 5-Year Plan," pp. 5–6; "National People's Congress: A Democratic Session," p. 5.

119. Conversations with *South China Morning Post*, UPI, AP, and *Da Gongbao* correspondents March–April 1989. See also, Bao Xin, "Letter from Beijing," *FBIS* 78 (April 22, 1988): 17, from *Liaowang (Overseas Edition)* 15 (April 11, 1988): 1; "Eight 'Firsts' Set by NPC Session," *FBIS* 68 (April 8, 1988): 27–8; "Foreign Journalists Hear NPC Deputies' Debates," *FBIS* 61 (March 30, 1988): 6. On plans to increase openness, see Liu Jui-shao, "Beijing Keen on Improving Quality of NPC Sessions," *FBIS* 39 (February 29, 1988): 15, from *Wen Wei Po*, February 29, 1988, p. 1; Luo Bing, "Notes on the Northern Journey," *FBIS* 41 (March 2, 1988): 14–20, from *Zhengming*, no. 125 (March 1, 1988): 6–9.

120. Guo Zhaojin, "First Session of the Seventh NPC Took Another Major Step Forward in the Process of Democratization," *FBIS* 73 (April 15, 1988): 16–17.

121. "Deputies Deliberate Report," *FBIS* 59s (March 28, 1988): 26–7; Yang Minqing, "PLA Deputies Offer Views," *FBIS* 60 (March 29, 1988): 21–2.

122. Quoted passage in Wang Gangyi, "PLA Deputies Air Concerns," *FBIS* 60 (March 29, 1988): 21, from *China Daily*, March 29, 1988, p. 4. On ministers and the seventeen panels they visited, see Yang Minqing and Zhang Chunyu, "Ministers Hear Deputies' Views," *FBIS* 69 (April 11, 1988): 32.

123. Comments reported in Zhang Yuan, "Farm Production Concerns Voiced," *FBIS* 66 (April 6, 1988): 28–9, from *China Daily*, April 5, 1988, p. 4.

124. "More Agriculture Investment Urged," *FBIS* 60 (March 29, 1988): 23.

125. Guo Weifeng, "NPC Delegates, CPPCC Members Warn Against Dangerous Situation in Agriculture," *FBIS* 63 (April 1, 1988): 38–9.

126. Yang Guojun, "Government Work Report Reveals Many Revisions," *FBIS* 72 (April 14, 1988): 28.

127. For comments, see "Yunnan Urges More Interior Aid," *FBIS* 59s (March 28, 1988): 34; Seth Faison, "Xinjiang Fears Coastal Development Rebound," *FBIS* 66 (April 6, 1988): 23, from *South China Morning Post*, April 6, 1988, p. 7; Robert Delfs, "Outburst of Democracy," *Far Eastern Economic Review* 140 (April 7, 1988): 16; Han Baocheng, "Importance Attached to Coastal Development," *Beijing Review* 31 (April 25–May 1, 1988): 20–1.

128. For Li's and Zhao's remarks, see Li Peng, "Report on the Work of the Government," in *The First Session of the Seventh National People's Congress of the People's Republic of China (1988)* (Beijing: Foreign Languages Press, 1988), p. 34; "Urges Paid Services to Society," *FBIS* 62 (March 31, 1988): 16. For one assessment of public and deputy opinion on the issue, see Guo Zhaojin, "Some NPC Delegates Are Worried about Part-Time Jobs for Intellectuals," *FBIS* 64 (April 4, 1988): 32–3.

129. Wei Xiang, "General Secretary, Have You Heard Such Sharp Views Before?" *FBIS* 62 (March 31, 1988): 16–17; "To Our Readers," *Beijing Review* 31 (April 11–17, 1988): 6; "Some NPC Delegates are Worried about Part-Time Jobs for Intellectuals," pp. 32–3; "Intellectuals' Second Jobs Opposed," *FBIS* 63 (April 1, 1988): 23; He Ping and Yang Xinhe, "Hu Qili Joins Tianjin Group," *FBIS* 61 (March 30, 1988): 21.

130. Robert Delfs, "Students Seek Recognition," *Far Eastern Economic Review* 140 (April 21, 1988): 13; "Beijing Students Stage Sit-In Near NPC Session," *FBIS* 68 (April 8, 1988): 39, from Hong Kong AFP, April 8, 1988; Seth Faison, "Students Wall Posters in Beijing Persist," *FBIS* 68 (April 8, 1988): 40–1, from *South China Morning Post*, April 8, 1988, p. 1.

131. For remarks, see "To Our Readers," p. 6; Faison, "Student Wall Posters in Beijing Persist," pp. 40–1; Delfs, "Students Seek Recognition," p. 13.

132. Passages by Ding in Zhong Nan, "Beijing lianghui xiezhao" [Portrait of two meetings], *Jiushi Niandai*, no. 220 (May 1988): 65; Faison, "Students' Wall Posters in Beijing Persist," p. 40.

133. On China in early 1989, see Adi Ignatius, "China's Congress is Set to Stress Austerity," *Asian Wall Street Journal*, March 20, 1989, pp. 1, 15; Louise de Rosario, "Speak No Evil," *Far Eastern Economic Review* 144 (March 30, 1989): 11; Marlowe Hood, "Few Initiatives in Li's Cautious Economic Remedy," *South China Morning Post*, March 21, 1989, p. 11.

134. Author's research notes, March–April 1989. On restrictions, see "Outspoken Newspaper Banned from Session," *Hong Kong Standard*, March 21, 1989, p. 7; Louise de Rosario, "Speak No Evil," p. 11; "Change or Not? Chinese Brace for Fight," *Columbus Dispatch*, March 19, 1989, p. 3A; Daniel Southerland, "Soviet Shifts Not a Model, Chinese Says," *Washington Post*, April 4, 1989, p. A19. Eye-opening questions from journalists included ones on: human rights, Wei Jingsheng, political prisoners, martial law in Tibet, the pace of Chinese reform vs. Soviet reform, neoauthoritarianism, and the Three Gorges dam project. Many Beijing residents followed these unrehearsed appearances with great interest (especially the questions) and were willing to assess leadership performance – for example, Qian Qichen (good), Li Peng (fair), Wang Hanbin (poor).

135. Based on the author's observations and conversations with Chinese and western journalists. See also Li Peng, "Resolutely Carry Out the Principles of Improvement, Rectification and Deepened Reform," Report of the Work of the Government, Delivered at the Second Session of the Seventh National People's Congress on March 20, 1989, pp. 4–5; Hood, "Few Initiatives in Li's Cautious Economic Remedy," p. 11; Daniel Southerland, "Chinese Are Told to Prepare for New Austerity Measures," *Washington Post*, March 21, 1989; Tammy Tam and Priscilla Leung, "Mild Rebuke for Radical Economic Reforms," *Hong Kong Standard*, March 22, 1989,

p. 11; Nicholas D. Kristof, "Power War, the Chinese Way: The Nation Listens to Rumors and Intrigues," *The New York Times* (National Edition), March 23, 1989, p. 4.

136. Quoted text in Zhang Yu'an and Chang Hong, "Leadership Acts on Deputies' Opinions," *China Daily*, March 27, 1989, p. 1; see also, "Gangqu daibiao guanzhu tongzhang yuanyin" [Hong Kong deputies pay attention to the causes of inflation], *Wen Wei Po*, March 23, 1989, p. 2; Ling Zhijun, "Jiyu qiucheng tanyuan" [Exploring the origins of overeagerness to get quick results], *Renmin Ribao (Haiwaiban)*, March 24, 1989, p. 1; Wu Zhong, "NPC Deputies Pressure Chairman to Admit Neglect," *Hong Kong Standard*, April 2, 1989, p. 4; Robert Delfs, "Avoiding the Issues," *Far Eastern Economic Review* 144 (April 6, 1989): 13.

137. On the feasibility study, see "Yangtze Project Study Approved," *Beijing Review* 32 (March 20–26, 1989): 13. For NPC reaction, see "Critical NPC Delegates Point the Finger at Li Peng," *South China Morning Post*, April 2, 1989, p. 5; "270 Deputies Want Dam Halted," *China Daily*, April 3, 1989, p. 4. On the decision to postpone the project, see "Beijing Postpones Decision on Big Dam in Three Gorges Area," *Asian Wall Street Journal*, April 4, 1989, p. 3; O'Brien notes on leadership press conference, April 3, 1989.

138. For Yao's words, see "Guanyu 1989 nian guomin jingji he shehui fazhan jihua caoan de baogao" [Report on the draft 1989 plan for national economic and social development], delivered at the Second Session of the National People's Congress on March 21, 1989, p. 25.

139. "China Rules Out New Political Parties," *International Herald Tribune*, March 24, 1989, p. 5.

140. "Minorities Want Exemption from Austerity Plan," *South China Morning Post*, March 31, 1989, p. 10; "Deputies Seek Exemption," *Hong Kong Standard*, March 31, 1989, p. 6; "Leaders Agree to Austerity...in Some Other Province," *Hong Kong Standard*, March 27, 1989, p. 5.

141. Willy Wo-Lap Lam, "Coastal Zones Fight to Keep Economy Free," *South China Morning Post*, March 29, 1989, p. 10; "Leaders Agree to Austerity...in Some Other Province," p. 5; Governor Ye Xuanping denied that Guangdong was colonizing Hunan at a press conference in the Great Hall of the People, March 30, 1989.

Chapter 7. Structural reforms

1. For a perceptive analysis of the 1978 constitution (and its ambiguities), see Jerome A. Cohen, "China's Changing Constitution," *China Quarterly*, no. 76 (December 1978): 794–841.

2. Deng's August 1980 speech at an Enlarged Meeting of the Politburo encapsulated his approach to political reform. This speech was not published until 1983, but circulated widely soon after it was given. See Deng Xiaoping, "On the Reform of the System of Party and State Leadership," in *Selected Works of Deng Xiaoping (1975–1982)* (Beijing: Foreign Languages Press, 1984), pp. 302–25. *People's Daily* confirmed and summarized Deng's "very important speech" in November 1980 in a long article written by the vice president of the Central Party School. See Feng Wenbin, "Guanyu shehuizhuyi minzhu wenti" [Problems concerning socialist democracy] *Renmin Ribao*, November 24 and 25, 1980, p. 5.

3. The nature of Deng's relationship with his advisors is not fully known. Stuart Schram believes that outside reformers usually elaborated ideas first put forward by Deng or Hu Yaobang. Hong Kong sources (and Chinese exiles) more often place Deng among the conservatives in the "reform faction," and note that Deng offered many criticisms but few, strong proposals for systemic reform. See Stuart R. Schram, "'Economics in Command?' Ideology and Policy Since the Third Plenum, 1978–84," *China Quarterly*, no. 99 (September 1984): 422; Xu Xing, "Conservative Systems Reforms," *CR:PSM* 11 (February 1, 1984): 110–17, from *Zhengming*, no. 73 (November 1983). Lecture by Su Shaozhi, Ohio State University, October 4, 1989. It seems clear that in the debate over the NPC, Deng provided the impetus, but intellectuals on the fringe of power developed the concrete proposals.

4. Liao Gailong, "Historical Experiences and Our Road of Development, Part III" (hereafter Liao Gailong, Part III), *Issues and Studies* 17 (December 1981): 86–8. Compare with Deng Xiaoping, p. 322. See also Feng Wenbin, *Renmin Ribao*, November 25, 1980, p. 5.

5. For two early examples, see Wu Jialin, "Zenyang fahui quanguo renda zuowei zuigao guojia quanli jiguan de zuoyong" [How to bring into play the NPC as the highest organ of state power] (hereafter Wu Jialin, *Xinhua Wenzhai*), *Xinhua Wenzhai*, no. 12 (December 1980): 48–51, from *Guangming Ribao*, October 30, 1980; Cao Siyuan, "Huge Appropriations Should be Examined and Approved by Legislative Organs Through Hearings" (hereafter Cao Siyuan, "Huge Appropriations"), *FBIS* 219 (November 10, 1980): L19–20, from *Guangming Ribao*, October 23, 1980, p. 3.

6. Most notably, Chen Haosu, a research fellow at the Academy of Military Science, son of Marshal Chen Yi, and deputy from the PLA, submitted a 19,000-character motion that reviewed past NPC weaknesses and included a proposed complete revision of the NPC organic law. This motion was widely discussed and excerpts were published. See "PLA Delegate Proposes Measures to Strengthen NPC," *FBIS* 177 (September 10, 1980): L13–14; Yi Jianru, "A Motion Reflecting the People's Aspirations," *FBIS* 178 (September 11, 1980): L10–12; Tian Sansong, "Democracy in Action, Accent on Reforms," *Beijing Review* 23 (September 29, 1980): 35. Dozens of other NPC deputies submitted similar proposals recommending legislative reform.

7. Gao Gongyou, "Jiaqiang renmin daibiao dahui zhidu de zhongyao yiyi" [The significance of strengthening the NPC system], *Faxue*, no. 7 (July 1982): 15. Joseph Y. S. Cheng, "How to Strengthen the National People's Congress and Implement Constitutionalism," *Chinese Law and Government* 16 (Summer–Fall 1983): 99–102.

8. On a "proper division of labor," see former NPCSC Chairman Peng Zhen, "Report on the Draft of the Revised Constitution of the People's Republic of China," *FBIS* 235 (December 7, 1982): K45; Wang Shuwen, Wang Dexiang, and Zhang Qingfu, "Shehuizhuyi minzhu he fazhi jianshe de xin jieduan" [A new stage in the construction of socialist democracy and legality], *Faxue Yanjiu*, no. 6 (December 1982): 15. Cao Siyuan advocated a more complete break with tradition (later rejected) than either Peng or Wang et al.: "In the past we have always refused to recognize the principle of separation of the three branches of state power, now we have come to realize its reasonableness after experiencing the danger of too high a degree of centralization of state power." Cao Siyuan, "Ten Proposals for Revising the Constitution" (hereafter Cao Siyuan, "Ten Proposals"), *CR:PSM* 201 (June 30, 1981): 5, from *Minzhu yu Fazhi*, no. 2 (February 1981). On overburdened party cadres, see Cao Siyuan, "Huge Appropriations," p. L19. Cao Siyuan was a prominent legal expert, senior adviser to Zhao Ziyang, and the architect of the Bankruptcy Law. At this writing, he is said to be under arrest. On mutual accountability, see Shi Xiaozhong, "Jianquan guojia zhengzhi zhidu wenti dangyi" [Current discussion on perfecting the nation's political system], *Minzhu yu Fazhi*, no. 10 (October 1981): 7. On the relationship between strengthening the NPC and strengthening party leadership, see Gao Gongyou, p. 15.

9. Gao Gongyou, p. 15.

10. Informative discussions of the 1979 electoral law and the 1980 elections can be found in Brantly Womack, "The 1980 County-Level Elections in China: Exper-

iment in Democratic Modernization," *Asian Survey* 22 (March 1982): 261–77; Barrett L. McCormick, "Leninist Implementation: The Election Campaign," in *Policy Implementation in Post-Mao China*, ed. David M. Lampton (Berkeley: University of California Press, 1987), pp. 383–413; Andrew J. Nathan, *Chinese Democracy* (Berkeley: University of California Press, 1985), pp. 193–223. For the 1979 electoral law and the 1982 and 1986 revisions, see Legislative Affairs Commission of the Standing Committee of the National People's Congress, *The Laws of the People's Republic of China (1979–1986)*, two volumes (Beijing: Foreign Languages Press, 1987).

11. The quoted text appears in Xu Chongde and Pi Chunxie, *Xuanju Zhidu Wenda* [Questions and Answers on the Electoral System] (Beijing: Qunzhong Chubanshe, 1980, 1982), p. 59. For a similar argument, see Wang Dexiang, "Jianquan xuanju zhidu, baozhang renmin dangjia zuozhu" [Perfect the electoral system, guarantee the people as masters], *Faxue Yanjiu*, no. 3 (June 1979): 6.

12. Feng Wenbin, pp. 17, 18.

13. Wu Jialin, *Xinhua Wenzhai*, p. 49. For an earlier, hedged statement, offered in the form of a series of questions comparing socialist and bourgeois democracy, see Wu Jialin, "Some Questions Concerning Socialist Democracy," *Beijing Review* 22 (June 15, 1979): 13. Wu Jialin is, of course, the same People's University professor who *People's Daily* denounced in 1957 for asserting that the NPCSC had violated the law on several occasions. He reappeared as a party spokesman on socialist democracy in 1979, made some of the most provocative proposals in the legislative reform debate, and continues to write on political-legal affairs.

14. Shen Baoxiang, "Cherish One's Right to Vote," *FBIS* 122 (June 23, 1980): L12–13, from *Renmin Ribao*, June 13, 1980, p. 5.

15. Cao Siyuan, "Ten Proposals," p. 9.

16. Cao Siyuan, "Ten Proposals," p. 13.

17. Wu Jialin, "Dui xuanju zhidu minzhuhua de yize jianyi" [A proposal to democratize the electoral system] (hereafter Wu Jialin, "A Proposal to Democratize the Electoral System"), in *Zhengzhi yu Zhengzhi Kexue*, ed. Zhongguo Zhengzhixue Hui, Zhengzhi yu Zhengzhi Kexue Bianji Weiyuanhui (Beijing: Qunzhong Chubanshe, 1981), pp. 228–34. Wu imagined a hypothetical exhange between a deputy and one of his constituents: "You say he represents poorly. He says he originally didn't want to run but you elected him! You say he didn't fulfill his duties. He says he never promised anything to you. What responsibilities did he have?" Wu also supported NPC campaigning in Wu Jialin, *Xinhua Wenzhai*, p. 49.

18. For quoted text, see He Huahui, "Cong xuanju shijian kan wo guo xuanju zhidu de minzhuxing" [From electoral practice see the democratic nature of our country's electoral system], *Zhengzhi yu Falü*, no. 5 (June 1983): 49. See also, Li Zuxing, "Jinyibu fahui renmin daibiao dahui zhidu de zuoyong" [Further bring into play the role of the NPC], *Zhengzhixue Yanjiu*, no. 4 (July 1986): 10; She Xuxin and Xu Laiqin, "Guanyu zhijie xuanze zhong ruogan wenti de tantao" [Research on problems of direct elections], *Faxue Yanjiu*, no. 1 (February 1987): 3–4.

19. Compare original article 30 and amended article 30 of the electoral law of the National People's Congress and Local People's Congress of the People's Republic of China in Legislative Affairs Commission of the Standing Committee of the National People's Congress, *The Laws of the People's Republic of China (1979–1982)*, pp. 68, 382. For criticism of the revision and an explanation of its origins, see Wu Jialin, "Zhengzhi tizhi gaige chutan" [An exploration of political structural reform], *Ningxia Shehui Kexue*, no. 5 (October 1986): 6. On election irregularities, see Womack, pp. 269–70. Declining official support for campaigning can be seen in "Xi Zhongxun's Explanation of Four Legislative Bills at the Fifth Session of the Fifth National People's Congress," available in *People's Republic of China Yearbook – 1983* (Hong Kong: Evergreen Publishing Company, 1983), p. 307. For an extended discussion of per-

missible and impermissible forms of campaigning, see Chen Hefu, *Xuanju Manyu* [Notes on Elections] (Beijing: Qunzhong Chubanshe, 1983), pp. 173–81.

20. On undemocratic elections in 1983, see Zhang Zonghou, "Quanli zhiyue lun" [On restricting power], *Faxue*, no. 10 (October 1986): 2; Pi Chunxie and Nian Xinyong, "Zhengzhi tizhi gaige de yixiang zhongyao renwu" [An important task in political structural reform], *Zhongguo Zhengzhi*, no. 1 (January 1987): 27–9, from *Falü Xuexi yu Yanjiu*, no. 3 (1986): 15–18. See also, Cai Dingjian, "Jingzheng jizhi yu minzhu xuanju" [Competition system and democratic elections], *Fazhi Jianshe*, no. 6 (December 1988): 10–12. On party supplements, see Chen Hefu, p. 97. A standard explanation of why candidates in indirect elections are not limited to deputies in the electing congress can be found in Xu Chongde and Pi Chunxie, pp. 99–108.

21. Credentials Committee of the Fifth National People's Congress of the People's Republic of China, "Credentials Committee Report," *FBIS* 92 (May 11, 1983): K3–4. Provincial reports in 1983 confirmed contested elections, although I only found two that provided statistics on the extent of competition. In Jiangsu and Xinjiang, NPC deputies were selected from a pool containing precisely 20% more candidates than available positions (i.e., minimal compliance with the law). See *FBIS*, May 2, 1983 (O5–6), May 5, 1983 (T5). In 1988, for four provinces that released information, the pool ranged from 32% to 50% more candidates than positions. See *FBIS*, January 25, 1988 (26), January 29, 1988 (27), February 1, 1988 (44), February 2, 1988 (35). Wang Shuwen, an NPC Law Committee member, told this author (March 17, 1989) that provincial congresses "generally adhere" to the requirement of 20% to 50% more candidates than positions. A legal researcher at the Chinese Academy of Social Sciences acknowledged (March 28, 1989) that uncontested elections still occur, but said, "when this occurs it is often exposed and corrected." For information on the Guangdong court president's defeat, see "NPC Delegates from Guangdong, Hainan Meet Press," *FBIS* 63 (April 1, 1988): 12.

22. Paragraph follows Cai Dingjian, pp. 10–12. Cai is a researcher attached to the NPCSC General Office. Yan Jiaqi, then a member of the Beijing People's Congress and director of the Political Science Institute of the Chinese Academy of Social Science, and now a prominent exile, has said that 99% of candidates on approved nomination lists are elected, while 1% of the candidates nominated by ten or more deputies are elected. Interview in Zhang Weiguo, "Zhongguo de xiwang zai yu minzhu yu fazhi" [China's hopes lie in democracy and legality], *Shijie Jingji Daobao*, April 3, 1989, p. 11. These remarks were made just before the 1989 student movement began. On the need to stress individual nominations and to limit those of political organizations, see Pu Xingzu, "Increase the Authority of Legislative Organs," *Chinese Law and Government* 20 (Spring 1987): 82, from *Zhengzhixue Yanjiu*, no. 2 (March 1986): 15–17; "Democratic Election System Discussed," *Beijing Review* 31 (February 1–7, 1988): 40; Zhang Bingyin, "Shilun woguo de minzhu zhengzhi jianshe yu renda gongzuo de guanxi" [Discussion of the relationship of our country's democratic political construction to people's congress work], *Zhengfa Luntan*, no. 3 (June 1989): 52.

23. "Many Ningxia Congress Deputies Unqualified," *FBIS* 103 (May 27, 1988): 53.

24. A detailed discussion of this meeting and changes in leadership candidate lists can be found in Li Shangzhi and Xu Minhe, "Chongfen fayang minzhu, shixian renmin xinyuan" [Fully develop democracy, realize the people's dreams], *Liaowang*, no. 7 (July 1983): 2–4.

25. Yau Shing-mu, "Paper on Voting for President, Vice Chairmen," *FBIS* 70 (April 12, 1988): 26–7, from *Hong Kong Standard*, April 9, 1988, pp. 1, 6.

26. On "forbidden zones" and the sensitivity of electoral reform, see Wu Jialin,

"Tigao difang guojia quanli jiguan de quanweixing" [Views on strengthening the powers of local authorities], *Faxue Pinglun*, no. 1 (January 1987): 30. For a defense of "democratic consultation," see Zhang Youyu, "Minzhu xieshang shi shixing renmin minzhu de youxiao fangshi" [Democratic consultation is an effective means to carry out people's democracy], *Jianghai Xuekan*, no. 4 (August 1984): 3–10. For typical recommendations to allow campaigning and reform nominating procedures, see Li Zuxing, "Renda biaojuezhi ji gaige shexiang [Ideas on reforming the NPC's voting system and other reforms], *Faxue*, no. 11 (November 1986): 6; Tian Jun and Liu Huiming, "Lun woguo renda jiandu zhidu de wanshan" [On perfecting our country's people's congress supervision system], *Jianghai Xuekan*, no. 1 (January 1989): 69.

Quoted remarks are Li Peng's at a press conference in the Great Hall of the People, April 3, 1989. They echo Qian Qichen at a press conference in the Great Hall of the People, March 27, 1989 and my conversation with a CASS legal researcher, March 28, 1989. All these comments were made in the immediate aftermath of the 1989 Soviet general election. In the words of one Beijing-based reporter (March 31, 1989), this election "aroused considerable talk among NPC deputies, though recommendations for similar reforms have not been particularly warmly received."

27. Yan Jiaqi quoted in Lai Pui-Yee, "Overhaul of Charter Demanded by Scholars," *South China Morning Post*, March 27, 1989, p. 6.

28. Chen Yunsheng, "Wo guo xianfa de falü baozheng" [Our constitution's legal guarantees], *Faxue Jikan*, no. 3 (July 1982): 18.

29. Wu Jialin, "A Proposal to Democratize the Electoral System," p. 231; Wu Jialin, *Xinhua Wenzhai*, p. 49; Pan Nianzhi, "Some Ideas About Revising the Constitution," *CR:PSM* 202 (July 6, 1981): 33, from *Minzhu yu Fazhi*, no. 4 (April 1981).

30. Liao Cailong, Part III, p. 87.

31. Wu Jialin, *Xinhua Wenzhai*, p. 49; Pan Nianzhi, p. 33; Zhang Shixin, "Some Views on the Issue of the Position of Head of State in China," *CR:PSM* 263 (January 26, 1982): 51, from *Minzhu yu Fazhi*, no. 9 (September 1981): 8–9.

32. Zhang Shixin, p. 51.

33. Liao Gailong, Part III, p. 88. Quotation from Cao Siyuan, "Ten Proposals," p. 12.

34. Zhang Shixin, p. 52.

35. Cao Siyuan, "Ten Proposals," p. 13.

36. Reducing the ratio of CCP members, it was said, would "strengthen coopcration and unity between the party and those outside the party" and "would mobilize activism and promote modernization." See "Hu Yaobang on Election of State Leaders," *FBIS* 107 (June 2, 1983): K2; Wang Xiangming, *Xianfa Ruogan Lilun Wenti de Yanjiu* (hereafter Wang Xiangming, *Xianfa*) [Research on Certain Theoretical Questions on Constitutions] (Beijing: Zhongguo Renmin Daxue Chubanshe, 1983), p. 123.

37. Statistics available in Peng Chong, "Peng Chong on Credentials of Sixth NPC Deputies," *FBIS* 91 (May 10, 1983): K1–3; Zheng Zhi, "New Lineup of Deputies to Sixth NPC Reviewed," *CR:PSM* 442 (August 1, 1983): 34–6, from *Banyuetan*, no. 10 (May 25, 1983): 6–7.

38. The average age of the NPC deputies elected in 1978 was never officially released, but one 1979 source put it at "about 50." "Xinhua Comments on Daily Activities of NPC Deputies," *CR:PSM* 6 (August 2, 1979): 10.

39. Liao Hansheng, "Guanyu diqijie quanguo renmin daibiao dahui daibiao zige de shencha baogao de shuoming" [An explanation of the report on the seventh NPC deputies' credentials], *Zhonghua Renmin Gongheguo Quanguo Renmin Daibiao Dahui Changwu Weiyuanhui Gongbao*, no. 2 (April 15, 1988): 4–7. See also "Spokesman Gives News Conference," *FBIS* 57 (March 24, 1988): 16–18; "Comments on Prep-

arations," *FBIS* 57 (March 24, 1988): 11–13; Hu Guohua, "A New Milestone for Building Democratic Politics – Thoughts on the Convening of the Seventh NPC," *FBIS* 63 (April 1, 1988): 28, from *Liaowang* (Overseas Edition), no. 13, March 28, 1988, pp. 3–4.

40. Peng Chong, p. K2; Zheng Zhi, pp. 34–6; Liao Hansheng, p. 6.

41. Liu Xia, "Zhengzhi tizhi gaige yu renmin daibiao suzhi" [Political structural reform and people's deputy quality], *Fazhi Jianshe*, no. 5 (October 1987): 20–1; She Xuxin and Xu Laiqin, p. 5; Zheng Gongcheng, "Suggestions on Reforming the People's Congress Deputy System," *FBIS* 215 (November 7, 1988): 29–30, from *Qunyan*, no. 9 (September 1988): 46. In an interview (March 28, 1989), a CASS legal researcher suggested that although deputies elected in 1988 were younger and better educated than their 1983 counterparts, "quality had not yet taken a fundamental change for the better."

42. Wang Xiangming, p. 123.

43. "Presidium Approves Candidate Lists," *FBIS* 118 (June 17, 1983): K1. For information on the 1983 NPC leaders, see Long Fei, "Ping zhonggong 'liujie renda' xuanchu de lingdao chengyuan" [A comment on the leading members elected at the Chinese communists Sixth NPC], *Zhonggong Yanjiu* (Taipei) 17 (July 1983): 39–40. Only three vice chairmen remained from those originally elected to the 1978 NPC.

44. "Hu Yaobang on Election of State Leaders," p. K2.

45. Zhonggong Yanjiu, "Zhonggong liujie renda yici huiyi de zhidao sixiang" [The guiding thought of the Chinese communists Sixth NPC First Session], *Zhonggong Yanjiu* (Taipei) 17 (July 1983): 2. There's some truth in this claim as at least several of the 1983 NPC leaders (e.g., Geng Biao, Song Renqiong, Huang Hua, Peng Chong) assumed their NPC position after vacating high party posts. Their party positions, in general, were filled by younger men who were more closely associated with Deng. The Chinese commentator cited is Li Zuxing, "Renda biaojuezhi ji qi gaige shexiang," p. 6.

46. The quoted text appears in "Bankruptcy Law Urged," *FBIS* 122 (June 25, 1986): K4; for other NPCSC discussions of why it was premature to implement a bankruptcy law, see Gao Ling, "Why the Draft Enterprise Bankruptcy Law Has Not Been Adopted – Sidelights on the NPC Standing Committee Session," *FBIS* 194 (October 7, 1986): K1–3, from *Liaowang* (Overseas Edition), no. 39, September 29, 1986, pp. 13–14; Hu Jihua and Li Yahong, "Commenting on Views on Temporarily Not Putting the Bankruptcy Law to Vote," *FBIS* 220 (November 14, 1986): K3–5, from *Zhongguo Fazhibao*, October 27, 1986, p. 3; Guo Yuanfa, "Properly Formulate the Law of Reform for the People," *FBIS* 238 (December 11, 1986): K3–5, from *Liaowang*, no. 48, December 1, 1986, p. 5.

47. On complementary legislation passed, see "Debate Continues on Bankruptcy Law Legislation," *FBIS* 228 (November 26, 1986): K7, from *Ta Kung Pao*, November 20–26, 1986, p. 1; Guo Yuanfa, p. K4. For detailed discussions of the making of the bankruptcy law, see Ta-kuang Chang, "The Making of the Chinese bankruptcy law: A Study in the Chinese Legislative Process," *Harvard International Law Journal* 28 (Spring 1987): 333–72. On revisions to the bankruptcy law, see "Song Rufen Explains Enterprise bankruptcy law," *FBIS* 225 (November 21, 1986): K14–15.

48. See "NPC Session Deliberates on enterprise law," *FBIS* 51 (March 13, 1987): K18–19; "NPC Session Discusses Party Role in Enterprises," *FBIS* 53 (March 19, 1987): K3–4. For a summary of the drafting of the enterprise law and NPCSC queries at each stage, see Zhang Sutang and He Ping, "Gaige huhuanzhe qiye fa chu tai" [Reform calling the enterprise law out from behind the stage], *Liaowang* (Overseas Edition), February 8, 1988, pp. 17–18.

49. Zhang and He, pp. 17–18. For a text of the law, see *FBIS* 80 (April 26, 1988): 42–9.

50. "Rules for Villages Reviewed," *FBIS* 47 (March 11, 1987): K4; "Discusses Village Rule, Contracts," *FBIS* 12 (January 20, 1987): K22–3.

51. "Village Committee Regulations," *FBIS* 66 (April 7, 1987): K7; "Considers Village Regulations," *FBIS* 68 (April 9, 1987): K17; Gong Miao, "Reform of Political Structure, Autonomy for Peasants – NPC Deputies Argue Over Draft of Villagers' Law," *FBIS* 71 (April 14, 1987): K24, from *Zhongguo Tongxun She*, April 11, 1987; Bao Xin, "Concerning the Villagers' Committee Organization Law," *FBIS* 79 (April 24, 1987): K10–12, from *Liaowang (Overseas Edition)*, no. 16, April 20, 1987, p. 1.

52. Bao Xin, p. K12.

53. On remaining opposition, see "NPC Standing Committee on Village Draft Law," *FBIS* 224 (November 20, 1987): 12–13.

54. Hu and Li, p. K3.

55. Li Shangzhi and Xu Minhe, p. 4. At the 1983 NPC, Peng Zhen also reportedly criticized the large number of politically reliable but untalented deputies and said the capable must take the lead. Reported in Long Fei, pp. 43–4.

56. "NPC to Revise 117 Laws in Next Five Years," *FBIS* 149 (August 3, 1988): 13–14. See also Liu Xia, p. 22; Nie Linfeng, "Shilun zhiding renmin daibiao fa" [Thoughts on enacting a people's deputy law], *Faxue Zazhi*, no. 4 (August 1987): 16–17.

57. For remarks at the 1980 NPC, see "Excerpts of Speeches by NPC Deputies at Panel Discussions" (hereafter *People's Daily* Excerpts 7), *FBIS* 184 (September 19, 1980): L15, from *Renmin Ribao*, September 12, 1980, p. 4. For Liao's speech, see Liao Gailong, Part III, p. 86.

58. For "some reduction," see Song Richang, "Guanyu xiugai xianfa de wojian" [My opinions on revision of the constitution], *Shehui Kexue*, no. 1 (January 1981): 65; "China Might Restore the State Chairman," *FBIS* 40 (March 2, 1981): VI-2, from *Wen Wei Po*, February 27, 1981, pp. 1, 2. Commentators who advocated 1,000 deputies include Xu Chongde, "Ten Proposals for Revising the Constitution," *CR:PSM* 200 (June 29, 1981): 4, from *Minzhu yu Fazhi*, no. 3 (March 1981): 7–10; Wu Jialin, *Xinhua Wenzhai*, p. 49; Zhang Shixin, p. 51.

59. Dong Chengmei, "Shilun xianxing xianfa ruhe xiugai de jige wenti" [Discussion of several issues on how to revise the current constitution], *Minzhu yu Fazhi*, no. 3 (March 1982): 9.

60. Liao Gailong, Part III, pp. 86–7, 92; Xu Chongde, pp. 4–5; "China Might Restore the State Chairman," p. V1; Song Richang, p. 65.

61. Xu Chongde, p. 4.

62. For this view, see Xu Chongde, pp. 4–5; Liao Gailong, p. 87.

63. Song Richang, p. 65. See also Pan Nianzhi, pp. 32, 33.

64. Pan Nianzhi, pp. 32–3, and Xu Chongde, pp. 4–5, reported these proposals, but opposed them.

65. Xu Chongde, p. 5; Liao Gailong, Part III, p. 87.

66. Liu Chuanchen, "Woguo daibiao jigou yu jiandu zhidu" [Our country's representative organs and the supervisory system], *Shehui Kexue*, no. 3 (March 1982): 21.

67. Xu Chongde, p. 4.

68. Pan Nianzhi, p. 32.

69. Dong Chengmei, p. 9.

70. Pan Nianzhi, pp. 32–3.

71. Wang Xiangming, *Xianfa*, p. 133.

72. Liao Gailong, Part III, p. 87.

73. Pan Nianzhi, pp. 32–3. Hsin-chi Kuan, a Hong Kong-based scholar, agreed that the creation of a second chamber would probably weaken the NPC further. See Hsin-chi Kuan, "New Departures in China's Constitution," *Studies in Comparative Communism* 17 (Spring 1984): 59.

74. Wang Xiangming, "Xiancao tixianle gexin guojia de jingshen" [The draft constitution embodies the spirit of reform], *Faxue Jikan*, no. 3 (July 1982): 13; Xiao Weiyun, "A New Development in the People's Congress System in Our Country," *FBIS* 123 (June 25, 1982): K9, from *Renmin Ribao*, June 14, 1982, p. 5; Wang Shuwen, "The People's Congress System is our Country's Basic Political System," *CR:RF* (July 16, 1982): 34, from *Hongqi*, no. 10 (May 16, 1982): 20–4. After the draft constitution was published, Xu Chongde recanted support for bicameralism and a considerably smaller NPC. See Xu Chongde and He Huahui, "Renmin daibiao dahui zhidu de xin fazhan" [New developments of the people's congress system], *Zhengzhi yu Falü*, no. 1 (June 1982): 31.

75. Peng Zhen, p. K44; Renmin Ribao Shelun, "Woguo guojia tizhi de zhongyao gaige he xin de fazhan" [Important reforms and new developments in our country's state system], *Renmin Ribao*, June 20, 1982, p. 1; Wang Xiangming, *Faxue Jikan*, p. 13. Several years later, Deng Xiaoping criticized bicameralism and defended "the system of a single NPC, which is adapted to China's reality." Quoted in Stuart Schram, "Political Reform in China – In the Primary Stage of Socialism," *IHJ Bulletin* 8 (Spring 1988): 3.

76. For deputy remarks, see "NPC Deputies Urge End to 'Rubber Stamp' Image," *FBIS* 72 (April 14, 1988): 36. For reducing the size of all people's congresses by two-thirds (in the name of efficiency, cost reduction, and better staff and simple administration), see Zheng Gongcheng, p. 29. A senior legal researcher at the Chinese Academy of Social Sciences supported reducing the size of all people's congresses, especially those at the provincial level, March 28, 1989. NPC Law Committee member Wang Shuwen explained (March 17, 1989) that leaders are aware of the "contradiction" between a large, broadly representative legislature and efficient plenary sessions. He acknowledged that legislative size was discussed frequently before 1982, but infrequently since.

77. This "very one-sided view" is presented as the position of "some comrades" in Kan Ke, "Quanguo renmin daibiao dahui daibiao ming'e queding yiju tantao" [An approach to determining the number of deputies to the NPC], *Zhengzhixue Yanjiu*, no. 5 (September 1987): 36. Kan opposes "using quantity to replace quality" and suggests that the influence and example of talented deputies are diminished in an overly large legislature.

78. Author's observations at the 1989 NPC, confirmed as essentially unchanged since the 1950s by many observers, including Chang Shao Wei, *Ta Kung Pao* reporter, March 31, 1989; He Zhigeng, staff member of the People's Institute of Foreign Affairs, March 18, 1989; John Pomfret, Associated Press correspondent, April 3, 1989. Chang explained that one of the few delegations still allowed to stay in a first-class hotel (the Beijing Hotel) is the Guangdong delegation, and that's because a number of its members are from Hong Kong. In 1989, a flashing sign welcomed NPC deputies to Beijing's Friendship Store and imported goods were in abundance. Many Beijing residents are said to resent deputy privileges. In a small gesture designed to reduce public antipathy, deputy motorcades in 1989 were required to pay attention to traffic signals. "Deputies Role in Congress," *China Daily*, April 1, 1989, p. 4.

79. Liao Gailong, Part III, p. 87. See also Cao Siyuan, "Ten Proposals," p. 12. Remarks by NPCSC Vice Chairman Zhang Youyu in a speech to the annual meeting of the Beijing Municipal Society of Law, reported in "China Might Restore the State

Chairman," p. VI. For later suggestions to change the NPC's date or to convene two sessions each year (partly to facilitate budget review), see Cao Siyuan, "Dui renda yishi guize caoan sidian yijian" [Four opinions on the NPC rules on proceedings], *Shijie Jingji Daobao*, March 20, 1989, p. 3; "Stronger Role for NPC Urged," *FBIS* 65 (April 5, 1988): 14; interview with CASS legal researcher, March 28, 1989. The NPC proceedings regulations, passed at the 1989 NPC, prescribe that the NPC meets in the first quarter of the year, several months after the fiscal year begins. On professionalizing deputies, see "Better Educated Deputies Urged," *FBIS* 35 (February 23, 1988): 7–8, from *China Daily*, February 23, 1988, p. 4; Yu Jian, "Lun renmin daibiao de falü diwei" [On the legal status of people's deputies], *Zhengzhi yu Falü*, no. 4 (August 1987): 26.

80. Wang Xiangming, *Xianfa*, p. 125; Xu Chongde and He Huahui, p. 31. For a counterargument that professional politicians can serve the working class as well as the bourgeoisie, see Pi and Nian, p. 29. "Defects" of the amateur deputy system are also discussed in Zheng Gongcheng, p. 30.

81. On subsidies, see Zhang Yu'an, "Less Deputy Fanfare – Start of a Trend?" *China Daily*, April 5, 1989, p. 4; Interview (April 3, 1989) with a leading member of the NPCSC General Office. On high officials serving in the NPC to protect their budgetary outlays, see Li Guoxiong, "Woguo renmin daibiaozhi dangyi" [An opinion on our country's people's congress system], *Faxue Pinglun*, no. 1 (January 1987): 14.

82. See Pan Nianzhi, p. 34; Wu Jialin, *Xinhua Wenzhai*, p. 49; Shi Xiaozhong, p. 7. Later in the 1980s, calls to establish a full-fledged plenary debate system became common. See "Shaanxi Deputy Proposes NPC Debates," *FBIS* 66 (April 6, 1988): 25; Cao Siyuan, "Dui Renda Yishi Guize Caoan Sidian Yijian," p. 3.

83. For quoted words, see Pan Nianzhi, p. 34; Cao Siyuan, "Ten Proposals," p. 12; "Excerpts of Speeches by NPC Deputies at Panel Discussions," *FBIS* 184 (September 19, 1980): L7. See also *People's Daily* Excerpts 7, p. L15; "NPC Deputies Talk About the Third Session of the Fifth NPC," *FBIS* 180 (September 15, 1980): L31.

84. Zhang Youyu, "Lun renmin daibiao dahui daibiao de renwu, zhiquan he huodong fangshi wenti" [On the tasks, powers, functions, and activities of National People's Congress deputies], *Faxue Yanjiu*, no. 2 (April 1985): 4.

85. Li Zuxing, "Renda Biaojuezhi Ji Gaige Shexiang," pp. 2–6; Pu Xingzu, pp. 78–9.

86. Dong Min, "Sidelights on the Fourth Session of the Sixth NPC," *CR:PSM* 61 (August 4, 1986): 6–8, from *Zhengming*, no. 103 (May 1986): 94.

87. Li Zuxing, "Jinyibu Fahui Renmin Daibiao Dahui Zhidu de Zuoyong," pp. 10–12, 37; Li Zuxing, "Renda Biaojuezhi Ji Gaige Shexiang," pp. 2–6.

88. Zi Mu, "Strengthening the People's Congress is the Fundamental Way to Develop Socialist Democracy," *Chinese Law and Government* 20 (Spring 1987): 87–8, from *Shijie Jingji Daobao*, August 11, 1986.

89. Pu Xingzu, pp. 78–9.

90. Li Zuxing, "Renda Biaojuezhi Ji Gaige Shexiang," pp. 2–6; Juan Chi-chung, "Sidelight – Dissenting Votes at the NPC," *FBIS* 76 (April 21, 1986): W5–6, from *Wen Wei Po*, April 13, 1986.

91. "NPC Special Committees Elected Over Opposition," *FBIS* 59s (March 28, 1988): 48–9; Antonio Kamiya, "KYODO Reviews Dissenting Votes in Elections," *FBIS* 69 (April 11, 1988): 21–2.

92. Fan Cheuk-wan, "HK Deputies Lash Shenzhen Plan," *Hong Kong Standard*, April 2, 1989, p. 4; Fan Cheuk-wan, "HK Deputies Force Beijing to Back Down," *Hong Kong Standard*, April 4, 1989, p. 1. The official vote tally was reported in *Renmin Ribao* (Haiwaiban), April 5, 1989, p. 1, and the voting was witnessed by many observers, including this author.

93. See Rules of Procedure for the National People's Congress of the People's Republic of China (Draft), later passed at the 1989 NPC. An NPCSC vice chairman acknowledged that there was "conflict" over limiting plenary speeches. But, he concluded, in accordance with international practice and to prevent "aimless, discursive chatting," restrictions were necessary. Zhang Youyu, "Guanyu zhiding quanguo renmin daibiao dahui yishi guize de wenti" [Issues drawing up the NPC rules of procedure], *Zhengzhixue Yanjiu*, no. 3 (May 1989): 4–5.

94. For an uncommonly complete explanation of the state-leadership selection process, see Li Shangzhi and Xu Minhe, pp. 2–4.

95. See "Excerpts of Speeches by NPC Deputies at Group Discussions" (hereafter *People's Daily* Excerpts 6), *FBIS* 182 (September 17, 1980): L5; "NPC Deputies Talk About the Third Session of the Fifth NPC," pp. L30, L31.

96. Wu Jialin, *Xinhua Wenzhai*, p. 49.

97. See Rules of Procedure for the National People's Congress of the People's Republic of China (Draft), later passed at the 1989 NPC. On receiving the government work report uncharacteristically early, see Liu Jui-shao, "Beijing Keen on Improving Quality of NPC Sessions," *FBIS* 39 (February 29, 1988): 15, from *Wen Wei Po*, February 29, 1988, p. 1.

98. For quoted text, see Wang Xiangming, *Xianfa*, pp. 137, 138, and Gao Zhaoxian, "Cong xiancao kan renmin daibiao dahui zhidu de xin fazhan" [New developments of the NPC system seen in the draft constitution], *Faxue Jikan*, no. 4 (October 1982): 12.

99. Gao Zhaoxian, p. 12; Zhang Youyu, "On the tasks, powers, functions and activities of National People's Congress deputies," p. 4.

100. Li Zuxing, "Renda Biaojuezhi Ji Gaige Shexiang," p. 6.

101. Liu Chuanchen, p. 21.

102. Wang Dexiang, "Zhixunquan jianlun" [A brief explanation of the right to address inquiries], in *Xianfalun Wenxuan*, ed. Zhongguo Faxuehui (Beijing: Falü Chubanshe, 1983), pp. 198–9. For procedures concerning deputy inquiries, see Rules of Procedure for the National People's Congress of the People's Republic of China (Draft), pp. 17–19, later passed at the 1989 NPC.

103. For quoted text and comment on piles of proposals, see Wang Xiangming, *Xianfa*, p. 132. See also "Xi Zhongxun's Explanation of Four Legislative Bills at the Fifth Session of the Fifth National People's Congress," p. 303.

104. Wang Shuwen and Zhou Yanrui, "New Development of the People's Congress System," *CR:PSM* 337 (September 15, 1982): 29, from *Faxue Yanjiu*, no. 3 (June 1982): 9–14.

105. Rules of Procedure for the National People's Congress of the People's Republic of China (Draft), p. 10.

106. Commentator, "Attention Must be Paid to the People's Deputies' Proposals," *FBIS* 193 (October 2, 1980): L5–6, from *Renmin Ribao*, September 27, 1980, p. 1. *Ta Kung Pao* reporter Chang Shao Wei told this author (March 31, 1989) that many deputies were frustrated that good suggestions made in 1988 were ignored and that procedures did not exist to guarantee a response.

107. "Progress Made in Legal System," *Beijing Review* 31 (April 18–24, 1988): 11.

108. It is noteworthy that none of the reformers discussed suffered setbacks in their careers comparable to their predecessors in 1957. Xu Chongde, for example, went on to write the entry on the NPC in the Law Volume of the Chinese Encyclopedia, and Liao Gailong, though tamed, continues as a vice chairman of the Central Committee's Party History Research Office. Wu Jialin was elected vice chairman of the Chinese Legal Society Constitutional Research Society. What has happened after

June 1989 is less clear. At this writing, Cao Siyuan and Yu Haocheng are said to be under pressure, though their exact whereabouts are not known.

109. Many authors argued that NPC ineffectiveness necessitated strengthening the NPCSC. For examples, see Chen Yunsheng, "Baozheng xianfa shishi de zhongyao zuzhi xingshi" [Important organizational forms to guarantee the constitution's enforcement], *Jianghai Xuekan*, no. 2 (April 1983): 56; Renmin Ribao Shelun, p. 1; Zhang Youyu and Xu Chongde, "The Fundamental Spirit of the Draft of the New Constitution," *SWB*, FE 7035, May 25, 1982, pp. BII/1–5, from *Renmin Ribao*, May 17, 1982; Wang Xiangming, *Faxue Jikan*, pp. 13–14.

110. In an often obscure debate, some opposed upgrading the NPCSC on grounds it would undermine the NPC's position and violate legislative supremacy. It was ultimately decided that since the NPCSC is one component of the legislature, strengthening it would strengthen the entire system. See Chen Yunsheng, p. 34; Wang Shuwen, "Jiaqiang shehuizhuyi he fazhi de liang zhongda cuoshi" [Two important measures to strengthen socialist democracy and legal system], *Minzhu yu Fazhi*, no. 7 (July 1982): 7–8; Zhang Youyu, "New Developments of the People's Congress System" (hereafter Zhang Youyu, *FBIS* 15), *FBIS* 15 (January 21, 1983): K13, from *Renmin Ribao*, January 14, 1983. Xiao Weiyun also explained that "history has shown that if functions and powers which cannot be conveniently and regularly exercised by the NPC are retained and not given to the NPCSC, this will affect the work of both the NPC and the NPCSC." Xiao Weiyun, p. K9.

111. Zhang Youyu, *FBIS* 15, p. K12. These provisions greatly expanded powers granted the NPCSC in 1955 and 1959 and were said to be of unprecedented scope among all socialist countries. Gao Zhaoxian, p. 10.

112. On the importance of promptness in law making and the advantages of delegating powers to the NPCSC, see Gao Zhaoxian, p. 10; Zhang Youyu, *FBIS* 15, p. K12; Zhang Youyu, "Jiaqiang xianfa lilun de yanjiu" [Strengthen research on constitutional theory] (hereafter Zhang Youyu, *Xianfalun Wenxuan*), in *Xianfalun Wenxuan*, ed. Zhongguo Faxuehui (Beijing: Falü Chubanshe, 1983), p. 8.

113. On extending powers of interpellation to the NPCSC, see the constitution (art. 73); NPC organic law (art. 33); Liu Chuanchen, p. 21; Han Peimei, "Lun jiaqiang quanguo renda changweihui de jianshe" [On strengthening NPCSC construction], *Faxue Zazhi*, no. 2 (April 1983): 32. Wu Jialin, *Xinhua Wenzhai*, p. 50, discusses the benefits of reviving NPCSC inspections.

114. Some reformers suggested reducing the number of NPCSC members to 100 or even 50 to 70, but this was rejected. See Dong Chengmei, p. 9; Liao Gailong, Part III, pp. 87, 88; Zhang Shixin, pp. 49, 51.

115. Interviews with a leading member of the NPCSC General Office, April 3, 1989, and a legal researcher at CASS, March 28, 1989. Small-group (*fenzu huiyi*) meetings appear to be held at every NPCSC session; I have conflicting reports on the frequency of joint meetings (*lianzu huiyi*). For statutory discussion of small-group meetings and joint meetings, see "Zhongguo renmin daibiao dahui changwu weiyuanhui yishi guize" [NPCSC proceedings regulations], *Renmin Ribao* (Haiwaiban), November 25, 1987, p. 4; "Tigao yishi xiaolü, wanshan changweihui zhineng" [Improve proceedings efficiency, improve standing committee functions], *Renmin Ribao* (Haiwaiban), December 4, 1987, p. 4.

116. This information is from Pan Nianzhi, p. 34; Wu Jialin, *Xinhua Wenzhai*, pp. 49–50; Han Peimei, p. 59.

117. See Gao Zhaoxian, p. 12; Wang Bixuan, Li Liancheng, Sun Xi, and Cui Min, *Xin Xianfa Wenda* [Questions and Answers on the New Constitution] (Taiyuan: Shanxi Renmin Chubanshe, 1983), pp. 137–8; Xu Chongde, pp. 5–6; Liu Chuanchen, p. 21.

118. The New China News Agency reported that "efforts have been made to reduce the number of people who hold several posts concurrently." "Presidium Approves Candidate Lists," p. K1. The wording of this remark suggests less than complete success.

119. Respectively, Wang Xiangming, *Faxue Jikan*, p. 14; Peng Zhen, pp. K42–3. Han Peimei, p. 59; Zhang Youyu, *FBIS* 15, p. K13. After the 1988 election, the NPCSC secretary-general claimed that "most of the members of the current NPCSC are full-time members." Chen Pixian, "Work Report of the Standing Committee of the National People's Congress," *FBIS* 81 (April 27, 1988): 18.

120. The information on NPCSC members' residential and salary arrangements was given me by leading members of the NPCSC General Office and the NPCSC Legislative Affairs Commission, April 3, 1989. They provided the estimate that 80% of NPCSC members live in Beijing. The 60% estimate was offered by Wang Shuwen, an NPC Law Committee member, March 17, 1989. On holding posts illegally, see Pi and Nian, pp. 27–9.

121. On the tasks and functions of the chairmanship group, see Mao Hua and Yin Lantian, "Caoan guanyu guojia jigou de guiding de ruogan tedian" [Certain features of the draft constitution concerning provisions on the state structure], *Faxue Zazhi*, no. 4 (August 1982): 28; Wang Bixuan et al., pp. 144–5; NPC organic law (art. 25); "Zhongguo Renmin Daibiao Dahui Changwu Weiyuanhui Yishi Guize," p. 4. It meets before every NPCSC meeting according to a leading member of the NPCSC Legislative Affairs Commission, April 3, 1989.

122. For early discussions of the NPCSC chairman as a potentially formidable political figure, see Joseph Y. S. Cheng, p. 105; Byron Weng, "Some Key Aspects of the 1982 Draft Constitution of the PRC," *China Quarterly*, no. 91 (September 1982): 498, 501.

123. Zhou Xinming and Chen Weidian, "Dui lifa chengxu wenti de yixie kanfa" [Some views on the issue of legislative procedures], *Renmin Ribao*, January 5, 1979, p. 3.

124. Cao Siyuan, "Huge Appropriations," pp. L19–20.

125. Wu Daying, "Zhongguo shehuizhuyi lifa chengxu" [China's socialist legislative procedures], in *Zhongguo Shehuizhuyi Falü Jiben Lilun* [The Fundamental Theory of Chinese Socialist Law], eds. Wu Daying and Shen Zongling (Beijing: Falü Chubanshe, 1987), p. 198. Information on the first two sessions of the Nationalities Committee (since the Cultural Revolution) can be found in "Ulanhu Speaks at NPC Nationalities Committee Work Meeting," *FBIS* 204 (October 19, 1979): L3–5; "Ulanhu Addresses NPC Nationalities Committee," *FBIS* 203 (October 18, 1979): L4–5; "Ulanhu Addresses NPC Nationalities Committee Second Session," *FBIS* 182 (September 17, 1980): L10–13; "Second Session of the NPC Nationalities Committee Ends," *FBIS* 186 (September 23, 1980): L1–2. A third session of the Nationalities Committee met during the 1981 NPC, and reported that work was underway on a Law on regional autonomy of minority nationalities (passed by the NPC in 1984). See "NPC Nationalities Committee Chairman's Report," *CR:PSM* 253 (December 30, 1981): 72–3.

126. Lists can be found in Cao Siyuan, "Ten Proposals," p. 13; Pan Nianzhi, p. 34; Wu Jialin, *Xinhua Wenzhai*, p. 49; Dong Chengmei, p. 9. At the 1980 NPC Yu Guangyuan suggested establishing fifteen committees under the NPCSC. Chen Haosu's program to strengthen the NPC also entailed setting up committees. See *People's Daily* Excerpts 6, p. L6; "PLA Delegate Proposes Measure to Strengthen NPC," p. L14.

127. Proposals in Cao Siyuan, "Ten Proposals," p. 13; Wu Jialin, *Xinhua Wenzhai*, p. 50; Liao Gailong, Part III, p. 88.

128. Xu Chongde and He Huahui, p. 32. Suggested additions include a legal supervision committee, a national defense committee, a constitution committee, and a committee for the appointment and removal of personnel. See Liu Jui-shao, p. 15.

129. See the NPC organic law (art. 37); "Xi Zhongxun's Explanation of Four Legislative Bills at the Fifth Session of the Fifth National People's Congress," p. 304; "Zhongguo renmin daibiao dahui changwu weiyuanhui yishi guize," p. 4.

130. On increasing the size of NPC committees, see "Chen Pixian on Larger Committees," *FBIS* 63 (April 2, 1986): K17; Chen Pixian, "Work Report of the Standing Committee of the NPC," *FBIS* 81 (April 27, 1988): 13; Peng Chong, "Quanguo renmin daibiao dahui changwu weiyuanhui gongzuo baogao" [Work Report of the Standing Committee of the NPC], delivered March 28, 1989, p. 2.

131. Interview with leading members of the NPCSC Legislative Affairs Commission and the NPCSC General Office, April 3, 1989.

132. The Nationalities Committee elected in 1983 had ten minority representatives (out of fourteen) and included a well-known historian and a distinguished economist as well as a number of cadres with experience working in minority areas. The Law Committee included China's most prominent jurists, including Zhang Youyu and Qian Duansheng. The Financial and Economics Committee had among its members one former vice premier, one former finance minister, one former vice minister of commerce, two former industrialists, and a number of economists. The Education, Science, Culture, and Public Health Committee was comprised primarily of intellectuals and included the President of Qinghua University. Former diplomats and returned overseas Chinese dominated the Foreign Affairs Committee and the Overseas Chinese Committee, respectively. See "Further on Six Committees," *FBIS* 110 (June 7, 1983): K11–12.

133. Unless otherwise noted, information on staff support is drawn from an interview conducted in the Great Hall of the People, April 3, 1989, with leading members of the NPCSC General Office and the Legislative Affairs Commission.

134. Chang, p. 345. See also, Zhang Youyu, "Guanyu woguo falü de lifa chengxu he qicao gongzuo" [On our country's legislative procedures and legal drafting work], *Zhengzhixue Yanjiu*, no. 3 (August 1985): 2.

135. For a recommendation to increase NPCSC staff and comparisons with the U.S. Congress, see Pi and Nian, p. 29. On the proposed 40% staff increase, see Liu Jui-shao, p. 15. The sixfold increase in Legislative Affairs Commission size was reported by a leading member of that committee, April 3, 1989.

136. On the limitations of NPC constitutional supervision, see Xu Chongde, pp. 8–9; Wang Shuwen and Zhou Yanrui, p. 28; Pu Zengyuan, "Guanyu xingai xianfa de wenti" [Questions concerning revising the constitution], *Minzhu yu Fazhi*, no. 11 (November 1980): 15.

137. For examples, see Dong Chengmei, p. 10; Kang Damin, "Jianyi sheli xianfa fayuan" [Proposal to establish a constitutional court], *Faxue Zazhi*, no. 2 (April 1981): 29–30; Xu Chongde, p. 9; Pu Zengyuan, p. 15.

138. Dong Chengmei, p. 10.

139. Pan Nianzhi, p. 37.

140. Kang Damin, p. 30.

141. For an example of this argument, see Gong Yuzhi, "Lun xianfa shishi de baozheng" [Guarantees for constitutional enforcement], *Xinhua Wenzhai*, no. 3 (March 1983): 17–19, from *Renmin Ribao*, January 17, 1983.

142. Zhang Youyu, *Xianfa Lunwenxuan*, pp. 13–14; Hu Jinguang, "Lun xianfa jiandu zhidu" [On the system of constitutional supervision], *Zhongguo Faxue*, no. 1 (March 1985): 72–3.

143. Yu Haocheng, "Yige jiqi zhongyao de jianyi" [An extremely important proposal], *Faxue Zazhi*, no. 4 (August 1982): 26–7.

144. Cui Min and Yu Chi, "Shilun xianfa de zuigao falü xiaoli" [A tentative discussion of the constitution's highest legal force], *Faxue Zazhi*, no. 3 (June 1982): 5.

145. Pu Xingzu, pp. 78–83.

146. "NPC Standing Committee's Work Outline Adopted," *FBIS* 132 (July 11, 1988): 37.

147. For support of NPCSC supervision of the party, see Zeng Heng and Zhong Ming, "Lun renda changweihui dui dang zuzhi de xianfa jiandu" [On the NPCSC's constitutional supervision of the party], *Faxue Jikan*, no. 1 (January 1987): 39–44; Liu Yang and Hou Yafei, "Shiyijie sanzhong quanhui yilai renmin daibiao dahui zhidu de gaige [Reform of the people's congress system since the third plenum of the eleventh party congress], in *Shiyijie Sanzhong Yilai Zhengzhi Tizhi Gaige de Lilun yu Shijian* [The Theory and Practice of Political Structural Reform Since the Third Plenum of the Eleventh Party Congress], eds. Li Longchun and Luo Jian (Beijing: Chunqiu Chubanshe, 1987), p. 133. Discussion of this issue is also reported in Li Zuxing, "Jinyibu Fahui Renmin Daibiao Dahui Zhidu de Zuoyong," p. 11; Zhang Pingli, "Yao jiaqiang renda de falü jiandu" [NPC legal supervision must be strengthened], *Renmin Ribao* (Overseas Edition), October 31, 1987, p. 2.

148. Yang Quanming, "Guanyu jiaqiang woguo xianfa jiandu de jige wenti" [Issues in strengthening our country's constitutional supervision], *Zhengzhixue Yanjiu*, no. 6 (November 1988): 6; Cai Dingjian, "Woguo xianfa zhidu tantao" [Research on our nation's constitutional supervision system], *Faxue Yanjiu*, no. 3 (June 1989): 30; Cai Dingjian, "Jianquan renda falü jiandu jigou de shexiang" [Ideas on strengthening the NPC's legal supervision structure], *Faxue Zazhi*, no. 3 (June 1987): 8–9. Cai is a researcher in the NPCSC General Office.

149. See Hu Jinguang, p. 77; Benkan Pinglun, "Lingdao ganbu bu neng chaoyue xianfa xingshi zhiquan" [Leadership cadres cannot overstep the constitution in exercising their powers], *Faxue*, no. 12 (December 1985): 2. Several speakers at the inaugural meeting of the Chinese Constitutional Research Society in October 1985 proposed creating a constitutional supervision committee. See Zheng Ping, "Zhongguo faxuehui xianfaxue yanjiuhui zai Guiyang chengli" [The Chinese constitutional research society is established in Guiyang], *Faxue Yanjiu*, no. 1 (February 1986): 28. On enlarging the Law Committee's responsibilities to include constitutional supervision, see Chen Yunsheng, "Tizhi gaige yu xianfa jiandu" [Structural reform and constitutional supervision], *Faxue Yanjiu*, no. 5 (October 1988): 9; Cai Dingjian, "Jiaqiang jiandu gongneng, wanshan renmin daibiao dahui zhidu" [Strengthen supervisory abilities, perfect the NPC system], *Zhengzhi yu Falü*, no. 1 (February 1988): 22–3.

Chapter 8. The NPC and systemic change

1. On laws passed since 1979, see Li Maoguan, "Why Laws Go Unenforced," *Beijing Review* 32 (September 11–17, 1989): 17. For law-making plans, see "NPC to Revise 117 Laws in Next 5 Years," *FBIS* 149 (August 3, 1988): 13–14. See also Chen Pixian, "Work Report of the Standing Committee of the NPC" (hereafter 1988 NPCSC Report), *FBIS* 81 (April 27, 1988): 11.

2. On rule by law and institutionalized legal safeguards, see Richard Baum, "Modernization and Legal Reform in Post-Mao China: The Rebirth of Socialist Legality," *Studies in Comparative Communism* 19 (Summer 1986): 69–104. See also Shao-chuan

Leng and Hungdah Chiu, *Criminal Justice in Post-Mao China* (Albany: State University of New York Press, 1985), p. 36.

3. Leng and Chiu, p. 37; R. Randle Edwards, "An Overview of Chinese Law and Legal Education," *AAPSS* 476 (November 1984): 52–3.

4. See Li Buyun, "Certain Questions Concerning the Relationship between Party Policies and State Laws," *CR:PSM* 68 (October 15, 1984): 33–4, from *Faxue Jikan*, no. 3 (July 1984): 3–7.

5. "Steady Progress in China's Legal System," *FBIS* 194 (October 4, 1984): K15.

6. Li Buyun, pp. 32–4; Commentator, "An Important Decision for Ensuring the Smooth Progress of Reform and Opening Up to the World," *FBIS* 71 (April 12, 1985): K13, from *Renmin Ribao*, April 11, 1985, p. 2.

7. Xiang Chunyi, Yang Jingyu, and Gu Angran, "Strive to Establish a Socialist Legal System with Chinese Characteristics," *CR:RF* 3 (February 1, 1984): 15–16, from *Hongqi*, no. 3 (February 1, 1984): 11–20; Han Sheng, "On the Stability of Laws," *FBIS* 83 (April 30, 1985): K17, from *Zhongguo Fazhibao*, April 19, 1985, p. 1. Also see remarks by Peng Zhen and Chen Shouyi cited in Tao-tai Hsia and Wendy I. Zeldin, "Recent Legal Developments in the People's Republic of China," *Harvard International Law Journal* 28 (Spring 1987): 281–2. A large literature has developed on the relationship between policy and law and many disagreements remain. For a summary of disputes and discussion of questions such as whether to follow law or policy when there is a conflict, see You Junyi, "Jinnian lai faxuejie dui ruogan zhongda lilun wenti de zhengyi" [Recent controversies in jurisprudence circles over certain important theoretical questions], *Faxue*, no. 11 (November 1985): 6–7.

8. See Frances Hoar Foster, "Codification in Post-Mao China," *American Journal of Comparative Law* 30 (1982): 413.

9. NPC relations with the Political-Legal Committee were described in an interview with a leading member of the NPC Legislative Affairs Commission, April 3, 1989. A chronology of the legislative process for one law can be found in Ta-kuang Chang, "The Making of the Chinese Bankruptcy Law: A Study in the Chinese Legislative Process," *Harvard International Law Journal* 28 (Spring 1987): 333–72.

10. Zhang Youyu, "Guanyu woguo falü de lifa chengxu he qicao gongzuo" [On our country's legislative procedures and legal drafting work], *Zhengzhixue Yanjiu*, no. 3 (August 1985): 3. See also Chang, p. 339.

11. Yao Dengkui and Deng Quangan, "Qianlun woguo lifa tizhi de tedian" [Discussing the features of our country's legislative system], *Faxue Jikan*, no. 2 (April 1985): 7; Huang Shuhai and Zhu Weijiu, "Shilun shouquan lifa" [On empowered legislation], *Faxue Yanjiu*, no. 1 (February 1986): 9; Zhang Shuyi, "Jingji tizhi gaige de fazhi xietiao fazhan" [Coordinated legal development within economic system reform], *Faxue*, no. 7 (July 1986): 10.

12. The Secretary-General of the NPCSC Legislative Affairs Commission explained the reasoning behind empowered legislation in Wang Hanbin, "Explanation of the 'Decision Authorizing the State Council to Formulate Provisional Regulations Concerning Economic Restructuring and Implementation of the Open Door Policy (Draft),'" *CR:PSM* 15 (January 29, 1986): 1–2, from *Guowuyuan Gongbao*, no. 11 (April 30, 1985): 331–2. A cogent and detailed treatment of empowered legislation is available in Huang Shuhai and Zhu Weijiu, pp. 7–13.

13. A clear statement of this view can be found in Liu Shengping, "Lun woguo lifa tizhi" [On our country's legislative system], *Zhengzhi yu Falü*, no. 5 (October 1985): 29–31.

14. For a summary of the debate over "levels," see Xu Xiuyi and Xiao Jinquan, "A Summary of Recent Theoretical Discussions of Major Constitutional Issues in

China," *Social Sciences in China* 7 (Summer 1986): 14–15; interview with a leading member of the CASS Institute of Political Science, March 28, 1989. A *People's Daily* article started the debate by recounting conflicting views without commentary. See Tian Nong, "Different Views on the Legislative System in Our Country," *FBIS* 165 (August 24, 1983): K10–12, from *Renmin Ribao*, August 19, 1983, p. 5.

15. "One-level" proponents who acknowledge the benefits of dispersed legislative capabilities include Chen Deshan, "Tantan woguo lifa tixi" [Discussing our country's legislative system], *Faxue Zazhi*, no. 2 (April 1985): 32; Wu Jialin, "'Liangji lifa tizhi' he 'duoji lifa tizhi' shuo zhiyi" [Querying 'two-level legislative system' and 'multilevel legislative system'], *Faxue*, no. 1 (January 1984): 14.

16. Interview with NPC Law Committee member, Wang Shuwen, March 17, 1989. See also Luo Yapei, "Shehuizhuyi minzhu zhengzhi jianshe chutan" [Research on socialist democratic politics], *Faxue Yanjiu*, no. 3 (June 1988): 12; Li Maoguan, p. 17.

17. Wu Jianfan, "The Building of China's Democracy and Legal System," *FBIS* 143 (July 25, 1985): K2, from *Renmin Ribao*, July 16, 1985, p. 2. Leng and Chiu also report: "The party Central Committee's approval is still essential to the adoption of all legislation in the PRC, but the major responsibility for legislative work now appears to rest with the NPC." Shao-chuan Leng and Hungdah Chiu, *Criminal Justice in Post-Mao China* (Albany: State University of New York Press, 1985), p. 44.

18. Chang, p. 345.

19. Interview with a leading member of the NPCSC Legislative Affairs Commission, April 3, 1989.

20. Sun Xiaohong, "Shilun woguo de lifa yuce" [On our country's legislative prediction], *Faxue Jikan*, no. 4 (October 1984): 34; Wu Daying, "Gexiang zhidu de gaige yu lifa gongzuo" [Systemic reform and legislative work], *Faxue Zazhi*, no. 5 (October 1983): 7; Wu Daying and Ren Yunzheng, "Lifa de yuce he guihua" [Legislative forecasting and planning], *Zhengzhi yu Falü*, no. 6 (September 1983): 9. Pan Jianfeng, "Tan lifa yuce yu lifa guihua" [Discussing legislative forecasting and legislative planning], *Fazhi Jianshe*, no. 1 (February 1987): 16; Wu Daying and Xin Chunying, "Jiaqiang lifa yuce shi fazhi xietiao fazhan de zhongyao cuoshi" [Strengthening legal forecasting is an important measure to develop legal coordination], *Faxue*, no. 8 (August 1984): 10.

21. Pan, p. 16.

22. Pan, p. 17; "NPC Standing Committee's Work Outline Adopted," *FBIS* 132 (July 11, 1988): 35–6.

23. Examples and forms of legislative interpretation are explained in Hu Jinguang, "Tantan jiaqiang lifa jieshi" [On strengthening legislative interpretation], *Zhengzhi yu Falü*, no. 1 (February 1988): 32. Hu opposes informal means of legal interpretation (notices, interviews) that lack legal force and suggests interpretation be done as the organic law provides: by the NPCSC at regular meetings, through decisions or revisions or laws. See also Liu Shengping, "Zhongguo shehuizhuyi falü jieshi wenti yanjiu" [Research on problems in Chinese socialist legal interpretation], *Zhengfa Luntan*, no. 5 (October 1985): 16–19; Wu Daying and Liu Cuixiao, "The Interpretation of Our Country's Socialist Laws," *CR:PSM* 10 (January 31, 1985): 11–12, from *Zhengzhi yu Falü*, no. 4 (August 1984): 42–6.

24. Chen Pixian, 1985 NPCSC Report, p. K7; Liu Shengping, *Zhengfa Luntan*, no. 5 (October 1985): 16–17. The NPCSC Work Outline instructs the Law Committee to study, solicit opinions, and coordinate the handling of requests for legislative interpretation, and to provide a report to the NPCSC. "NPC Standing Committee's Work Outline Adopted," p. 36. The editors of *Faxue* have suggested using the

NPCSC as a center, and establishing a special organ for legal interpretation. Benkan Bianjibu (editors), "Fazhi yao xietiao, taolun dai shenhua" [The legal system must be coordinated, discussion deepens], *Faxue*, no. 10 (October 1985): 4.

25. Liu Shengping, *Zhengfa Luntan*, no. 5 (October 1985): 16. For a list of revisions to the criminal law in the first six years after it was passed, see Gao Mingxuan, "Tantan woguo xingfa gongbu shishi yihou de buchong he xiugai" [Discussing supplements and revisions of our country's criminal law since its promulgation], *Faxue Zazhi*, no. 6 (December 1985): 5–8.

26. "Zhang Youyu tongzhi jiu kaizhan woguo fazhi jianshe xietiao fazhan wenti taolun de tanhua" [Comrade Zhang Youyu's speech on unfolding issues in our country's coordinated legal construction], *Faxue*, no. 6 (June 1984): 2–3.

27. A typical expression of this view can be found in Guo Daohui, "Lun woguo yiyuan lifa tizhi" [On our country's centralized legislative system], *Faxue Yanjiu*, no. 1 (February 1986): 6–7.

28. Benkan Bianjibu (editors), p. 3.

29. Chen Pixian, 1985 NPCSC Report, p. K7.

30. "Zhaokai minfa tongce caoan zuotanhui" [Convening a conference on the draft civil code], *Zhongguo Fazhibao*, December 6, 1985, p. 1. This practice has been encouraged by NPC Law Committee Vice Chairman Zhang Youyu, among others. See Zhang Youyu, "Lun renmin daibiao dahui daibiao de renwu, zhiquan he huodong fangshi wenti" [On the tasks, powers, functions, and mode of activity of National People's Congress deputies], *Faxue Yanjiu*, no. 2 (April 1985): 7.

31. Chen Pixian, 1988 NPCSC Report, p. 12.

32. On the regional autonomy law, inheritance law, and Hong Kong basic law, see Ngapoi Ngawang Jigme, "Explanations of 'Law on Regional Autonomy for PRC Minority Nationalities,'" *CR:PSM* 92 (December 31, 1984): 1, from *Guowuyuan Gongbao*, no. 13 (June 30, 1984): 430–7; Chen Pixian, "Report on the Work of the Standing Committee of the National People's Congress" (hereafter 1985 NPCSC Report), *FBIS* 78 (April 28, 1985): K5; Chen Pixian, "Work Report of the Standing Committee of the National People's Congress" (hereafter 1984 NPCSC Report), *FBIS* 113 (June 11, 1984): K5; Zhang Youyu, "Guanyu wo guo falü de lifa chengxu he qicao gongzuo," pp. 2–3. On augmenting committees and the involvement of forty-seven NPCSC members in drafting fifteen laws, see Chen Pixian, "Report on the Work of the Standing Committee" (hereafter 1986 NPCSC Report), *FBIS* 80 (April 25, 1986): K13, Chen Pixian, 1988 NPCSC Report, p. 18. According to a leading member of the NPCSC General Office (April 3, 1989), NPC-initiated bills typically require elaboration: PLA deputies, for example, have frequently proposed a military installations law to protect firing ranges from peasant encroachment, but they have never adequately defined a military installation – for example, does it include a commander's residence, barracks, clinics, and rehabilitation centers?

33. Lu Jiawei and Zhao Chengjin, "Jiaqiang lifa gongzuo, cujin quanmian gaige he duiwai kaifang" [Strengthen legislative work, promote all-around reform and opening to the outside], *Fazhi Jianshe*, no. 5 (October 1987): 10–11.

34. Chen Pixian, 1988 NPCSC Report, p. 13; "Zhongguo renmin daibiao dahui changwu weiyuanhui yishi guize" [NPCSC proceedings regulations], *Renmin Ribao* (Haiwaiban), November 25, 1987, p. 4. The Law Committee has also been instructed to include "major dissenting opinions" in its report on draft bills. "Rules of Procedure for the National People's Congress of the People's Republic of China (Draft)," since passed at the 1989 NPC.

35. See Chapter 7 for discussion of NPCSC deliberation of the bankruptcy law, the state-owned enterprise law, and the villagers' committee law. See also "TV Special Covers NPC Committee Session," *FBIS* 191 (October 2, 1986): K1; Gao Ling, "Why

the Draft Enterprise Bankruptcy Law Has Not Been Adopted," *FBIS* 194 (October 7, 1986): K1–3, from *Liaowang* (Overseas Edition), no. 39, September 29, 1986, pp. 13–14; Hu Jihua and Li Yahong, "Commenting on Views on Temporarily Not Putting the Bankruptcy Law to Vote," *FBIS* 220 (November 14, 1986): K3–5, from *Zhongguo Fazhibao*, October 27, 1986, p. 3; Chang, pp. 333–72. Zhang Sutang and He Ping, "Gaige huhuanzhe qiye fa chu tai [Reform calling the enterprise law out from behind the stage], *Liaowang* (Haiwaiban), February 8, 1988, pp. 17–18; Chen Pixian, 1988 NPCSC Report, p. 13; Marlowe Hood, "Hong Kong Paper Comments," *FBIS* 58 (March 25, 1988): 35–6, from *South China Morning Post*, March 25, 1988, p. 7. Bao Xin, "Concerning the Villagers' Committee Organization Law," *FBIS* 79 (April 24, 1987): K10–12, from *Liaowang* (Overseas Edition), no. 16, April 20, 1987, p. 1; Gong Miao, "Reform of Political Structure, Autonomy for Peasants – NPC Deputies Argue over Draft of Villagers' Law," *FBIS* 71 (April 14, 1987): K24–5, from *Zhongguo Tongxunshe*, April 11, 1987; "Discusses Village Rule, Contracts," *FBIS* 12 (January 20, 1987): K22–3; "NPC Standing Committee on Village Draft Law," *FBIS* 224 (November 20, 1987): 12–13.

36. NPC Law Committee, "Report by the Law Committee of the NPC on the Result of Examination of the 'Patent Law of the People's Republic of China,'" *CR:PSM* 79 (November 23, 1984): 12–15, from *Guowuyuan Gongbao*, no. 6 (April 20, 1984): 173–6; "NPC to Consider Inheritance Law," *Beijing Review* 28 (April 1, 1985): 8–9; Chang, pp. 347–50.

37. On the 1982 constitutional reforms, see Chapter 7. For discussions of the "kontrol" function of European socialist legislatures, see Peter Vanneman, *The Supreme Soviet: Politics and the Legislative Process in the Soviet Political System* (Durham, NC: Duke University Press, 1977), pp. 102–23, 166; William A. Welsh, "The Status of Research on Representative Institutions in Eastern Europe," *Legislative Studies Quarterly* 5 (May 1980): 290–5; Stephen White, "Some Conclusions," in *Communist Legislatures in Comparative Perspective*, eds. Daniel Nelson and Stephen White (London: Macmillan Press, 1982), pp. 192–6.

38. He Ping and Yang Xinzhe, "Hu Qili Joins Tianjin Group," *FBIS* 61 (March 30, 1988): 21; "Urges Paid Services to Society," *FBIS* 61 (March 30, 1988): 21; "Listens to Criticisms," *FBIS* 62 (March 31, 1988): 16–17; "Intellectuals' Second Job Opposed," *FBIS* 63 (April 1, 1988): 23; Guo Zhaojin, "Some NPC Delegates Are Worried About Part-Time Jobs for Intellectuals," *FBIS* 64 (April 4, 1988): 32–3; Robert Delfs, "Brighter Means Poorer," *Far Eastern Economic Review* 140 (June 16, 1988): 34–6.

39. During the 1988 session, at the request of NPC deputies, thirty ministers and vice ministers came to small-group meetings of seventeen provincial panels. "Ministers Hear Deputies' Views," *FBIS* 69 (April 11, 1982): 32. For a request for a minister to appear, see Wang Gangyi, "PLA Deputies Air Concerns," *FBIS* 60 (March 29, 1988): 21, from *China Daily*, March 29, 1988, p. 4.

40. For a discussion of the NPC's moderating influence and its procedurally conservative impact, see Kevin J. O'Brien, "Is China's National People's Congress a 'Conservative' Legislature?" *Asian Survey* 30 (in press). On NPC small-group debates, see Chapter 6.

41. See "NPC Standing Committee to Make Inspection Tours," *FBIS* 99 (May 22, 1981): K1–2.

42. Zhang Youyu, "Lun renmin daibiao dahui daibiao de renwu, zhiquan he huodong fangshi wenti," p. 7; "NPC Standing Committee to Make Inspection Tours," p. K2.

43. Chen Pixian, 1986 NPCSC Report, pp. K8–9; Chen Pixian, 1988 NPCSC Report, p. 17; Chen Pixian, "Quanguo renmin daibiao dahui changwu weiyuanhui

gongzuo baogao" [Work Report of the NPCSC] (hereafter 1987 NPCSC Report), *Zhonghua Renmin Gongheguo Quanguo Renmin Daibiao Dahui Changwu Weiyuanhui Gongbao*, no. 3 (May 1987): 76–7; Yau Shing-mu, "NPC Deputies Given Inspection Rights Passes," *FBIS* 104 (June 1, 1987): K14, from *Hong Kong Standard*, May 30, 1987, p. K6.

44. Chen Pixian, 1986 NPCSC Report, p. K4, K8–9; "NPC Deputies to Tour Localities Before Session," *FBIS* 23 (February 4, 1985): K13; Chen Pixian, 1985 NPCSC Report, p. K6; Chen Pixian, 1987 NPCSC Report, pp. 71–2; Chen Pixian, 1988 NPCSC Report, p. 14. That "more than 50%" of NPC deputies have conducted inspections was disclosed by a leading member of the NPCSC General Office, April 3, 1989. On tours in Beijing and Heilongjiang, see "NPC Deputies Involved in Democratic Politics," *FBIS* 208 (October 27, 1988): 24.

45. According to a leading member of the NPCSC General Office (April 3, 1989), the Letter and Visits Bureau of the NPCSC General Office has twenty to thirty staff members and receives over 100,000 letters and 20,000 mass visits each year. Some individuals appear many times and common complaints involve civil disputes, court decisions, and prison sentences. Most deputies do not have district offices for incoming letters and visits. See also Tian Jun and Liu Huiming, "Lun woguo renda jiandu zhidu de wanshan" [On perfecting our country's people's congress supervision system], *Jianghai Xuekan*, no. 1 (January 1989): 70–1.

46. Chen Pixian, 1988 NPCSC Report, p. 18; Chen Pixian, 1986 NPCSC Report, p. K13; "Zhongguo renmin daibiao dahui changwu weiyuanhui yishi guize," p. 4; "Tigao yishi xiaolü, wanshan changweihui zhineng" [Improve proceedings efficiency, improve standing committee functions], *Renmin Ribao* (Haiwaiban), December 4, 1987, p. 4.

47. "NPC Standing Committee's Work Outline Adopted," p. 37. For criticisms, see "NPC Executive Body Rapped as Weak Watchdog," *China Daily*, April 1, 1989, p. 3; Wu Zhong, "NPC Deputies Pressure Chairman to Admit Neglect," *Hong Kong Standard*, April 2, 1989, p. 4. On new Finance and Economics Committee responsibilities, see "Rules of Procedure for the National People's Congress of the People's Republic of China (Draft)," later passed at the 1989 NPC.

48. On failing to report decisions, see Tian and Li, p. 71; Yuan Jiliang, "Guanyu jiaqiang guojia quanli jiguan falü jiandu baozheng zhineng de jige wenti" [Problems in strengthening state power organs and guaranteeing the role of legal supervision], *Faxue Yanjiu*, no. 1 (February 1988): 23. For differing views on NPC supervision of party committees, see Shao Jingjun, "Renmin daibiao dahui zhidu jianshe lilun taolun lunhui gaishu" [Summary of the symposium on the theory of people's congress construction], *Renmin Ribao* (Haiwaiban), December 3, 1987, p. 4; Zhang Pingli, "Yao jiaqiang renda de falü jiandu" [NPC legal supervision must be strengthened], *Renmin Ribao* (Haiwaiban), October 31, 1987, p. 2; Zeng Heng and Zhong Ming, "Lun renda changweihui dui dangzuzhi de xianfa jiandu" [On the NPCSC's constitutional supervision of party organizations], *Faxue Jikan*, no. 1 (January 1987): 39–44.

49. Chen Pixian, 1984 NPCSC Report, p. K3; Chen Pixian, 1986 NPCSC Report, p. K4; Zhou Minyi, "NPC No Longer a Platform of One Voice," *Beijing Review* 31 (April 18–24, 1988): 7; "NPC Presidium Holds Fourth Meeting 5 April, Wan Li Presides," *FBIS* 65 (April 5, 1988): 11–12.

50. The editors of *Faxue* have written that education of leading cadres in "socialist democracy and legal system" is more important than establishing a special organ for enforcing the constitution. See Benkan Pinglun (editors), "Lingdao ganbu bu neng chaoyue xianfa xingshi zhiquan" [Leadership cadres cannot overstep the constitution], *Faxue*, no. 12 (December 1985): 2. A 1988 survey of nearly 1,000 NPC deputies found that although 62.1% of respondents said the NPC should supervise government work, only 18.9% said it does. "NPC Deputies Express Views," *Beijing Review* 31 (August 1–7, 1988): 11. Complaints are often heard that the marriage, food hygiene, trademark, compulsory education, land, and forestry laws have not been rigorously enforced. "NPC Deputies Urge End to 'Rubber Stamp' Image," *FBIS* 72 (April 14, 1988): 36; Li Maoguan, p. 17. On the NPC lacking "authority to go against the party," see Yu Haocheng, "Questioning the Third Echelon," *China Spring Digest* 1 (November/December 1987): 63. Criticisms of inadequate NPC supervision were common in small-group discussions observed by this author, March 31, 1989.

51. White, p. 192.

52. Hanna F. Pitkin, *The Concept of Representation* (Berkeley: University of California Press, 1967), pp. 221–34.

53. On party domination of NPC elections and reliance on quotas, see Xu Chongde and He Huahui, *Xianfa yu Minzhu Zhidu* [The Constitution and Democratic System] (Hubei: Hubei Renmin Chubanshe, 1982), p. 60; Wu Jialin, "Zenyang fahui quanguo renda zuowei zuigao guojia quanli jiguan de zuoyong" [How to bring into play the NPC as the highest organ of state power], *Xinhua Wenzhai*, no. 12 (December 1980): 49; Li Guoxiong, "Woguo renmin daibiaozhi dangyi" [An opinion on the Chinese NPC system], *Faxue Pinglun*, no. 1 (January 1987): 14; Zhang Zonghou, "Quanli zhi yuelun" [On the system of power], *Faxue*, no. 10 (October 1986): 2; Pi Chunxie and Nian Xinyong, "Zhengzhi tizhi gaige de yixiang zhongyao renwu – tantan jianquan renmin daibiao dahui zhidu" [Some important tasks in political systemic reform – discussing perfecting the NPC system], *Zhongguo Zhengzhi*, no. 1 (January 1987): 28; Liu Xia, "Zhengzhi tizhi gaige yu renmin daibiao suzhi" [Political system reform and people's deputy quality], *Fazhi Jianshe*, no. 5 (October 1987): 22.

54. See comments by Deng cited in Stuart Schram, "Political Reform in China," *IHJ Bulletin* 8 (Spring 1988): 3–4. For reasons direct elections are opposed (low efficiency on the first ballot, too much trouble, humiliates losers), see She Xuxin and Xu Laiqin, "Guanyu zhijie xuanze zhong ruogan wenti de tantao" [Research on problems of direct elections], *Faxue Yanjiu*, no. 1 (February 1987): 3–4. Some commentators, however, note that China's transition period has already been longer than those of most East European nations, and they favor a more rapid introduction of direct, popular elections. See Kan Ke, "Quanguo renmin daibiao dahui daibiao ming'e queding yiju tantao" [An approach to determining the number of deputies to the NPC], *Zhengzhixue Yanjiu*, no. 5 (September 1987): 33; Wu Jialin, "Tigao difang guojia quanli jiguan de quanweixing" [Views on strengthening the competence of local organs of state power], *Faxue Pinglun*, no. 1 (January 1987): 30.

55. The concept of service responsiveness is discussed in Heinz Eulau and P. D. Karps, "The Puzzle of Representation: Specifying Components of Responsiveness," *Legislative Studies Quarterly* 2 (August 1977): 243–5.

56. This encounter is reported in Zhang Zonghou and Yan Jun, "Wo shi renmin daibiao, jiuyao ti quanzhong jianghua" [I am a people's representative and must speak for the masses], *Zhongguo Fazhibao*, April 1, 1985, p. 1.

57. Zhang Youyu, p. 5.

58. See comments by NPCSC Chairman Peng Zhen, NPC Secretary-General Chen Pixian, and Zhang Youyu in Zhang Youyu, pp. 5–8; Chen Pixian, 1984 NPCSC Report, p. K7. On the obligation of deputies to dismiss requests that "conflict with administrative or bureau interests," or are "irrational" or "unconstitutional," see Yu Jian, "Lun renmin daibiao de falü diwei" [On the legal status of people's deputies], *Zhengzhi yu Falü*, no. 4 (August 1987): 24.

59. See Eulau and Karps, p. 245, for a definition of allocation responsiveness.

60. Detailed analysis of deputy speeches can be found in Chapter 6. Dorothy J.

Solinger, "The Fifth National People's Congress and the Process of Policy-Making: Reform, Readjustment and Opposition," *Asian Survey* 22 (December 1982): 1238–75.

61. On pleas for heavy industry, see Solinger, pp. 1238–75; for typical remarks on inland areas, see Liang Qian, "Jingji gaige zhong chule shemma wenti?" [What problems are emerging in economic reform?], *Zhengming*, no. 91 (May 1985): 44; Han Baocheng, "NPC Sidelights – Taking the Road to Common Prosperity," *Beijing Review* 28 (April 8, 1985): 17–19; "Poor Areas Want Attention," *FBIS* 62 (April 1, 1987): K9–10; "Tibetans Want More Favorable Policies," *FBIS* 66 (April 6, 1988): 21–2; "Yunnan Urges More Interior Aid," *FBIS* 59s (March 28, 1988): 34; Seth Faison, "Xinjiang Fears Coastal Development Rebound," *FBIS* 66 (April 6, 1988): 23–4, from *South China Morning Post*, April 6, 1988, p. 7. For requests for attention to agriculture, see Luo Bing, "Liujie renda huinei huiwai" [Inside and outside the Sixth NPC], *Zhengming*, no. 69 (July 1983): 11; "Deputies Make Suggestions," *FBIS* 114 (June 13, 1983): K12–13; "Local Leaders Advocate Attention to Agriculture," *FBIS* 61 (March 31, 1986): K10; "Study of Zhao's Report Continues," *FBIS* 61 (March 31, 1987): K6; "More Agriculture Investment Urged," *FBIS* 60 (March 29, 1988): 23; Zhang Yuan, "Farm Production Concerns Voiced," *FBIS* 66 (April 6, 1988): 28–9, from *China Daily*, April 5, 1988, p. 4; Guo Weifeng, "NPC Delegates, CPPCC Members Warn Against Dangerous Situation in Agriculture," *FBIS* 63 (April 1, 1988): 38.

62. Zhang Youyu, p. 4. That deputies are kept busy with provincially organized activities is a further impediment to allocation responsiveness. Deputies have limited contact with members of other delegations and small-group agendas often diverge. Interview with Chang Shao Wei, *Ta Kung Pao* reporter, March 31, 1989.

63. Du Xichuan, "Renda daibiao ying daibiao shei de liyi?" [Whose interests should people's deputies represent?], *Faxue Zazhi*, no. 1 (January 1989): 19–20. Du is a member of the NPCSC Research Office. Recall of deputies, though lauded by Marx and Lenin, is infrequent in China. Other than criminals and dissidents (e.g., Yan Jiaqi), few deputies are removed, and this is the source of some criticism. Zhang Bingyin, "Shilun woguo de minzhu zhengzhi jianshe yu renda gongzuo de guanxi" [Discussion of the relationship of our country's democratic political construction to people's congress work], *Zhengfa Luntan*, no. 3 (June 1989): 52.

64. Zhang Youyu, pp. 2, 8. A commentator at the 1988 NPC also noted that too many deputy legislative proposals concern local and professional issues and too few deal with "the interests of the whole." Tang Xiaoke, "NPC Proposals and NPC Deputies," *FBIS* 74 (April 18, 1988): 18.

65. Du Xichuan, p. 19.

66. On lobbying for intellectuals' interests, see He Ping and Yang Xinhe, "Hu Qili Joins Tianjin Group," *FBIS* 61 (March 30, 1988): 21; Suzanne Pepper, "Rocky Road to Reform," *Far Eastern Economic Review* 140 (June 16, 1988): 32–4; "Listens to Criticisms," *FBIS* 62 (March 31, 1988): 16–17; "Intellectuals' Second Jobs Opposed," *FBIS* 63 (April 1, 1988): 23; Guo Zhaojin, "Some NPC Delegates are Worried About Part-Time Jobs for Intellectuals," *FBIS* 64 (April 4, 1988): 32–3.

67. See O'Brien, "Is China's National People's Congress a 'Conservative' Legislature?" *Asian Survey* 30 (in press).

68. For a criticism of structural explanations of the relationship between economic reform and political change, see Nina P. Halpern, "Economic Reform and Democratization in Communist Systems: The Case of China," *Studies in Comparative Communism* 22 (Summer/Autumn 1989): 139–52.

69. For a discussion of extending rights of consultation in order to preempt demands for systemic change in European socialist nations, see Stephen White, "Eco-

nomic Performance and Communist Legitimacy," *World Politics* 38 (April 1986): 462–82.

70. Even after June 4, 1989, Li Peng reaffirmed the party's policy toward intellectuals and deemed them a part of the working class and "an important contingent for socialist construction." "Li Peng on Current Domestic and International Policies," *Beijing Review* 32 (October 16–22, 1989): 20. The future for private entrepreneurs is more unsure.

71. Zhang Youyu, "Minzhu xieshang shi shixing renmin minzhu de youxiao fangshi" [Democratic consultation is an effective means to carry out people's democracy], *Jianghai Xuekan*, no. 4 (August 1984): 7.

72. Zhang Youyu, *Jianghai Xuekan*, no. 4 (August 1984): 8.

73. For a discussion of assemblies that conform to a systems-maintenance model of legislatures, see Michael L. Mezey, *Comparative Legislatures* (Durham, NC: Duke University Press, 1979), pp. 11, 18–20, 259–70, 281–2. See also, Michael L. Mezey, "The Functions of Legislatures in the Third World," *Handbook of Legislative Research*, eds. Gerhard Loewenberg, Samuel C. Patterson, and Malcolm E. Jewell (Cambridge, MA: Harvard University Press, 1985), pp. 744–50.

74. See "Fundamental Change in China's Class Situation," *Beijing Review* 22 (November 16, 1979): 9–13, (November 23, 1979): 14–18; "Comrade Ye Jianying's Speech – At the Meeting in Celebration of the Thirtieth Anniversary of the People's Republic of China," *Beijing Review* 22 (October 5, 1979): 21.

75. Jowitt, p. 71.

76. On the costs of "revolutions from above," see Richard Lowenthal, "Development vs. Utopia in Communist Policy," in *Change in Communist Systems*, ed. Chalmers Johnson (Stanford, CA: Stanford University Press, 1970), pp. 53–4, 111–16; Richard Lowenthal, "On 'Established' Communist Party Regimes," *Studies in Comparative Communism* 7 (Winter 1974): 335–58.

77. See Jowitt, pp. 72–89.

78. Worth noting is Politburo Standing Committee member Li Ruihuan's September 1989 promise to avoid "overcorrecting mistakes" and to forsake the "dogmatic, rigid methods that had been used in the past to criticize bourgeois liberalization." Cited in Robert Delfs, "Stuck in the Groove," *Far Eastern Economic Review* 146 (October 5, 1989): 14.

79. For a discussion of "consultative authoritarianism," see H. Gordon Skilling, "Group Conflict and Political Change," in *Change in Communist Systems*, ed. Chalmers Johnson (Stanford, CA: Stanford University Press, 1970), pp. 215–34. For a description of a "middle road" between party–state authoritarianism and parliamentary democracy, see Brantly Womack, "Party-State Democracy: A Theoretical Exploration," a paper presented at the 17th Sino-American Conference on Mainland China, June 6, 1988.

80. See Jin Jian, "China Cannot Adopt the Balance of the Three Powers," *FBIS* 156 (August 15, 1989): 22–5, from *Renmin Ribao*, August 11, 1989, p. 6. "Deng's Talk on Quelling Rebellion in Beijing," p. 21. In June and July 1989, Deng's speech was study material in every unit in China.

81. Huang Ping, "On the People's Congress System in Our Country," *FBIS* 197 (October 13, 1989): 30, from *Jingji Cankao*, September 17, 1989, p. 4. The emphasis on party leadership over the legislature increased after the 1989 Tiananmen suppression, but has been present since the NPC's founding.

82. "Deng's Talk on Quelling Rebellion in Beijing," p. 18. See also Yang Shangkun's account of a May 1989 meeting (including seven semiretired octogenarians) in which it was agreed "there was no road of retreat." Cited in Robert Delfs, "The Old Men Still the Power Behind the Scene," *Far Eastern Economic Review* 146 (October

5, 1989): 66–7. On improving legislative oversight, see Jiang Zemin, "Speech at the Meeting in Celebration of the 40th Anniversary of the Founding of the People's Republic of China," September 29, 1989, in *Beijing Review* 32 (October 9–15, 1989): 19–20.

Bibliography

English language references

This selected bibliography excludes most FBIS translations and other sources that recount remarks made at NPC small-group meetings. For citations to these accounts, reference must be made to the Notes at the end of the text.

Almond, Gabriel. "The Return to the State." *American Political Science Review* 82 (September 1988): 853–74.

Baum, Richard. "China in 1985: The Greening of the Revolution." *Asian Survey* 26 (January 1986): 30–53.

"Modernization and Legal Reform in Post-Mao China: The Rebirth of Socialist Legality." *Studies in Comparative Communism* 19 (Summer 1986): 69–104.

Bedeski, Robert E. *State-Building in Modern China: The Kuomintang in the Prewar Period.* China Research Monograph No. 18. Berkeley: Berkeley Center for Chinese Studies, 1981.

Bernstein, Thomas P. "China in 1984." *Asian Survey* 25 (January 1985): 33–50.

"Domestic Politics." In *China Briefing, 1984*, edited by Steven M. Goldstein, 1–19. Boulder, CO: Westview Press, 1985.

"How Stalinist is Mao's China?" *Problems of Communism* 34 (March–April 1985): 118–25.

"Stalinism, Famine, and Chinese Peasants." *Theory and Society* 13 (May 1984): 339–78.

Bianco, Lucien. *Origins of the Chinese Revolution 1915–1949.* Translated by Muriel Bell. Stanford, CA: Stanford University Press, 1971.

Blondel, Jean. *Comparative Legislatures.* Englewood Cliffs, NJ: Prentice-Hall, 1973.

Burns, John F. "Peking's Legislative Forums are Increasingly Feisty." *The New York Times,* April 15, 1985, p. A12.

Burns, John P. "China's Nomenklatura System." *Problems of Communism* 36 (September–October 1987): 36–51.

Burns, John P., and Stanley Rosen. *Policy Conflicts in Post-Mao China.* Armonk, NY: M.E. Sharpe, 1986.

Cao Siyuan. "Huge Appropriations Should Be Examined and Approved by Legislative Organs Through Hearings." *FBIS* 219 (November 10, 1980): L19–20. From *Guangming Ribao,* October 23, 1980, p. 3.

"Ten Proposals for Revising the Constitution." *CR:PSM* 201 (June 30, 1981): 4–13. From *Minzhu yu Fazhi*, no. 2 (February 1981): 6–10.

Central Committee of the Communist Party of China. *Eighth National Congress of the Communist Party of China (Documents)*. Peking: Foreign Languages Press, 1956; reprint 1981.

Chang Ching-wen. "Reshuffles in the Peiping Regime After the First Session of the Third National People's Congress." *Issues and Studies* (Taipei) 1 (February 1965): 24–33.

Chang, Parris H. *Power and Policy in China*. University Park, PA: Pennsylvania State University Press, 1975.

Chang, Ta-kuang. "The Making of the Chinese Bankruptcy Law: A Study in the Chinese Legislative Practice." *Harvard International Law Journal* 28 (Spring 1987): 333–72.

Chen Pixian. "Report on the Work of the Standing Committee of the National People's Congress." *FBIS* 78 (April 28, 1985): K1–11.

"Work Report of the Standing Committee of the National People's Congress." *FBIS* 113 (June 11, 1984): K1–9.

"Work Report of the Standing Committee of the National People's Congress." *FBIS* 81 (April 27, 1988): 11–19.

Chen Shouyi. "A Review of New China's Law Research During the Past Thirty Years." *CR:PSM* 100 (July 18, 1980): 35–54. From *Faxue Yanjiu*, no. 1 (February 1980): 1–10.

Chen Shouyi, Liu Shengping, and Zhao Zhenjiang. "Thirty Years of the Building up of Our Country's Legal System." *CR:PSM* 70 (March 25, 1980): 25–40. From *Faxue Yanjiu*, no. 4 (October 1979): 1–8.

Chen Shutong. "Industrial and Commercial Circles Must Be Fully Determined to Reform Themselves." *CB* 502 (April 7, 1958): 1–4.

Chen Yun. "On Commercial Work and Industrial-Commercial Relations." *CB* 398 (July 12, 1956): 1–8.

Cheng, Joseph Y. S. "How to Strengthen the National People's Congress and Implement Constitutionalism." *Chinese Law and Government* 16 (Summer–Fall 1983): 88–122.

Ch'i Hsin (Qi Xin). "A Brief Analysis of China's New Personnel Arrangements." *Chinese Law and Government* 11 (Summer–Fall 1978): 84–97.

Chiang Chih-nan. "An Analysis of the Personnel Composition of the Fifth People's Congress and the State Council." *Chinese Law and Government* 11 (Summer–Fall 1978): 54–83.

Ch'ien Tuan-sheng (Qian Duansheng). "After Liberation – New Democracy." In *China in Transition*, edited by China Reconstructs, pp. 40–5. Peking: China Reconstructs, 1957.

"Our New State Structure." *China Reconstructs* 4 (February 1955): 2–5.

The Government and Politics of China. Cambridge: Harvard University Press, 1950.

China Daily Commentator. "New People's Congress." *FBIS* 110 (June 7, 1983): K17–18. From *China Daily*, June 7, 1983, p. 4.

"China Goes to the Polls." *China News Analysis* (Hong Kong) 245 (September 19, 1958).

"China Might Restore the State Chairman." *FBIS* 40 (March 2, 1981): V1–2. From *Wen Wei Po* (Hong Kong), February 27, 1981, pp. 1–2.

"China, November 1957." *China News Analysis* (Hong Kong) 207 (November 29, 1957).

Cohen, Jerome A. "China's Changing Constitution." *China Quarterly*, no. 76 (December 1978): 794–841.

Cohen, Paul A. "The Post-Mao Reforms in Historical Perspective." *Journal of Asian Studies* 47 (August 1988): 518–40.

Commentator. "Attention Must be Paid to the People's Deputies' Proposals." *FBIS* 193 (October 2, 1980): L5–6. From *Renmin Ribao*, September 27, 1980, p. 1.

"An Important Decision for Ensuring the Smooth Progress of the Reform and Opening Up to the World." *FBIS* 71 (April 12, 1985): K12–14. From *Renmin Ribao*, April 11, 1985, p. 2.

"Comrade Ye Jianying's Speech – At the Meeting in Celebration of the Thirtieth Anniversary of the People's Republic of China." *Beijing Review* 22 (October 5, 1979): 7–31.

"A Congress Session that Strives for a Leap Forward." *CB* 496 (March 7, 1958). From *Renmin Ribao*, February 12, 1958.

Credentials Committee of the Fifth National People's Congress of the People's Republic of China. "Credentials Committee Report." *FBIS* 92 (May 11, 1983): K3–4.

"Crossfire at the Congress." *Asiaweek* 13 (April 12, 1987): 18–23.

Crozier, Michel. *The Bureaucratic Phenomenon*. Chicago: The University of Chicago Press, 1964.

Delfs, Robert. "The Old Men Still the Power Behind the Scene." *Far Eastern Economic Review* 146 (October 5, 1989): 66–7.

"Outburst of Democracy." *Far Eastern Economic Review* 140 (April 7, 1988): 16.

"Stuck in the Groove," *Far Eastern Economic Review* 146 (October 5, 1989): 14–15.

"Students Seek Recognition." *Far Eastern Economic Review* 140 (April 21, 1988): 13.

"Democratic Election System Discussed." *Beijing Review* 31 (February 1–7, 1988): 40.

Deng Xiaoping. *Selected Works of Deng Xiaoping (1975–1982)*. Beijing: Foreign Languages Press, 1984.

"Deng's Talk on Quelling Rebellion in Beijing." *Beijing Review* 32 (July 10–16, 1989): 18–21.

Ding Ji. "Vivid Manifestation of Political Democracy." *FBIS* 174 (September 9, 1986): K1. From *Renmin Ribao*, September 7, 1986, p. 4.

Dittmer, Lowell. "China in 1986: Domestic Politics." In *China Briefing, 1987*, edited by John S. Major and Anthony Kane, pp. 1–25. Boulder, CO: Westview Press, 1987.

"The Formal Structure of Central Chinese Political Institutions." In *Organizational Behavior in Chinese Society*, edited by Sidney L. Greenblatt, Richard W. Wilson, and Amy Auerbacher Wilson, pp. 47–76. New York: Praeger, 1981.

"Ideology and Organization in Post-Mao China." *Asian Survey* 24 (March 1984): 346–69.

"The Twelfth Congress of the Communist Party of China." *China Quarterly*, no. 93 (March 1983): 108–24.

Dong Min. "Sidelights on the Fourth Session of the Sixth NPC," *CR:PSM* 61 (August 4, 1986): 6–8. From *Zhengming*, no. 103 (May 1986): 94.

Dong Xi Fang Commentator. "Preliminary Observations on the Third Plenary Session of the Fifth NPC." *CR:PSM* 138 (November 17, 1980): 13–16. From *Dong Xi Fang*, no. 21 (September 1980): 12–13.

Doolin, Dennis J. "Chinese Communist Policies Toward the Chinese Intelligentsia: 1949–1963." Ph.D. diss., Stanford University, 1964.

Eastman, Lloyd E. *The Abortive Revolution*. Cambridge: Harvard University Press, 1974.

"Economic Situation, Penury." *China News Analysis* (Hong Kong) 499 (January 10, 1964).

Edwards, R. Randle. "An Overview of Chinese Law and Legal Education." *AAPSS* 476 (November 1984): 48–61.

Eulau, Heinz. "Introduction: Legislative Research in Historical Perspective." In *Handbook of Legislative Research*, edited by Gerhard Loewenberg, Samuel C. Patterson, and Malcolm E. Jewell, pp. 1–14. Cambridge: Harvard University Press, 1985.

Eulau, Heinz, and P. D. Karps. "The Puzzle of Representation: Specifying Components of Responsiveness." *Legislative Studies Quarterly* 2 (August 1977): 233–54.

Fainsod, Merle. *How Russia is Ruled*. Revised ed. Cambridge: Harvard University Press, 1963.

Faison, Seth. "Students Wall Posters in Beijing Persist." *FBIS* 68 (April 8, 1988): 40–1. From *South China Morning Post*, April 8, 1988, p. 1.

Falkenheim, Victor C. "The Limits of Political Reform." *Current History* 86 (September 1987): 261–5, 279–81.

"Political Reform in China." *Current History* 81 (September 1982): 259–63, 280–1.

Fan Cheuk-wan. "HK Deputies Lash Shenzhen Plan." *Hong Kong Standard*, April 2, 1989, p. 4.

"HK Deputies Force Beijing to Back Down." *Hong Kong Standard*, April 4, 1989, p. 1.

Fewsmith, Joseph. *Party, State and Local Elites in Republican China*. Honolulu: University of Hawaii Press, 1985.

Fincher, John H. *Chinese Democracy: The Self-Government Movement in Local, Provincial and National Politics 1905–1914*. London: Croon Helm, 1981.

Foster, Frances Hoar. "Codification in Post-Mao China." *American Journal of Comparative Law* 30 (1982): 395–428.

Friedgut, Theodore H. *Political Participation in the USSR*. Princeton: Princeton University Press, 1979.

Friedman, Edward. *Backward Toward Revolution*. Berkeley: University of California Press, 1974.

"Fundamental Change in China's Class Situation." *Beijing Review* 22 (November 16, 1979): 9–13, (November 23, 1979): 14–18.

Gao Chongmin. "The Sole Outlet for Bourgeois Intellectuals Is to Transform Their Political Stand and Take the Road of Socialism." *CB* 503 (April 10, 1958): 12–15.

Gao Ling. "Why the Draft Enterprise Bankruptcy Law Has Not Been Adopted." *FBIS* 194 (October 7, 1986): K1–3. From *Liaowang* (Overseas Edition), September 29, 1986, pp. 13–14.

Gasper, Donald. "The Chinese National People's Congress." In *Communist Legislatures in Comparative Perspective*, edited by Daniel Nelson and Stephen White, pp. 160–90. London: Macmillan Press, 1982.

Geng Yunzhi. "The Movement for a Parliament in the Last Years of the Qing Dynasty." *Social Sciences in China* 1 (September 1980): 115–54.

Ginsburgs, George. "Theory and Practice of Parliamentary Procedure in Communist

China: Organizational and Institutional Principles." *University of Toronto Law Journal* 15 (1) (1963): 1–48.

Gold, Thomas B. "After Comradeship: Personal Relations in China Since the Cultural Revolution." *China Quarterly*, no. 104 (December 1985): 657–75.

Green, Marcus. "The National People's Congress." *China Quarterly*, no. 17 (January–March 1964): 241–50.

Gu Wen. "Beginning the Talk with the 'Rubber Stamp.'" *FBIS* 201 (October 17, 1986): K4–5. From *Gongren Ribao*, September 27, 1986, p. 3.

Halpern, A. M. "Between Plenums: A Second Look at the 1962 National People's Congress in China." *Asian Survey* 2 (November 1962): 1–10.

Halpern, Nina P. "Economic Reform and Democratization in Communist Systems: The Case of China." *Studies in Comparative Communism* 22 (Summer/Autumn 1989): 139–52.

Han Sheng. "On the Stability of Laws." *FBIS* 83 (April 30, 1985): K17–18. From *Zhongguo Fazhibao*, April 19, 1985, p. 1.

Harding, Harry. *China's Second Revolution*. Washington, D.C.: Brookings Institution, 1987.

    Organizing China. Stanford, CA: Stanford University Press, 1981.

    "Political Development in Post-Mao China." In *Modernizing China: Post-Mao Reform and Development*, edited by A. Doak Barnett and Ralph N. Clough, pp. 13–38. Boulder, CO: Westview Press, 1986.

Hazard, John N. *Communists and Their Law*. Chicago: The University of Chicago Press, 1969.

    "The Experience with Constitutionalism." In *The Legal System of the Chinese Soviet Republic 1931–1934*, edited by W. E. Butler, pp. 21–46. Dobbs Ferry, NY: Transnational Publishers, 1983.

He Yang. "Showdown between Deng Xiaoping and Peng Zhen." *China Spring Digest* 1 (May–June 1987): 41–3.

Hinton, Harold C. *The People's Republic of China 1949–1979: A Documentary Survey, Volume 2*. Wilmington, DE: Scholarly Resources Inc., 1980.

Houn, Franklin W. "Communist China's New Constitution." *Western Political Quarterly* 8 (June 1955): 199–233.

Hsia, Tao-tai. "Chinese Legal Publications: An Appraisal." In *Contemporary Chinese Law*, edited by Jerome A. Cohen, pp. 20–83. Cambridge: Harvard University Press, 1970.

Hsia, Tao-tai, and Wendy I. Zeldin. "Recent Legal Developments in the People's Republic of China." *Harvard International Law Journal* 28 (Spring 1987): 249–87.

Huang Ping. "On the People's Congress System in Our Country." *FBIS* 197 (October 13, 1989): 30. From *Jingji Cankao*, September 17, 1989, p. 4.

Huntington, Samuel P. "The Change to Change." *Comparative Politics* 3 (April 1971): 283–322.

    "The Social and Institutional Dynamics of One-Party Systems." In *Authoritarian Politics in Modern Society: The Dynamics of Established One-Party Systems*, edited by Samuel P. Huntington and Clement Moore, pp. 3–47. New York: Basic Books, 1970.

Jain, Hari Mohain. "Some Aspects of the Chinese Constitution." *India Quarterly* 14 (October–December 1958): 373–9.

Jiang Zemin. "Speech at the Meeting in Celebration of the 40th Anniversary of the Founding of the People's Republic of China." *Beijing Review* 32 (October 9–15, 1989): 11–24.

Jin Jian. "China Cannot Adopt the Balance of the Three Powers." *FBIS* 156 (August 15, 1989): 22–5. From *Renmin Ribao*, August 11, 1989, p. 6.

Joseph, William A. *The Critique of Ultra-Leftism in China 1958–1981*. Stanford, CA: Stanford University Press, 1984.

Jowitt, Kenneth. "Inclusion and Mobilization in European Leninist Regimes." *World Politics* 28 (October 1975): 69–96.

Juan Chi-chung. "Sidelight – Dissenting Votes at the NPC." *FBIS* 76 (April 21, 1986): W5–6. From *Wen Wei Po*, April 13, 1986.

"The Judiciary (I)." *China News Analysis* (Hong Kong) 140 (July 20, 1956).

Kamiya, Antonio. "KYODO Reviews Dissenting Votes in Elections." *FBIS* 69 (April 11, 1988): 21–2.

Kane, Anthony J. "1987: Politics Back in Command." In *China Briefing, 1988*, edited by Anthony J. Kane, pp. 1–18. Boulder, CO: Westview Press, 1988.

Kim, Chong Lim, Joel D. Barkan, Ilter Turan, and Malcom E. Jewell. *The Legislative Connection: The Politics of Representation in Kenya, Korea, and Turkey*. Durham, NC: Duke University Press, 1984.

Kim, Ilpyong J. *The Politics of Chinese Communism: Kiangsi Under the Soviets*. Berkeley: University of California Press, 1973.

Kokubun, Ryosei. "The Politics of Foreign Economic Policy-Making in China: The Case of Plant Cancellations with Japan." *China Quarterly*, no. 105 (March 1986): 45–71.

Krasner, Stephen D. "Approaches to the State: Alternative Conceptions and Historical Dynamics." *Comparative Politics* 16 (January 1984): 223–46.

"Sovereignty: An Institutionalist Approach." *Comparative Political Studies* 21 (April 1988): 66–94.

Kristof, Nicholas D. "Power War, the Chinese Way: The Nation Listens to Rumors and Intrigues." *The New York Times* (National Edition), March 23, 1989, p. 4.

Kuan, Hsin-chi. "New Departures in China's Constitution." *Studies in Comparative Communism* 17 (Spring 1984): 53–68.

Lai Pui-Yee. "Overhaul of Charter Demanded by Scholars." *South China Morning Post*, March 27, 1989, p. 6.

LaPalombara, Joseph G. "Monoliths or Plural System: Through Conceptual Lenses Darkly." *Studies in Comparative Communism* 8 (August 1975): 305–32.

Politics Within Nations. Englewood Cliffs, NJ: Prentice-Hall, 1974.

Lardy, Nicholas R. "China's Economic Readjustment: Recovery or Paralysis." In *China Briefing, 1980*, edited by Robert B. Oxnam and Richard C. Bush, pp. 39–51. Boulder, CO: Westview Press, 1980.

"Legal Principles and Practice." *China News Analysis* (Hong Kong) 284 (July 10, 1959).

Legislative Affairs Commission of the Standing Committee of the National People's Congress. *The Laws of the People's Republic of China (1979–1986)*. Two Volumes. Beijing: Foreign Languages Press, 1987.

Leng, Shao-chuan. "The Role of Law in the People's Republic of China as Reflecting Mao Tse-tung's Influence." *Journal of Criminal Law and Criminology* 68 (September 1977): 356–73.

Leng, Shao-chuan, and Hungdah Chiu. *Criminal Justice in Post-Mao China*. Albany, NY: State University of New York Press, 1985.

Li Buyun. "Certain Questions Concerning the Relationship between Party Policies and State Laws." *CR:PSM* 68 (October 15, 1984): 32–9. From *Faxue Jikan*, no. 3 (July 1984): 3–7.

Li Chiu-yi. "Composition of the Chinese Communist Third National People's Congress." *Issues and Studies* (Taipei) 1 (December 1964).

Li Maoguan. "Why Laws Go Unenforced." *Beijing Review* 32 (September 11–17, 1989): 17–19, 26.

"Li Peng on Current Domestic and International Policies." *Beijing Review* 32 (October 16–22, 1989): 18–21.

Li Peng. "Report on the Work of the Government." In *The First Session of the Seventh National People's Congress of the People's Republic of China (1988)*. Beijing: Foreign Languages Press, 1988.

"Resolutely Carry Out the Principles of Improvement, Rectification and Deepened Reform." Report of the Work of the Government, delivered at the Second Session of the Seventh National People's Congress on March 20, 1989.

Li Qi. "Strive to Strengthen the People's Democratic Legislative System of China." *SCMP* 1425 (December 6, 1956): 3–12. From *Renmin Ribao*, November 6, 1956.

Li, Victor H. "The Evolution and Development of the Chinese Legal System." In *China: Management of a Revolutionary Society*, edited by John M. H. Lindbeck, pp. 221–55. Seattle: University of Washington Press, 1971.

Liao Gailong. "Historical Experiences and Our Road of Development (Parts I–III)." *Issues and Studies* (Taipei) 17 (October–December 1981).

Lieberthal, Kenneth. "China in 1982: A Middling Course for the Middle Kingdom." *Asian Survey* 23 (January 1983): 26–37.

A Research Guide to Central Party and Government Meetings in China 1949–1975. White Plains, NY: International Arts and Science Press, 1976.

Lin Hsin-tao. "Supreme Paramount Power – How the NPC Can Really Be Worthy of its Name, Part 1." *CR:PSM* 148 (December 15, 1980): 26–8. From *Wen Wei Po* (Hong Kong), November 9, 1980, p. 3.

Liu Jui-shao. "Beijing Keen on Improving Quality of NPC Sessions." *FBIS* 39 (February 29, 1988): 15. From *Wen Wei Po*, February 29, 1988, p. 1.

Liu Tingxiao and Ma Hongru. "Valuable Spiritual Wealth of the Party and the People – Studying Comrade Dong Biwu's Political and Legal Thinking." *CR:RF* 16 (July 29, 1985): 14–19. From *Hongqi*, no. 11 (June 1, 1985): 9–12.

Lowenthal, Richard. "Development vs. Utopia in Communist Policy." In *Change in Communist Systems*, edited by Chalmers Johnson, pp. 33–116. Stanford, CA: Stanford University Press, 1970.

"On Established Communist Party Regimes." *Studies in Comparative Communism* 7 (Winter 1974): 335–58.

"The Ruling Party in a Mature Society." In *Social Consequences of Modernization in Communist Societies*, edited by Mark G. Field, pp. 81–118. Baltimore: Johns Hopkins University Press, 1976.

Lukes, Steven. *Power – A Radical View*. London: Macmillan Press, 1974.

Luo Bing. "Behind-the-Scene News at the NPC." *CR:PSM* 275 (March 2, 1982): 67–72. From *Zhengming*, no. 51 (January 1982): 8–10.

"Notes on the Northern Journey." *FBIS* 41 (March 2, 1988): 14–20. From *Zhengming*, no. 125 (March 1, 1988): 6–9.

Ma Lu. "How to View the Succession of Zhao Ziyang." *CR:PSM* 143 (December 3, 1980): 17–20. From *Zhengming*, no. 36 (October 1, 1980): 18–19.

MacFarquhar, Roderick. *The Hundred Flowers Campaign and the Chinese Intellectuals*. New York: Praeger, 1960.

The Origins of the Cultural Revolution, Vol. 1: Contradictions Among the People. New York: Columbia University Press, 1974.

The Origins of the Cultural Revolution, Vol. 2: The Great Leap Forward 1958–1960. New York: Columbia University Press, 1983.

Mao Zedong. "On Coalition Government." In *Selected Works of Mao Tse-tung*, Vol. 3, pp. 205–70. Peking: Foreign Languages Press, 1967.

"On New Democracy." In *Selected Works of Mao Tse-tung*. Vol. 2, pp. 339–84. Peking: Foreign Languages Press, 1975.

"On the People's Democratic Dictatorship." In *Selected Readings from the Works of Mao Tse-tung*, pp. 371–88. Peking: Foreign Languages Press, 1971.

March, James G., and Johan P. Olsen. "The New Institutionalism: Organizational Factors in Political Life." *American Political Science Review* 78 (September 1984): 734–49.

Marx, Karl, Friedrich Engels, and V. I. Lenin. *On Democracy – Bourgeois and Socialist*. Moscow: Progress Publishers, 1988.

McCormick, Barrett L. "Leninist Implementation: The Election Campaign." In *Policy Implementation in Post-Mao China*, edited by David M. Lampton, pp. 383–413. Berkeley: University of California Press, 1987.

Meisner, Maurice J. "The Chinese Rediscovery of Karl Marx: Some Reflections on Post-Maoist Chinese Marxism." *Bulletin of Concerned Asian Scholars* 17 (July–September 1985): 2–16.

Mao's China. New York: The Free Press, 1977.

Mezey, Michael L. *Comparative Legislatures*. Durham, NC: Duke University Press, 1979.

"The Functions of Legislatures in the Third World." In *Handbook of Legislative Research*, edited by Gerhard Loewenberg, Samuel C. Patterson, and Malcolm E. Jewell, pp. 733–72. Cambridge: Harvard University Press, 1985.

"Policy and Regime Support Functions." Paper prepared for delivery at the Conference on Parliaments, Policy and Regime Support, Durham, North Carolina, December 2–5, 1982.

Michael, Franz. "The Role of Law in Traditional, National and Communist China." *China Quarterly*, no. 9 (January–March 1962): 124–48.

"A Milestone in the Historical Development of the People's Republic of China." *SCMP* 899 (September 30, 1954): 1. From *Renmin Ribao*, September 29, 1954.

"The Ministries – from Within." *China News Analysis* (Hong Kong) 184 (June 7, 1057).

Ming Bao. "Forum of the 1980s – Forum on the Sixth NPC." *CR:PSM* 452 (September 2, 1983): 131–4. From *Ming Bao*, June 27, 1983, p. 21.

Moody, Peter R., Jr. *Chinese Politics After Mao*. New York: Praeger, 1983.

Nathan, Andrew J. *Chinese Democracy*. Berkeley: University of California Press, 1985.

Peking Politics, 1918–1923. Berkeley: University of California Press, 1976.

National People's Congress of the People's Republic of China. *Documents of the First Session of the Fifth National People's Congress of the People's Republic of China*. Peking: Foreign Languages Press, 1978.

Documents of the First Session of the First National People's Congress of the People's Republic of China. Peking: Foreign Languages Press, 1955.

Main Documents of the First Session of the Third National People's Congress. Peking: Foreign Languages Press, 1965.

Main Documents of the Second Session of the Fifth National People's Congress of the People's Republic of China. Beijing: Foreign Languages Press, 1979.

Main Documents of the Third Session of the Fifth National People's Congress of the People's Republic of China. Beijing: Foreign Languages Press, 1980.

Second Session of the Second National People's Congress of the People's Republic of China (Documents). Peking: Foreign Languages Press, 1960.

Nelson, Daniel N. "Editor's Introduction: Communist Legislatures and Communist Politics." *Legislative Studies Quarterly* 5 (May 1980): 161–74.

Ngapoi Ngawang Jigme. "Explanations of 'Law on Regional Autonomy for PRC Minority Nationalities,'" *CR:PSM* 92 (December 31, 1984): 1–9. From *Guowuyuan Gongbao*, no. 13 (June 30, 1984): 430–7.

"The 1957 Session of National People's Congress (VIII) – The Rightists Surrender: Comment." *CB* 470 (July 26, 1957).

"NPC Deputies Express Views." *Beijing Review* 31 (August 1–7, 1988): 11.

"NPC Deputies Urge End to 'Rubber Stamp' Image." *FBIS* 72 (April 14, 1988): 35–6.

"NPC Executive Body Rapped as Weak Watchdog." *China Daily*, April 1, 1989, p. 3.

NPC Law Committee. "Report by the Law Committee of the NPC on the Result of Examination of the 'Patent Law of the People's Republic of China.'" *CR:PSM* 79 (November 23, 1984): 12–15. From *Guowuyuan Gongbao*, no. 6 (April 20, 1984): 173–6.

"NPC: Lively Political Atmosphere." *Beijing Review* 22 (July 13, 1979): 18–23.

"NPC Special Committees Elected Over Opposition." *FBIS* 59s (March 28, 1988): 48–9.

"NPC Standing Committee to Make Inspection Tours." *FBIS* 99 (May 22, 1981): K1–2.

O'Brien, Kevin J. "China's National People's Congress: Reform and Its Limits." *Legislative Studies Quarterly* 13 (August 1988): 343–74.

   "Is China's National People's Congress a 'Conservative' Legislature?" *Asian Survey* 30 (in press).

   "Legislative Development and Chinese Political Change." *Studies in Comparative Communism* 22 (Spring 1989): 57–75.

Ou-Yang, Hsin-Yi. "From Proletarian Dictatorship to People's Democratic Dictatorship: Elite Transition in the National People's Congress, People's Republic of China." Unpublished master's thesis, Ohio State University, Department of Sociology, 1984.

"Outspoken Newspaper Banned from Session." *Hong Kong Standard*, March 21, 1989, p. 7.

Packenham, Robert A. "Legislatures and Political Development." In *Legislatures in Developmental Perspective*, edited by Allan Kornberg and Lloyd D. Musolf, pp. 521–82. Durham, NC: Duke University Press, 1970.

Pan Nianzhi. "Some Ideas About Revising the Constitution." *CR:PSM* 202 (July 6, 1981): 26–37. From *Minzhu yu Fazhi*, no. 4 (April 1981): 4–8.

Peng Zhen. "Report on the Draft of the Revised Constitution of the People's Republic of China." *FBIS* 235 (December 7, 1982): K33–48.

"Peng Zhen Urges Sound Socialist Legal System." *FBIS* 128 (July 3, 1985): K4.

"The People's Congress, Part 1." *China News Analysis* (Hong Kong) 989 (February 7, 1975).

"The People's Congress, Part 2." *China News Analysis* (Hong Kong) 990 (February 14, 1975).

Pitkin, Hanna F. *The Concept of Representation*. Berkeley: University of California Press, 1967.

Polsby, Nelson W. "Legislatures." In *Handbook of Political Science, Volume 5*, edited by Fred I. Greenstein and Nelson W. Polsby, pp. 257–319. Reading, MA: Addison-Wesley, 1975.

Potter, Pitman B. "Peng Zhen: Evolving Views on Party Organization and Law." In *China's Establishment Intellectuals*, edited by Carol Lee Hamrin and Timothy Cheek, pp. 21–50. Armonk, NY: M.E. Sharpe, 1986.

Pravda, Alex. "Elections in Communist Party States." In *Communist Politics: A*

Reader, edited by Stephen White and Daniel Nelson, pp. 27–54. Washington Square, NY: New York University Press, 1986.

Pu Xingzu. "Increase the Authority of Legislative Organs." *Chinese Law and Government* 20 (Spring 1987): 78–9. From *Zhengzhixue Yanjiu*, no. 2 (March 1986): 15–17.

"Resolution of the Fourth Session of the Fifth National People's Congress of the People's Republic of China Concerning the Report 'Present Economic Situation and Principles for Future Economic Construction.'" *CR:PSM* 253 (December 30, 1981): 70–1.

Reynolds, Bruce L. "The Chinese Economy in 1980: Death of Reform?" In *China Briefing, 1981*, edited by Robert B. Oxnam and Richard C. Bush, pp. 41–52. Boulder, CO: Westview Press, 1981.

Rosario, Louise de. "Speak No Evil." *Far Eastern Economic Review* 144 (March 30, 1989): 11.

Rosen, Stanley. "China in 1986: A Year of Consolidation." *Asian Survey* 27 (January 1987): 35–55.

"China in 1987: The Year of the Thirteenth Party Congress." *Asian Survey* 28 (January 1988): 35–51.

Schram, Stuart R. "The Chinese Soviet Republic: Some Introductory Reflections." In *The Legal System of the Chinese Soviet Republic 1931–1934*, edited by W. E. Butler, pp. 7–20. Dobbs Ferry, NY: Transnational Publishers, 1983.

"'Economics in Command?' Ideology and Policy Since the Third Plenum, 1978–84." *China Quarterly*, no. 99 (September 1984): 417–61.

"Introduction: The Cultural Revolution in Historical Perspective." In *Authority, Participation and Cultural Change in China*, edited by Stuart R. Schram, pp. 1–108. Cambridge: Cambridge University Press, 1973.

"Political Reform in China – In the Primary Stage of Socialism." *IHJ Bulletin* 8 (Spring 1988): 1–7.

Schwartz, Benjamin I. *Communism in China: Ideology in Flux*. Cambridge, MA: Harvard University Press, 1968.

Selden, Mark. *The Yenan Way in Revolutionary China*. Cambridge: Harvard University Press, 1971.

Shen Baoxiang. "Cherish One's Right to Vote." *FBIS* 122 (June 23, 1980): L12–13. From *Renmin Ribao*, June 13, 1980, p. 5.

Sheridan, James E. *China in Disintegration*. New York: The Free Press, 1975.

Shih Tien-hui. "A Milestone in the Modernization of the Chinese Political System – On Covering the NPC in the Great Hall of the People." *CR:PSM* 128 (October 15, 1980): 45–9. From *Dongxiang*, no. 24 (September 1980): 4–6.

Skilling, H. Gordon. "Group Conflict and Political Change." In *Change in Communist Systems*, edited by Chalmers Johnson, pp. 215–34. Stanford, CA: Stanford University Press, 1970.

Skowronek, Stephen. *Building a New American State*. Cambridge: Cambridge University Press, 1982.

Simon, Maurice D., and David M. Olson. "Evolution of a Minimal Parliament: Membership and Committee Changes in the Polish Sejm." *Legislative Studies Quarterly* 5 (May 1980): 211–30.

Simons, William B. "Reflections on State Administration in the Chinese Soviet Republic and the Soviet Union." In *The Legal System of the Chinese Soviet Republic 1931–1934*, edited by W. E. Butler, pp. 47–52. Dobbs Ferry, NY: Transnational Publishers, 1983.

Solinger. Dorothy J. *Chinese Business Under Socialism*. Berkeley: University of California Press, 1984.

"Economic Reform." In *China Briefing, 1984*, edited by Steven M. Goldstein, pp. 87–108. Boulder, CO: Westview Press, 1985.

"The Fifth National People's Congress and the Process of Policy-Making: Reform, Readjustment and Opposition." *Asian Survey* 22 (December 1982): 1238–75.

Three Visions of Socialism. Boulder, CO: Westview Press, 1984.

Southerland, Daniel. "Soviet Shifts Not a Model, Chinese Says." *Washington Post*, April 4, 1989, p. A19.

Stahnke, Arthur. "The Background and Evolution of Party Policy on the Drafting of Legal Codes in Communist China." *American Journal of Comparative Law* 15 (3) (1967): 506–25.

Starr, John Bryan. *Continuing the Revolution: The Political Thought of Mao*. Princeton: Princeton University Press, 1979.

Stavis, Benedict. *China's Political Reforms*. New York: Praeger, 1988.

"Steady Progress in China's Legal System." *FBIS* 194 (October 4, 1984): K15–16.

"The Structure of the State in China." *China News Analysis* (Hong Kong) 107 (November 4, 1955).

Tam, Tammy, and Priscilla Leung. "Mild Rebuke for Radical Economic Reforms." *Hong Kong Standard*, March 22, 1989, p. 11.

Tian Nong. "Different Views on the Legislative System in Our Country." *FBIS* 165 (August 24, 1983): K10–12. From *Renmin Ribao*, August 19, 1983, p. 5.

Tian Sansong. "Democracy in Action, Acccent on Reforms." *Beijing Review* 23 (September 29, 1980): 33–7.

Tien, Hung-mao. *Government and Politics of Kuomintang China 1927–1937*. Stanford, CA: Stanford University Press, 1972.

Tilly, Charles. "Reflections on the History of European State-Making." In *The Formation of National States in Western Europe*, edited by Charles Tilly, pp. 3–83. Princeton: Princeton University Press, 1975.

Townsend, James R. *Political Participation in Communist China*. Berkeley: University of California, 1967.

"Ts'ao Ts'ao on the Stage." *China News Analysis* (Hong Kong) 274 (May 1, 1959).

Tung, William L. *The Political Institutions of Modern China*. The Hague, Netherlands: Martinus Nijhoff, 1964.

Vanneman, Peter. *The Supreme Soviet: Politics and the Legislative Process in the Soviet Political System*. Durham, NC: Duke University Press, 1977.

Vogel, Ezra F. *Canton Under Communism*. Cambridge, MA: Harvard University Press, 1969.

Waller, Derek J. *The Kiangsi Soviet Republic: Mao and the National Congresses of 1931 and 1934*. China Research Monograph, No. 10. Berkeley: University of California Center for Chinese Studies, 1973.

Wang Hanbin. "Explanation of the 'Decision Authorizing the State Council to Formulate Provisional Regulations Concerning Economic Restructuring and Implementation of the Open Door Policy (Draft).'" *CR:PSM* 15 (January 29, 1986): 1–2. From *Guowuyuan Gongbao*, no. 11 (April 30, 1985): 331–2.

Wang Hsiao-t'ang (Wang Xiaotang). "An Evaluation and Analysis of China's Revised Constitution." *Chinese Law and Government* 11 (Summer–Fall 1978): 34–53.

Wang Shuwen. "The People's Congress Sytem Is our Country's Basic Political System." *CR:RF* (July 16, 1982): 30–8. From *Hongqi*, no. 10 (May 16, 1982): 20–4.

Wang Shuwen and Zhou Yanrui. "New Development of the People's Congress System." *CR:PSM* 337 (September 15, 1982): 23–32. From *Faxue Yanjiu*, no. 3 (June 1982): 9–14.

Welsh, William A. "The Status of Research on Representative Institutions in Eastern Europe." *Legislative Studies Quarterly* 5 (May 1980): 275–308.

Weng, Byron. "Some Key Aspects of the 1982 Draft Constitution of the PRC." *China Quarterly*, no. 91 (September 1982): 492–506.

"The Role of the State Council." *Chinese Law and Government* 16 (Summer–Fall 1983): 153–92.

White, Gordon. "The Post-Revolutionary State." In *State and Society in Contemporary China*, edited by Victor Nee and David Mozingo, pp. 27–52. Ithaca, NY: Cornell University Press, 1983.

White, Stephen. "Economic Performance and Communist Legitimacy." *World Politics* 38 (April 1986): 462–82.

"Non-competitive Elections and National Politics: The USSR Supreme Soviet Elections of 1984." *Electoral Studies* 4 (1985): 215–29.

"Some Conclusions." In *Communist Legislatures in Comparative Perspective*, edited by Daniel Nelson and Stephen White, pp. 191–6. London: Macmillan Press, 1982.

"The Supreme Soviet and Budgetary Politics in the USSR." *British Journal of Political Science* 12 (January 1982): 75–94.

"The USSR Supreme Soviet: A Developmental Perspective." *Legislative Studies Quarterly* 5 (May 1980): 247–74.

Whyte, Martin King. "Bureaucracy and Modernization in China: The Maoist Critique." *American Sociological Review* 38 (April 1973): 149–63.

Womack, Brantly. "Modernization and Democratic Reform in China." *The Journal of Asian Studies* 44 (May 1984): 417–39.

"The 1980 County-Level Elections in China: Experiment in Democratic Modernization." *Asian Survey* 22 (March 1982): 261–77.

"Party-State Democracy: A Theoretical Perspective." A paper presented at the 17th Sino–American Conference on Mainland China, June 6, 1988.

Wu Daying and Liu Cuixiao. "The Interpretation of Our Country's Socialist Laws." *CR:PSM* 10 (January 31, 1985): 9–17. From *Zhengzhi yu Falü*, no. 4 (August 1984): 42–6.

Wu Jialin. "Some Questions Concerning Socialist Democracy." *Beijing Review* 22 (June 15, 1979): 9–13.

Wu Jianfan. "The Building of China's Democracy and Legal System." *FBIS* 143 (July 25, 1985): K1–4. From *Renmin Ribao*, July 16, 1985, p. 2.

Wu Ke-chien (Wu Kejian). "People's Congress – People's Democracy – People's Power." *China Reconstructs* 8 (January 1959): 26–9.

Wu Zhong. "NPC Deputies Pressure Chairman to Admit Neglect." *Hong Kong Standard*, April 2, 1989, p. 4.

Xiang Chunyi, Yang Jingyu, and Gu Angran. "Strive to Establish a Socialist Legal System with Chinese Characteristics." *CR:RF* 3 (February 1, 1984): 11–20. From *Hongqi*, no. 3 (February 1, 1984): 8–12.

Xu Chongde. "Ten Proposals for Revising the Constitution." *CR:PSM* 200 (June 29, 1981): 1–9. From *Minzhu yu Fazhi*, no. 3 (March 1981): 7–10.

Xu Xing. "Conservative Systems Reforms." *CR:PSM* 11 (February 1, 1984): 110–17. From *Zhengming*, no. 73 (November 1983).

Yan Jun. "Having More Arguments Is a Good Thing." *FBIS* 179 (September 16, 1986): K6–7. From *Zhongguo Fazhibao*, September 4, 1986, p. 1.

Yao Meng-hsuan, "Peiping's National Congress and Trends." *Issues and Studies* (Taipei) 1 (February 1965): 13–24.

Ye Ruixian. "Socialist Democracy Is the Broadest Form of Democracy." *CR:PSM* 13 (August 29, 1979): 13–17. From *Nanfang Ribao*, June 27, 1979, p. 3.

Young, Ernest P. *The Presidency of Yuan Shih-k'ai*. Ann Arbor: University of Michigan Press, 1977.

Yu, George T. "The 1962 and 1963 Sessions of the National People's Congress of Communist China." *Asian Survey* 4 (August 1964): 981–90.

Yu Haocheng. "Questioning the Third Echelon." *China Spring Digest* 1 (November/December 1987): 62–9.

Zhang Shixin. "Some Views on the Issue of the Position of Head of State in China." *CR:PSM* 263 (January 26, 1982): 48–52. From *Minzhu yu Fazhi*, no. 9 (September 1981): 8–9.

"Zhang Youyu Explains Draft Inheritance Law." *FBIS* 73 (April 16, 1985): K13–15.

Zhang Youyu. "New Developments of the People's Congress System." *FBIS* 15 (January 21, 1983): K12–15. From *Renmin Ribao*, January 14, 1983, p. 5.

Zhang Youyu and Xu Chongde. "The Fundamental Spirit of the Draft of the New Constitution." *SWB*. FE 7035, May 25, 1982, pp. BII/1–5. From *Renmin Ribao*, May 17, 1982.

Zhang Yu'an. "Less Deputy Fanfare – Start of a Trend?" *China Daily*, April 5, 1989, p. 4.

Zhao Ziyang. "Government Work Report." *FBIS* 61 (March 29, 1985): K1–17.

"The Present Economic Situation and the Principles for Future Economic Construction." *FBIS* 241 (December 16, 1981): K1–35.

"Report on the Seventh Five-Year Plan." In *The Fourth Session of the Sixth National People's Congress (Main Documents)*. Beijing: Foreign Languages Press, 1986.

"Report on the Sixth Five-Year Plan." In *Fifth Session of the Fifth National People's Congress (Main Documents)*. Beijing: Foreign Languages Press, 1983.

"Report on the Work of the Government." *FBIS* 107 (June 1, 1984): K1–20.

"Report on the Work of the Government." In *The Fifth Session of the Sixth National People's Congress (Main Documents)*. Beijing: Foreign Languages Press, 1987.

"Report on the Work of the Government." In *The First Session of the Sixth National People's Congress (Main Documents)*. Beijing: Foreign Languages Press, 1983.

Zheng Gongcheng. "Suggestions on Reforming the People's Congress Deputy System." *FBIS* 215 (November 7, 1988): 29–30. From *Qunyan*, no. 9 (September 1988): 46.

Zheng Zhi. "New Lineup of Deputies to Sixth NPC Reviewed." *CR:PSM* 442 (August 1, 1983): 34–6. From *Banyuetan*, no. 10 (May 25, 1983): 6–7.

Zhu Wei. "A Look at the General Situation in Communist China." *Translations on People's Republic of China* 429 (May 15, 1978): 7–10. From *Zhengming*, no. 6 (April 1978).

Zi Mu. "Strengthening the People's Congress is the Fundamental Way to Develop Socialist Democracy." *Chinese Law and Government* 20 (Spring 1987): 84–8. From *Shijie Jingji Daobao*, August 11, 1986.

Chinese language references

Benkan Bianjibu [editors]. "Fazhi yao xietiao, taolun dai shenhua" [The legal system must be coordinated, discussion deepens]. *Faxue*, no. 10 (October 1985): 1–4.

"Guanyu kaizhan woguo fazhi jianshe xietiao fazhan wenti taolun yijian" [Opinions on the discussion on problems in unfolding our country's coordinated legal development]. *Faxue*, no. 5 (May 1984): 1–3.

Benkan Bianjibu [editors]. "Zai gaige zhong tabu qianjin" [A big step forward in reform]. *Zhengzhi yu Falü*, no. 5 (October 1984): 1–4.

Benkan Pinglun [editors]. "Lingdao ganbu bu neng chaoyue xianfa xingshi zhiquan" [Leadership cadres cannot overstep the constitution]. *Faxue*, no. 12 (December 1985): 1–2.

Cai Dingjian. "Jianquan renda falü jiandu jigou de shexiang" [Ideas on strengthening the NPC's legal supervision structure]. *Faxue Zazhi*, no. 3 (June 1987): 8–9.

"Jiaqiang jiandu gongneng, wanshan renmin daibiao dahui zhidu" [Strengthen supervisory abilities, perfect the NPC system]. *Zhengzhi yu Falü*, no. 1 (February 1988): 22–3.

"Jingzheng jizhi yu minzhu xuanju" [Competition system and democratic elections]. *Fazhi Jianshe*, no. 6 (December 1988): 10–12.

"Woguo xianfa zhidu tantao" [Research on our nation's constitutional supervision system]. *Faxue Yanjiu*, no. 3 (June 1989): 25–31.

Cao Siyuan. "Dui renda yishi guize caoan sidian yijian" [Four opinions on the NPC rules on proceedings]. *Shijie Jingji Daobao*, March 20, 1989, p. 3.

Chen Deshan. "Tantan woguo lifa tixi" [Discussing our country's legislative system]. *Faxue Zazhi*, no. 2 (April 1985): 32–4.

Chen Hefu. *Xuanju Manyu* [Notes on Elections]. Beijing: Qunzhong Chubanshe, 1983.

Chen Yunsheng. "Baozheng xianfa shishi de zhongyao zuzhi xingshi" [Important organizational forms to guarantee the constitution's enforcement]. *Jianghai Xuekan*, no. 2 (April 1983): 55–7, 34.

"Tizhi gaige yu xianfa jiandu" [Structural reform and constitutional supervision]. *Faxue Yanjiu*, no. 5 (October 1988): 5–11.

"Wo guo xianfa de falü baozheng" [Our constitution's legal guarantees]. *Faxue Jikan*, no. 3 (July 1982): 16–19.

Cui Min and Yu Chi. "Shilun xianfa de zuigao falü xiaoli" [A tentative discussion of the constitution's highest legal force]. *Faxue Zazhi*, no. 3 (June 1982): 3–5.

Dong Biwu. "Dangqian zhengfa gongzuo de jige wenti" [Several problems in current political-legal work]. In *Dong Biwu Lun Shehuizhuyi Minzhu he Fazhi*, pp. 139–50. Beijing: Renmin Chubanshe, 1979.

Dong Biwu Xuanji [The Selected Works of Dong Biwu]. Beijing: Renmin Chubanshe, 1985.

"Jinyibu jiaqiang renmin minzhu fazhi, baozhang shehuizhuyi jianshe shiye" [Further strengthen people's democratic legal system and ensure socialist construction]. In *Dong Biwu Lun Shehuizhuyi Minzhu he Fazhi*, pp. 127–38. Beijing: Renmin Chubanshe, 1979.

Dong Chengmei. "Shilun xianxing xianfa ruhe xiugai de jige wenti" [Discussion of several issues on how to revise the current constitution]. *Minzhu yu Fazhi*, no. 3 (March 1982): 8–10.

Du Xichuan. "Renda daibiao ying daibiao shei de liyi?" [Whose interests should people's deputies represent?]. *Faxue Zazhi*, no. 1 (January 1989): 19–20.

Fan Jiahua. "Xin tizhi de lao wenti" [The new system's old problems]. *Qishi Niandai*, no. 162 (July 1983): 19–21.

Feng Wenbin. "Guanyu shehuizhuyi minzhu wenti" [Problems concerning socialist democracy]. *Renmin Ribao*, November 24 and 25, 1980, p. 5.

Fu Shihui. "Renda sanji" [Random notes on the NPC]. *Mingbao Yuekan*, no. 178 (October 1980): 6–7.

"Gangqu daibiao guanzhu tongzhang yuanyin" [Hong Kong deputies pay attention to the causes of inflation]. *Wen Wei Po*, March 23, 1989, p. 2.

Gao Gongyou. "Jiaqiang renmin daibiao dahui zhidu de zhongyao yiyi" [The significance of strengthening the NPC system]. *Faxue*, no. 7 (July 1982): 14–16.

Gao Mingxuan. "Tantan woguo xingfa gongbu shishi yihou de buchong he xiugai" [Discussing supplements and revisions of our country's criminal law since its promulgation]. *Faxue Zazhi*, no. 6 (December 1985): 5–8.

Gao Zhaoxian. "Cong xiancao kan renmin daibiao dahui zhidu de xin fazhan" [New developments of the NPC system seen in the draft constitution]. *Faxue Jikan*, no. 4 (October 1982): 9–12.

Gong Yuzhi. "Lun xianfa shishi de baozheng" [Guarantees for constitutional enforcement]. *Xinhua Wenzhai*, no. 3 (March 1983): 16–19. From *Renmin Ribao*, January 17, 1983.

Gu Angran. "Disanjie quanguo renmin daibiao dahui kuoda daibiao ming'e shi wo guo zhengzhi shenghuo zhong de yijian dashi" [Enlarging the number of deputies at the Third National People's Congress is a big event in our country's political life]. *Zhengfa Yanjiu*, no. 1 (March 1964): 5–11.

"Fensui youpai fenzi gongji quanguo renmin daibiao dahui shi 'xingshi' de miulun" [On denouncing the absurd statement of the rightist elements that the NPC is only a "formality"]. *Zhengfa Yanjiu*, no. 6 (December 1957): 31–4.

Gu Angran and Li Jianfei. "Bochi Wu Jialin weixie zuigao guojia quanli jiguan weifa fazhi de miulun" [Refuting Wu Jialin's slanderous falsehood that the highest state organs violated the law]. *Renmin Ribao*, September 24, 1957, p. 3.

Gu Huiwen. "Renzhen guanche renmin daibiao dahui zhidu" [Conscientiously carry out the people's congress system]. *Guangming Ribao*, April 15, 1957, p. 3.

Guo Daohui. "Lun woguo yiyuan lifa tizhi" [On our country's centralized legislative system]. *Faxue Yanjiu*, no. 1 (February 1986): 1–7.

Han Peimei. "Lun jiaqiang quanguo renda changweihui de jianshe" [On strengthening NPCSC construction]. *Faxue Zazhi*, no. 2 (April 1983): 31–2, 59.

Han Sheng. "Tantan falü de zhiding guocheng" [Discussing the process of enacting laws]. *Zhongguo Fazhibao*, May 10, 1985, p. 1.

He Huahui. "Cong xuanju shijian kan wo guo xuanju zhidu de minzhuxing" [From electoral practice see the democratic nature of our country's electoral system]. *Zhengzhi yu Falü*, no. 5 (June 1983): 45–9.

Hong Yuan. "Wujie renda hou de Beijing" [Beijing after the Fifth NPC]. *Dongxiang*, no. 10 (July 1979): 4–6.

Hu Jinguang. "Lun xianfa jiandu zhidu" [On the system of constitutional supervision]. *Zhongguo Faxue*, no. 1 (March 1985): 72–9.

"Tantan jiaqiang lifa jieshi" [On strengthening legislative interpretation]. *Zhengzhi yu Falü*, no. 1 (February 1988): 32.

Hu Tugui. "Renmin daibiao yao xuedian falü" [People's deputies must study a little law]. *Faxue Zazhi*, no. 4 (August 1982): 47–8.

Hua Guoquan. "Bochi youpai dui lianhe timing he deng'e xuanju de wuxie" [Denouncing and refuting rightist slander of joint nomination and equal quota elections]. *Faxue*, no. 5 (May 1958): 40–3.

Huang Shuhai and Zhu Weijiu. "Shilun shouquan lifa" [On empowered legislation]. *Faxue Yanjiu*, no. 1 (February 1986): 7–13.

Ji Peng. "Wei wujie renda dierci huiyi gaikuang" [The general situation at the Fifth NPC Second Session]. *Zhonggong Yanjiu* (Taipei) 13 (July 1979): 25–7.

Jin Zhiming. "Lun Zhongguo minzhu qiantu" [Discussing China's democratic future]. *Dong Xi Fang* (Hong Kong), no. 22 (October 1980): 26–9.

Jiu Zhongyi. "Xin jingjipai doukua shiyoupai" [The new economic faction topples the petroleum faction]. *Dongxiang*, no. 24 (September 1980): 9–11.

Kan Ke. "Quanguo renmin daibiao dahui daibiao ming'e queding yiju tantao" [An approach to determining the number of deputies to the NPC]. *Zhengzhixue Yanjiu*, no. 5 (September 1987): 32–7.

Kang Damin. "Jianyi sheli xianfa fayuan" [Proposal to establish a constitutional court]. *Faxue Zazhi*, no. 2 (April 1981): 29–30.

Lan Yanzhi. "Pingdan wushi de jingji huiyi" [A flat, pragmatic, economic congress]. *Qishi Niandai*, no. 144 (January 1982): 44–5.

Li Buyun. "Shehuizhuyi minzhu yu zibenzhuyi minzhu de qubie" [The differences between socialist and capitalist democracy]. *Faxue*, no. 12 (December 1983): 12–16.

Li Guoxiong. "Woguo renmin daibiaozhi dangyi" [An opinion on our country's people's congress system]. *Faxue Pinglun*, no. 1 (January 1987): 13–15, 72.

Li Shangzhi and Xu Minhe. "Chongfen fayang minzhu, shixian renmin xinyuan" [Fully develop democracy, realize the people's dreams]. *Liaowang*, no. 7 (July 1983): 2–4.

Li Youyi. "Lun woguo de xuanju zhidu" [On our country's electoral system]. *Renmin Ribao*, November 29, 1957, p. 7.

Li Zuxing. "Jinyibu fahui renmin daibiao dahui zhidu de zuoyong [Further bring into play the role of the NPC]. *Zhengzhixue Yanjiu*, no. 4 (July 1986): 10–12, 37.

"Renda biaojuezhi ji gaige shexiang [Ideas on reforming the NPC's voting system and other reforms]. *Faxue*, no. 11 (November 1986): 2–6.

Liang Qian. "Jingji gaige zhong chule shemma wenti?" [What problems are emerging in economic reform?]. *Zhengming*, no. 91 (May 1985): 43–6.

Liao Hansheng. "Guanyu diqijie quanguo renmin daibiao dahui daibiao zige de shencha baogao de shuoming" [An explanation of the report on the seventh NPC deputies' credentials]. *Zhonghua Renmin Gongheguo Quanguo Renmin Daibiao Dahui Changwu Weiyuanhui Gongbao*, no. 2 (April 15, 1988): 4–7.

Lin Nian. "Cong dang de houshe kan renda zhengxie huiyi" [Looking at the NPC and CPPCC as the party's tongue]. *Zhengming*, no. 91 (May 1985): 47–9.

Ling Zhijun. "Jiyu qiucheng tanyuan" [Exploring the origins of overeagerness to get quick results]. *Renmin Ribao (Haiwaiban)*, March 24, 1989, p. 1.

Liu Chuanchen. "Woguo daibiao jigou yu jiandu zhidu" [Our country's representative organs and the supervisory system]. *Shehui Kexue*, no. 3 (March 1982): 19–21.

Liu Han. "Lun woguo falü shishi de baozheng" [On guarantees of our country's legal enforcement]. *Zhengfa Luntan*, no. 4 (August 1985): 12–16.

Liu Renxian and Gu Angran. "Renmin daibiao dahui zhidu shi gonggu wuchan jieji zhuanzheng, jinxing shehuizhuyi jianshe de youli wuqi" [The people's congress system is a powerful weapon to consolidate the dictatorship of the proletariat to realize socialist construction]. *Zhengfa Yanjiu*, no. 3 (June 1959): 10–13.

Liu Shengping. "Lun woguo lifa tizhi" [On our country's legislative system]. *Zhengzhi yu Falü*, no. 5 (October 1985): 28–31.

"Zhongguo shehuizhuyi falü jieshi wenti yanjiu" [Research on problems in Chinese socialist legal interpretation]. *Zhengfa Luntan*, no. 5 (October 1985): 14–19.

Liu Xia. "Zhengzhi tizhi gaige yu renmin daibiao suzhi" [Political structural reform and people's deputy quality]. *Fazhi Jianshe*, no. 5 (October 1987): 20–2.

Liu Yang and Hou Yafei. "Shiyijie sanzhong quanhui yilai renmin daibiao dahui zhidu de gaige [Reform of the people's congress system since the third plenum of the eleventh party congress]. In *Shiyijie Sanzhong Yilai Zhengzhi Tizhi Gaige de*

Lilun yu Shijian [The Theory and Practice of Political Structural Reform Since the Third Plenum of the Eleventh Party Congress], edited by Liu Yang and Hou Yafei, pp. 126–34. Beijing: Chunqiu Chubanshe, 1987.

Liu Zhenmin and Yan Jun. "Baogao gongzuo shi yao yansu renzhen" [Report work must be serious and conscientious]. *Zhongguo Fazhibao*, June 17, 1985, p. 1.

Long Fei. "Ping zhonggong 'liujie renda' xuanchu de lingdao chengyuan" [A comment on the leading members elected at the Chinese communists Sixth NPC]. *Zhonggong Yanjiu* (Taipei) 17 (July 1983): 37–44.

"Wei wujie 'renda' sanci huiyi dui gaoceng lingdaoren de tiaozheng" [High-level leadership changes at the Fifth NPC Third Session]. *Zhonggong Yanjiu* (Taipei) 14 (October 1980): 33–43.

Luo Bing. "Jun daibiao yujing sizuo" [Army deputy's statement received with raised eyebrows]. *Zhengming*, no. 51 (January 1982): 11–13.

"Liujie renda huinei huiwai" [Inside and outside the Sixth NPC]. *Zhengming*, no. 69 (July 1983): 7–11.

"Paohuang nüfu zongli shijian ji qita" [The incident of bombarding the woman vice-premier and others]. *Zhengming*, no. 22 (August 1979): 6–9.

"Zhao Ziyang baogao shou piping" [Zhao Ziyang's report receives criticism]. *Zhengming*, no. 63 (January 1983): 13–15.

Luo Shiying. "Bochi youpai fenzi dui woguo xuanju zhidu de weixie" [Denouncing and refuting the rightists' slander of our country's electoral system]. *Zhengfa Yanjiu*, no. 6 (December 1957): 27–30.

Luo Yapei. "Shehuizhuyi minzhu zhengzhi jianshe chutan" [Research on socialist democratic politics]. *Faxue Yanjiu*, no. 3 (June 1988): 8–14.

Mao Hua and Yin Lantian. "Caoan guanyu guojia jigou de guiding de rougan tedian" [Certain features of the draft constitution concerning provisions on the state structure]. *Faxue Zazhi*, no. 4 (August 1982): 27–9.

Mou Runsun. "Wujie renda sanci dahui hou zhonggong zui zhuyao de gongzuo" [The most important tasks for the Chinese communists after the Fifth NPC Third Session]. *Mingbao Yuekan*, no. 178 (October 1980): 2–5.

Mu Fu. "Zhongguo renda de zhiheng zuoyong" [The NPC's system-balancing role]. *Qishi Niandai*, no. 162 (July 1983): 22–4.

Nie Linfeng. "Shilun zhiding renmin daibiao fa" [Thoughts on enacting a people's deputy law]. *Faxue Zazhi*, no. 4 (August 1987): 16–17.

Pan Jianfeng. "Tan lifa yuce yu lifa guihua" [Discussing legislative forecasting and legislative planning]. *Fazhi Jianshe*, no. 1 (February 1987): 15–17.

Peng Chong. "Quanguo renmin daibiao dahui changwu weiyuanhui gongzuo baogao" [Work Report of the Standing Committee of the NPC]. Delivered March 28, 1989, Great Hall of the People, Beijing.

Pi Chunxie and Nian Xinyong. "Zhengzhi tizhi gaige de yixiang zhongyao renwu" [An important task in political structural reform]. *Zhongguo Zhengzhi*, no. 1 (January 1987): 27–9. From *Falü Xuexi yu Yanjiu*, no. 3 (1986): 15–18.

Pu Zengyuan. "Guanyu xiugai xianfa de wenti" [Questions concerning revising the constitution]. *Minzhu yu Fazhi*, no. 11 (November 1980): 14–15.

Qi Xin. "Deng Hu Zhao tizhi de xin geju" [The new setup of the Deng-Hu-Zhao system]. *Qishi Niandai*, no. 162 (July 1983): 16–19.

Quangguo Renda Changweihui Bangongting Yanjiushi. *Quangguo Renda Jiqi Changweihui Dashiji* [A Chronicle of the NPC and its Standing Committee]. Beijing: Falü Chubanshe, 1987.

Quanguo Renmin Daibiao Dahui. *Zhonghua Renmin Gongheguo Diyijie Quanguo Renmin Daibiao Dahui Diwuci Huiyi Huikan, Xia* [Documents of the Fifth

Session of the First People's Congress of the People's Republic of China]. Peking: Renmin Chubanshe, 1958.

Renmin Ribao Shelun. "Woguo guojia tizhi de zhongyao gaige he xin de fazhan" [Important reforms and new developments in our country's state system]. *Renmin Ribao*, June 20, 1982, pp. 1, 4.

Renmin Shouce 1955. Peking: Da Gongbaoshe, 1955.

Renmin Shouce 1956. Peking: Da Gongbaoshe, 1956.

Renmin Shouce 1958. Peking: Da Gongbaoshe, 1958.

She Xuxin and Xu Laiqin. "Guanyu zhijie xuanze zhong ruogan wenti de tantao" [Research on problems of direct elections]. *Faxue Yanjiu*, no. 1 (February 1987): 1–6.

Shi Xiaozhong. "Jianquan guojia zhengzhi zhidu wenti dangyi" [Current discussion on perfecting the nation's political system]. *Minzhu yu Fazhi*, no. 10 (October 1981): 6–7.

Song Richang. "Guanyu xiugai xianfa de wojian" [My opinions on revision of the constitution]. *Shehui Kexue*, no. 1 (January 1981): 63–5.

Sun Bingzhu and Wang Yanfei. "Shitan xianfa guanmen de peiyong he xianfa shishi de guanxi" [A preliminary discussion of the relationship between developing legal concept and enforcing the constitution]. *Zhengfa Luntan*, no. 1 (February 1986): 20–4.

Sun Chenggu. *Lifa Quan yu Lifa Chengxu* [Legislative Power and Legislative Procedures]. Beijing: Renmin Chubanshe, 1983.

Sun Tianfu. "Tantan shicha gongzuo zhong de jige wenti" [Discussing several problems in inspection work]. *Guangming Ribao*, April 1, 1957, p. 3.

Sun Xiaohong. "Shilun woguo de lifa yuce" [On our country's legislative prediction]. *Faxue Jikan*, no. 4 (October 1984): 31–5.

Tao Jin. "Poushi liujie renda" [An analysis of the Sixth NPC]. *Zhengming*, no. 69 (July 1983): 51–3.

"Tan wujie wuci renda" [Discussing the Fifth NPC Fifth Session]. *Zhengming*, no. 62 (December 1982).

Teyue Pinglunyuan [Special Commentator]. "Dangqian lifa gongzuo zhong de yixie wenti" [Several problems in current legislative work]. *Guangming Ribao*, December 22, 1978, p. 3.

Tian Jun and Liu Huiming. "Lun woguo renda jiandu zhidu de wanshan" [On perfecting our country's people's congress supervision system]. *Jianghai Xuekan*, no. 1 (January 1989): 69–72.

"Tigao yishi xiaolü, wanshan changweihui zhineng." [Improve proceedings efficiency, improve standing committee functions]. *Renmin Ribao* (Haiwaiban), December 4, 1987, p. 4.

Wang Bixuan, Wu Jie, Li Liancheng, Sun Xi, and Cui Min. *Xin Xianfa Wenda* [Questions and Answers on the New Constitution]. Taiyuan: Shanxi Renmin Chubanshe, 1983.

Wang Dexiang. "Jianquan xuanju zhidu, baozhang renmin dangjia zuozhu" [Perfect the electoral system, guarantee the people as masters]. *Faxue Yanjiu*, no. 3 (June 1979): 5–8.

"Zhixunquan jianlun" [A brief explanation of the right to address inquiries]. In *Xianfalun Wenxuan*, edited by Zhongguo Faxuehui, pp. 195–200. Beijing: Falü Chubanshe, 1983.

Wang Guangmei. "Shishi xin xianfa de baozheng" [Carry out the guarantees of the new constitution]. *Faxue Zazhi*, no. 1 (February 1983): 4–5.

Wang Hanbin. "Wo guo lifa gongzuo sanshiwu nian lai de chengjiu he dangqian de renwu" [Achievements and current tasks in thirty-five years of our country's legislative work]. *Falü yu Shenghuo*, no. 10 (October 1984): 4–6.

Wang Shuwen. "Jiaqiang shehuizhuyi he fazhi de liangxiang zhongda cuoshi" [Two important measures to strengthen socialist democracy and legal system]. *Minzhu yu Fazhi*, no. 7 (July 1982): 7–8.

"Lun xuanju" [On elections]. *Faxue Yanjiu*, no. 1 (April 1979): 7–12.

Wang Shuwen, Wang Dexiang, and Zhang Qingfu. "Shehuizhuyi minzhu he fazhi jianshe de xin jieduan" [A new stage in the construction of socialist democracy and legality]. *Faxue Yanjiu*, no. 6 (December 1982): 10–16.

Wang Xiangming. *Xianfa Ruogan Lilun Wenti de Yanjiu* [Research on Certain Theoretical Questions on Constitutions]. Beijing: Zhongguo Renmin Daxue Chubanshe, 1983.

Wang Xiangming. "Xiancao tixianle gexin guojia de jingshen" [The draft constitution embodies the spirit of national reform]. *Faxue Jikan*, no. 3 (July 1982): 13–16.

Wang Xianju. "Jiaqiang difang renda changweihui jianshe shi yixiang poqie renwu" [Strengthening the establishment of LPC standing committees is an urgent task]. *Faxue Jikan*, no. 1 (January 1986): 14–16.

Wang Xiaotang. "Dui zhonggong zhaokai wujie 'renda sici huiyi' zhi yanxi" [Analysis of the fourth session of the Fifth NPC]. *Zhonggong Yanjiu* (Taipei) 15 (December 1981): 22–33.

"Wei 'renda changweihui' heyi she fazhi weiyuanhui?" [Why has the NPCSC created a legal commission?]. *Zhonggong Yanjiu* (Taipei) 13 (March 15, 1979): 77–83.

Wu Daying. "Gexiang zhidu de gaige yu lifa gongzuo" [Systemic reform and legislative work]. *Faxue Zazhi*, no. 5 (October 1983): 6–9.

"Zhongguo shehuizhuyi lifa chengxu" [China's socialist legislative procedures]. In *Zhongguo Shehuizhuyi Falü Jiben Lilun* [The Fundamental Theory of Chinese Socialist Law], edited by Wu Daying and Shen Zongling, pp. 194–205. Beijing: Falü Chubanshe, 1987.

Wu Daying, Liu Han, Chen Chunlong, Xin Chunying, and Zhou Xinming. *Zhongguo Shehuizhuyi Lifa Wenti* [Problems in Chinese Socialist Legislation]. Beijing: Qunzhong Chubanshe, 1984.

Wu Daying and Ren Yunzheng. "Lifa de yuce he guihua" [Legislative forecasting and planning]. *Zhengzhi yu Falü*, no. 6 (September 1983): 6–12.

Lifa Zhidu Bijiao Yanjiu [Comparative Research on Legislative Systems]. Beijing: Falü Chubanshe, 1981.

Wu Daying and Xin Chunying. "Jiaqiang lifa yuce shi fazhi xietiao fazhan de zhongyao cuoshi" [Strengthening legal forecasting is an important measure to develop legal coordination]. *Faxue*, no. 8 (August 1984): 8–11.

Wu Jialin. "Dui xuanju zhidu minzhuhua de yize jianyi" [A proposal to democratize the electoral system]. In *Zhengzhi yu Zhengzhi Kexue*, edited by Zhongguo Zhengzhixue Hui, Zhengzhi yu Zhengzhi Kexue Bianji Weiyuanhui, pp. 228–34. Beijing: Qunzhong Chubanshe, 1981.

"'Liangji lifa tizhi' he 'duoji lifa tizhi' shuo zhiyi" [Querying "two-level legislative system" and "multilevel legislative system"]. *Faxue*, no. 1 (January 1984): 10–14.

"Minzhu santi" [Three problems of democracy]. *Minzhu yu Fazhi*, no. 12 (December 1980): 17–19.

"Tigao difang guojia quanli jiguan de quanweixing" [Views on strengthening the competence of local organs of state power]. *Faxue Pinglun*, no. 1 (January 1987): 6–12, 30.

"Yixing heyi" [Combination of legislative and executive powers]. In *Zhongguo*

Dabai Kequan Shu (Faxue), edited by Zhang Youyu, pp. 702–3. Beijing: Zhongguo Dabai Kequan Shu Chubanshe, 1984.

"Zenyang fahui quanguo renda zuowei zuigao guojia quanli jiguan de zuoyong" [How to bring into play the NPC as the highest organ of state power]. *Xinhua Wenzhai*, no. 12 (December 1980): 48–51. From *Guangming Ribao*, October 30, 1980.

"Zhengzhi tizhi gaige chutan" [An exploration of political structural reform]. *Nignxia Shehui Kexue*, no. 5 (October 1986): 1–7.

Wu Kejian (Wu Ke-chien). "Renmin daibiao de guancha gongzuo" [Inspection work of people's deputies]. In *Renmin Shouce 1957*, pp. 309–10. Peking: Da Gongbaoshe, 1957.

Xin Chunying. "Dui woguo difang lifa quanxian de chubu tantao" [Preliminary research on our country's local legislative authority]. *Faxue Zazhi*, no. 2 (April 1984): 31–2.

Xiong Xiyuan. "Renmin daibiao dahui shi yixing heyi de guojia quanli jiguan" [The NPC is a state power organ that combines legislation with discussion]. *Renwen Kexue Zazhi (Yunnan Daxue)*, no. 1 (January 1958): 19–28.

Xu Chongde. "Jianquan renmin daibiao dahui zhidu" [Perfect the people's congress system]. *Faxue Yanjiu*, no. 3 (August 1979): 33–6.

Xu Chongde and He Huahui. "Renmin daibiao dahui zhidu de xin fazhan" [New developments of the people's congress system]. *Zhengzhi yu Falü*, no. 1 (June 1982): 29–36.

Xianfa yu Minzhu Zhidu [The Constitution and Democratic System]. Hubei: Hubei Renmin Chubanshe, 1982.

Xu Chongde and Pi Chunxie. *Xuanju Zhidu Wenda* [Questions and Answers on the Electoral System]. Beijing: Qunzhong Chubanshe, 1982.

Yan Yi. "Wo mudu neici kepa de renda huiyi" [I saw with my own eyes that frightful NPC]. *Zhengming*, no. 36 (October 1980): 34–5.

Yang Quanming. "Guanyu jiaqiang woguo xianfa jiandu de jige wenti" [Issues in strengthening our country's constitutional supervision]. *Zhengzhixue Yanjiu*, no. 6 (November 1988): 3–9.

Yao Dengkui. "Qianlun woguo lifa tizhi de tedian" [Discussing the features of our country's legislative system]. *Faxue Jikan*, no. 2 (April 1985): 6–10.

Yi Shi. "Jielu zhonggong renda de neimu" [Exposing the inside story of the Chinese Communists NPC]. *Dong Xi Fang* (Hong Kong), no. 7 (July 1979): 9–11.

You Junyi. "Jinnian lai faxuejie dui ruogan zhongda lilun wenti de zhengyi" [Recent controversies in jurisprudence circles over certain important theoretical questions]. *Faxue*, no. 11 (November 1985): 5–8.

Yu Haocheng. "Xin xianfa fazhanle shehuizhuyi minzhu" [The new constitution develops socialist democracy]. In *Wo Guo de Minzhu Zhengzhi yu Fazhi Jianshe*, edited by Yu Haocheng, pp. 148–55. Taiyuan: Shanxi Renmin Chubanshe, 1983.

"Yige jiqi zhongyao de jianyi" [An extremely important proposal]. *Faxue Zazhi*, no. 4 (August 1982): 23–7.

Yu Jian. "Lun renmin daibiao de falü diwei" [On the legal status of people's deputies]. *Zhengzhi yu Falü*, no. 4 (August 1987): 23–6.

Yu Jiwen. "Zhongguo jingji: gaige yu shikong" [Chinese economy: reform out of control]. *Jiushi Niandai*, no. 184 (May 1985): 21–6.

Zeng Heng and Zhong Ming. "Lun renda changweihui dui dang zuzhi de xianfa jiandu" [On the NPCSC's constitutional supervision of party organizations]. *Faxue Jikan*, no. 1 (January 1987): 39–44.

Zeng Lin. "Renmin daibiao dahui zhidu shi wo guojia de jiben zhidu" [The people's congress system is our country's fundamental system]. *Faxue Yanjiu*, no. 4 (August 1980): 1–5.

Zhang Bingyin. "Shilun woguo de minzhu zhengzhi jianshe yu renda gongzuo de guanxi" [Discussion of the relationship of our country's democratic political construction to people's congress work]. *Zhengfa Luntan*, no. 3 (June 1989): 50–5.

Zhang Dapeng. "Wo guo xuanju zhidu shi zhenzheng minzhu de xuanju zhidu" [Our country's electoral system is a truly democratic electoral sytem]. *Faxue*, no. 6 (December 1957): 37–9.

Zhang Limen. "Buxu youpai fenzi Wang Jixin xiang renmin minzhu fazhi jingong" [Rightist Wang Jixin's attack on the people's democratic legal system is not allowed]. *Zhengfa Yanjiu*, no. 2 (April 1958): 69.

Zhang Pingli. "Yao jiaqiang renda de falü jiandu" [NPC legal supervision must be strengthened]. *Renmin Ribao* (Overseas Edition), October 31, 1987, p. 2.

Zhang Shuyi. "Jingji tizhi gaige de fazhi xietiao fazhan" [Coordinated legal development within economic system reform]. *Faxue*, no. 7 (July 1986): 9–11.

Zhang Sutang and He Ping. "Gaige huhuanzhe qiye fa chu tai" [Reform calling the enterprise law out from behind the stage]. *Liaowang* (Overseas Edition), February 8, 1988, pp. 17–18.

Zhang Weiguo. "Zhongguo de xiwang zai yu minzhu yu fazhi" [China's hopes lie in democracy and legality]. *Shijie Jingji Daobao*, April 3, 1989, p. 11.

Zhang Yanjie. "Quanguo renmin daibiao dahui shouquan changwu weiyuanhui zhiding danxing fagui shi hefa" [The NPC's authorization of the NPCSC to enact special regulations is legal]. *Faxue*, no. 3 (March 1958): 15–16, 25.

Zhang Youyu. "Guanyu woguo falü de lifa chengxu he qicao gongzuo" [On our country's legislative procedures and legal drafting work]. *Zhengzhixue Yanjiu*, no. 3 (August 1985): 1–3.

"Guanyu zhiding quanguo renmin daibiao dahui yishi guize de wenti" [Issues drawing up the NPC rules of procedure]. *Zhengzhixue Yanjiu*, no. 3 (May 1989): 1–5.

"Jiaqiang xianfa lilun de yanjiu" [Strengthen research on constitutional theory]. In *Xianfalun Wenxuan*, edited by Zhongguo Faxuehui, pp. 1–12. Beijing: Falü Chubanshe, 1983.

"Lun renmin daibiao dahui daibiao de renwu, zhiquan he huodong fangshi wenti" [On the tasks, powers, functions, and activities of National People's Congress deputies]. *Faxue Yanjiu*, no. 2 (April 1985): 1–8.

"Minzhu xieshang shi shixing renmin minzhu de youxiao fangshi" [Democratic consultation is an effective means to carry out people's democracy]. *Jianghai Xuekan*, no. 4 (August 1984): 3–10.

"Zhang Youyu tongzhi jiu kaizhan woguo fazhi jianshe xietiao fazhan wenti taolun de tanhua" [Comrade Zhang Youyu's speech on unfolding issues in our country's coordinated legal construction]. *Faxue*, no. 6 (June 1984): 1–3.

Zhang Zonghou. "Quanli zhiyue lun" [On restricting power]. *Faxue*, no. 10 (October 1986): 1–6.

Zhang Zonghou and Yan Jun. "Wo shi renmin daibiao, jiuyao ti quanzhong jianghua" [I am a people's representative and must speak for the masses]. *Zhongguo Fazhibao*, April 1, 1985, p. 1.

Zhao Binglin. "Jianshe gaodu minzhu de shehuizhuyi zhengzhi zhidu" [Construct a highly democratic socialist political system]. *Minzhu yu Fazhi*, no. 7 (July 1981): 8–11.

Zhao Zong. "Shiping wujie renda" [Evaluating the fifth NPC]. *Mingbao Yuekan*, no. 148 (April 1978): 2–7.

"Zhaokai minfa tongce caoan zuotanhui" [Convening a conference on the draft civil code]. *Zhongguo Fazhibao*, December 6, 1985, p. 1.

Zheng Ping. "Zhongguo faxuehui xianfaxue yanjiuhui zai Guiyang chengli" [The Chinese constitutional research society is established in Guiyang]. *Faxue*, no. 12 (December 1985): 28.

Zhong Nan. "Beijing lianghui xiezhao" [Portrait of two meetings]. *Jiushi Niandai*, no. 220 (May 1988): 65.

Zhonggong Yanjiu. "Zhonggong liujie renda yici huiyi de zhidao sixiang" [The guiding thought of the Chinese communists sixth NPC first session]. *Zhonggong Yanjiu* (Taipei) 17 (July 1983): 1–3.

"Zhongguo renmin daibiao dahui changwu weiyuanhui yishi guize." [NPCSC proceedings regulations]. *Renmin Ribao* (Haiwaiban), November 25, 1987, p. 4.

Zhongguo Renmin Daxue Falüxi "Zhengfa Gongzuo" Yanjiu Xiaozu. "Woguo renmin minzhu fazhi de jige wenti" [Several questions about our country's people's democratic legal system]. *Zhengfa Yanjiu*, no. 2 (April 1959): 3–8.

Zhou Xinming and Chen Weidian. "Dui lifa chengxu wenti de yixie kanfa" [Some views on the issue of legislative procedures]. *Renmin Ribao*, January 5, 1979, p. 3.

Zong Nankai. "Chuping renda huiyi" [First evaluation of the NPC]. *Dong Xi Fang* (Hong Kong), no. 7 (July 1979): 6–8.

Index